PUBLIC RELATIONS HISTORY:
From the 17th to the 20th Century.
The Antecedents

PUBLIC RELATIONS
HISTORY:
From the 17th to the 20th Century.
The Antecedents

SCOTT M. CUTLIP
Dean Emeritus, The University of Georgia

LEA LAWRENCE ERLBAUM ASSOCIATES, PUBLISHERS
1995   Hillsdale, New Jersey   Hove, UK

Lawrence Erlbaum Associates, Inc., Publishers
365 Broadway
Hillsdale, New Jersey 07642

Library of Congress Cataloging-in-Publication Data

Cutlip, Scott M.
   Public relations history : from the 17th to the 20th century.
   The Antecedents / Scott M. Cutlip.
      p.   cm.
   Includes bibliographical references and index.
   ISBN 0-8058-1779-4 (alk. paper). — ISBN 0-8058-1780-8 (pbk. :
alk. paper)
   1. Publication relations—United States—History. 2. Public relations—
Social aspects—United States. I. Title.
HM263.C784 1995
659.2—dc20   95-13889
                                                                 CIP

Books published by Lawrence Erlbaum Associates are printed on acid-free
paper, and their bindings are chosen for strength and durability.

Printed in the United States of America
10 9 8 7 6 5 4 3 2 1

This book is dedicated to the memory of
Maj. Gen. L. Gordon Hill, USA
Soldier, Scholar

Contents

Preface

This volume brings to print a research effort I began some 35 years ago. Fortunately, good history, like good wine, profits from time. I returned to this early research with a better perspective and increased knowledge gained through the intervening years. I had completed 10 of these chapters in rough draft when I accepted President Fred Davison's invitation—summons would be more accurate—to accept the deanship of the Henry W. Grady School of Journalism at the University of Georgia. This work was put aside as I tackled my administrative tasks. With the encouragement of friends, I returned to this original project in 1993 after completing *The Unseen Power: Public Relations*. That book, published by Lawrence Erlbaum Associates in 1994, tells the early 20th-century history of public relations as revealed in the work and personalities of the pioneer agencies.

This volume, in a real sense, is a companion volume that documents events and practices that we in retrospect define as public relations practice—a decision with which many may quarrel. The term *public relations* did not generally come into our language until the late 19th century. A famous Yale University history professor once observed, "The way to get at the nature of any institution is to see how it has grown." This has been our goal in the study of the origins of public relations practice that today plays such a powerful, if often unseen and unscrutinized, role in our democratic society. This history opens in the 17th century with the efforts of land promoters and colonists to lure settlers from Europe—mainly England—to this primitive land along the Atlantic Coast. They used publicity, tracts, sermons, and letters to disseminate rosy, glowing accounts of life and opportunity in the new land. We close by describing the public relations efforts of colleges and other nonprofit agencies in the late 19th and early 20th centuries, thus providing a bridge across the century line.

Studying the origins of public relations can provide helpful insight into its functions, its strengths and weaknesses, and its profound, although often unseen, impact on our society. Early on in my teaching career, I saw the value of history in explaining this now influential vocation's place in society and its profound effect over time on the nation's political, social, economic, and cultural life. As I stated in *The Unseen Power: Public Relations*, initially when I embarked on this project in the early 1960s, I set out to trace the evolution of public relations practice from the colonial period to mid-20th century. The first 10 chapters brought me to the eve of the 20th century. Publication of this volume finally—some 35 years later—completes the work of a lifetime.

Earlier histories of public relations have usually telescoped and oversim-plified a fascinating and complex story by tending to emphasize novelty and personalities. Exempted from this generalization is Alan Raucher's *Public Relations and Business 1900–1929* (1968). As this and its companion vol-ume, *The Unseen Power: Public Relations. A History*, make clear, there is a great deal more to the evolving history of this powerful vocation, one that today employs 150,000 professional practitioners in the United States.

Public relations—or its equivalents, *propaganda, publicity, public infor-mation*—began when people came to live together in tribal camps where one's survival depended on others of the tribe. To function, civilization requires communication, conciliation, consensus, and cooperation—the bed-rock fundamentals of the public relations function. I used to tell my students that public relations probably began when one Neanderthal man traded the hindquarters of a sheep to another for a flint. The Greek philosophers wrote about the *public will*, even though they did not use the term *public opinion*. The urban culture of the Roman Empire gave more scope to the opinion process. Certain phrases and ideas in the political vocabulary of the Romans and in the writings of the Medieval Period are not unrelated to modern concepts of public opinion. The Romans inscribed on their walls the slo-gan—"S.P.Q.R."—The Senate and the Roman People. Later, Romans coined the expression, "vox populi, vox Dei"—the "voice of the people is the voice of God." Machiavelli wrote in his *Discoursi*, "Not without reason is the voice of the people compared to the voice of God," and he held that people must be either "caressed or annihilated." The struggles to win in the public forum today may not be that brutal, but they are every bit as intense.

The communication of information to influence opinions or alter the behavior of others can be traced to the earliest civilizations. Archaeologists have unearthed farm bulletins in Iran dating from 1800 B.C. instructing farm-ers how to sow their crops, how to irrigate, how to deal with field mice, and how to harvest their crops—an effort not unlike the "how to" information disseminated by our Land Grant Agricultural colleges over this century, information that has made U.S. agriculture the envy of the world. What is known today of ancient Egypt, Assyria, and Persia (Iran) comes largely from recorded material intended to publicize and glorify the rulers of the day. Much of the literature and art of antiquity was designed to build support for kings, priests, and other leaders. Virgil's *Georgics* was written to persuade urban dwellers to move to farms to produce food for the growing city. The walls of Pompeii were inscribed with election appeals. Caesar carefully prepared the Romans for his crossing of the Rubicon in 49 B.C. by sending reports to Rome of his epic achievements as governor of Gaul. Historians have assumed that he wrote his *Commentaries* as propaganda for himself.

Rudimentary elements of public relations can be found in ancient India. In writings of that nation's earliest times there is mention of the king's spies, whose function included, besides espionage, keeping the king in touch with public opinion, championing the king in public, and spreading rumors favorable to the king. Public relations was used centuries ago in England, where the kings maintained Lords Chancellor as "Keeper's of the King's Conscience." These chancellors surely offer a historical counterpart of today's practitioners and ombudsmen. Long before the complexities of communication, there was acknowledged need for a third party to facilitate communication and mediate adjustment of conflicting interests between the government and its people. So it was with the church, tradesmen, and craftsmen.

The term *propaganda* was born in the Catholic Church in the 17th century when the Church set up its *Congregatio de propaganda* (congregation for propagating the faith). Although often used today as a pejorative term, propaganda is an essential part of the public relations function if the word is defined neutrally. Much of practitioners' endeavors are in propagating a doctrine, a cause, an institution, or an individual (e.g., candidates for public office). For today's practitioners to eschew the term propaganda in describing their work is either snobbery or sophistry. The propaganda that Sam Adams and his brave band used to bring their nation to Revolution and the Independence was not greatly different from that used in the Carter Administration to pass the Panama Canal Treaty by one vote or that used by President Clinton to win passage of the North American Free Trade Agreement (NAFTA)—only the millions of dollars expended, the multiple channels of communication and influence used, and the intensified lobbying efforts are different. Readers of the chapter "Propaganda Gives Birth to a New Nation," will find therein techniques of propaganda initiated by Adams that are in use today. Public relations in part, let's face it, is the propagation of a cause, a doctrine, a program or its opposite, defeat of a cause, a doctrine, a program (e.g., The Right to Life lobby vs. the Freedom of Choice movement). Systematic efforts to win support for causes, candidates, or corporations is part and parcel of life in a democratic society where public opinion prevails, at least much of the time.

These were essential and honorable callings in the beginnings of democracy as the people gained more and more power over their lives, and they are essential and honorable callings today, even though not all practitioners work in an honorable manner. From its rudimentary beginnings in the United States as described in this volume, the propagandist or public relations functionary has provided an important link in the free communications and debate on which this nation or any other democratic nation depends for its democracy, culture, cohesion, and solidarity. This role for the communicator and a free press was first seen by John Milton in 1644 in *Areopagitica*: "Let her [Truth] and falsehood grapple, who ever knew Truth put to the worse, in a free and open encounter." This philosophy has been embedded in our political system by a series of brilliant Supreme Court justices and their decisions: Oliver Wendell Holmes, Louis D. Brandeis, Hugo Black, William O. Douglas, and William Brennan. A contemporary statement of this democratic faith is found in Justice Douglas' dissent in *Dennis v. United States* (341 U.S. 494, 584 [1951]: "When ideas compete in the market for acceptance, full and free discussion keeps a society from becoming stagnant and unprepared for the stresses and strains that work to tear all civilizations apart."

The propagandist from Samuel Adams to David Gergen plays an important if unseen role in public debate. He or she has the responsibility of making certain that the ideas, information, or cause of every individual, industry, or institution are heard in the public arena. In the roar of today's public forum with its hundreds of competing causes and its publicity outlets numbering in the thousands resembling the Tower of Babel, this functionary is essential to making our democracy work by disseminating information and mediating society's stresses and strains. What the U.S. Supreme Court termed *robust debate* in one decision often leads to rough no-holds-barred fights in the public arena. In "Public Relations' Magna Carta," Justice Hugo Black in a historic decision of 1961 upheld the rights of contestants in the public arena to have such battles. In writing the unanimous opinion of the Court in the *Noerr Motor Freight et al. v. Eastern Railroads Presidents Conference et al.*, Justice Black wrote: "We have restored what appears to be the true nature of this case—a 'no-holds barred' fight between two industries, both of which are seeking control of a profitable source of income. Inherent in such fights which are commonplace in the halls of legislative bodies, is the possibility, and in many instances even the probability that one group or the other will be hurt by the arguments that are made."

This volume is replete with such robust public struggles: the work of the Revolutionaries, led by the indomitable Sam Adams, to bring on the War of Independence that gave birth to a New Nation; the propaganda of Alexander Hamilton, James Madison, and John Jay in the Federalist Papers to win ratification of the U.S. Constitution, winning out against the propaganda of the Anti-Federalists led by Richard Henry Lee; the historic struggle between the forces of President Andrew Jackson, led by Amos Kendall, and those of Nicholas Biddle and his Bank of the United States presaged corporate versus government campaigns common today; the propaganda work, led by Abraham Lincoln, that ultimately saved this nation as the outcome of our "First Public War"; or the classic presidential campaign of 1896 that pitted pro-Big Business candidate William McKinley against the Populist orator of the Platte, William Jennings Bryan. Or in the political struggles between the Hamiltonian Federalists and the Jeffersonian Republicans in which the nation's first campaign consultant, John Beckley, emerged. Today his successors dominate our political process. Of such struggles is history made and a nation is built.

Today, public relations plays a major supporting role in the marketing of goods or services by business firms and some nonprofit agencies, such as hospitals. Unfortunately there are scholars and practitioners who confuse the supporting role of public relations in marketing with the whole of marketing. This role of public relations today has its antecedent in the publicity of the railroads in the 19th century that was produced to promote the sale of the U.S. government-granted lands that subsidized the railroads as they moved West. Railroad publicity and promotion was also used to promote passenger traffic in support of the railroads' marketing programs.

These same years also saw the flowering of press agentry, promotion, and advertising with the U.S. circuses leading the way. The flamboyant showmen who produced our great circuses of the 19th century were the first major users of display advertising in newspapers and on billboards—common features of America today.

These then are the antecedents of today's flourishing, influential vocation of public relations whose practitioners make their case for their clients or their employers in the highly competitive public opinion marketplace. "Let Truth and Falsehood Grapple."

ACKNOWLEDGMENTS

Two persons who contributed substantially to this volume are not, unfortunately, alive to read my words of profound gratitude. One was a former Wisconsin colleague, Oliver H. Knight, who last taught history at the University of Texas–El Paso. Professor Knight read the first 10 chapters when they were in draft form; he greatly improved them by his editing and also saved me from several errors of fact. The other deceased person is Major General L. Gordon Hill, who died a few years ago. General Hill was an undergraduate student of mine at the University of Wisconsin. I got him interested in the generally unsung work of Amos Kendall, an important 19th-century figure whose accomplishments have been lost in time—at least until this book is published. When General Hill retired from the U.S. Army, in which he served a tour as chief of public affairs, he returned to the life of Amos Kendall. Before his death, he had completed three chapters as the result of his extensive research. When ill health caught up with him, he sent the chapters in rough draft and back-up research materials to me. He did not want his work wasted. General Hill's research and writing form the basis of the three Kendall chapters. Amos Kendall deserves a full-length biography; these chapters must serve until a more detailed one is written—if ever. Obviously, my debt to my friend and student is a large one indeed, and I freely acknowledge his contribution.

In chapter 1, I made extensive use of Hermine McLarty's master's thesis, written at the University of Georgia in 1984, *Eighteenth Century Communication: The Promotion of the Colony of Georgia.*

Chapter 2 is based on an article first published in *The Public Relations Review.* Before its publication it was read by a dear friend and a leading colonial historian, the late Merrill Jensen, who made many improvements in it.

For chapter 3 I benefited greatly from criticism provided by Merrill Jensen and by correspondence with Professor William Crosskey.

The John Beckley chapter is based in part on the research and seminar paper of Doyle Mote, a graduate student of mine at the University of Georgia. As a reading of the John Beckley chapter makes clear, I relied heavily on the research and writings of Edmund and Dorothy Smith Berkely, authors of the only full-length biography of Beckley.

As indicated earlier, chapters 5, 6, and 7 are largely based on the work of the late General Hill.

For the history of the U.S. Navy's role in the Civil War, I am indebted to a former student and Naval officer, F. Donald Scovel, whose thesis, *History of the Development of the Public Affairs Function in the United States Navy, 1861–1941,* was written under my direction at the University of Wisconsin in 1968. Similarly, for the history of the Army's efforts to cope with the press in the Civil War, I am indebted to the late Colonel Bennett Jackson's thesis on the history of Army public affairs, also written at Wisconsin in 1968.

The role of George F. Parker in the three Grover Cleveland Presidential campaigns was researched and recorded by Colonel Gordon A. Moon for his master's thesis, written under my direction, at the University of Wisconsin in 1963. General Leonard Wood's story is based on a master's thesis by Colonel Peter J. Foss, *Power and Prominence Through Publicity: A Study of the Publicity Campaign of General Leonard Wood,* written under my direction at Wisconsin in 1968.

In chapter 13, the pioneering work in university public relations by President Charles R. Van Hise and Willard G. Bleyer of the University of Wisconsin is told in a master's thesis by Donald C. Bauder, *University of Wisconsin Public Relations Policies Under President Charles R. Van Hise,* written under my direction at Wisconsin in 1960. Bauder is now business editor of the

San Diego Union-Tribune. Another thesis used was that of Donald K. Ross, *W. G. Bleyer and the Development of Journalism Education*, written at Wisconsin under my direction in 1952. James Drummond Ellsworth's memoir, *Twisting Trails*, was given to the State Historical Society of Wisconsin by his daughter, Mrs. R. H. Scannell.

As these acknowledgments make clear, I, like most scholars, owe much of my inspiration and knowledge to bright, hardworking graduate students. This debt I have acknowledged widely and freely. Unfortunately, some professors do not do so. Readers of this volume as well as *The Unseen Power* will note that many of the graduate students quoted were military officers. This is because from 1947 through 1974 at Wisconsin it was my privilege to guide some 135 U.S. military officers, mostly U.S. Army, through their graduate programs—a program initiated by then Army Chief of Staff General Dwight D. Eisenhower on the recommendation of Arthur W. Page, an eminent public relations pioneer.

Once again I am indebted to William Gray Potter, director of the University of Georgia Libraries, for providing me with a convenient place to work and to his congenial staff for their unfailing help. Similarly, I owe a debt of gratitude to Hollis Heimbouch, Senior Editor, and Sondra Guideman, Production Editor, for guiding this book through publication.

And again sincere thanks to Sandra Gary who cheerfully and promptly typed this manuscript over 1993.

Scott M. Cutlip

Hype for Colonies, Colleges, and the Frontier

Utilization of publicity and press agentry to promote causes, tout land ventures, and raise funds is older than the nation itself. In fact, the U.S. talent for promotion can be traced back to the first settlements on the East Coast in the 16th century.

The exaggerated claims that often characterize publicity began with Sir Walter Raleigh's ill-fated effort to settle Roanoke Island off the Virginia coast. When Captain Arthur Barlowe returned to England in 1584 from that desolate, swampy area, he reported to Raleigh: "The soile is the most plentiful, sweete, fruitful and wholesome of all the worlde . . . they have those Okes that we have, but farre greater and better, the highest and reddest Cedars of the world and a great abundance of 'Pine or Pitch Trees.' " He even described the Indians as "most gentle, loving, and faithfull, voide of all guile or treason."[1]

Even more glowing was the description of Raleigh's "lieutenant governor." Writing from Virginia in 1585, Ralph Lane trumpeted that the mainland had "the goodliest (s)oyle under the cope of heaven," and that "what commodities soever" France, Spain, Italy, or the East produced, "these parts doe abound with the growth of them all."

Contrary to the accounts of bolder settlers eagerly flocking to the newly discovered America given in grade school histories, it would appear that

---

[1]Richard Hakluyt (comp.), *The Principal Navigations Voyages Traffiques & Discoveries of the English Nation* (12 vols.). Glasgow: (1903–1905) VIII, pp. 299, 303, 304, 305. Not quoted in sequence.

many came from Europe to the new land in response to exaggerated publicity claims. Lefler observed:[2] "The glorified advertising of every colony was the chief means of procuring money and men. The degree of success varied considerably from time to time and from place to place."

The first eyewitness description of the present United States, Thomas Hariot's *A Brief True Report of the New Found Land of Virginia*, was printed by Sir Walter Raleigh to aid in raising funds and men for another expedition before his charter expired. Publicity to lure settlers to Virginia was stepped up with the chartering of the London Company of Virginia in 1606. Lefler noted: "Virginia had the largest amount, the widest variety, the most exaggerated and perhaps the most effective of the promotional tracts of any colony."[3] The publicity placed much emphasis on moral sanction, missionary zeal, and imperialism in addition to greatly exaggerated claims about the resources of Virginia. Shortly after the founding of Jamestown, the Company started circulating publicity to encourage emigration, and the next several years "produced the largest crop of promotional tracts in Virginia's history." One of the first, *A true Declaration of the estate of the Colonie in Virginia, with a confutation of such scandalous reports as have tended to the disgrace of so worthy an enterprise*, was aimed at scotching reports of the hardships in the colony. The pamphlet's anonymous author argued that all the accusations against the colony were false. In a day of religiosity, it was inevitable that the clergy would be enlisted in these promotional efforts. These early promoters sensed the importance of credibility in communication. One, a Reverend Daniel Price, compared Virginia with distant lands, saying that Virginia was "not unlike to equalize Tyrus for colours, Basan for woods, Persia for oils, Arabia for spices, Spain for silks, Narsis for shipping, Netherlands for fish, Pomona for fruit, and tillage, Babylon for corn." Another clergyman, the Reverend William Cranshaw, denounced Virginia's critics by asserting that the enterprise to colonize the new land "hath only three enemies: 1. The Divell, 2. The Papists, and 3. The Players."[4]

Although it is not possible to assess the effectiveness of this promotional material, Lefler reported that a tract published by a layman, Robert Johnson, entitled, *Nova Brittania: Offering Most Excellente Fruites by Planting in Virginia*, published in 1609, did produce "a great increase in investments in the Company and in the number of people migrating to Virginia."[5] After the crisis caused by the Indian Massacre of 1622, there was another spate of publications intended to reassure prospective settlers. Then, "with the royalization of Virginia in 1624, the slow recovery from the Indian Massacre,

---

[2]Hugh T. Lefler, "Promotional Literature of the Southern Colonies," *Journal of Southern History, 33*, 1967, p. 24.

[3]*Ibid.* p. 4.

[4]*Ibid.* p. 4.

[5]*Ibid.* p. 9.

and the gradual spread of population and of tobacco culture, publication of promotional literature came to an abrupt halt."[6]

MARYLAND

Virginia's early promotional efforts were matched in varying degrees by the later colonies of the South Atlantic region. When the settlement of Maryland was being planned, the imagination of Europe was not yet fired up with the vision of a new land rich with opportunity and romance. The Charles I edition of the "Charter of Maryland," printed in 1622, was the first promotional tract for that colony. Another tract, *Objections Answered Concerning Maryland,* appeared in 1663. *A Declaration of the Lord Baltimore's Plantation in Maryland* is dated February 10, 1633. Wroth wrote:[7] "There has always existed a conception of the Maryland settlements as the result of a dark and secret flight to sanctuary of persecuted Catholics. The mere fact of the appearance in print of a prospectus in 1633, however, shows that Lord Baltimore went about the recruiting of his expedition in the manner of colony promoters of all time, and in the note appended to the Declaration date and the port of departure of the 'Arke of Maryland' was advertised for all men to read."

Wroth thought, a tract, *A Relation of Maryland of 1635,* "is one of the most elaborate publications issued in the promotion of any English American colony." In addition to the brief account of the successful settlement of the year before, it contained a full description of the country and a prognostication of its certain reward to industry, the outline of a generous policy toward the Indian inhabitants, the conditions of land tenure, and detailed instructions taken almost verbatim from John Smith's *General Historie.* Smith instructed the new settlers on the matters of seed, blotching, arms, tools, and agricultural implements needed in the new land. Historians consider Smith a self-serving propagandist.

A decade after the 1635 pamphlet, another promotional tract was issued entitled, *A Moderate and Safe Investment.* This was an appeal to stave off repeal of the Maryland Charter by the House of Lords "until the yearly ship from Maryland, expected before June, could bring the information needed in the defense of Lord Calvert." It was, Wroth wrote, among other things, a plea to make the emigration of Catholics to Maryland easier. The Charter was heard no more of in Parliament. Wroth noted: "With this exceptionally

---

[6]*Ibid.* p. 12.

[7]Lawrence C. Wroth, "The Maryland Colonization Tracts," in William W. Bishop and Andrew Keogh, eds., *Essays Offered to Herbert Putnam.* New Haven: Yale University Press, 1929, pp. 539–552.

interesting writing, political documents such as the colonization tract, the promotional literature of Maryland comes to an end."

In Lefler's opinion, "The Maryland proprietary had less promotional literature than other Southern colony, and, with one notable exception, such material was less exaggerated and more specific in its appeals."

THE CAROLINAS

In Lefler's opinion, Carolina's publicity did not match Virginia in a variety of appeals or in media used. "There were no poems or officially inspired sermons, few broadsides, and only a minimum of prospectuses." Yet when the English settled Charles Town in 1670, they were encouraged by accounts of the country written by explorers such as William Hilton—for whom Hilton Head Island is named—and Robert Sandford. These explorations were made after King Charles II granted a charter to eight of his supporters in 1663. The accounts of these voyages are now Carolina classics—and as one writer noted, "classics in public relations history." The account was written by Robert Horne in 1664 and starts out: "Carolina is a fair and spacious province." His narrative told what wildlife and vegetation was to be found, what the lands and waterways looked like. All was laudatory with the consequence many settlers came to Carolina believing what they had read, but very quickly learning that they had been gulled, as would other colonists. The settlers' letters back home were filled with complaints about the fevers, the heat, the insects, the wild animals, and the rankness of the vegetation. As a writer for the *Charleston News and Courier* observed recently: "Far from being a land of milk and honey, they reported, the country was strange, unlike anything in England and France." The settlers, instead, found the Carolinas to be "a land of toil and tribulation, sickness and terror."

Nonetheless the proprietors continued to control the general public's perceptions of Carolina by publishing a steady stream of promotional literature. For example, T. A. and Samuel Wilson authored a pamphlet, *The Discourses of Many Ingenious Travellers*, which opened with this. "The Luxuriant and Indulgent Blessings of Nature (have) justly rendered Carolina Famous." The Wilson brothers wrote. "The coastal Indians way of life was being changed through prolonged contact with the English colonists." T. S. Wilson concluded his description by observing "that the Neighboring Indians are very kind and serviceable, doing our Nation such Civilities and Good Turns as lie within their power." No Indian scalpings here!

Beyond these narratives, there were four promotional efforts on behalf of Carolina from 1649 to 1651—an anonymous two-page article in a London newspaper, a pamphlet about Virginia that included a description of the Chowan River area, a book about Virginia that included a glowing account of "a long neglected Virgin," the Carolina section, and a brochure to lure settlers to "Carolina." Over the next two decades, the Proprietors left the promotion of Carolina to their London agents.

GEORGIA

Georgia was unlike any other of the thirteen colonies—it was a colony for the settlement of the poor, the exiled, and outcast of England and Europe, financed by private donations and Parliamentary appropriations. Georgia's founders, led by Lord Oglethorpe, were motivated by the ideals of humanity, charity, and unselfish devotion by helping the less fortunate build new lives in America. Because of its dependence on charity and Parliamentary appropriations, the Georgia colony mounted an intensive, broad-scale campaign of promotion and persuasion that was not matched by any other colony. The trustees' promotional activities parallel many of present-day methods. Components of a modern promotional campaign for a non-profit organization such as fundraising, publicity, symbols, special events, and use of influential leaders all have counterparts in the Georgia campaign of the 1730s, 1740s, and early 1750s. Like many other such campaign, the exaggerations and high expectations raised in this campaign brought disillusionment and failure to the Georgia promotion. Exaggeration was the common trait of all colonial hype.

Lord Oglethorpe's effort to found the Georgia colony was not the first. Scottish baronet Sir Robert Montgomery launched in 1717 the first major attempt to establish another Southern colony. The rudiments of Georgia promotional literature lie in Montgomery's pamphlets boasting the exaggerated virtues of his proposed colony, "Margravate of Azila." Montgomery's effort prompted his published *A Discourse Concerning the design'd Establishment of a New Colony to the South of Carolina in the Most Delightful Country of the Universe* to entice prospective settlers and investors. Montgomery was seeking settlement by the landed gentry. He met with no success and his grant expired in 1720.[8]

Concurrently, Oglethorpe, a young member of Parliament, became concerned with the conditions of English prisons. McLarty wrote: "Oglethorpe's concern for the less fortunate as well as his awareness of the Spanish threat to Florida stirred his interest in the settlement of a new colony to meet both needs." He and a few associates petitioned King George II for a charter that was granted on June 9, 1732. The trustees saw that they had two publics

---

[8]This account of Georgia's promotional campaign is based on Hermine McLarty's master's thesis, "Eighteenth Century Communication: The Promotion of the Colony of Georgia," written at the University of Georgia in 1984.

to persuade for support of this settlement—the financial supporters of the philanthropic colony and the potential settlers. Georgia was not restricted to charity cases; people could settle in the colony at their own expense. Through the terms of the charter, no trustee could receive a salary or own land in Georgia, therefore their duties lay in raising money for the colony and accepting applicants as settlers. Contrary to a historical myth, no debtors in prison were actually released to be sent to Georgia. The settlers sent at the trustees' expense were charity cases although some may have spent time in prisons for debt.

Given their need to raise money to finance the Georgia colony, the trustees knew that they had to establish a favorable public opinion for their enterprise. These sagacious Trustees realized that they must respond to the public's self-interest and show how contributions could help the colonists and themselves.

A Broad-Scale Campaign

The decision was made to take the colony's case to the people of England through advertisements and pamphlets and to avoid negative publicity. The Trustees resolved at their very first meeting:[9] "that measures be taken to prevent the publishing in the newspapers anything relating to this Society, that shall be disadvantageous to their designs; and that Mr. Oglethorpe be desired to take the said measures to cause such paragraphs to be published in the said newspapers as may be proper for the promoting of the said designs."

Although Oglethorpe directed the flow of publicity, he apparently wrote none of the pamphlets. Benjamin Martyn, an author and scholar, was chosen as secretary of the Trust and wrote most of the promotional literature. Because no authors were cited on title pages of the pamphlets, many assumed Oglethorpe to be the author. Records later established that Martyn was the author. The first pamphlet written by Martyn, *Some Account of the Designs of the Trustees for Establishing the Colony in America*, was published in 1732. Its target was potential benefactors. The two folio editions, one containing elaborate engravings and a map, described the plight of the unfortunate and explained the plans for the colony and the ways donations would be handled. The pamphlet stressed that America had so much to offer for the poor of England and the Protestants of Europe if they only had money for their passage. The trustees promised annual reports to the Lord High Chancellor of their receipts and expenditures.

Another promotional pamphlet, *A New and Accurate Account of the Provinces of South Carolina and Georgia*, published in 1732, lauded the

---

[9] *The Colonial Records of the State of Georgia*, Vol. II, p. 30.

generosity and humanitarianism of the trustees. Several chapters covered various areas about South Carolina and Georgia and was marked by effusive praise—the air described as "always serene, pleasant and temperate, never subject to excessive heat or cold, nor to sudden change." The pamphlet promised that the poor would not be bound in servitude from donations and would receive only passage fare and supplies to begin new lives in Georgia. That same year Oglethorpe compiled *Selected Tracts* as a device to use respected sources to endorse and promote the colony. This subtle pamphlet uses the essays to meet the objections some English had concerning the new colony and instead to promote favorable public opinion for the enterprise.

The next year, 1733, Martyn wrote a pamphlet, *Reasons for Establishing the Colony of Georgia*, detailing the economic benefits to Great Britain and announced establishment of a silk growing industry in Georgia. Thirteen hundred copies of this one were printed and copies were sent to each member of Parliament. Martyn played on the bandwagon technique in this tract. Thus began production of a steady stream of propaganda pamphlets emphasizing the lofty aims of the colony and the attractions of this new promised land.

The Georgia Sermons

A main component of the Georgia publicity—and one of the most profitable—was the anniversary sermons preached by well-known clergymen, including John Wesley. The ministers preached the sermons at the annual meeting of the Georgia trustees. The texts were later published to raise money and advertise Georgia. George Watts' 1735 sermon appealed for support for relieving the poor of their misery by "turning the wilderness into a fruitful, well-watered habitation for them." A prescient fear of many English people at the time was that the colony would prosper and then seek its independence of Britain. Watts assured his audience that this would not happen. He may have been a great preacher but he was a poor prophet. He said on this occasion:[10] "[Even] if their affection to the Mother County; if their gratitude, their interest, their love of their present happy Government and fear of change, does not prevent any attempts of this kind, these several Provinces, cannot all be supported to join and assist in one Design."

The final Georgia sermon, given in 1750 by Rev. Thomas Franklin, manifested the undying optimism the clergy had for success in Georgia although the rosy promises of the propaganda were already turning to disillusionment.

---

[10]George Watts, "A Sermon Preach'd Before the Trustees for Establishing the Colony in America, March 17, 1737" (London, 1737), p. 68.

The pamphlets, sermons, and newspaper advertisements apparently were effective; contributions for the first full year were over 3,700 pounds—big money in the 18th century. A total of 11,502 pounds, 19 shillings and 3 pence were donated between 1733 and 1734, the period in which most of the promotional effort was made. During the first year of the colony, more than 113 pounds was spent on printing and advertising, again a big sum for its time. Comparable amounts were spent in 1735–1736 and in 1741–1742. As the result of the trustees' campaign, almost 500 persons accepted the trustees' charity and came to Georgia the first 2 years. In the design of the Savannah settlement, each colonist received 50 acres of land, 45 outside the township for farming, 5 acres in town for a house and garden.

Oglethorpe and his associates were well aware of the value of the staged event to attract public attention—the *pseudo-event* is a *sine qua non* of today's promotion. In 1734, Oglethorpe returned to England to rally for support and brought with him Tomo Chichi, the Chief of the Yamacraws, and a few of his warriors. The Indians created quite a stir in England. Tomo Chichi met both the Arch Bishop of Canterbury and King George II. All this received wide press coverage, generating free publicity for the new colony. Oglethorpe returned to Georgia in 1736 with two shiploads of colonists, some of whom settled Frederica on St. Simon's Island.

The propagandists also used poetry to extol the glories of Georgia. Alexander Pope, James Thomson, and other lesser-known English poets enlisted in their talent in the cause. *The Gentleman's Magazine* printed much of this poetry, and in 1735, it sponsored a poetry contest, which kept Georgia in the news for more than 2 years.

Disgruntlement Sets In

Like many a propaganda campaign before and since, the high, unrealistic expectations created by this unprecedented campaign for its time turned to bitter disillusionment. In the 1740s disgruntled colonists began writing back to England about true conditions in the colony. These letters to England centered on the prohibition of rum and slaves in the colony and the system of land tenure and were filled with attacks on Oglethorpe and the trustees. This resulted in a pamphlet war between Benjamin Martyn and William Stephens, the trustees' secretary in Georgia, defending the colony and trustees, and Thomas Stephens, a colonist and William's son, carrying the torch for the disillusioned settlers. In 1741, Martyn wrote a pamphlet, *An Impartial Inquiry in to the State and Utility of the Province of Georgia*. A thousand copies of the pamphlet urged Parliament to investigate the colony with the hope that this would persuade the government to appropriate annual support. But at the same time the unhappy colonists' publication, *A True and Historical Narrative of the Colony in Georgia in America* was circulating in Charles Town, and

Thomas Stephens soon found a book seller in England to reprint his tract. The trustees denounced the Stephens pamphlet as "libelous."

The hard fact was that colonists began leaving Georgia in the late 1730s, crossing the river into South Carolina where there were no restrictions on rum or on owning slaves. The population dropped significantly. The silk-worm "industry" had proved a flop. A report was sent to the trustees reported that there were more houses than people in Savannah. The disillusionment from all the rosy promises made in the trustees' propaganda is summed by this letter from a former colonist who had moved to South Carolina.[11] "The inhabitants are scattered over the face of the earth, her plantations a wild, her towns a desert, her villages in rubbish, her improvements a byword, and her liberties a jest; an object of pity to friends and of insult, contempt, ridicule to enemies."

The final blow to the Georgia Trust occurred in 1751 when Parliament refused to appropriate more money, and George III refused to help the colony unless the crown controlled it. This well-promoted 20-year experiment ended on June 23, 1752, when the Georgia Charter was surrendered to the King.

Lefler thought Georgia was "subject to more unfair attacks by malcontents than any other province." He concluded: "The promotional propaganda of the Southern colonies would compare favorably in quality, quantity, and results with that of other English colonies, with the possible exception of Pennsylvania and New Jersey."

FLORIDA

Nor did the English lose any time in promoting Florida after it was acquired under the terms of the Peace of Paris in 1763. The official British proclamations offering land "described the great salubrity of the climate and the longevity of former inhabitants and referred to the fertility of the soil."[12] From then on, there appeared several books and pamphlets in what Mowat described as a "vigorous and prolonged campaign of publicity." Effusiveness is not a new characteristic of Florida's sustained publicity efforts dating to this day. In 1766, a Dr. William Stork authored an *Account of East Florida* which told of the wonders and beauties of this sunny clime, although it is probable that the author had not been to Florida when he wrote his pamphlet. Some claim the Stork account was inspired by the British Government but Mowat did not put much stock in the claim. A later edition of the Stork

---

[11]*Colonial Records of Georgia*, Vol. XX, Part 2, p. 394, as quoted in Miles Lane, *General Oglethorpe's Georgia*.

[12]Charles L. Mowat, "The First Campaign of Publicity for Florida," *Mississippi Valley Historical Review, 30,* 1943, p. 363.

book included a heavily distorted version of a botanist's journal covering a trip up the St. John's River. The botanist, John Bartram, had a generally unfavorable opinion, but a typical edited entry reads: "fine warm morning, birds singing, fish jumping, and turkies gobbling."[13]

FUND-RAISING FOR CHARITY

The English also knew the value of publicity in raising funds for charitable causes. What was probably the first fund-raising campaign for education in North America had its origins in the latter part of October 1621 when a Patrick Copland approached the London Proprietors of the Virginia Company with an offer to raise money to build a school in Virginia. Copland had just returned from the East Indies and hearing of the "wondrous prosperity of the plantation called Virginia" voluntarily raised 270 pounds from "gentlemen and mariners" of the East India Company. He then set about to raise additional sums for a school in Charles City, Virginia, but after the Indian Massacre in 1622, the money was diverted to fortifications. The school was never built.

The first systematic effort to raise money on this continent was for Harvard College, founded in 1636. In 1641, the Massachusetts Bay Colony sent a trio of fundraisers to England to raise money for Harvard so that it could, among other endeavors, "educate the heathen Indian." Some suspect that the purpose was more to get desperately needed capital for the Massachusetts Bay Colony than to provide an education—a commodity then not in great demand in Massachusetts. Samuel Eliot Morison, Harvard historian wrote:[14] "The Weld-Peter begging mission, which one may call, in modern terms, the first concerted 'drive' to obtain income and endowment for the College, began early. On June 2, 1641, the General Court entreated their respective churches to release Hugh Peter of Salem, Thomas Weld of Roxbury, and William Hibbens of Boston, to go to England upon some weighty occasion for the good of the country."

This was 17th century circumlocution for seeking money. The Rev. Hibbens returned before the year was out, bearing some 500 pounds for the college and the colony. Fundraisers Weld and Peter sent back an urgent request for "literature" to play up the best "selling points" of New England. In response to this request came *New England's First Fruits*, written in Massachusetts but printed in England in 1643. This surely was the first of millions of fund-raising brochures. Morison described it as a "promotion pamphlet," adding, "one half expects to find in it a return postcard." This

---

[13]*Ibid.* pp. 365–369.
[14]*The Founding of Harvard College.* Cambridge: 1935, p. 303.

pamphlet was intended to show that Harvard College was a going concern, not a paper college "like the Virginia institution for which so much money had been collected twenty-five years before."

New England's First Fruits, a tract of 26 pages, carried a glowing picture of that region's natural resources and "wonder-working providences," an account of Harvard's work, and "a moving description of the benighted state of the Indians, and their desire to hear the Gospel." This promotional pamphlet provides much of our knowledge of this period in Massachusetts. Historians owe a debt to these early publicists. As Lefler observed: "The promotional tracts would not measure up to standards of modern historical scholarship, but they conveyed the full flavor of early America."

COLLEGES TAKE THEIR CUE

From the start, America's early colleges were hard pressed for funds to keep going because then, as now, student fees paid only a small part of the cost. Consequently, these pioneering educators were compelled to see the need for publicity. In 1758, King's College, now Columbia University, staged the first college commencement in New York City. The officials of King's College sensed the value of a staged public event in dramatizing its work, thus they sought to publicize this event. Someone at King's College—his identity lost in time—sent identical news releases to the publishers of the New York *Gazette*, the weekly *Post-Boy*, and the New York *Mercury* with a June 26th release date. The handouts quaintly said: "Mr. Printer Please insert the following in your next paper."[15] Surely this is one of the earliest examples of college publicity.

Princeton also pioneered in publicity methods suggestive of those used in more recent times by college publicists. One historian noted:[16] "Newspapers were supplied with information about the affairs of the college, particularly those which would interest parents of prospective students. Alumni of other institutions, granted degrees by Princeton, carried home a warm regard for their second alma mater. Trustees were drawn from various churches and colonies."

In this colonial period of 1745–1775, appeals to the general public from the hard-pressed colleges relied mainly on subscription lists and lotteries. Both had to be promoted and publicized. Occasional bequests brought in a bit more. Such funds usually went to meet recurring deficits. McAnear said that with the exception of King's, all the existing colleges of the time were

---

[15]Meyer Berger, *The New York Times*, June 6, 1958.

[16]Nelson R. Burr, *Education in New Jersey 1630–1871*. Princeton: Princeton University Press, 1942, p. 135.

operating on deficit budgets after 1770.[17] Often necessity is the mother of publicity. McAnear concluded, "The colleges were saved by the development of widespread popular interest in higher education."

THE DANIEL BOONE LEGEND BORN
OF FRONTIER HYPE

Just as publicity was used to lure settlers to the United States' primitive lands, so was it used to lure their offspring to move West, first to the Alleghenies, thence to the broad prairies of the Middle West, and finally, to the shores of the Pacific. The legend of Daniel Boone, today woven deeply in the fabric of our culture, was the creation of a land owner promoting settlement in the bluegrass land of Kentucky. More than any other U.S. folk hero, Daniel Boone epitomizes the United States' incurable romance with the bold adventures of the Westward migration against hardship and receding lines of Indian warriors. Dixon Wecter, in his *The Hero in America*, said:[18] "The winning of the West is the great fantasy of our Republic. It is the epic which the folk mind has looked upon as more truly American than the settlement of Jamestown and Plymouth, the spacious life of the old plantation, or the building of stone and steel." The very word, West, connotes excitement and enchantment. The publicist selling lands for the railroads and land speculators played a key role in fabricating this epic, one being constantly replayed on our motion picture screens and television.

Because the Daniel Boone legend was created to sell land in Kentucky, it has grown to fabulous dimensions, magnified many times over by historians and the imaginative writers for today's television. The Boone story was told by his publicists as one of hair-raising adventures in Chateaubriand-like prose to Americans and Europeans alike almost as soon as the Indian wars in Kentucky were over. Even though in his declining years Boone was a failure as a tavern keeper, horse breeder, trader, and land speculator, he remains the nation's first popularly acclaimed hero—thanks to his publicists. Boone owes his place in the United States' Pantheon of Heroes largely to John Filson, whose purpose was not to glorify Daniel Boone but to sell land in Kentucky. He saw the Boone tale as a means to that end because Boone was the best known man in the West at that time.

As John Mack Faragher wrote, much of the Boone legend is folklore because "facts come inextricably entwined with the legend." Nonetheless, the Boone legend has its roots in a chance meeting in a little log cabin in Lexington in 1783 between two men "who were destined to grace the pages

---

[17]Beverly McAnear, "College Founding in the American Colonies, 1745–1775," *Mississippi Valley Historical Review, 42* (June, 1955), pp. 24–44; and "The Raising of Funds by the Colonial Colleges," *Mississippi Valley Historical Review, 38* (March 1952) pp. 591–612.

[18]New York: C. Scribner's Sons, 1941, p. 182.

of many an unwritten text and story." The men were Daniel Boone, intrepid frontier scout, and John Filson, a school teacher from the Brandywine in Pennsylvania. Boone, now in his 50th year, had been leading the settlers' struggles against the Indians defending their hunting lands from white invasion.

Little is known of the birth and youth of John Filson. He is thought to have been born on the waters of Brandywine Creek, near what is now Chester, PA. Filson had spent the war years teaching school near Wilmington, DE. Caught in the excitement of the westward movement and the vision of making money in land speculation, Filson came to Kentucke (with an *e* not a *y*) on a river barge from Pittsburgh down to Louisville and then by land to Lexington. Filson later wrote:[19] "When I visited Kentucke, I found it to so far exceed my expectations, although great, that I concluded it was a pity they had not adequate information about it. I conceived that a proper description and a map of it, were objects highly interesting to the United States." Out of this project would come Daniel Boone's lasting fame.

Daniel Boone lived in a log cabin on the Kentucky River with his wife and extended family. For 15 years he had worked and fought to settle and defend this land. Faragher wrote: "it was understandable that Boone looked forward to the opportunity for retreats to Filson's room, where he reflected on his Kentucky adventures for a sympathetic listener." Faragher continued: "Boone rambled, but as Filson accumulated the details he began to sense the dramatic possibilities in these stories that might transform his work into something more than the compleat guide he had at first envisioned writing."[20]

Although Filson loudly disclaimed any financial motive for this writing project, it was to sell some 12,000 acres of land that he had acquired through land warrants bought with depreciated currency he had acquired from his share of his father's estate. It is clear his purpose was to sell land, not settle and develop it with axe and plow. Filson knew that the more people he could lure to Kentucke, the more his large land holdings would be worth.[21] "For gain he plunged into arduous schemes, sued and was sued, and endured all the hardships of an incredibly savage frontier."

Though he was living in a wilderness, Filson knew the value of publicity. Thus, he set about writing a guide to Kentucke—its geography, rivers, soil, climate, and its flora and fauna. He next prepared a detailed map with the help of Boone and other experienced surveyors—all the product of hard travel and countless interviews. His was the first map of this region, thus

---

[19]John Filson, *The Discovery, Settlement and present state of Kentucke* with foreword by William H. Masterson. New York: Corinth Books, 1962. Quote from preface.

[20]John Mack Faragher, *Daniel Boone the Life and Legend of an American Pioneer.* New York: Henry Holt and Company, 1992, p. 3.

[21]William Masterson in Introduction to Corinth paperback edition of Filson's book, *The Discovery, Settlement, and Present State of Kentucke.* New York: 1962.

John Filson has some claim as a pioneer cartographer, though his first map of Kentucky was far from accurate and lacked perspective. The promoter understandably described the new land in the purplest of prose, asserting Kentucke was "the most extraordinary country that the sun enlightens with his celestial beams."

But it was in the second section of the book that Filson waxed eloquent and poetic in creating the legend of Daniel Boone—"The Adventures of Col. Daniel Boone," taken down from his mouth. Filson saw that this epic would promote interest in his book. As it indeed did. He used Boone's words to sing the glories of Kentucke. He quoted Boone: "I surveyed the famous Ohio River that rolled in silent dignity, marking the western boundary of Kentucke with inconceivable grandeur. At a vast distance I beheld the mountains lift their brows and penetrate the clouds. All things were still. I kindled a fire near a fountain of sweet water and feasted on the loin of a buck, which a few hours before I had killed."

Boone was passably literate in the manner of his time, but this lofty language was that of Filson. For example, the old scout had once carved on a tree, "D. Boon cilled a bar." He also had carved on his rifle, "Boons best fren." Contrast this simplistic language with the opening sentence in the Boone narrative: "Curiosity is natural to the soul of man, and interesting objects have a powerful influence on our affections."

Or ponder this bit of philosophizing by Boone: "Felicity, the companion of content, is rather found in our own breasts than in the enjoyment of external things; and I firmly believe that it requires but a little philosophy to make a man happy in whatsoever state he is." Here is the natural man, innately good, freed from the tensions of society and from the shackles of convention. Even though few believed that these were Boone's words, many did think them his thoughts. Rather they were the thoughts and words of Filson, the land promoter, who made the roughhewn Boone speak as a pedant.

The fact was that Boone, son of a Reading, Pennsylvania, blacksmith, was able to write little more than his own name. Early in his youth he took to hunting, fishing, and in exploring the wilderness as an agent of the Transylvania Company who became—thanks to Filson—the flesh-and-blood symbol of the free-lance frontiersman "ordained by God to settle the Wilderness." Wecter described Boone as "a brave, kindly, honest soul, too simple for the complexities and knaveries of civilization. Robbed, cheated, disposed, he moved farther and farther west, pathetically seeking a fortune with which he never caught up."[22] The real life Boone bore little resemblance to Walt Disney's Daniel Boone, played by Fess Parker in the 1960s.

Filson finished his book in 2 months. There was no printing press west of the Alleghenies at this time, so in the late spring of 1784, Filson carried

---

[22]Wecter, p. 182.

his manuscript to Wilmington, DE, where it was published by James Adams under the title *The Discovery, Settlement and Present State of Kentucke.* The map was engraved and printed in Philadelphia. The Boone saga was printed as an appendix. Fifteen hundred copies of the book and map were printed in the first edition. The next year, the book was published in Paris and in Frankfurt, Germany. Soon reprints were appearing in London and New York. Only 33 pages of the book were given to the Boone narrative, but it was this heroic tale that caught the public's fancy—here and in Europe. Filson's idea had paid off; soon the book was known as "Filson's Boone." A year after the initial publication Europeans knew as much about the Boone exploits as did Americans. This prototype of the U.S. hero, who embodied many of the virtues of the European natural man, caught the public's imagination and has held it in a tight grip ever since. Even Lord Byron, in his *Don Juan*, praised Boone as:

> Not only famous, but of *good* fame,
> Without which Glory's but a tavern song—

Filson's great grandson, John Walton, had observed:[23] "Boone has directly and indirectly inspired many of the characters in American fiction. One of the first writers who became indebted to this legend was James Fennimore Cooper, whose Leatherstocking bore unmistakable similarities to Boone." Cooper's Leatherstocking represented the essence of old-fashioned U.S. enterprise. The hold of the Boone epic on the literary mind of Europe was reflected in a news dispatch from Paris to *The New York Times* on April 6, 1917, apropos the United States' entry in the war: "Old Leatherstocking still slumbers in the depth of the American soul. Wait till the lion wakens. Don't believe he will go at it half-heartedly; it is not his nature." The Boone chronicle has been republished many times, often without due credit to Filson whose press agentry is available today as a paperback.

For example, in 1786, it was plagiarized and condensed to 12 pages by John Trumbull of Norwich, CT, and published as a paper-covered pamphlet. This version can be found in *The Boone Narrative* by Willard Rouse Jillson, published by the Standard Printing Company, Louisville, KY, 1932. Filson's first edition sold fairly well in the United States, but he found no demand for a second edition.

How much land Filson's promotional publicity sold is not known, but historians have concluded that the book "did speed the settlement of the state."

Eventually Filson returned to Kentucky and variously tried fur trading, school teaching, and more land speculation. He had no further contact with

---

[23]John Walton, "Daniel Boone," *American Heritage* (October 1955), p. 11.

Boone after the book's publication. Alas, our imaginative press agent gained little. In August 1788, Filson entered into a contract with two other men to develop about 800 acres of land on the north bank of the Ohio River, opposite the mouth of the Licking River. They proposed to develop a river town there called Losantiville—today's Cincinnati, Ohio. On one of his reconnoitering trips to Losantiville, Filson vanished into the forest of the lower Miami River valley. He was never seen again. His death remains a mystery to this day. Presumably he was done in by the Indians. John Filson may have ducked the battle of Brandywine but apparently failed to duck an Indian's tomahawk. Thus, one of our pioneer press agents died an ignoble death that took him to the shadows of history whereas his publicity creation, Folk Hero Daniel Boone, lives on and his legend is embellished with each succeeding generation. A few dedicated Kentucky history buffs set out in 1884 to see that Filson got his due by forming the John Filson Club to honor "The First Historian of Kentucky." For details of Filson's life see John Walton, *John Filson of Kentucke*, Lexington, KY, 1956, and John Mack Farragher, previously cited.

Thus began the art of "shirt stuffing" that U.S. publicists have developed to a high art indeed.

Propaganda Gives Birth
to a New Nation*

Employment of public relations skills to shape the course and impact of government is older than the national government itself. The tools and techniques of persuasive communication have long been utilized in the nation's struggles for political power. The public relations function in government is inevitably involved in the political contests in the public arena, though this is not the whole of the function as it has evolved in our politics and governments. Political public relations practice in the United States dates back to the nation's pre-Revolution years when a small, dedicated, and resourceful band of propagandists and strategists fed the fires of revolt that led to this nation's birth. Practices originated by them are in use today, albeit in a more precise and professional manner of execution and utilizing modern channels of communication. The essential difference between the Revolutionary propagandists and today's practitioners is the greater awareness of the utility of persuasive communication and in its extensive, sophisticated use.

The 20-year struggle from 1763 to 1783 that brought the United States its nationhood was sustained by a small group of revolutionaries who struggled uphill against great odds, against the strong pro-British loyalties of many influential citizens, and against the apathy of most citizens who were occupied with the hard tasks of life in a primitive country. These revolutionaries were among the first to demonstrate the power of an organized, articulate minority carrying the day against the unorganized, apathetic majority of citizens. John Adams estimated that one third of the people were Loyalists.

---

*This chapter is based in large part on my article, "Public Relations and the American Revolution," published in *The Public Relations Review*, Volume 2, Winter, 1976, and is used here with the permission of Editor Ray L. Hiebert.

In this context it is useful to remember that in the pre-Revolution period most of the U.S. people were farmers.

Little wonder Philip Davidson thought "The influence of the propagandists was out of all proportion to their number."[1] That the struggle for Independence in America—from 1763 to 1776—took 14 years offers a basic lesson for today's persuaders: public opinion is more likely to move at glacial speeds than that of lightning.

Today's patterns of public relations practice have been shaped far more than most practitioners realize by innovations in mobilizing public opinion developed by Samuel Adams and his fellow revolutionaries. In fomenting revolt against Great Britain, the Revolutionary propagandists, operating largely from the shadows, developed and demonstrated the power of these techniques:

1. The necessity of organization to implement actions made possible by a propaganda campaign, for example, the Sons of Liberty, organized in Boston in January 1766 and the Committees of Correspondence, also born in Boston, in 1772.

2. The use of symbols that are easily identifiable and emotion arousing—for example, the Liberty Tree.

3. The use of slogans that compress complex issues in easy-to-quote, easy to remember stereotypes, for example, "Taxation without representation is tyranny."

4. Staged events that catch public attention and thus crystallize unstructured public opinion, for example, the Boston Tea Party.

5. The importance of getting your story to the public first so that your interpretation of events becomes the widely accepted one, for example, the Horrid Boston Massacre.

6. The necessity of a sustained, saturation campaign using the previous techniques through all available media to penetrate the public mind with a new idea or a new conviction. The emotion-laden Revolutionary campaign set patterns for the nation's political battles that were to follow.

We concur in the view of a contemporary practitioner that Adams' "classic campaign foreshadowed, in certain elements, some of the principles of persuasion which remain evident two centuries later."[2] A popular Yale history

---

[1]Philip Davidson, *Propaganda and the American Revolution*, 1763–1783. Chapel Hill: University of North Carolina Press, 1941, p. 3 (Now available in paperback.)

[2]A book authored by Cass Canfield endeavors to give Adams his due: *Sam Adams' Revolution* (1765–1776), published by Harper & Row in 1976. The book tells us little new about Adams despite Richard Morris' assertion in a foreword that Canfield restored "Sam Adams to his central role as a tenacious and uncompromising leader of the independence movement."

teacher once said: "The way to get at the nature of an institution, as of anything else that is alive, is to see how it has grown."

The American Revolution was not a popular uprising. The fact is the colonists were not an oppressed people. Ralph Volney, Harlow asserted, that "by 1760 the colonies were nearly independent in fact." The revolt against the British Government was not a spontaneous movement, but rather it was carefully planned and sagaciously carried out by a few active, shrewd men and one woman, Mercy Otis Warren. It could never have succeeded had it been left unorganized. The work of these revolutionaries was greatly abetted by periodic British blunders and by slow, feeble lines of communication between England and the colonies. To keep the record balanced, it should be noted that the Loyalists were active in countering the Patriots' propaganda efforts.

The preeminent Revolutionary historian, Merrill Jensen, in one of his last essays wrote: "America's leaders knew that there was a wide gap between their public professions and American reality. They knew that there was bitter opposition to Independence and that the mass of people were probably indifferent. They knew too that there were serious rivalries and fundamental differences among the states and among groups of states that would be obstacles to winning Independence and to creating a nation."[3] Historian Carl Becker concluded in his study of the Revolution that "the American Revolution was the result of two general movements, the contest for home-rule and independence, and the democratization of American politics and society." He reasoned: "The American Revolution was far more than a war between the colonies and Great Britain; it was a struggle between those who enjoyed political privileges and those who did not."

Fundamentally, in Jensen's view,[4] "the Revolution had deep roots; some ideas can be traced back at least as far as Magna Carta. Obviously, too, Americans had achieved an economic and political society of such maturity that they resented outside interference with their operation of it." Likewise, some of them at least had begun to look on Americans as different or a "new" people long before the troubles began in 1763.

Great Britain's victory over France in the Seven Years War, which concluded with the Peace of 1763, ousted France from the North American continent and thus greatly lessened the colonists' dependence on Great Britain. The war also saddled the victor with large debts that required new and heavier taxes. Another important factor was that by 1763 American newspapers had achieved a measure of freedom.

---

[3]"The Sovereign States: Their Antagonisms and Rivalries and Some Consequences," in Ronald Huffman and Peter J. Albert, eds., Charlottesville, VA: University of Virginia Press, 1981, p. 226.

[4]Merrill Jensen, *The Founding of a Nation.* New York: Oxford University Press, 1968, p. 66.

This was the backdrop against which the colonists moved falteringly toward independence. "Twelve rasping years of irritation, incident and propaganda converted an unquestioning love of the parent state first into distrust and foreboding, then into hatred and repudiation."[5] The fruit of a steady drum fire of anti-British propaganda and a series of British blunders united the colonies, more like independent nations than sister states, in a common cause by 1775. By then, in Richard Morris' view, "deep and varied grievances stirred discontent in the Thirteen Colonies and ultimately inspired common action." John Adams, years later, said that the Revolution was "in the minds and hearts of the people, and this was effected, from 1760 to 1775, in the course of fifteen years before a drop of blood was drawn at Lexington.[6] Then, as now, public opinion moved at slowly, not in the quick mercurial ways that those who worry about "hidden persuaders" would have us believe.

The idea of independence from Britain, though long a private dream of a few, chiefly Samuel Adams, did not become a publicly stated goal until late in the long campaign against British taxes and controls. After the opening battle at Lexington and Concord in April 1775, the propagandists began their campaign for independence in earnest. Demands by essayists and letter writers for independence from Britain began appearing in the press as early as 1773. "The opening of the war in April, 1775, made independence inevitable, yet it was nearly fifteen months before the act of independence could be passed. The contest which delayed the decision was between those who wished reconciliation and those who demanded independence. In this contest, the propagandists were necessary, and their work decisive."[7]

The debate took place on many levels, and its basic themes were iterated and reiterated in the manner of modern-day advertising, through many channels. The propagandists found their basic appeal in John Locke's philosophy that people had natural rights, rights to their religion, their own property, and the right to control their own affairs. Adams had studied Locke at Harvard with the consequence that in this debate some historians assert a large part of Sam Adams' contributions were based on Locke. Jensen has noted that the only pamphlets that quoted Locke were those by Joseph Galloway, a Pennsylvania conservative; he used Locke to prove the "Patriots" were wrong. Adams was more likely to quote Milton.

---

[5]Arthur M. Schlesinger, *Prelude to Independence*, Vintage eds., New York: 1957, p. 4, Published by Alfred Knopf.

[6]Lester J. Cappon, ed., *The Adams–Jefferson Letters*. University of North Carolina Press, Chapel Hill: 1959, II, p. 455.

[7]Philip Davidson, *Propaganda and the American Revolution*, paperback ed. University of North Carolina Press, Chapel Hill: 1941, p. 43.

ALL AVAILABLE MEDIA UTILIZED

Newspapers, pamphlets, sermons from the pulpit, town meetings, and the committees of correspondence were the primary means of carrying the attack on British rule. Other means of communication, such as broadsides, songs, plays, poems, and cartoons, were also used but in a lesser way. The documentation for these techniques is far from complete and, with the exception of the broadside, historians have assigned them lesser importance.[8] Davidson asserted that the broadside was a highly effective means for reaching the lower classes with "inflammatory propaganda."

These efforts were given added power by the paucity and slowness of communication from England. Then, as now, the vacuum of public curiosity was filled by rumor and allegation if it was not first filled with authentic information. The colonies lived in a constant state of uncertainty, often based on uncertain reports and rumor. In those days, it took some 5 weeks or more for a letter to cross the 3,000 miles of ocean. It took from 8 to 10 weeks to get an act of Parliament published in the colonies. Even more time elapsed before the often angry reaction of the colonists was fed back to the British authorities by the royal governors and quite often this public opinion feedback was erroneous or sugar-coated. Schlesinger said, "The representatives of the Crown continually sent home pathetic accounts of the impotence in the face of these excesses [mob actions, effigy hangings, e.g.] but the London authorities were too far away and too immersed in their own concerns to give the situation here more than offhand attention."[9] As Royal Governor Francis Bernard wrote his British superiors about the Sugar Act, "The mischievous consequences of such a measure, I fear, will not appear as certain on your side of the water, as they do here."

Nonetheless the odds against which the propagandists, led first by James Otis until he got whacked on the head in a brawl, then by the resourceful, indefatigable Samuel Adams, struggled to carry the day of independence, serves to write large their successful campaign and innovative techniques. The dedicated few who carried off the revolution against Great Britain included Otis, Adams, his second cousin, John Adams, Benjamin Franklin, Josiah Quincy, Thomas Paine, Thomas Jefferson, Alexander McDougall, who became known as the "Wilkes of America," Christopher Gadsden, and Mercy Warren. Of these, only Adams in Boston, McDougall in New York, Dickinson in Philadelphia, and Gadsden achieved intercolonial prominence.

We ought not overlook a few women who played a part in this anti-British campaign. Mercy Otis Warren, friend of John and Abigail Adams, published satirical plays and poems lampooning Tory leaders as classic villains. She

---

[8]See Schlesinger, Chapter 2, and Davidson, Chapters 10–13.
[9]Schlesinger, p. 26.

became known as the poet laureate of the cause. Her three-volume history, published in 1805, has value for its contemporary views. Another revolutionary writer was an African-American woman, Phillis Wheatley, who was once a slave. She was sold to a benevolent Boston family who educated her and gave her freedom. She wrote of the colonial tyranny and was the first African-American woman to publish a book of poetry. She also created awareness of the evils of slavery through her works. Another stalwart fighter in the cause of independence was Mary Katherine Goodard, editor and publisher of the *Maryland Journal and Baltimore Advertiser.* Her paper was the first to publish the Paris Peace Treaty on February 19, 1783.[10]

Limits of space permit us to focus only on the leader—Samuel Adams, described by a current practitioner as "a genius in the use of mass communications who ought now at last to be recognized as the 'father of American propaganda.' " This "genius" gave indications of suffering from a deep inferiority complex; the evidence suggests that he found his political career a means of escape from his sense of failure in earlier pursuits. Canfield termed him a "loner," one who "was suspicious of people, privilege and of wealth."[11] Harlow described him as the "last of the Puritans" who resembled Martin Luther somewhat in temperament. He termed Adams a shrewd operator who concealed petty partisanship under "high sounding generalities." Peter Oliver, chief justice of the Massachusetts Superior Court from 1771 until the Revolution, saw Sam Adams as a "thorough Machiavellian" who "used every low and dirty art . . . such arts as an Oyster Wench disdains."

As an aside, it is interesting to note that three of the ablest political publicists of our first 200 years—Adams, Amos Kendall, who served Andrew Jackson, and Louis McHenry Howe, who served Franklin Roosevelt—were the antithesis of the common stereotype of the public relations practitioner as a congenial backslapper ready to buy a free drink. Chidsey described Adams as a "man unskillfully put together."[12]

ADAMS FINDS SUCCESS AS PROPAGANDIST

Adams was a dismal failure as a business man and something less than diligent as a tax collector although his easy going ways made him popular with the people. He won lots of votes in town meetings by listening to taxpayers' hard luck stories. There Adams found his genius in political ma-

---

[10]For more details on these women, see Lonnelle Aikman, "Patriots in Petticoats," *National Geographic,* October 1975, pp. 475–493.

[11]*Sam Adams's Revolution,* p. 5.

[12]Donald Barr Chidsey, *The World of Samuel Adams.* Nashville: T. Nelson, 1974, an undocumented brief book that adds little new on Adams or his "world."

nipulation and in propaganda and, as a consequence, "rose to commanding power during the early days of the struggle with Britain."

In 1765, Sam Adams plunged into a whirl of political activity that would by the time of the Stamp Act make him the acknowledged leader of the radical forces. Vernon Parrington wrote of Adams:[13] "His hours of triumph in Boston town meeting or in the assembly were preceded by an incredible amount of labor with the pen as well as with the tongue, for this master politician was the journalist as well as the organizer of the New England revolution. The labors undergone and the energy consumed were enormous. It was no holiday task to create and guide a public opinion that was so constantly falling into apathy."

His first move, always, was to gain the support of public opinion. Davidson wrote: "Sam Adams owned no superior as a propagandist. No one in the colonies realized more fully than he the primary necessity of arousing public opinion, no one set about it more assiduously." Vernon Parrington once called him "a master political strategist, the first of our great popular leaders." Another biographer said of Adams: "The biographer must make plain Adams' manner of work, his manufacturing of public opinion, his mishandling of the facts, his mistaken persistence in attributing evil motives to those whom he fought. These things Adams did; indeed they were the tools with which he labored."[14] Surely one of his guiding precepts was "Put your enemy in the wrong and keep him there," a precept that is no stranger to today's political public relations. Many historians argue, with validity, that Adams' manipulative intent and vituperative attacks were not characteristic of most polemicists of this period. Bernard Bailyn, for one, strongly dissents from Philip Davidson's point of view.[15] Typical of his latter-day successors, Adams usually operated from behind the scenes.

MANY VIEWS OF ADAMS

Adams' role in history, the ethics of his tireless campaign for independence, and the impact of his agitation on public opinion have been a source of conflicting interpretation by historians for more than 200 years. His prime target, Governor Thomas Hutchinson, saw him as an evil, criminal man, "neither to be trusted by contemporaries nor praised by historians." Tory Peter Oliver called him a character assassin. A more recent writer with a conservative view, Clifford K. Shipton, argued that instead of bringing about

---

[13]*In Main Currents in American Thought*, New York: Harcourt Brace Jovanovich, 1927, I, pp. 241–242.

[14]Ralph Volney Harlow, *Samuel Adams*. New York: Henry Holt, 1923, pp. 357–358.

[15]See his *Ideological Origins of the American Revolution*, "A Note on Conspiracy," pp. 144–159. Cambridge: The Belknap Press of Harvard University Press, 1967.

the Revolution, Adams "set back the Revolution for years." John C. Miller held him to be "a master manipulator of public opinion." Bernard Bailyn seems to argue that the propaganda produced by Adams and his compatriots was as much an effect of inflamed political passions as a cause, thus tending to minimize the propaganda they contrived. Writing in 1970, Hiller Zobol said Adams was "unmatched" in his "mastery of the weasel word." A current reappraisal of Adams has been set in motion by Richard Brown, Pauline Maier, a student of Bailyn's, and Stephen Patterson. The latter asserted Adams and many of his fellow revolutionaries were appalled by the excesses of partisanship.[16] I concur with the Progressive historians who saw Adams as a prime mover in bringing our independence.

Adams and his fellow revolutionaries understood the importance of public opinion and knew how to arouse and channel it toward their predetermined ends. To do this they used pen, platform, pulpit, staged events, symbols, and political organization in a determined, imaginative, and unrelenting way. Adams worked tirelessly to first arouse and then to organize public opinion, proceeding always on the assumption that "the bulk of mankind are more led by their senses than by their reason." Adams early discerned that public opinion resulted from the march of events and the way these events were seen by those active in public affairs. He once wrote Joseph Warren: "it will be wise for us to be ready for all events, that we may make the best improvement of them."[17] Adams would create events to meet a need if none were at hand to serve his purpose.

Then, as now, the news media provided the central platform for the propagandist. During the revolutionary period, only one Boston paper made any effort to be neutral. This was the *Boston Evening Post*, published by Thomas and John Fleet who ultimately found that their balanced news policy could not endure. Their paper folded in April 1775. *The Massachusetts Spy* and *Boston Gazette* were the workhorses of the Patriots' campaign. *The Massachusetts Spy* was founded by Zechariah Fowle and Isaiah Thomas in 1770; Fowle left the paper a few months later. One historian, Mary Ann Yodelis, said that "the most effective Patriot editors were Benjamin Edes and John Gill," who assumed the proprietorship of the *Boston Gazette* with the April 7, 1755, edition.[18] These and other newspapers were the principal means of disseminating radical ideas, developing hatred of the British rulers and their Tory supporters in the colonies, and finally, in persuading the colonies to unite. Many of the newspapers in every colony throughout the

---

[16]For a documented, balanced view of these conflicting assessments of Adams, see James M. O'Toole's essay, "The Historical Interpretations of Samuel Adams," *New England Quarterly*, (March 1976) pp. 82–96.

[17]Davidson, *op. cit.* p. 3.

[18]Mary Ann Yodelis, "Economics and the Boston, Massachusetts Newspapers, 1763–1773," paper given at Association for Education in Journalism, Washington, DC, 1970.

pre-Revolutionary period were printed by men who viewed their roles as "ranging from the high purpose of uniting the colonies to the more mundane motive of earning a living."[19]

NEWSPAPERS PLAY MAJOR ROLE

The newspapers played a most influential role in political life from the Stamp Act onward. As Jensen noted, "The newspapers, far more than the pamphlets, appealed to the mass of the people, stirred their emotions, and urged them to action." Schlesinger agreed "that, although a multitude of factors from the Sugar Act onward pushed the colonists along the road to Independence, the movement could hardly have succeeded without an ever alert and dedicated press."[20] In the pre-Revolution period the press, as now, influentially shaped the public agenda and the public's response to the issues of the day. Then as now the news-media–public opinion relationship worked both ways, the media influencing public opinion and public opinion shaping media content.

These newspapers, mostly weeklies, were produced mainly by printers who welcomed outside contributions. Then, as now, the propagandists were quick to capitalize on the media's lack of reportorial manpower. From the founding of the *Independent Advertiser* in 1748 until 1776 when the Declaration of Independence was written as a public relations document "out of a decent respect to the opinions of mankind," Samuel Adams wrote hundreds of essays attacking England under at least 25 pseudonyms. Near the climax of the struggle, Adams and his band filled the pages of the *Boston Gazette* with emotion-laden articles, letters from other colonies, clippings from other newspapers—all designed to arouse hatred of the British and arouse demands for self-government. "No other pen in Boston is as busy as his," Governor Francis Bernard of Massachusetts once wrote of Adams. "Every dip of his pen stung like a horned snake." Other opponents referred to Adams and his fellow publicists as "Canker worms of the state" and "men of desperate fortunes."[21]

PAMPHLETS ALSO HEAVILY USED

The propagandists also made such use of the pamphlet that it became "the distinctive literature of the Revolution." Pamphleteering had been heavily used in the English Civil War of the 17th century. More than 400 pamphlets

---

[19]Jensen, *Founding a Nation*, p. 99.
[20]Schlesinger, p. 46.
[21]"A True Patriot," *Boston Evening Post*, Sept. 21, 1767.

were published between 1750 and 1776, and by 1783, at the end of the 20-year struggle, more than 1,500 had appeared. These were primarily political, not literary documents. Many of these were polemical and aimed at the passions of the colonists, but many were rather dull. Bailyn, who has made an extended study of these pamphlets, mostly the Massachusetts anti-British ones, said:[22] "Explanatory as well as declarative and expressive of the beliefs, attitudes, and motivations as well as the professed goals of those who led and supported the Revolution, the pamphlets reveal, more clearly than any other single group of documents, the contemporary meaning of that transforming event." Bailyn's research led him to conclude that the success of the Revolution was not inevitable and that the years were filled with "unpredictable reality."

The pamphlet writers used satire, irony, allegory, fact, and direct vituperation, often with remarkable results. Davidson said, "The pamphlet, when used to develop the constitutional argument, appealed to the intellectual classes and was the best possible type of propaganda for that specific purpose." He added: "Samuel Adams and Benjamin Franklin, for instance, whose appeal was primarily to the average reading public, relied almost entirely upon the newspapers whereas Oxenbridge Thacher, Stephen Hopkins, James Otis, James Wilson, Alexander Hamilton, Thomas Jefferson, and many others . . . published their more important contributions in pamphlets. The basic elements of American political thought of the revolutionary period appeared first in this form."[23]

Merrill Jensen did not agree with this assertion, arguing that "on the whole, the newspapers between 1763 and 1776 were more aggressive in promoting extreme ideas than the writers of pamphlets." Jensen wrote: "But whether the pamphleteers led or followed is not as important as the fact that they did sum up, in extended and in more permanent form, ideas that were scattered about in newspapers. It is idle to try to assign predominance to either newspapers or pamphlets; at the time, they were in fact interchangeable tools in a continuing debate."[24]

The pamphlets were used in tandem with the briefer journalistic essays being printed in newspapers. Pamphlets permitted the propagandists to present a detailed, cogent case in a way that synthesized and summarized arguments being made in the public forum. Most pamphlets' authors were well known although they were rarely signed. Whig supporters in the Parliament often quoted from these pamphlets in presenting the colonists' grievances.

The most famous and probably most effective of all these pamphlets came after the battle was joined—Thomas Paine's *Common Sense*, published

---

[22]Bernard Bailyn, *op. cit.*

[23]Davidson, *Propaganda*, p. 210.

[24]Merrill Jensen, *Tracts of the American Revolution*, 1763–1776. Indianapolis: Bobbs-Merrill Co., 1967, p. XV.

on January 9, 1776. This pamphlet, said Jensen, "presented the issue of independence to Americans as it had never been presented before, and in language that could be understood by anyone who could read. The ideas in it were not new, what was new was the direct, hard-hitting prose." Thomas Paine, who came to the United States in 1774, "agitator and propagandist supreme," sensed the popular temper and expressed it vividly in the people's language. He did much to sustain the Revolutionary cause in the dark days of war. Jensen said *Common Sense* was the first pamphlet to have the appeal of newspaper articles and the broadside.[25]

A Paine biographer, Eric Foner, held that Paine's pamphlet "was the precursor of a tradition of polemical political writing addressed to a mass audience. American writing as diverse as abolitionist tracts, 'yellow journalism,' and political commentators in the mass media today, all owe something to *Common Sense*."[26]

A final word on pamphlets. Most of the Revolutionary material was published in newspapers; political pamphlets accounted for a very small percentage of the total printing in the colonies during this period and later during the War for Independence. As the war progressed and the economy took a turn for the worse, and as paper became scarce, pamphlets became fewer. Pamphlets were published in great numbers only during times of crisis. Newspapers took over the propaganda function particularly during the times of the paper shortage. Pamphlets were not as important economically to the Colonial printers.

COMMITTEES OF CORRESPONDENCE

Sam Adams knew well that it took organization to channel and implement the public opinion he first aroused; organization of the rank and file presented a new problem in a new land. The Caucus Club, in which his father was active, served as a training school for these revolutionaries. There, said Parrington, "The policies were determined upon for the town meeting and the assembly, and there the plans for a continental union were laid in Non-Importation Agreements, organization of the Committees of Correspondence, and the like." The success of the Caucus Club was born more of organized effort than of popular support.

To create a network of communication that would solidify the thirteen scattered, independent colonies, Adams organized the Committees of Correspondence to circulate information in the common cause, a channel of

[25]In letter to author, dated April 21, 1976.
[26]Eric Foner, *Tom Paine and Revolutionary America*. New York: Oxford University Press, 1976.

communication well suited to the day of letter writing. Started in Massachusetts in 1772 at Sam Adams' urging, the committees evolved into a "powerful grassroots political organization" for the revolutionists. After the one was formed in Massachusetts, Virginia proposed a year later that official committees be organized in each colony. The system was not completed until summer 1774. Forerunners of this intercolony communications network first appeared in 1764 at the time of the Sugar Act. These committees, Schlesinger termed *furnaces of propaganda.*

It is difficult for us today to comprehend the communications problem facing the Adams-led propagandists. Road networks did not exist and land travel was primarily by horseback in a day when no major stream in the colonies was bridged. In days when the trip from New York to Philadelphia took 2 days by stage, travel conditions discouraged intercolony contacts for those with a "message" to send. The postal service, manned by riders on horseback in the North and served by ships in the South, was slow, and often unreliable. The sailing ship was the way to travel in those days.

Communications was a difficult, slow process. It took anywhere from 2 to 5 weeks to send material from Boston to Charleston, South Carolina. For example, it took 6 weeks for the news of Lexington and Concord to fully permeate the colonies.[27] The main means of intercolony communication were the Committees of Correspondence, printed sermons, and newspapers; printers lifting material from other newspapers as these arrived by post over the enlarged postroads system started by Benjamin Franklin in 1753. Only a few pamphlets circulated throughout the colonies; one written by John Dickinson in 1768 and Paine's *Common Sense* had the widest circulation. It was the newspapers that did the job.

The way the Committees of Correspondence worked in generating opposition to British rule is illustrated by the Boston committee's first efforts. In November 1772, the Boston town meeting directed its newly created committee to open communication with other Massachusetts towns by means of a political pamphlet, "State of the Rights of the Colonies," which detailed a long list of grievances against Britain. It was divided into three parts: a statement of rights, a list of grievances, and a Letter of Correspondence to other towns. Distribution of this pamphlet led to many town meetings in Massachusetts where the contents were discussed. In some towns, grievances were listed in others local committees of correspondence were formed; in still others no action was taken.

Though the towns expected leadership from Boston there was a wide diversity in their response of the Boston committee's efforts.[28] Incidentally,

---

[27]Frank Luther Mott, "Newspaper Coverage of Lexington and Concord," *New England Quarterly, 17* (December 1944) pp. 489–505.

[28]See Richard D. Brown, "Massachusetts Towns Reply to the Boston Committee of Correspondence, 1773," *William & Mary Quarterly, 25* (January 1968) pp. 22–39.

Richard Brown dissented from those scholars who have assumed that Sam Adams ran the Boston committee and that the committee in turn led the Massachusetts countryside by the adroit use of propaganda, but he did agree that the Boston committee did exercise considerable influence on the countryside.[29]

Through these committees passed a constant if somewhat irregular flow of information and exhortation to concerted action, first against the royal authorities, then against the British. Adams saw the committees as a means of building confidence in one another, in forming plans of opposition, and making clear to the British that the opposition came from all colonies. "If the enemies should see the flame bursting in different parts of the country and distant from each other, it might discourage their attempts to damp and quench it." A Tory spokesman, Daniel Leonard, who wrote under the name of "Massachusettensis," singled out the Committees of Correspondence as "the foulest, subtlest, and most venomous serpent that ever issued from the egg of sedition." In an opposite view, John Adams defended them as "admirably calculated to diffuse knowledge, to communicate intelligence, and promote unanimity." Sam Adams' vituperative propaganda dealt far more in personalities than in "diffusion of knowledge" as he heaped abuse on Governor Thomas Hutchinson and his supporters. Then, as now, political propaganda gave more emphasis to personalities and attacks than to discussion of complex issues.

Adams knew then as political practitioners know today that public attitudes are largely the result of events coupled with the way these events come to be interpreted. Here, too, he worked swiftly to "make the best improvement" on events to build fervor for his cause. The way Adams and his group exploited the Boston Massacre is a perfect example of this persuasion principle. Sam Adams turned a skirmish between some British soldiers and a gang of port toughs into an emotional symbol of brutality and oppression.

GET YOUR STORY THERE FIRST

On the night of March 5, 1770, a file of British regulars, after a sentry had been attacked near the Boston Customs House, fired into the crowd of their tormentors. Five were killed, others hurt. The propagandists quickly labeled this the "Horrid Boston Massacre" and, in the words of Bruce Lancaster in *The American Revolution*, "turned the dead port toughs into martyrs, orating

---

[29]See his *Revolutionary Politics in Massachusetts: The Boston Committee and The Towns, 1772–1774.* Cambridge, MA: Harvard University Press, 1970. Brown argued that regardless of the persuasive skills Adams had, the countryside was ready to receive the message and "iffy" arguments.

and thundering how they had been shot down in cold blood by hireling troops." The Boston Town Meeting quickly issued a pamphlet giving its version of the "massacre" and disseminated it to the English-speaking world. Entitled, "A Short Narrative of the Horrid Massacre in Boston," it was written by James Bowdoin, Dr. Joseph Warren, and Samuel Pemberton. Paul Revere made an engraving of innocent citizens being mowed down by British soldiers that was captioned by a poem full of gore and patriotic outrage. The date, under Adams' deft touch, became a hallowed anniversary in the colonies and provided an effective source for anti-British propaganda for 5 years thereafter.

A student of the impact of the Boston Massacre propaganda found that the "evidence shows that the principal message transmitted by all channels of public communication was that the massacre was the inevitable consequence of a standing army stationed 'illegally' among civilians in a time of peace; that the army was inherently evil and threatened liberty."[30] He found the massacre message received its fullest exposure in Massachusetts diminishing in Connecticut and Pennsylvania. The story was circulated to lesser degree in South Carolina and Virginia. However, in New York the message got short shrift. Generally, Smith's evidence shows that for 5 years the massacre was kept before the public through the efforts of the militant Whigs. Newspapers were main vehicles for this effort.

Of the Boston Massacre, John Adams wrote: "On that night the formation of American Independence was laid." Later he offered the opinion that the massacre was "an event never yet forgiven by any part of America." Years later Daniel Webster said: "From that moment we may date the severance of the British Empire." Like many a propaganda effort, over time the massacre has become a part of our national legend, although Arthur M. Schlesinger described the event as "a public relations effort aimed at inciting the lower classes." And indeed it was!

THE STAGED EVENT

Sam Adams knew intuitively the power of a dramatic event to seize public attention and to set off public discussion. What Historian Daniel Boorstin termed the *pseudo-event* is a staple ingredient of today's public relations practice. Sam Adams' Boston Tea Party provided the model. In bringing off the Boston Tea Party, Adams effectively demonstrated the power of the shocking, dramatic event in mobilizing public opinion. After careful planning, Adams set off the Tea Party with the cue to a Boston rally that "this

---

[30]Robert W. Smith, "News Diffusion and Significance of the Boston Massacre in Six American Colonies, 1770–1775," unpublished thesis University of Wisconsin-Madison, 1972, p. 176.

meeting can do nothing more to save our country," an event that brought a new spirit of unity to colonial America.[31] In fact, many persons in Boston and in the other colonies were shocked and outraged by this staged event. Others argue the impact of the tea's destruction was more one of shock and dismay, and that it was the Intolerable Acts that brought unity to the colonies. Adams' first biographer, his great grandson, William V. Wells, wrote in 1865 that "the destruction of the tea was the great crowning act of the Revolution prior to the commencement of hostilities." A later and more definitive if somewhat inaccurate biographer, John C. Miller, believes the Tea Party "was a headlong plunge toward a revolt which set free the forces, long gathering in America, that led to the war."

The work of a disciplined mob in destroying the tea in Boston harbor was effective because Adams and his colleagues knew the importance of getting their side of the event to the public first. Paul Revere rode express to carry the patriots' version of the Tea Party to New York and Philadelphia. A broadside was published that appealed for support in the common cause, and letters to individuals were written by members of the Committee of Correspondence. Back came the reply: "This horrid attack upon the town of Boston, we consider not as an attempt upon that town singly, but upon the whole continent." Bailyn, among others, held that the passage of the Tea Act and resulting Tea Party in Boston in December 1773 marked the turning point of the campaign for independence. Jensen argued, persuasively, that it was not the Tea Party but rather the British punishment of Boston for the event that brought the turning point.

In the same fashion, these propagandists saw to it that the patriots' version of the clash at Lexington and Concord got to England ahead of the official account sent by General Gage to defend his actions. Carried by Captain John Darby of Salem, a skipper who knew how to crowd sail, the colonists' version was rushed to London where the astute Benjamin Franklin quickly circulated it among the not inconsiderable group of America supporters. Gage's account was anticlimatic when it arrived 11 days later.[32]

USE OF SYMBOLS

The revolutionaries made extensive and effective use of symbols—for example the Tree of Liberty in Boston's Hanover Square—rallies of protest, parades, anniversary salutes, slogans, and songs to keep up their drum fire

[31]Benjamin Woods Labaree, *The Boston Tea Party.* New York: Oxford University Press, 1966, pp. 168.

[32]An interesting and useful book to consult on the first battle, Arthur B. Tourtellot's *William Diamond's Drum.* New York: Doubleday and Co., 1959. Tourtellot was a prominent public relations counselor as a partner in the Earl Newsom firm and later as a vice-president of CBS.

of protest. Without doubt, Adams "was a master of stagecraft, deeply versed in the art of swaying the popular mind." Miller recorded:[33] The Sons of Liberty celebrated the repeal of the Stamp Act with "such illuminations, bonfires, pyramids, obelisks, such grand exhibitions and such fireworks as were never before seen in America." Effigies of popular enemies were used to inflame the people's passion; cartoons exhibiting in easily understood form the wickedness of the Tories and mother country were passed from hand to hand; stirring phrases were coined and spread among the common people with greater effect than whole volumes of political reasoning [e.g., No taxation Without Representation], and Whig newspapers carried the radicalism of the seaboard towns to every corner of the province.

No means of attacking the British and arousing the citizens interested in public affairs was overlooked. Town meetings, county meetings, and the colonial legislatures were constantly adopting resolutions and petitions, that, in turn, would be used in pamphlets or newspaper articles. Judges, too, got into the act by expounding on "issues of the time as well as on matters more relevant to their duties."[34]

Preaching from the pulpit about the sins of the British was another powerful weapon. Ministers, among the best educated and most widely traveled persons in the colonies, preached innumerable sermons, many of which also became pamphlets. Most of the clergy in New England at least joined in the Whig movement. Peter Oliver bitterly complained that Adams "had perverted the clergy, who made their pulpits foam with politics, unceasingly sounding Yell of Rebellion in the ears of an ignorant deluded people."[35] Typical was the Rev. Jonathan Mayhew who preached: "True religion comprised a love of liberty and of one's country and the hatred of tyranny and oppression; that civil liberty they cherished so deeply received its chief sanction from religious faith."[36]

The propagandists even used transparencies to get across their message. Paul Revere fashioned a crude sort of slide by displaying oilpaper transparencies on a sheet in front of lighted candles. These, said Schlesinger, "lent color and drama to nocturnal Whig affairs." These slides usually depicted American magnaminity and British malignity side by side.

In weak contrast to the bold, effective ways of communication developed by the revolutionists, the Tories, supporters of King George and the British Empire, relied not so much on propaganda as on legal and military pressures—all to no avail. The Jonathan Sewalls were no match for the intrepid

---

[33]John C. Miller, *Sam Adams, Pioneer in Propaganda.* Stanford, CA: Stanford University Press, 1960, p. 112.

[34]Merrill Jensen, *Tracts,* p. XIII.

[35]*Sam Adams's Revolution,* p. 21.

[36]Alice Baldwin, *The New England Clergy and the American Revolution.* Durham, NC: University of North Carolina Press, 1928, p. 83.

and imaginative Samuel Adams and his band. Sewall, onetime friend of the Adamses and John Hancock, took up the role of publicist in the service of his King in the 1760s and consequently ended his days in exile.[37] The Loyalist propagandists were not without their successes. For example, John Mein and John Fleming brought the Non-Importation Agreements to a crashing halt by using the same tools of publicity and propaganda in their *Chronicle*. Mein was eventually driven from Boston.

Little wonder that an exuberant Sam Adams would exult when he heard the firing at Lexington, "Oh, what a glorious morning is this." He and his fellow propagandists had done their work well.

Nonetheless, once independence for the United States of America was won, historians early on began to cloud and criticize Samuel Adams' achievements as the leading propagandist of the Revolution. In 1819, his cousin, President John Adams wrote: "A systematic course has been pursued for thirty years to run him down."[38] Pauline Maier wrote: "As the nation moved further from Samuel Adams' lifetime, portraits of him became increasingly confident, even stereotypic, and hostile."[39] It is true, as Maier suggested, observers who knew "Samuel Adams in life found in him an elusiveness that has evaded his biographers." Maier concluded: "Thus, Adams's role was that of an intermediary, passing the achievements of the past on to the future. He was not breaking new paths, discovering new worlds, but traveling a well-marked highway." This author dissents strongly to Maier's view. In setting precedents for today's public relations, Sam Adams developed standard techniques used by practitioners today as enumerated at the beginning of this chapter. We stand with Ralph Volney Harlow that Adams was a genius who "found it easy . . . to manufacture public opinion with a pen"— the hallmark of today's successful practitioner.

---

[37]Carol Berkin, *Jonathan Sewall, Odyssey of an American Loyalist.* New York: Columbia University Press, 1974.

[38]Camfield, XIII.

[39]Pauline Maier, "Coming to Terms with Samuel Adams," *American Historical Review* (February 1976), pp. 12–33.

"Greatest Public Relations Work Ever Done"

The power of propaganda to mobilize public opinion was relied on heavily in the history-making campaign to ratify the United States Constitution in 1787–1788. This campaign, ranking alongside the propaganda campaign for Independence in shaping our nation, was once extravagantly praised by Allan Nevins as "the greatest work ever done in America in the field of public relations." Surely, it was the most important one. The burden of the campaign to win quick ratification of the new Constitution, drafted in secrecy in Philadelphia in 1787, was carried by the *Federalist Papers*, which, like the Declaration of Independence, were written as propaganda documents. The Papers were the work of Alexander Hamilton, James Madison, and John Jay. A contemporary, James Wilson, saw the *Federalist Papers* as "the frankest, baldest, and boldest propaganda ever penned." Robert Rutland, in *The Ordeal of the Constitution*, termed this effort to win ratification of the Constitution the nation's "first national political campaign."

Rutland put this historic struggle for public opinion in perspective:[1]

> The political ordeal that produced the Constitution in 1787 and brought about its ratification in 1788 was unique in human history. Never before had the representatives of a whole nation discussed, planned, and implemented a new form of government in such a manner and in such a short time. In little more than a year, Americans established a political network which enlightened Europeans viewed with skepticism. . . . The unprecedented struggle to write

---

[1]Robert A. Rutland, *The Ordeal of the Constitution: The Antifederalists and the Ratification Struggle of 1787–88*. Boston: Northeastern University Press, 1983, pp. 3–4.

and ratify a document affecting millions of citizens in the new nation revealed divergent views of the nature of republicanism.

Rutland saw this battle as "the seedtime of American party politics." Whatever its weight in the final decision may have been—and this is a matter of conjecture to this day—the Hamilton-directed propaganda campaign, shrewd in its strategy, skilled in its execution, set patterns for political propaganda that lasted well into the late 19th century.

The somewhat unfairly maligned Articles of Confederation, drafted in the midst of the American Revolution and finally ratified March 1, 1781, reflected the philosophy of the Declaration of Independence and the aims of the radicals who led the rebellion. With victory, in the view of Merrill Jensen, "the radical organization which had brought about the Revolution disintegrated." He concluded that "the vital change which took place between 1776 and 1787 was not in ideas nor in attitudes, but in the balance of political power."[2] Consequently, the Hamilton-led conservatives were able to engineer a counter-revolution and erect "a nationalistic government whose purpose in part was to thwart the will of the people in whose name they acted."

In late May 1787, these conservatives, later to be enshrined in history as the nation's Founding Fathers, met in Philadelphia to begin the arduous task of drafting a constitution that would give the United States a strong national government instead of a loose confederation of state governments with limited powers. For 4 months the Constitutional Convention met in tight secrecy in Philadelphia's state house.

On September 17, 1789, the members of the Philadelphia Convention signed their names to the new Constitution and then set out at once for home, anxious to marshal support for their momentous labors. The task at hand was a matter of some uncertainty for the delegates; their summerlong debates had been held in the utmost secrecy, and if, as James Madison confessed, the public was "certainly in the dark" about the proceedings of the Convention, the delegates themselves were "equally in the dark as to the reception" that would be given the Constitution. Even the most sanguine of framers, however, felt sure that opponents of the Constitution would include writers whose intelligence and eloquence were quite the equal of their own. In Pennsylvania, such a writer was not long in taking up his pen.

The text of the new constitution was published by Philadelphia newspapers within 4 days of the convention's adjournment. On October 5, Eleazer Oswald, the feisty editor of *The Independent Gazetteer; or the Chronicle of Freedom*, printed a letter from an anonymous correspondent who signed

---

[2] *The Articles of Confederation*. Madison: University of Wisconsin Press, 1948, p. 240.

himself "Centinel." "Mr. Oswald:" it began, "As the *Independent Gazetteer* seems free for the discussion of all public matters, I expect that you will give the following a place in your next." Then, addressing himself to the "Freemen of Pennsylvania," the writer exhorted:

> Friends, Countrymen and Fellow Citizens.
> Permit one of yourselves to put you in mind of certain *liberties* and *privileges* secured to you by the constitution of this commonwealth, and to beg your serious attention to his uninterested opinion upon the plan of federal government submitted to your consideration, before you surrender these great and valuable privileges up forever. (October 5, 1787, p. 1)

There was no provision in the new Constitution, the letter continued, for those liberties dearest to the hearts of men. Seduced by their misplaced respect for its framers, Philadelphians were greeting the proposed plan with a "frenzy of enthusiasm," long before it could be "dispassionately and deliberately examined on its own intrinsic merit." But when enthusiasm gave way to reason, warned Centinel, the nation's citizens would learn to their dismay that the Constitution was, in fact, "the most daring attempt to establish a despotic aristocracy among freemen, that the world has ever witnessed."

So began the first of the Centinel letters. Twenty-three others appeared in the *Independent Gazetteer* during the next 14 months, and their anonymous author soon came to be regarded as one of the most important essayists in the Antifederalist camp. Throughout the bitter struggle for ratification, Centinel continued to assail the Constitution and its framers—and in the process, provided history with a vigorous statement of the principles on which Antifederalism was founded.

Centinel was the pseudonym of Samuel Bryan, a former clerk of the Pennsylvania Assembly, and his father, George Bryan, then a justice of the state supreme court. The Bryans argued vehemently that Pennsylvanians had the "peculiar felicity of living under the most perfect system of local government in the world." Quite understandably the strong-arm tactics of the Federalists aroused terrific passion, and although the Federalists controlled most of the newspapers, the editor of the Philadelphia *Independent Gazetteer* was a staunch Antifederalist. One of the framers, Colonel George Mason of Virginia, angered by the lack of inclusion of a bill of rights, published his list of objections in the *Pennsylvania Packet*. The rumor of the time was that Mason would sooner cut off his right hand than sign the Constitution.

Most opponents of ratification used pseudonyms. In the 18th century, it was the practice to emphasize the argument over the authority or personality of the writer. The authors of the Federalist Papers were known soon after publication. "Agrippa," the major Massachusetts Antifederalist, was thought to have been James Winthrop. It is still unclear whether New York's "Cato" was

Governor George Clinton, a fierce opponent of ratification. Maryland's "Farmer" may have been John Francis Mercer, but the evidence is circumstantial.

Richard Henry Lee, Virginia's Revolutionary War hero who, along with Mason, was in the forefront of the coalescing opposition to the newly drawn document wrote: "To say as many do, that a bad government must be established, for fear of anarchy, is really saying that we must kill ourselves, for fear of dying." He saw the new Constitution as "a mere shred, or rag of representation." Lee saw in the rush to write and then ratify the new Constitution a form of "temporary insanity." Many of the Antifederalists saw trickery in the defenders of the Constitution calling themselves Federalists, when "in truth" "Federalists" were people who believed in a federal form of government as provided by the Articles of Confederation.

Rutland observed: "The Antifederalists unfortunately fell heir to a party label that had already become unpopular by the time they were identified with it. In 1787 they were burdened with the unenviable reputation of being a disorganized but sizeable political group that existed in nearly every state at the close of the Revolution" (p. 5).

Among the states, the strongest opposition to ratification was found in Rhode Island, which did not ratify the Constitution until 1790, North Carolina, which rejected it in 1788, Pennsylvania, Massachusetts, New York, and Virginia.

In Kaminski's and Leffler's view, the Antifederalists thought the Constitution would destroy the states and create one, large consolidated republic that would deteriorate into monarchy or despotism. These writers continued:[3] "They [the Antifederalists] espoused a traditional position based on Montesquieu and other political theorists that a republic—by which they meant a government in which the people consent to be governed by representatives they elect directly or indirectly on a regular basis—could exist only in a relatively small territory populated by people who shared similar values and interests."

This reliance upon Montesquieu's theories is reflected in a letter, signed "Brutus," which appeared in the *New York Journal*, October 18, 1787: "The territory of the United States is of vast extent; it now contains three million souls, and is capable of containing more than ten times that number. Is it practicable for a country, so large and so numerous as they will soon become, to elect a representation that will speak their sentiments, without their becoming so numerous as to be incapable of transacting public business? It certainly is not." This was the first of 16 letters signed by "Brutus" that

---

[3]John P. Kaminski and Richard Leffler, eds. *Federalist and Antifederalists. The Debate Over the Ratification of the Constitution.* Madison: Madison House, 1989, p. 3. The Richard Henry Lee quotes are from a letter he wrote Dr. William Shippen Jr. on October 3, 1787.

appeared in the *New York Journal* between October 18 and April 10, 1788. The identity of "Brutus" is not known.

Brutus began his discussion of republican government with this passage from the eighth book of Montesquieu's *Spirit of the Laws*:

> It is natural to a republic to have only a small territory, otherwise it cannot long subsist. In a large republic, there are men of large fortunes and consequently of less moderation; there are trusts too great to be placed in any single subject; he has interests of his own; he soon begins to think that he may be happy, great and glorious, by oppressing his fellow citizens; and that he may raise himself to grandeur on the ruins of his country. In a large republic, the public good is sacrificed to a thousand views. . . . In a small one, the interest of the public is easier perceived.

The Constitutional debate quickly moved to the pages of America's youthful and yeasty press. "Newspapers everywhere published the Constitution as soon as they could lay their hands on it. So many columns had never been given over to a political subject in America. Correspondents wrote in, angry, approving, or frightened as the case might be."[4] The battle in the public arena was quickly joined as the Federalists and Antifederalists turned to the press and platform to vigorously argue their cause.

John K. Alexander, in his study of the role of newspapers in *The Selling of the Constitutional Convention*, found that "the press entered the fray even before the Constitution existed." He added:[5] "After the fact, John Babcock and Thomas Clayton, the editors of the Lansingburgh, New York, *Northern Centinel*, frankly admitted that they had turned their newspapers into a propaganda instrument during the time the Constitution was being framed." Writing in March, 1788, they said they had "conceived it a duty incumbent upon them to prepare the minds of their readers for its *reception*."

America's 18th Century newspapers, as is the case today, for the most part depicted themselves as independent. In fact, the word *independent* often appeared in their mastheads. In that time their claim of independence was rather hollow, not nearly as valid as it is today. Then as now, editors argued that the nation's welfare depended on the fair dissemination of news and comment by a free press. Few publishers of that period lived up to this commitment.

Alexander concluded:[6]

> Considering their own vaunted ideals, the most damning evidence of publishers abandoning impartiality comes from their news coverage. The events

---

[4]Catherine Drinker Bowen, *Miracle at Philadelphia*. Boston: Little, Brown, 1966, p. 267.

[5]John K. Alexander, *The Selling of the Constitutional Convention. A History of News Coverage*. Madison, WI: Madison House, 1990, p. 3.

[6]*Ibid.*, pp. 213–215.

of late 1786 through the early fall of 1787 certainly demonstrated that the convention had serious problems to tackle. Publishers, however, were not always willing to settle for news as it actually occurred. In 1787, some in the news media occasionally fabricated letters that championed the convention. Just as publishers engaged in selective reprinting of commentary, they also engaged in selective reprinting of news, and at times, in outright news management.

Sound familiar?

The preponderance of newspaper support for ratification of the Constitution is understandable to those who accept Charles Beard's economic interpretation of the Constitution versus the Articles of Confederation. In their time, most owners of newspapers also carried on a profitable printing business. Benjamin Franklin acquired his wealth though his printing business. They also tended to think nationally, and not parochially. Thus, the Federalists entered the ratification battle with the people's main source of information and commentary on their side. Nonetheless, winning acceptance of the new Constitution posed an extremely difficult public relations challenge—a challenge seen and met by Alexander Hamilton, praised by Nevins as "a born public relations man—a born master of persuasion by the spoken and written word." Nevins wrote:[7]

> Once the Constitution came before the country, the rapidity with which Hamilton moved was a striking exemplification of good public relations. He knew that if a vacuum develops in popular opinion, ignorant and foolish views will fill it. No time must be lost in providing accurate facts and sound ideas. The Constitutional Convention ended September 17, 1787, and twelve days later the Continental Congress voted almost unanimously to lay the new framework before a convention in each state. Within the month, on October 27, Hamilton began the immortal series of Federalist Papers, his first essay appearing in three New York publications. . . . In that brief period, he had gone home, straightened out his law business, enlisted Madison and Jay as co-authors, and made his arrangements with the press.

Hamilton understood that the Constitution must be explained and defended by persuasive propaganda if it was to obtain the necessary public support. For all his basic contempt for the views of the common people, Hamilton was a realist. He also saw that if the Federalists were to win their uphill battle, they must obtain ratification quickly. The political steamroller was soon put in motion, but uphill it must go. Available historical records do not show what the division of public opinion was on the issue of a strong central government as against the states-rights-oriented Articles of

---

[7]Allan Nevins, *The Constitution Makers and the Public*. New York: Foundation for Public Relations Research and Education, 1963, p. 7.

Confederation. Jackson Turner Main thought "the Antifederalists had a very small majority—perhaps fifty-two percent but of course it is impossible to be exact." He wrote:[8] "If we try to form an estimate of the entire white population, the two sides appear to have been nearly equal in numbers. Of course in 1787–88 this was of no importance; what counted then was the ratification by nine states. Since the Federalists were a minority in at least six and probably seven states, they ought to have been defeated. Yet they came from behind to win."

The Federalists victory was the triumph of an organized, smartly generaled influential politicians over what Main viewed as a uncoordinated, somewhat disorganized slight majority of the voters. From the outset, the Federalists saw that their cause would be won or lost in the key states of Massachusetts, Virginia, and New York, states in which they had their greatest strength. They had little time to organize and mount their campaign. The Massachusetts convention was to sit in January, the Virginia convention early in June, and New York later that month. Fierce opposition to ratification had arisen early in New York state. During the last week in September and the first weeks of October 1787, the pages of New York's newspapers were filled with fiery articles denouncing the new Constitution. There were defenders, but most of their writing was critical of the opponents, rather than reasoned arguments for the new central government. The Federalists were often criticized for their arrogance. Hamilton realized that the best way to counter this mounting criticism in the New York press quickly and persuasively was through the printed word. Thus was conceived what has become one of the United States' historic political documents—*the Federalist Papers*.

The articles first appeared in the semiweekly New York *Independent Journal* from October 1787 to April 1788 and were widely reprinted in the pro-Federalist press. In the manner of the propaganda of that era, the articles were later reprinted as pamphlets. Finally, with six additional essays, they were published in book form and titled *The Federalists*, which became a campaign handbook; one that lives and influences our courts to this day. These articles were written by Hamilton, James Madison, and John Jay. Writing under the pseudonym, Publius, Hamilton wrote the majority of these essays, Madison wrote 29, Jay 5, possibly 6. Hamilton was the leader of the Federalists and their chief propagandist. Authorship of several particular essays has not been determined. The first seven essays published between October 27 and November 17, 1787, appeared on Saturdays and Wednesdays in *The Independent Journal*, a semiweekly paper, and a day or two later in both *The New York Packet* and *the Daily Advertiser*. The announced plan of regular publication of these "Publius" essays was not followed.

---

[8]Jackson Turner Main, *The Antifederalists*. Chapel Hill: University of North Carolina Press, 1961.

ESSAYS AUTHORED BY HAMILTON, MADISON, AND JAY

Alexander Hamilton emerged early as the leader of the Federalist political forces and as the advocate of a strong central government. Born in 1757 in the West Indies, the son of a Scottish merchant, Hamilton emigrated to the American colonies as a young man. He served President George Washington as the nation's first Secretary of the Treasury from 1789 until 1795, the climax of his public career. A brilliant political economist, he served President Washington as a political strategist and helped with his speeches, particularly Washington's Farewell Address. This brought him into a bitter rivalry with Thomas Jefferson, who had emerged as the leader of the Antifederalist forces in the new government. Hamilton, then only 47, met a tragic death in a duel with Aaron Burr, fought at Weehauken Heights on the banks of the Hudson July 11, 1804. Hamilton had incurred Burr's wrath by frustrating the latter's political ambitions.

James Madison, later to serve as President, was a leading advocate of independence as a young Virginia legislator and was the primary author of the newly framed Constitution. The Constitutional Convention was originally called for the express purpose of revising the Articles of Confederation. However, in the early stages of the secret conclave, several alternate plans emerged that called for a complete restructuring of the federal government. Governor Edmund Randolph and James Madison of Virginia submitted a list of 15 resolves that became known as the Virginia Plan, which suggested an entirely new approach to the structure of the national government. Madison, in effect, became the principal author of the historic document.

Although he never attained the Presidency, John Jay was among the most talented and influential figures of the revolutionary generation. He served as President of the Continental Congress, was the principal negotiator of the treaty that gained America its independence, and Secretary of Foreign Affairs in the Confederation Government. He climaxed his career as the first Chief Justice of the United States. One biographer deemed Jay's "integrity unimpeachable and his judgment unfailingly sound."

These then were the brilliant authors of the *Federalist Papers.*

Gouverneur Morris later recalled that he "was warmly pressed by Hamilton to assist" in writing Federalist essays "for the campaign," but declined.

As a matter of fact, the Federalist propaganda campaign had started well before the convening of the Constitutional Convention. Jensen concluded:[9]

The development of Federalist propaganda may be traced in the contemporary press. Items with a tinge of special pleading began to appear before the convention met, continued during its deliberations, and burst forth in full strength once the Constitution was presented to the electorate.

---

[9]*Articles of Confederation*, fn 6, pp. 4–5.

While the Convention was in session, a serious effort was made to prepare the public to accept its work without question. Two lines of argument much used were (1) that the members of the convention were the wisest and best men in the country, and their deliberations should therefore be accepted without question, and (2) that if their deliberations were not accepted, chaos would ensure. Opponents of the Convention were said to be inspired only by ulterior motives.

Truly the campaign for the Constitution produced "a work of propaganda which is a classic." Although these essays were written as campaign documents, they are rarely dealt with as such by either historians or the judiciary.

The opposing public relations effort was spearheaded by Lee who early in October 1787, began writing essays that he titled *Letters of a Federal Farmer*. Lee chose the tactics of gentle persuasion in sharp contrast with the strident protests of some Antifederalists. "Unlike many Antifederalist writers who matched sneer with sneer, Richard Henry Lee made his points by delicate concessions. He neither claimed that the Confederation might be saved nor held that a second convention [a diversionary tactic of the Antifederalists] could unravel all the good in the Constitution."[10] Taking quite the opposite tack was the shrill, strident Mercy Otis Warren, who put out a scorching pamphlet and wrote stinging essays against the Constitution. She railed against the Federalists as "partisans of monarchy" and accused them of "fraudulent designs." Few surpassed "Lord Peter" who denounced his Federalist opponents as "blind, positive, conceited sons of bitches" who deserved roasting in Hell.[11]

Many Antifederalists joined in the campaign to prevent ratification, relying, for example, on letters "to the frontier counties, where the people is most easily deceived," and alarming voters "with a number of hard words, such as *aristocracy, monarchy, oligarchy*, and the like, none of which they will understand."[12] An author, thought to be Governor George Clinton, in a "Cato" letter, argued that the Constitution could lead to a vile and arbitrary aristocracy or monarchy. George Mason repeatedly warned that the judicial power of the Constitution would destroy state government. A writer—probably Benjamin Workman—who signed his letters "Philadelphiensis" exhorted:[13] "Before Martial law is declared to be the supreme law of the land, and your character of free citizens be changed to that of subjects of a *military king*, which are necessary consequences of the adoption of the proposed constitution, let me admonish you in the name of *sacred liberty*, to make a solemn pause." Though there were many writing and speaking against the Consti-

---

[10]Rutland, *The Ordeal of the Constitution*, p. 40.
[11]Boston *Independent Chronicle*, November 8, 1787.
[12]Springfield *Hampshire Chronicle*, October 23, 1787.
[13]Philadelphia *Independent Gazetteer*, February 7, 1788.

tution, the Antifederalists neither individually nor collectively produced a work to match the *Federalist Papers* in persuasiveness and lasting impact.

Leonard Levy observed that a basic weakness of the Antifederalist campaign was that its thrust was largely negative.[14] Yet, negative political campaigns have been quite successful down through the more than 200 years of the United States. Also, as Rutland pointed, out, "Even when the Antifederalists hit upon a popular issue, they found it difficult to broadcast their message, because a majority of the newspapers were pro-Federalist." He estimated that hardly one tenth of all the papers then being printed supported the foes of the Constitution.

Federalist control of the mails that delayed circulation of letters and newspapers was a bitter reason often advanced by the Antifederalists for their defeat. Main argued that the widespread press support for the Constitution was a more important factor. "The number of papers which opposed ratification was very few. This was natural, for the city people were overwhelmingly Federal, and the printers were influenced by local opinions as well as their own convictions; moreover, it was profitable to agree with the purchasers and the advertisers."[15] It must be added that Federalist supporters often supported newspapers financially.

Clearly, the Federalists had the weight of talent, the power of the positive argument, widespread newspaper support, and prestigious leaders on their side. Foremost among those supporting ratification were Benjamin Franklin, though now a very old man, and General George Washington, hero of the Revolution who had presided over the Philadelphia Convention. Most historians agree that Washington's great hold on the affections of the people influenced both the drafting and the ratification of the Constitution.

Rutland, in his assessment of the causes of the Antifederalists' failure, wrote:[16] "The evidence shows that the Antifederalists began their campaign for an amended Constitution without coordination, without a definite counter proposal, and without unified leadership. The Bill of Rights was their only common cry. Once they departed from that, as the Federalists never tired of saying, the Antifederalists marched off in all directions" (p. 313).

Nonetheless, the Antifederalists' demands for inclusion of a Bill of Rights in the Constitution was not unavailing. Public opinion demanding such a series of amendments was built during the campaign for ratification of the Constitution. When the Constitution was being written and adopted in Philadelphia in the summer of 1787, only Virginian George Mason argued for including a Bill of Rights. Madison, principal drafter, did not see such a charter as essential. Most historians have concluded that his lack of concern

---

[14]For collection of Antifederalist propaganda, see Cecelia M. Kenyon, *The Antifederalists*. Indianapolis, IN: Bobbs-Merrill, 1966.

[15]Main, *The Antifederalists*, p. 250.

[16]*The Ordeal of the Constitution*, p. 313.

grew out of his concept of federalism. As a price of winning ratification, Madison would, during the campaign, become a convert and chief advocate of what became our Bill of Rights. It was out of the crucible of debate over ratification of the Constitution and the Antifederalists' demands for a second convention that developed the strong public pressure that resulted in the subsequent writing and adoption of the Bill of Rights.

In sharp contrast to the negative, aimless, uncoordinated campaign of the Constitution's opponents led by Lee, Patrick Henry, and Mason stood the carefully planned campaign of Hamilton and Madison "to cultivate a favorable disposition in the citizens at large." Craig Smith and Scott Lybarger, in their little book, *To Form a More Perfect Union: The Ratification of the Bill of Rights 1789-1791*, concurred with most historians that although the rhetoric of Lee, Henry, and Mason "was powerful, they did not organize their writings as effectively as the authors of the Federalist." The planning of the Ratification campaign was largely the work of Hamilton, who had shown a flair for public relations when a mere lad of 17. Nevins termed Hamilton "the possessor of a remarkably clear, original, and comprehensive mind." In the face of the shrill, exaggerated writings of the Antifederalists, Hamilton pursued a planned course to win the key states and remained "tactful, suave, and objective." He almost never attacked his opponents and used eloquence more than invective in his writing, suggesting the value of reasoned argument and moderation in molding public opinion. He did resort to biting invective on occasion. Mitchell wrote:[17]

> In parrying blows against and enlisting support for the Constitution, the authors of the Federalist did the best job of public relations known to history. Objectors were not so much repulsed as refuted. Honest fears were removed. Ignorance was supplied with information and illustration. The manner was earnest rather than passionate, was persuasive by a candor that avoided the cocksure. He [Hamilton] addressed his readers' judgment in a spirit of moderation.

The era of the late 18th century may seem quaint and remote to today's citizen and the task of popular persuasion a simple one but the truth is, as Nevins asserted, "the ways in which brilliant men attain success is much the same in all periods." Hamilton and Madison, through their strategy and appeals, mobilized a constructive minority of Americans to bring about adoption of the Constitution in the face of what Main speculated was a majority of citizens who were either opposed or indifferent. Nevins suggested "their skills and methods, the media they used in reaching the four million people scattered from New England to Georgia, and their modes of appealing to popular psychology, are well worth the attention of public relations experts

---

[17]Broadus Mitchell, *Alexander Hamilton: Youth to Maturity, 1755-1788*. New York: Macmillan, 1957, pp. 422-23.

today." Morison and Commager in *The Growth of the American Republic* held that "unless the Federalists had been as shrewd in manipulation as they were sound in theory, their arguments could not have prevailed."

As today, precise evaluation of the impact of a public relations campaign was and is difficult to determine—less so today than in the 18th century; there are many imponderables involved moving a public to decide an issue or campaign one way or the other. The debate over the effect of the *Federalist Papers* in winning ratification continues to this day. Historians writing in the late 19th and early 20th centuries stressed the importance of these articles in gaining ratification, but more recent historians give the writings far less weight in the final result. Not many students of history and public relations today agree with pioneer historian John Fiske's assertion that the *Federalist Papers* "probably accomplished more toward ensuring the adoption of the Constitution than anything else that was said or done in that eventful year." A strong dissenter to the Fiske view has been William W. Crosskey, who termed the Fiske version "a fable." He wrote:[18]

It is hardly a cause for wonder that the "Federalist Papers," properly understood, are seen to contain much of sophistry; much that is merely distractive; and some things, particularly in the parts that Madison wrote, which come perilously near to falsehood. In addition, it is virtually certain that much of The Federalist was written only to fill up space in the New York "federal" newspapers and thereby make less obvious the exclusion therefrom of opposing views.

In these circumstances, it is obviously necessary to correct evaluation of various of the statements and intimations that The Federalist contains, and to correct assessment of the influence these probably had on the adoption of the Constitution. . .No attempt to evaluate the Federalist upon such a basis ever has been made. Instead, the fable that it was "widely copied"—"extensively reprinted by the press of different states"—is repeated by writer after writer, with no apparent notion of truth.

A more balanced view falling between those of the Fiske school and Crosskey is that of Douglass Adair:[19]

The Federalist's propaganda value, as first published in the newspapers, should not be overrated; the essays probably influenced few votes among the general electorate. In the Virginia and New York Conventions, however, the bound

---

[18]William W. Crosskey, *Politics and the Constitution.* Chicago: University of Chicago Press, 1953, I, pp. 9–10. Fiske's point of view can be found in his *The Critical Period of American History.* (Boston, 1888).

[19]"The Authorship of the Disputed Federalist Papers," *William and Mary Quarterly* (1944) p. 236.

volumes were enormously valuable. The pro-Constitution party in both states was eager for a clause by clause discussion of the proposed government. Under this procedure, with Publius' systematic analysis of the document at hand, the Constitutionalist leaders were able to arrange the order of debate beforehand, to coach specific speakers to talk on various parts of the Constitution, and generally to organize and manage its defense in a systematic way.

Even in pivotal New York state, the influence of the *Federalist Papers* is in dispute. Many historians assert that the Federalist essays were more influential in swaying convention votes than in influencing the public at large is indicated by what happened in New York's convention. These essays were first published in the New York's Federalist newspapers and then supplemented by a series of widely distributed broadsides. Nonetheless, the Antifederalists scored an overwhelming victory by electing 46 delegates to the ratification convention as against 19 Federalists elected. Yet New York voted to ratify the Constitution once it became simply of a question of that state joining or staying out of a union that by this time, had been assured of ratification by the actions of New Hampshire and Virginia. Thus, there is some reason for Crosskey to write:[20] "I should be inclined to say that, if the 'public relations job' done in New York had been duplicated in other states, there would have been no Constitution—at least as we know it." Crosskey's view is shared by David M. Ellis who asserted that the *Federalist Papers*, however important as commentary for later generations, did not change many, if any, votes in 1788.

Jackson Turner Main wrote, that Hamilton's activity in New York "was perhaps more of a liability than an asset to the Federalists." Other scholars shared this view and thus put doubt on the high praise Nevins lavishes on Hamilton. Another historian believed that Hamilton's speeches at the New York Convention in Poughkeepsie, though brilliant, were irritating and suggested that John Jay's calm manner and gentle words had more influence on the Antifederalist majority.[21]

At the least then the *Federalist Papers* can be described as the campaign bible for the winning cause in the nation's first national political campaign. Whatever its contemporary influence in the struggle for ratification, no one can doubt its lasting impact on the development of political thought and in shaping our government. Nor can one doubt the value of studying Hamilton's response to a complex and difficult public relations task. Looking at him as a public relations man, one Hamilton biographer stoutly declared:[22] "He was

---

[20]Letter to author, March 16, 1963.

[21]Linda Grant DePauw, *The Eleventh Pillar: New York State and the Federal Constitution.* Ithaca, NY: Cornell University Press, 1966. Published for the American Historical Association.

[22]Claude G. Bowers, *Jefferson and Hamilton.* Boston: Houghton Mifflin, 1925, p. 25. (It should be noted that Bowers was not a great admirer of Hamilton.)

a natural journalist and pamphleteer—one of the fathers of the American editorial. His perspicacity, penetration, powers of condensation, and clarity of expression were those of a premier editorial writer. These same qualities made him a pamphleteer without peer."

Thus, in the propaganda effort to carry the New York Convention for ratification, Hamilton and his fellow essayists created the *Federalist Papers*, described by Jacob E. Cooke as one of three of America's most historic documents, ranking behind only the Declaration of Independence and the Constitution. Another historian held that the ratification of the Constitution was the true "miracle" rather than the "Miracle of Philadelphia." Through Hamilton's effective campaign, the nation enjoys the enduring legacy of the Constitution.

THE BEGINNINGS OF THE FIRST PARTY SYSTEM

Given his talents and his strong political convictions, it was inevitable that Hamilton would serve the nation's first president, George Washington, as a public relations counselor as well as Secretary of the Treasury. Vernon Parrington wrote: "So able a man could not be restricted within a single portfolio, and during the larger part of Washington's two administrations Hamilton's was the directing mind and chief influence." While still a young man, Hamilton had won Washington's confidence while serving the Commander-in-Chief as an aide, particularly in the dark days of Valley Forge. In this position, "Hamilton exerted constant ingenuity that went beyond obvious obligation," demonstrating that "his capacities and zeal to use them could not be confined by minor station or by his youth."[23]

Another author recorded that Washington "was soberly delighted with the master clerk's capacity for work and detail. The huge mass of headquarters correspondence took on a polish and clarity which it owed to the new secretary. Gradually, Hamilton was left more and more to draft details of important papers."[24] Miller shared this view: "Distrustful of his own literary powers, Washington fell easily to the habit of turning his correspondence over to Colonel Hamilton; and the habit thus acquired during the War of Independence was carried over into the period when the relationship of the two men was that of President and Secretary of the Treasury."[25] Hamilton was no man to let such power slip from his grasp.

---

[23]Broadus Mitchell, *Alexander Hamilton, Portrait of a Prodigy*, New York: Harper, 1939, p. 143.

[24]David Goldsmith Loth, *Alexander Hamilton: Portrait of a Prodigy*. New York: Harper, 1939, p. 74.

[25]John C. Miller, *Alexander Hamilton: Portrait of a Paradox*. New York: Harper, 1959, p. 67.

President Washington was fully aware of the importance of public opinion in shaping the new government and winning public acceptance of this fragile democratic vessel. He once declared: "The mass of our citizens require no more than to understand a question to decide it properly." Washington saw the newspapers as a means of building such understanding of public matters. Although he was never comfortable with the editors of his day, Washington recognized the press' importance in molding support for his trailblazing administration. Though often stung by bitter attacks in that day of vitriolic journalism, Washington "clung to his belief in the effectiveness of the press as the chief medium of publicity."[26] Washington sensed equally well the importance of building the prestige of the Presidency and used pomp and circumstance to this end. Little did he dream that it would come to the day of the Imperial Presidency!

John Adams said of Washington in this connection: "We may say of him, if he was not the greatest President, he was the best actor the presidency ever had. His address to the states when he left the army; his solemn leave taken of Congress when he resigned his commission; his Farewell Address to the people when he resigned the presidency. These were all in a strain of excellence in dramatic exhibitions."

In his Farewell Address, Washington said: "In proportion as the structure of a government gives force to public opinion, it is essential that public opinion should be enlightened." Hamilton had a hand in polishing and publicizing this famed message, as evidenced by this note to Hamilton:[27] "To what editor in *this* city do you think it had best be sent for publication? Will it be proper to accompany it with a note to him, expressing that it is hoped, or expected, that the state printers will give it a place in their Gazettes; or preferable to let it be carried by my private Secretary to that press which is destined to usher it to the world and suffer it to work its way afterwards?" Reliance upon Hamilton for public relations advice was typical. Rossiter wrote:[28] "No one can read through the correspondence between these two men in 1795 and 1796 without recognizing the almost touching dependence of Washington on Hamilton for information, advice, and opinion on a broad range of problems. Washington made clear on a dozen occasions that he looked upon Hamilton as his principal coadjutor and assistant in the 'turmoils I have consented to encounter.' " The Farewell Address in truth was a product of the collaborative efforts of Washington, Hamilton, Madison, and to a lesser extent, Jay.

---

[26]James E. Pollard, *The Presidents and the Press.* New York: Macmillan, 1947, p. 30.

[27]*The Writings of George Washington,* Bicentennial Edition. Washington, DC. 1940, 35, p. 192.

[28]Clinton Rossiter, *Alexander Hamilton and the Constitution.* New York: Harcourt, Brace & World, 1964, p. 32.

Washington made several efforts to bring the Presidency closer to the people. One example was his arduous tour of New England from October 15 to November 13, 1789, by stage coach over "intolerable bad roads." In 1791, he made another tour to the South, traveling north to Philadelphia, thence south to Virginia, the Carolinas, and on into Georgia. This trip took more than 2 months and covered 1,887 miles of tiresome travel. On these trips, he met with many influential persons but seldom spoke publicly. Washington's *Diary* for the years 1789–1791 reveal him to be a leader who was most solicitous of the public's views. Through such efforts, Washington began the task of bringing the federal government to the people, a task that has reached the level of a fine art indeed in our time of presidential "electronic town halls" and television addresses from the Oval Office.

President Washington, like the 42 presidents who have followed him, had his difficulties with the press. Washington received the draft of the Jay Treaty in Philadelphia in March 1795 but sat on it to wait for a propitious time to submit it to the Senate. "Benny" Bache, Benjamin Franklin's grandson and long a harsh critic of the President, broke the secrecy by publishing the treaty's contents June 29 in his Philadelphia *Aurora*, but with many inaccuracies. Bache's frequent attacks on Washington were rancorous; typical was his assertion that "Washington was the source of all the misfortunes of our country." As the result of Bache's disclosure of the Jay Treaty, both in his paper and in a pamphlet, strong opposition was aroused.

Hamilton moved quickly to counter this unfavorable publicity. Under the pen name, "Camillus," he published a stirring defense of the treaty in the New York press. President Washington asked Hamilton to circulate this defense widely, for otherwise "the opposition pieces will spread their poison in all directions." In ways such as these, Hamilton aided Washington with his correspondence, his speeches, his messages to Congress, and in public advocacy of the Federalist cause. Rossitter thought that it was largely due to Hamilton that Washington proved "an influential leader of legislation."

To promote the political goals of the Washington Administration and the Federalist policies, Hamilton took the initiative to establish a Federalist pro-Administration newspaper, the *Gazette of the United States*. The paper was started in New York, then the national capital, April 15, 1789, by John Fenno, an ex-school teacher. The paper, later moved to Philadelphia, was established to "endear the General Government to the people." It soon had the largest circulation of any newspaper in that time. It prospered because Hamilton awarded the *Gazette* Treasury Department printing contracts and, on occasion, lent Fenno money out of his own pocket. Pollard found that "Hamilton not only helped found the paper, but was Fenno's chief reliance for funds, and was a constant contributor to its columns." Understandably, the *Gazette* carried fulsome praise of Hamilton. "No printer was ever so correct in his politics," said Fisher Ames of Fenno. Little wonder that James

McGregor Burns has described Hamilton as "the activist, the operator, the dynamo of the first administration."

Hamilton's effective use of the *Gazette* in promoting Federalist policies ultimately led his strong opponent, Thomas Jefferson, to clandestinely establish the Antifederalist organ, the *National Gazette*. This paper was edited by Philip Freneau, then known as the "Poet of the Revolution," who had been brought to Jefferson's attention by James Madison, a Princeton classmate of Freneau. Jefferson brought Freneau to the capital by offering him a clerkship in the State Department, a job paying $250 a year; a job that required little work so that Freneau was free to pursue "any other calling." This "calling" consisted of publishing a newspaper that set out to destroy Hamilton's good name and build support for Jefferson's emerging Republican Party. "While the *National Gazette* pilloried Hamilton as a monarchial serpent in the republican paradise, Hamilton inveighed against Jefferson as a disunionist."[29]

Freneau's sponsor, Jefferson, once averred that in the 1790s Freneau saved the Constitution "which was galloping fast into Monarchy, and has been checked by no means so powerfully as by that paper [the *Gazette*]." On the other side, President Adams blamed his failure to be re-elected on Freneau, cursed by President Washington as "that rascal."[30]

In the increasingly bitter conflict between Alexander Hamilton and Thomas Jefferson, both inside Washington's cabinet and in their newspapers, were planted the seeds of America's two-party political system—a development the framers of the Constitution had feared and thus had not seen its necessity. James Madison had expressed great fear as to the damage "factions" could do to the fabric of the infant republic. By 1792, the conflict between the ideas and economic interest in these Founding Fathers began to crystallize in the form of political parties. Publicity has long been the meat and drink of politics—in fact from the beginning. The 1800 Presidential election has been described by Joseph Charles, in his *The Origins of the American Party System*, as one of "the bitterest and most momentous elections which the country has ever seen."[31]

But the Federalist and Republican parties did not survive. Richard P. McCormick, in his *The Second American Party System*, wrote:[32] "The first American party system, which had its origins late in Washington's presidency, entered upon a stage of arrested development after 1800, and by 1820 had all but disintegrated." This disintegration came about in the Era of Good Feeling in presidencies of James Madison and James Monroe. McCormick

---

[29]John C. Miller, *The Federalist Era*. New York: Harper, 1960, p. 92.

[30]For a biography, see *Philip Freneau, Champion of Democracy* by Joseph Axlered. Austin: University of Texas Press, 1967.

[31]Published by Harper Torchbooks, with foreword by Frederick Merk, 1956.

[32]Chapel Hill: University of North Carolina Press, 1966.

continued: "In 1824 essentially as a result of the revival of the contest for the presidency, there began a new era of party formation. . . . By 1840, when the new parties had attained an equilibrium of forces nationally, politics in every state was conducted on a two-party basis." Thus, was born the Second Party System. Its birth is described in chapter 5.

The First American Party System brought forth the nation's first political campaign specialist—John Beckley. The Second American Party System brought forth the second political campaign specialist—Amos Kendall. They were the progenitors of today's large army of public relations practitioners who specialize in politics and now play a dominant role in political campaigns from the White House to the courthouse. Their stories follow.

But truly, winning ratification of the United States Constitution was "the greatest public relations work ever done." The Hamilton-engineered victory lives in our lives and around the world today.

John Beckley: The First
Campaign Specialist*

In a letter to Aaron Burr on September 24, 1792, Patriot Dr. Benjamin Rush wrote, in part: "This letter will be handed to you by Mr. [John] Beckley. He possesses a fund of information about men and things, and what is more in favor of his principles, he possesses the confidence of our two illustrious patriots, Mr. Jefferson and Mr. Madison."[1] Beckley's biographers, Edmund Berkeley and Dorothy Smith Berkeley, described the ubiquitous Beckley as "a skillful electioneer, both a product and a promoter of the newly developing party system in the United States, Beckley was an early prototype of a now familiar figure—the party manager."[2] Truly, John Beckley was the first political campaign specialist, a lonely warrior of the infant Republican Party of Jefferson. Today his successors are a mighty army dominating the political process in the United States.

John James Beckley was born in England, August 4, 1757. His exact birthplace is not known, but evidence suggests that it was in the vicinity of London. His obituary of 1807 simply stated that he was born in Great Britain. Little is known of his family or his childhood in England. By one of history's fateful rolls of the dice, John Beckley arrived in Virginia just before reaching

---

*Much of the research for this chapter was done by Doyle Mote, a graduate student at the University of Georgia in 1976. He is now an executive with Bell South.

[1]Irving Brant, *James Madison Father of the Constitution*. Indianapolis: Bobbs Merrill, 1950, Vol. 3.

[2]The definitive biography of Beckley was written by Edmund Berkeley and Dorothy Smith Berkeley, *John Beckley*. Philadelphia: The American Philosophical Society, 1973. Their evaluation is on pp. 279–285.

the age of 12, where in the course of events he would become the political ally of Thomas Jefferson, James Madison, and James Monroe in their political struggles with the Hamilton Federalists.

Beckley's luck of the draw came about this way. John Clayton, then 74 years old, had been clerk of Gloucester County, Virginia, for 48 years. He was also America's best known botanist of that time. Clayton's age and his increasing duties in a growing county demanded that he seek assistance in his duties. Clayton had often done business with John Norton & Sons, a London mercantile firm. He wrote James Withers of the Norton firm that he needed a young scribe. Withers recommended his nephew, John Beckley. The uncle and nephew arrived in Virginia in May 1769. This proved a happy arrangement. "Young John Beckley would be going to no average planter's home, but to one where he could easily continue his education while he received an excellent training as a clerk."[3]

Clayton's family was a distinguished one. His grandfather was an Original Fellow of the Royal Society of London, and his father had served many years as Virginia's Attorney General. Beckley, though a mere lad, began working immediately as Clayton's scribe and in due time developed great skill as a calligrapher. Clayton put him to work in the courthouse and taught him record keeping. Clayton was a stern taskmaster and had little patience with carelessness or sloppiness. He demanded absolute accuracy, a trait Beckley learned and practiced, at least in his clerkships! Beckley learned to keep the office accounts and the best ways of filing. In this work, young Beckley also learned how to handle business correspondence and tactfully deal with the public. He also learned much from reading in the Clayton family library—a large one for that day. Clayton had many volumes of books on law, science, religion, and poetry. In time, Beckley became a well educated person for his era and a lawyer.

In December 1773, John Clayton died, and after spending the better part of a year settling Clayton's affairs, Beckley, now nearing 17, moved to Richmond to find work. This was the year of the faint beginnings of the colonies' drive for independence. Relations between the colonies and England were becoming strained. Localities began forming groups to determine the future of America. In Henrico County (Richmond), it was the Committee of Safety. John Beckley got its clerkship in 1775. On November 6 of that same year, he was elected clerk at a a meeting of freeholders in Henrico County. Royal government ended in Virginia in 1775. The colony established a Committee of Safety in Williamsburg on August 24, 1775. In February 1776, Beckley moved to Williamsburg to become assistant clerk of the Virginia committee. Then on December 23, he was named assistant clerk of the newly formed

---

[3]Beckley's obituary in *The National Intelligencer and Washington Advertiser*, Washington, DC, April 10, 1807.

Privy Council of Virginia and reappointed as assistant clerk in 1777. That same year, he also served as clerk of the Virginia Senate. Two years later, in October 1779, he succeeded Edmund Randolph as clerk of the Virginia House of Delegates, a position he held until his election as clerk of the United States House of Representatives. Randolph had resigned his post upon being elected to the Continental Congress. Beckley and Randolph became good friends and law partners; their association lasted until Beckley's death.

Thus, Beckley's proficiency as a clerk, his shrewd political instincts, and his ability to get along with people brought him into close association with the leaders of the new nation. His growing popularity was shown when the rules of Phi Beta Kappa Society were changed so that he could be admitted. Phi Beta Kappa was founded at the College of William and Mary on December 5, 1776, shortly after Beckley had moved to Williamsburg. In 1778, the rules were broadened to permit election of nonstudents and a few months later Beckley was elected. The Berkeleys wrote: "Within a month, as might have been predicted, he was chosen clerk, or secretary. He became a very active member in spite of his many commitments. The group, at the time, was a remarkable one, including William Short, later minister to Spain, John Page, later governor of Virginia, and John Brown, later U. S. Senator from Kentucky. Brown and Page remained close friends throughout Beckley's life."[4] A few months later, Beckley was elected to the Williamsburg Lodge of Freemason, whose membership included Randolph, James Madison, James Monroe, and Henry Tazewell.

The year 1779 was eventful for Beckley in more important ways. Jefferson was elected governor in June to succeed Patrick Henry. In December, the general assembly voted to move its meeting place from Williamsburg to Richmond for its next meeting in the spring of 1780. According to the Berkeleys: "The move to Richmond began a new period in Beckley's life. He rented a house and acquired several slaves. He began to practice law on his own and involved himself in city affairs." Beckley had started reading law in the Clayton library and then in Williamsburg entered into practice with Randolph.

ELECTED MAYOR OF RICHMOND

Beckley, demonstrating his political prowess at an early age, was first elected to the Richmond City Council and then, at age 26, he was elected Richmond's second mayor in July, 1783, a position he held for 6 years. With all his

---

[4]Edmund and Dorothy Smith Berkeley, "The First Librarian of Congress John Beckley." *The Quarterly Journal of the Library of Congress*, Vol. 32, April 1975, p. 84.

politicking, Beckley found time to explore the scenic lands of western Virginia, now West Virginia. He saw the potential of this little-settled country and soon acquired land grants. The Berkeleys wrote: "Beckley's interest in land and in western Virginia and Kentucky increased, and he was continuously involved for the rest of his life though he never lived in the area."*

Nonetheless, Beckley kept his eye on the big prize—political involvement in the politics of founding a nation. The Berkeleys asserted: "Beckley's urge to participate in the federal government became irresistible" (p. 85). His first taste of this exciting business of founding a nation came when in April 1787, he accompanied Gov. Edmund Randolph and James Madison to Philadelphia for the revision of the Articles of Confederation, which evolved into the Constitutional Convention. He tried to get the clerkship of that convention but failed to do so. Later, when the Virginia Convention met in Richmond to consider ratification of the new Constitution, Beckley, naturally, was elected its secretary.

Beckley resigned as mayor of Richmond on March 9, 1789, and headed to New York to seek a role in the new federal government. He went armed with a strong letter of recommendation of Edmund Randolph and the support of James Madison. To provide expenses for his trip, he carried the official vote of the Virginia convention to the first capital. He was there a month campaigning for the clerkship of the newly organized House of Representatives. The organizational meeting of the new House of Representatives was delayed until April 1, 1789, and then it elected Frederick A. Muhlenberg of Pennsylvania as Speaker and Beckley as Clerk. Rep. James Madison wrote an account of elections to President George Washington on April 6, 1789. "The papers will have made known that Mr. Muhlenberg was the choice of the Representatives for their Speaker and Mr. Beckley for their Clerk. The competition of the latter was Mr. S. Stockton of New Jersey, who, on the first ballot, had the same number with Mr. Beckley."[5]

NOW IN THE THICK OF THE FIGHT

Brant recorded: "For Clerk of the House, Virginia's vote helped produce a tie and then a victory for John Beckley. Madison thus gained the use of the keenest pair of ears in the country."[6] John Beckley was now in the thick of political struggle developing between the Federalists, led by President Wash-

---

*Beckley's son, Alfred, in time became a general in the Virginia militia serving briefly in the Confederate Army. The city of Beckley, West Virginia, is named for him.

[5]Gaillard Hunt, ed., *Writings of James Madison*, New York: G. P. Putnam's Sons, 1904, Vol. V.

[6]Irving Brant, *James Madison Father of the Constitution 1787–1800*, Indianapolis: Bobbs Merrill, 1950, p. 245.

ington and Secretary of the Treasury Alexander Hamilton, and the new Republican faction, which chose that term to avoid the negative connotations of "Antifederalists," led by Madison, Monroe, and Jefferson. Beckley became active in promoting development of the new Republican Party and served as its unofficial chairman in setting out to work for Jefferson's election. Beckley considered Hamilton "insidious" and "contemptible."

Joseph Charles wrote in his *Origins of the American Party System:*[7] "As Clerk of the House, Beckley was in a position to watch every move in Congress with much more facility than most of its members. He was a keen observer and astute listener. Plus, he had access to papers and documents that few others had a chance to see." Beckley became one of Jefferson's closest confidantes. In his memoirs, Jefferson acknowledged: Beckley's "competence and efficiency in the House," and of "his activities as a political intelligence agent." Jonathan Daniels, in his *Ordeal of Ambition* asserted:[8] "Jefferson wooed and counted his votes to the last Tammany ward. He waged a press war (always piously backstage) against the Federalists as scurrilous as that directed against him." Daniels told of Jefferson using spies to gather political intelligence. "Notable among them was one John Beckley, who would be rewarded with no less post than the first Librarianship of Congress for scandal-mongering and informing for the Jefferson machine," an unfair and demeaning characterization of Beckley's wide range of work.

Typical of Beckley's early efforts in the nascent political struggle between the Federalists and the Jeffersonians was his collaboration on a political pamphlet attacking Hamilton's Treasury administration. This pamphlet, *An Examination of the Late Proceedings in Congress Respecting the Official Conduct of the Secretary of the Treasury,* was widely read from Vermont to Georgia in 1793, yet today only a handful of copies are extant in libraries. The stinging pamphlet that had wide political repercussions was originally attributed to John Taylor of Caroline. Later revelations made clear that it was the work of James Madison, assisted by Beckley. This attack came, in part, in response to attacks made by Hamilton anonymously on both Jefferson and Madison during the summer and fall of 1792. By early fall of that year, Beckley had written Madison: "Our domestic affairs, seem to me, to be fast verging on the issue of a contest between the Treasury department and the people, whose interest shall preponderate in the next Congress," a political estimate that proved to be accurate. In the same letter, Beckley wrote: "Mr. Hamilton unequivocally declares that you are his *personal and political enemy.*" The earliest copy of *An Examination* bears the date of March 8, 1793, though the pamphlet was not released to the public until

[7]Joseph Charles, *Origins of the American Party System,* Williamsburg, VA: Institute of Early American History and Culture, 1956.

[8]Johnathan Daniels, *Ordeal of Ambition: Jefferson, Hamilton, Burr,* Garden City, NY: Doubleday, 1970.

April 9. A later printing was dated October 20. None bore the name of the author or the printer. The pamphlet dealt with Hamilton's alleged peculations in the William Duer affair. It stressed "the duty of a free people to watch attentively the movements of every department of public trust," especially "the conduct of the legislature. Whilst that branch preserves its independence and integrity, they are safe." Shortly after the pamphlet was off the press, Beckley showed a copy to Jefferson, who approved of its charge that the "misapplication of public monies by the Secretary of the Treasury."

Authorship ultimately became clear in a letter Beckley wrote to James Monroe on April 10, the day after the revised pamphlet came off the press:

> The pamphlet is out, and I think merits all the attention bestowed upon it—Altho it only appeared yesterday the demand has nearly exhausted the 250 copies reserved for this place—200 to go tomorrow to New York, and will be scattered there, at Albany, in Connecticut & Vermont—200 to go to Boston—100 to Charleston—100 to Augusta, 100 to Petersburg—100 to go to Frederick—I have ordered by water two parcels of 20 each, one for Mr. Madison, the other for you—to be made into one packet and addressed to Mr. James Blair, at Freg.[9] The whole expense is about—this money, which, at the price demand of 3/16 of a dollar will be defrayed by the copies sold here. As the Assembly of this State adjourns tomorrow, and I have taken care to scatter it pretty well among them, thro' the means of Dallas [Alexander J. Dallas, a fellow Republican].

This letter sheds light on the method of financing and circulating political pamphleteering of that day.[10]

THE POLITICAL PUBLICIST EMERGES

From these early battles between the Hamiltonians and Jeffersonians, there gradually evolved the Federalist and Republican parties. In this increasingly bitter conflict were planted the seeds of the nation's first two-party system—a development that the framers of Constitution had feared and thus had not foreseen its necessity. By 1792, the conflict between the ideas and economic interests of these titans began to crystallize in the form of political parties. The President, much to his distaste, was gradually pulled into the Federalist orbit by his trusted adviser, Hamilton. Consequently, Jefferson quit as Secretary of

---

[9]In *Papers of James Monroe*, Vol. 38, Series 2, Library of Congress. Quoted from "The Piece Left Behind," By Edmund and Dorothy Smith Berkeley, *Virginia Magazine of History*, Vol. 75, 1967, p. 179.

[10]For full account of this pamphlet and its repercussions, see: Edmund and Virginia Berkeley, "The Piece Left Behind; Monroe's Authorship of a Political Pamphlet Revealed," *Virginia Magazine of History*, Vol. 75, No. 2 (1967), pp. 174–180.

State and gradually edged into a position of open opposition. He became the national spokesman and leader of the Republicans. Charles asserted in his history of this new two-party system that "Jefferson did not create a party; a widespread popular movement recognized and claimed him as its leader." John Beckley had much to do with this "widespread popular movement."

Intentionally or not, Beckley made a major contribution to the evolving party split when he obtained from England the first part of Thomas Paine's *Rights of Man*. He had it republished as an antidote to John Adams' *Discourses on Davila*, which in Beckley's view seemed to advocate monarchy, nobility, and aristocracy. Beckley persuaded Jonathan Bayard Smith to republish the Paine essay but first lent it to Madison who in turn lent it to Jefferson. At Beckley's request, Jefferson sent it to Smith with a recommendation to publish it. He did, including Jefferson's comments on the flyleaf. Adams and the other Federalists were outraged. In Charles' view this exchange opened "the battle for public opinion in earnest."

Jefferson had great faith in agrarian democracy and in public opinion. Charles wrote: "He apparently believed in the early 1790s that if public opinion could be informed, the measures of government would reflect the views of its citizens." He wrote Madison in 1799: "Let me pray and beseech you to set aside a certain portion of every post day to write what be proper for the public." In the same letter Jefferson saw the press "the engine to use in molding public sentiment."

Hamilton, a realist, on the other hand saw the need to build Washington's prestige as a means of bulwarking Federalist strength. In 1802, in retrospect, he lamented that the Federalists "erred in relying so much on the rectitude and utility of their measures as to have neglected the cultivation of popular favor, by fair and justifying expedients."[11] This was a strange confession for the man who had seen the necessity of influencing public opinion to win ratification for the Constitution, and had set about effectively doing just that.

THE PRESS PROVIDES THE ENGINE

The colonial newspapers that provided an effective platform for Samuel Adams and his fellow revolutionaries in fomenting the American Revolution soon provided Jefferson's "engine" for molding public opinion. In Elwyn Robinson's view, Hamilton and Jefferson, perhaps without realizing it, "guided the transformation of the American Press from unenterprising purveyors of news and to an important corpus in the shock troops of party conflict."[12] Their use of newspapers as the prime weapon in political conflict

---

[11]Hamilton, *Hamilton's Works*, VI, New York: John F. Trow, 1850, pp. 517–541.

[12]Elwyn Robinson, "The Dynamics of American Journalism from 1787 to 1865," *Pennsylvania Magazine of History*, 61 (1937).

put a partisan stamp on our newspapers that only began to erode late in the 20th century. Today newspapers are second only to television as the "engines" used by today's successors to John Beckley.

At the beginnings of the 1790s, it had been common for editors to profess impartiality in public affairs, but by the end of the decade, they were publicly proclaiming their party attachments. For example, Alexander Martin of the Baltimore *American* proclaimed in its first issue of May 13, 1799, that "in supporting the principles of *Replicanism*, the Editor is aware that he shall lay himself open to all the hatred, malice, slander and persecution which form the leading policy of the advocates of *toryism* and *royalty*."

Beckley, now emerging as a Jefferson strategist and publicist, joined Madison and Henry Lee in persuading Philip Freneau to come to Philadelphia and start publishing the *National Gazette*. This move was made to counter the Hamilton-sponsored *Gazette of the United States*, edited by John Fenno. This was the dominant paper of the time and in publicizing the Federalist view of things was antagonistic to everything Beckley and his allies espoused. According to the Berkeleys: "Freneau's paper gave them a much needed public voice for their views, and they supported it not only with their writing but also by obtaining subscriptions in Philadelphia and elsewhere." Beckley and Freneau became close friends and had a very close association.

Beckley, ever the busy scribe, was a frequent contributor to Freneau's *Gazette*. He wrote under a variety of pseudonyms, "Mercator," "The Calm Observer" and "Timon." As Mercator he challenged the Treasury Department's claim that it had reduced the public debt by almost 2,000,000 dollars. His attacks drew replies from Hamilton writing in Fenno's paper as "Civis."

Undoubtedly at Beckley's urging, President-elect Jefferson suggested to a young journalist, Samuel Harrison Smith, that he move his printing office from Philadelphia to the new capital on the mudflats of the Potomac. In the fall of 1800, Smith started a paper, *The National Intelligencer*, which became the semiofficial organ of the Jefferson Administration. Incidentally, when the nation's capital was moved in the late spring of 1800, none of the New York or Philadelphia papers covered the story.

BECKLEY EMERGES AS CAMPAIGN MANAGER

Noble Cunningham, in his interesting account of Beckley's career also saw Beckley as the forerunner of today's campaign manager.[13]

> Beckley has gone down in history as a mysterious person who carried tales and worked behind the scenes, actually, he merits attention less as a political

---

[13]Noble E. Cunningham, Jr., "John Beckley: An Early American Party Manager," *William and Mary Quarterly, 13*, 1956, p. 42.

informant than as one of the leading party organizers of the 1790s. At ease in the realm of politics and skillful organizer, he could manage an election campaign with the same methodical competence with which he performed his duties of the clerkship of the House. John Beckley was a man who knew how to win elections and to advance a party cause.

Beckley, "infected with the party spirit," led him to become in the second session of the Congress, "something of a party whip before the party division had proceeded very far." Charles recounted:[14] "He was one of those most active in organizing through the country the public meetings which protested the Jay Treaty, and he appeared in the election of 1796 to have been the most energetic organizer of public opinion in support of Jefferson."

After President Washington signed the Jay Treaty, John Beckley and his associates made a second attempt to arouse opinion against it and its supporters—the Federalists. Beckley wrote DeWitt Clinton of New York: "Rely on every effort and cooperation here in pursuit of what we religiously think our country's political salvation rests—the defeat of the treaty." Beckley also distributed circular letters throughout the States to denounce the treaty.

Beckley played a major role in prodding Jefferson to take the leadership of the Republican Party and, as indicated, he was an energetic and resourceful propagandist for Jefferson's ideas. He was more—he was Jefferson's eyes and ears collecting political intelligence, gossip, and indications of public opinion. In a sense, he was a pioneer pollster—a standard part of today's intensely organized campaigns. Cunningham noted: "Everywhere he went, Beckley had the happy facility of obtaining all sorts of information about men and things." Jefferson's notes are full of the attribution, "Beckley tells me . . ." Charles thought that Beckley had considerable influence in drawing Jefferson into opposition to Hamilton. Beckley's partisanship was intensified as President Washington, nearing the end of his second term, dismissed Attorney General Edmund Randolph on what Beckley thought trumped up charges that Randolph had accepted money from the French to oppose the Jay Treaty, and recalled his friend James Monroe from his position as minister to Paris in August 1796. Beckley's friendship with Monroe dated from when he was Clerk of the Committee of Safety in Williamsburg and Monroe was a student at William and Mary College. Also in 1780, Monroe was a member of the Virginia House of Delegates when Beckley was clerk.

President Washington announced his retirement officially in September 1796. Beckley "was convinced that the short notice the President had given of his retirement was designed to prevent a fair election, and the consequent choice of Mr. Jefferson." He saw there was no time to lose—he went to work immediately. The Berkeleys in "The Piece Left Behind," stated that "it is in this contest that Beckley appears at his best as a party worker."

---

[14]Charles, *Origins of the American Party System*, Williamsburg, VA: Institute of Early American History and Culture, 1956, pp. 81–82.

THE CAMPAIGN FOR PENNSYLVANIA

Beckley was among the few Republican leaders to realize the importance of gaining the support of Pennsylvania for Jefferson and the influence that that support could have on other states. He quickly assumed management of the Republican campaign in that state. In 3 weeks,he would boast that "our Republican ticket is pushing with infinite zeal and earnestness." And indeed it was, demonstrating his ability as a political publicist. He circulated widely lists of electors because he thought "copies of them scattered about in different neighborhoods would do great good," and distributed handbills in like profusion "shewing the strong reasons" for Jefferson's election.

A skillful publicist, Beckley took the lead in utilizing publicity as a means of winning elections when many citizens considered it unseemly for a person to openly campaign for an office. Beckley made great use of the handbill, a single sheet printed on one side, which offered an effective yet economical way of disseminating publicity. Handbills played an important role in the Pennsylvania campaign, although how many votes were won or lost by the appeals and attacks of handbills would be sheer speculation. However, their widespread use suggests that they were considered by Beckley and others as effective weapons.

Beckley fully sensed the importance of reaching the influentials in politics; his letters are filled with quotes such as these: "dispersed in a few judicious hands," "on a few popular men," "in proper hands." Three weeks before the election, Beckley distributed 30,000 party tickets—enough to provide 3 for every eligible voter—sending them by express to every county in Pennsylvania. On one occasion, he had printed 1,000 copies of a Republican speech that he distributed to those he regarded as influential leaders.

In the manner of political campaigns from that day to this, Beckley was not above disseminating exaggerated claims or even false information. From time to time, he sent around bulletins stating that Jefferson was far out in front and on one occasion, circulated the report that Hamilton was advising Jefferson's election to prevent war with France. For example, he wrote a friend and Republican leader, William Irvine, October 4, 1796: "I am at this moment advised by a letter from New York, that Mr. Hamilton publicly declares that he thinks it would be best on the score of conciliation and expediency to elect Mr. Jefferson president, since he is the only man in America that could secure us the affections of the French republic. Will it not be advisable to throw this paragraph into the Carlisle paper?"[15] Beckley and Irvine, who served as a general in Washington's Continental Army, close friends for years, carried on an extensive correspondence. The general had become an active figure in Pennsylvania politics in these postwar years.

---

[15]Noble E. Cunningham, Jr., ed., *The Making of the American Party System 1789–1809.* Englewood Cliffs, NJ: Prentice-Hall, 1965.

Beckley's campaign to promote the Republican ticket was probably not equalled in any election of the 1790s. Much of his political promotion was innovative. In addition to the large volume of printing, he relied on the press to promote the Republicans. His intensive campaign was capped with victory—of Pennsylvania's 15 electoral votes, Jefferson won 14. But as unfavorable returns from other states reached Philadelphia, he could only lament that "after all our exertions, I fear Jefferson will fall altogether." And he did. The national vote went to Federalist John Adams by the narrow margin of 71 to 68 for Jefferson. But delivery of Pennsylvania's vote by Beckley assured Jefferson of the vice presidency.

BECKLEY'S REWARD IS HIS OUSTER

The Federalists were not long in punishing Beckley for his Republican campaign. The Federalists moved quickly to strengthen their position. The Berkeleys wrote: "The Federalists were well aware of how narrowly they had averted the disaster of a Republican administration. The behind-the-scenes maneuvering that had destroyed the political influence of Randolph and Monroe had been successful and could not be directed to strengthening their control of the government."[16] Beckley was high on their "enemies list"—to use a Nixonian phrase. Beckley optimistically felt secure in his clerkship of the House. The House Federalists called an early caucus before the new Congress convened in 1797 and agreed to demand an early vote on the clerkship. Despite many protests from House members, the Federalists were successful in electing a young law student, Jonathan Williams Condy, by a one-vote margin, 41–40. Republican outrage and Federalist gloating were widely expressed in public and in private. Jefferson lamented "the loss of the ablest clerk in the United States." Beckley's longtime friend, Governor John Page of Virginia, declared that "as much of a Democrat as I am, I would not have voted against Beckley if he had been most insolent aristocrat and desperate Tory that could be found in the United States."

Beckley's financial situation which had been difficult, now became critical. Many people were wholly or partially dependent upon him. His wife—whom he had married in New York in 1791—her mother, and her younger brother were members of his household. His parents and an afflicted brother in England and other relatives in Virginia all looked to him for financial help. All his savings were invested in the western Virginia and Kentucky land, but efforts to sell any of this land had not been successful. Beckley was humiliated to have to borrow money from his friends, including Jefferson and Dr. Rush.

---

[16]Edmund and Dorothy Smith Berkeley, "The First Librarian of Congress, John Beckley," *The Quarterly Journal of the Library of Congress*, Vol. 32, 1975, p. 89.

The next 4 years were dominated by the Federalists, and this made life doubly hard for the partisan Beckley. He continued to be hard up for money and at various times considered returning to Richmond or moving to Kentucky. But somehow he hung on in Philadelphia. And, as Cunningham observed: "In or out of office Beckley never withdrew from the fascinating world of politics." Repeatedly rebuffed in his efforts to regain the House of Representatives clerkship, he became more and more convinced that the Federalists were determined to destroy him and his allies Randolph, Monroe, and Jefferson. He set out to get even.

While he was Secretary of the Treasury, Alexander Hamilton had an affair with the wife of a James Reynolds. When confronted with the evidence by Congressmen F. A. C. Muhlenberg and Abraham Venable, Hamilton admitted that this was true and that he was being blackmailed by Reynolds. Representative Muhlenberg had sought the assistance of Monroe in the investigation. At that time, Monroe had asked Beckley to keep complete notes on the affair but to keep them secret. Beckley had made no commitment to do so but did until provoked by his financial situation and what he perceived as Hamilton's efforts to destroy him and his Republican allies. The Berkeleys recounted: "Beckley persuaded James Thomaon Callender to edit the papers relating to the Reynolds affair as a supplement to his *History of the United States for 1796*, published by Snowden & McCorkle. It had even more impact than Beckley could have anticipated." Hamilton refused to believe that Monroe was not involved in the release of the papers."[17] Ironically, as time would prove, a duel between Hamilton and Monroe was narrowly averted through the diplomacy of Aaron Burr. Eight years later, Hamilton died at Burr's hand in a duel, a way of settling disputes in that day.

Beckley finally got a break when he worked in the campaign of Thomas McKean for governor of Pennsylvania in the state elections of 1799. After McKean was elected, he used his influence, supported by Jefferson, to have Beckley appointed as clerk of the mayor's court of city of Philadelphia and clerk of the orphans' court for the county. This put him in good shape to again work for the election of Jefferson as President of the United States.

BECKLEY HELPS JEFFERSON WIN

Beckley took the chairmanship of the Republican Committee of Correspondence for Philadelphia as a way of working for Jefferson's election. He authored an anonymous pamphlet, *An Address to the People of the United States; with an Epitome and Vindication of the Public Life and Character of Thomas Jefferson*. In this pamphlet, Beckley wrote of his hero "as a man

---

[17]"The First Librarian of Congress," pp. 89–90.

of pure, ardent and unaffected piety; of sincere and genuine virtue; of an enlightened mind and superior wisdom; the adorer of our God; the patriot of his country; and the friend and benefactor of the whole human race." These economiums were widely reprinted in the Republican press. Beckley saw to that. The pamphlet which included a seven-page biography of Jefferson was published by Mathrew Carey in Philadelphia, who printed 2,000 copies. A copy in the author's possession was printed by Meriwether Jones in Richmond, then printer to the Commonwealth of Virginia, which suggests that the printing may have been gratis. It was dated simply 1800. Others also reproduced this campaign document.

In August 1800, Beckley sent a dozen copies of the pamphlet to Monroe in Virginia, explaining:[18]

> To you, as a friend, I must apologize for the inaccuracies & inefficiencies of the "Epitome"—destitute of materials, oppressed by sickness myself and the death of an only child,* having only designed a brief newspaper essay, and being urged by friends to give it is present form, and believing that it is materially sound in fact, I determined to send it forth, 1000 copies were struck for me, 1000 more by the printer, 1000 at New York, 1000 in Connecticut, and 100 in Maryland, have since been struck, and imperfect as it is, it will I trust do some good.

The Berkeleys wrote of this campaign:[19]

> Beckley, who was always inclined to take an optimistic view, began to see hope of a Republican victory in November and determined to do everything in his power to bring it about. He dug out an essay he had written in 1795 dealing with Federalist attempts to establish a standing army and sent it to his friend Ephhraim Kirby in Connecticut to be published as a pamphlet. Beckley's efforts toward organization at the grassroots level were so effective that the Federalists accused the Republicans of establishing presses in every town and county in the country.

Although Beckley's campaign in Pennsylvania for Jefferson and against President John Adams was not as successful as his 1796 effort, Jefferson did ultimately triumph. When the Electoral College met after the November election, the national vote ended in a tie between Aaron Burr and Jefferson, 71–71, with 65 for Adams, 64 for Thomas Pinckney, and one for John Jay. Thus, the vote had to be resolved in the House of Representatives where Jefferson finally won on the 36th ballot. Not an overwhelming mandate! Yet the Republicans celebrated widely in all sections of the country. A grand jubilee was planned for Inauguration Day March 4, 1801, with "Ciceronian

---

[18]Beckley to Monroe, August 26, 1800, *Monroe Papers*, New York Public Library.
*The Beckleys had two children; a daughter, who died in infancy, and the son, Alfred.
[19]"The First Librarian of Congress," p. 91.

Beckley" as the orator. Adams and Jefferson, as the chief ideological stand-ard-bearers in the American Revolution and in the forming of a new federal government, had become close friends. Now their friendship was in tatters. Only in 1812 was a reconciliation be effected by Dr. Benjamin Rush. Both died, appropriately, on the Fourth of July in 1826—and they died as friends.

In 1801, with the Republicans now in control, Beckley was restored to the clerkship of the House of representatives and served in that post until his death on April 8, 1807. In 1802, President Jefferson rewarded his friend and political adviser with the post of the Librarian of Congress after the position was authorized by Congress. Beckley held this post, too, until his death. In that role, always the partisan, Beckley made it difficult for Feder-alists in Congress to obtain documents from the library.[20] Nonetheless, the Berkeleys defended this appointment. They wrote: "His appointment as Librarian was, however, by no means a political appointment. He was un-doubtedly the best qualified applicant for the position. Jefferson had a very real interest in and concern for the Library, and he was thoroughly familiar with Beckley's qualifications."

Cunningham concluded as to Beckley's career:[21] "In or out of office, Beckley never withdrew from the fascinating world of politics. A partisan always, he worked ceaselessly for party ends in a time when that kind of allegiance was only beginning to looked upon as a virtue." Proof of Beckley's ceaseless, untiring efforts to promote the Republican cause was his effort to start promoting Monroe for the presidency midway in Jefferson's second term. Beckley wrote Monroe in 1806, a year before his death: "I trust the *confidential* letter I wrote you during the Session via New York per packet has come safe to hand. It was not signed and was written in the 3rd person, so as to guard *vs* accidental miscarriage. I unfold the intrigues which caused us so much agitation during the Session, and initials used I was confident you could not mistake.[22]

Although he played a major role in the emergence of the nation's first two-party political system and in so doing established a political debate as to the role of government that persists to this day, John Beckley has been generally neglected by historians. His role in the politics of the new nation was ever bit as powerful as say James Carville's role in the election of President William Clinton in 1992.

John Beckley died on Wednesday, April 8, 1807, in Washington, DC at the age of 50. Understandably, his obituary, printed April 10 in *The National Intelligencer*, the Republican organ, was effusive in its praise:

---

[20]Berkeleys, "The Piece Left Behind," p. 52.

[21]"John Beckley: An Early American Party Manager," *William and Mary Quarterly, 13*, 1956, p. 52.

[22]Beckley to Monroe, July 13, 1806, *Monroe Papers*, New York Public Library.

Having been educated to the bar, he pursued that profession with reputation, so far as various public duties admitted, until organization of the General Government, when he was chosen Clerk of the House of Representatives, a place he filled with rare, perhaps unprecedented distinction, with the intermission of a term of two years until his decease. His articulation was distinct, his elocution commanding, and his parliamentary knowledge extensive. But his highest distinction was his inflexible patriotism and adherence to republican principles. Through the whole period of his life he pursued an unbending course. Devoted to the cause of liberty, much of his happiness flowed from its triumphs; and the zeal, which prompted him the ardor of his youth, to resist tyranny, remained unabated, during the more mature period of his life, against internal oppression.

Discounting the purple political prose, Beckley did "pursue an unbending course," to play a significant role in the evolving U.S. political system and thus earned a place in history that has been generally denied him.

BECKLEY'S PLACE IN HISTORY

Joseph Charles in his seminal study, *The Origins of the American Party System*, recognized Beckley's influential role in this passage:[23] "A great deal of the work usually attributed to Jefferson in organizing opposition to Federalist measures, both in the House of Representatives and among the general public, should be credited instead to John Beckley . . ." Charles then illustrates this point: "Early in the second session of the First Congress, Senator Malay of Pennsylvania noted of the Virginia men, Buckley [sic] and Madison govern them' Madison fulfilled the function of opposition leader in that his attacks on administration measure were so solidly based that they served to rally support . . . Beckley gradually took over work of this sort and became something of a party whip before the party division has proceeded very far." The incubus of the two-party system can be found in the national debate over the ratification of the Jay Treaty with Great Britain. Beckley early took the lead in opposing the treaty by writing letters to put pressure on the Senators he thought were shaky. Beckley was active in organizing public meetings throughout the country to protest the Jay Treaty. Charles believed that: "In addition to organizing the opposition, Beckley may have had some importance in preparing Jefferson for the role he was to play." How much Jefferson was influenced by the intelligence Beckley steadily brought him can only be a matter of conjecture, but Charles found "there appears to have been considerable influence exerted upon Jefferson in the attempt to bring him into opposition to Hamilton."

---

[23]Institute of Early American History and Culture, Williamsburg, VA, 1956, pp. 80–81.

Beckley's role in the United States' early history was a significant one. As Samuel Eliot Morison has written of the Hamilton–Jefferson political struggle,[24] "All those differences in temper, theory, and policy were bracketed by two opposed conceptions of what America was and might be." These political battles continue to this day and retain, in Morrison's words, "a remarkable vibrancy as the American people continue to work their destiny." Albert Fried, in *The Jefferson and Hamiltonian Traditions in American Politics*, underscored this generalization:[25] "Both ideologies have been relevant throughout American history, even though the specific circumstances that shaped them and first brought them into opposition disappeared. In the broadest sense, Hamiltonianism and Jeffersonianism have presented the country with alternative ends, and the country has always had to choose between them."

John Beckley move over and make way for James Carville.[26]

[24]Samuel Eliot Morison, Henry Steele Commager, William E. Leuchtenburg, *The Growth of the American Republic*, 7th ed., New York: Oxford University Press, 1980.

[25]Albert Fried, *The Jeffersonian and Hamiltonian Traditions in American Politics: A Documentary History*, Garden City, NY: Anchor Books, 1968.

[26]Charles, p. 82.

Amos Kendall: Andrew Jackson's "Thinking Machine"

The Presidential election of 1828 in which war Hero Andrew Jackson decisively defeated incumbent President John Quincy Adams marked a watershed in U.S. politics and government, bringing frontier democracy to the young United States government, providing the genesis of the nation's two-party political system, and enlarging the Presidency. In winning his victory, Andrew Jackson had significant assistance from an astute political strategist and skilled publicist, Amos Kendall, who would serve as the President's chief adviser for his two terms. These men left an indelible stamp on U.S. history, yet one of them, Kendall, has been lost in the mists of history.

Historian John A. Gerraty asserted that Jackson's significance in U.S. political and social history is enormous. "His larger-than-life personality and equally heroic convictions and prejudices changed the American Presidency and the character of American politics forever." Whether Jackson accomplished much or little as President has been debated by historians from that day to this.

A more recent biographer, Robert V. Remini, pictured Jackson as a great democrat, the person above all others who changed "the pure republican character" of the political system as originally established by the Founding Fathers by insisting on greater representation of the people and a greater responsiveness to their will. Remini saw Jackson as an "aggressive, forceful, and dynamic leader, accustomed to command," arguing that Jackson "was the right man at the most propitious moment in the ongoing development of American democracy."[1] Kendall, too, was the man for this "propitious moment."

---

[1] This view of Jackson is made clear in the preface by Robert V. Remini, *Andrew Jackson and the Course of American Democracy, 1833–1845.* New York: New York University Press, Vol. III, 1984.

On the other hand, Thomas A. Bailey thought Jackson had been over-rated as President; Arthur Schlesinger in his *The Age of Jackson* ranked him among the Near Greats in the presidency; Corwin and Koenig concluded that "When he left office he left behind a political vacuum that a resuscitated Congress presently filled."[2] The Rienows concluded that Jackson left the people he loved "with a void—and with a vision that would plague them forever."[3]

Lynn Marshall viewed Jackson as "a transitional figure" as a political leader. Jackson developed "no elevated political theory; he reacted directly to events, trusting in his intuitive grasp of immediate practical expedients. Jackson's character may perhaps best be measured by his choice of chief political lieutenants. In Van Buren and Kendall he demonstrated his taste for the practical, the shrewd, the opportunistic, and the efficient—even though socially obscure."[4]

Of these chief lieutenants to President Jackson, Amos Kendall would provide the driving force in Jackson's policies in his influential role as the first White House press counselor, ghost writer, and political strategist. Kendall's role in the defeat of the Bank of the United States was particularly decisive. This is told in the next chapter. The first clear beginnings of the Presidential campaign and the White House public relations function came in the work and ideas of Kendall, who had broken with Jacksonian rival, Henry Clay, to join Jackson's forces in 1827.

It was no coincidence that a publicist and public relations strategist emerged in the Jackson era. In the 1820s and 1830s, more male voters were gaining the right to vote, free public schools were springing up along the frontier, and a burgeoning, strident partisan press was stimulating increased interest in politics and government. When Alexis de Tocqueville visited the United States in 1831 and 1832, he marveled at the "immense" influence of the press in U.S. political life. The French observer wrote that "the press causes political life to circulate through all parts of that vast territory," forcing leaders to face the popular will, rallying "the interests of the community round certain principles," and serving "as a vital communication link for a dispersed population." Gerald J. Baldasty, a journalism scholar, found in a detailed study that the press and party were inextricably bound in the age of Jackson, adding: "The press did, in fact, provide a forum for public opinion," as de Tocqueville noted, "but its role in American political society was far more extensive. In particular, editors formed the nucleus of political

---

[2]Edwin S. Corwin and Louis W. Koening, *The Presidency Today*. New York: New York University Press, 1956, p. 18.

[3]Robert and Leona Train Rienow, *The Lonely Quest*. Chicago: University of Chicago Press, 1966, p. 78.

[4]Lynn Marshall, "The Strange Stillbirth of the Whig Party," *American Historical Review*, *LXXII*, January 1967, pp. 445–453.

organization in the 1820s and 1830s, and thus were central to the dramatic growth in partisan activity that characterized the age of Jackson."[5]

No longer could government be the exclusive concern of the patrician few, the "Eastern Establishment" of that day. Given a popular war hero who constantly talked of "the people's rights" and the widening political enfranchisement, more systematic efforts to inform and influence the voters were a logical development, and Amos Kendall emerged to meet this challenge. He was, indeed, a man for his times who would leave a large imprint on 19th century United States as a political publicist and strategist, as the modernizer of the U. S. Postal System, as the promoter of the newly invented telegraph, and as a philanthropist who founded the nation's first school for the deaf and dumb.

Lynn Marshall observed of John Beckley, profiled in the previous chapter, and Amos Kendall that their roles and methods of political propaganda reflected clearly the difference between the Jeffersonians and the Jacksonians. Each was a man for his time. Beckley, Marshall wrote, was "in contrast to the Jacksonian organizers, a particular protege and confidant of Virginia's leading gentlemen politicians. The Republican Party reached out to other local gentlemen-leaders of similar persuasion." In this process Beckley was perfectly placed to play a leading role. On the other hand, the Jacksonians went directly to the people and to fashion and direct their political salvos they had in Amos Kendall a sharpshooter of extraordinary talent.[6]

From whence did this remarkable man come?

FROM A NEW ENGLAND FARM

In mid-1789, the world was unsettled. The French Revolution was getting under way. Great Britain was desperately trying to hold on to its far-flung empire in the wake of losing its U.S. colonies. The newly independent United States inaugurated George Washington as its first president on April 30. A typical American in these times was the New England farmer, who aspired for many sons and with their help managed to scratch out an austere but adequate living.

One such farmer was Zebedee Kendall of Dustable, MA, about 30 miles from Boston. His forebears had arrived in Massachusetts from England in about 1640. In June 1779, Zebedee had married Molly Dakin of Mason and settled down to the rigors of farm life on a hard-scrabble farm.

---

[5]"The Press and Politics in the Age of Jackson," *Journalism Monographs*, No. 89, August 1984, p. 1.

[6]Marshall, p. 453.

Within 10 years, Zebedee and Molly had four sons and a daughter, Molly. In mid-1789, Molly was preparing for another child. On a hot summer day, August 16, another boy was born to the Kendalls. Impressed with a recent sermon in their Congregational Church on the Old Testament prophet Amos, they named their new son Amos. He was baptized into the church by the Reverend Daniel Emerson of nearby Hollis, NH, on November 1, according to the Reverend Elias Mason's *History of the Town of Dustable*. Zebedee Kendall 10 days before had been elected a deacon in the Congregational Church and from that time on was referred to as Deacon Kendall.

Amos grew up in an atmosphere of hard work on the farm, of strict observance of Congregational religious principles, and of exacting but not harsh family discipline. His parents' attitude on the upbringing of children had relaxed somewhat by the time Amos came along and consisted mostly of giving advice and admonition. His early years were almost void of recreation as the only possible day for it was Sunday, but the family rigidly adhered to the Sabbath being a day of rest and quiet contemplation. However, the Kendall boys did get in quite a bit of fishing in the spring and summer and trapping of mink and muskrat in the winter months. They sold the skins to earn money of their own.[7]

Zebedee's farm straddled the Massachusetts, New Hampshire line, and he paid school taxes in both states. Thus Amos' early schooling was variously in the free schools of one state and then the other. One winter when there were five Kendall children of school age, a female teacher was hired to teach them in the Kendall home. Amos developed into the best scholar of the family and came to excel in spelling and arithmetic. He also was a prolific reader, often pursuing this activity while his brothers played. This led him to become a frequent visitor to a small township library, which was nearby.

Amos was a sober, thoughtful boy, and somewhat diffident and bashful. This personality gained him the nickname "Deacon," but the nickname also suggests that he may have been most like his father, who was in fact a church deacon. Amos showed some mechanical inclinations in his youth; he "invented" a water pump for use on the farm but discovered years later that such a pump had long been used in Europe.

When Amos was 14, his father became disabled with rheumatism and that year, Amos and his 16-year-old brother did all the farm work. The next year Amos spent in the home of a parish preacher—his labors in exchange for advanced instruction in arithmetic and English grammar. But the preacher

---

[7]Amos Kendall, *Autobiography of Amos Kendall*. William Stickney, ed., Boston: Lee and Shepard, 1872. Though the volume is entitled "Autobiography" and Stickney (Kendall's son-in-law) is listed as editor, it is more a biography even though Stickney made liberal use of Kendall's writings. Kendall has not been the subject of a definitive biography although he merits one.

turned out to be a tyrant who was interested mostly in obtaining ready labor; Amos received little education. Up to this time, Amos had looked on ministers as good, honorable men whose actions and motives were above question. This experience caused him to revise his attitude, and for the rest of his life, he reserved opinion on ministers until he could judge their actions.

At age 16, Kendall attended the New Ispswich (NH) Academy. Being an uncultured farm boy, he felt inferior—he considered everyone his superior. At his first class recitation, the teacher "ridiculed him unmercifully." This served to stiffen Kendall's backbone, and he resolved to improve, which he did. After almost a year at the academy, Kendall in the fall of 1806 launched into teaching—for $13 a month plus board. With his savings from this teaching, he entered Groton Academy in the spring of 1807 to prepare for college.

Kendall was admitted to Dartmouth College later that year, but finances forced him to teach again the following winter. He kept up with his studies however and rejoined his Dartmouth classmates in March 1808. His feeling of inferiority persisted at Dartmouth, and with great trepidation, he finally read to his class a piece of original composition. His tutor and classmates praised it. "This success," wrote Stickney, "gave him considerable confidence; but never during his college life, and scarcely ever since, has he written an article which he did not think could be improved."

Each winter of his last 3 years at Dartmouth, like the first, Kendall left school for several months to teach. His college education cost $570, of which he earned $270 teaching. His father contributed the difference.[8]

Kendall was a member of several societies, including a forensic and literary society and the Handel Society, which was devoted to cultivating sacred music. He also was selected as a member of Phi Beta Kappa.

Kendall initially avoided the prankishness of college life, but by his second year, he was participating in some of the more common shenanigans, such as locking up the neighborhood cows in the cellar of the college building. By the end of his junior year, he was highly popular with his classmates; however it was a natural popularity—not one cultivated by Kendall simply for its own sake. He often bucked the majority in moral matters, particularly as to drinking. In other areas, he seemed to be an average college boy. He took dancing lessons in his junior year and participated fully in the college social life. He did not however tell his parents about his dancing, as they had been avidly against it when he was growing up. Stickney said; "It was the only time that Amos Kendall deceived his parents, and although he did it to save them unhappiness, and felt justified, he could not recommend the practice to others."[9]

Late in his junior year, Kendall had occasion, possibly for the first time, to observe aroused public opinion. A Dartmouth student had been sent to

---

[8]*Ibid.* p. 163.
[9]*Ibid.* pp. 31–40.

Boston to purchase a body for use in the college's dissecting room. Instead of making the long trip, he took a body from a fresh grave in a nearby town. The empty grave was discovered, and the subsequent investigation finally turned up the body at the college. Excitement and terror reigned in the area; town meetings were held and violent resolutions adopted. People threatened to burn the college, and they would not even listen to explanations that college officials tried to offer. It was a long time before the excitement subsided. Perhaps Kendall perceived how meetings, speeches, resolutions, and so forth could arouse and solidify public opinion.

To his surprise, Kendall finished Dartmouth at the head of his class. He felt adequate in most subjects, lacking in some, but superior in none. He concluded that the faculty had made liberal allowances for his extended absences while teaching.

With Kendall's character and personality pretty well formed by this time, it is interesting to note these words, which are contained in a review of his college life that he wrote at the end of his college days:[10]

> I soon found that popularity and excellence of scholarship are seldom connected. . . . I have seen that man's opinion of right is generally founded upon his interests; that to make a man your friend, you must promote his interest; that differences of opinion, inflamed by continual dispute, begets coldness and suspicion; that honors often depend on popularity, and popularity on accommodation and acquiescence; but that the most stable kind of popularity—that which insures respect and lasting esteem is founded upon decision of character. Yet this decision must be based on reason, and exercised with prudence. The man of decision is alone independent.

Not inclined toward the ministry, which his parents wanted, or medicine, Kendall went into law almost by default. In Groton, MA, he studied from 1811 to 1813 in the office of William Merchant Richardson, a U. S. Representative and Democrat. During this period Kendall's political learnings began to take shape. "Although," he wrote, "my principles as well as interests incline me toward the Democratic or Republican side [referring to one party], I am not yet prepared to sacrifice my conscience and every principle of moral honesty to the unhallowed zeal of any party."

In October 1812 Kendall mustered twice with a militia company, but primarily because of his weak and somewhat delicate physique, the military was not for him. "If I cannot carry a gun half a day, or see a wounded man without fainting, farewell to the tented field." Later he was formally rejected for physical reasons.

During his 2 years with Richardson, Kendall's varied interests were reflective of a curious and intelligent young man. He tried to invent a perpetual

---

[10]*Ibid.* pp. 66–67.

motion machine; he wrote several plays, but none was accepted by producers; he dabbled in poetry. Kendall experienced his first love affair and proceeded to enjoy several others. He visited Boston and the Massachusetts legislature, which was a disappointment: "I could not see much majesty in the collected dignity of the State."[11]

Richardson moved to Portsmouth, NH, in December 1813 and made arrangements for Kendall to continue his law studies with another lawyer. But Kendall thought this lawyer inferior and did not take up the offer. In Stickney's words: "The depression of business in New England caused by the war with Great Britain, and the absence of any rich or influential family connection who could aid in his advancement" turned Kendall's thoughts to the West or the South.

With a loan of $200 from his father, Kendall left home on February 19, 1814, and proceeded to Washington. He spent several days becoming acquainted with the city and meeting, through his former benefactor, Congressman Richardson, a number of famous men in government. Among them was Senator Bledsoe of Kentucky. In time Kendall entered into an agreement with Bledsoe wherein Bledsoe took him into his family to assist in teaching his four children in return for board and $100 a year.

Kendall left Washington and proceeded to Lexington, KY. Bledsoe arrived soon thereafter but reneged on the agreement. Kendall was stranded without a job in a strange country, but he began to meet people. Through a young man named Watkins, who was a half brother of Henry Clay, Kendall met Mrs. Clay. She offered him board, the use of Clay's library, and $300 a year to teach her five school-age children (two others were preschool age). Thus Kendall was taken into the Clay household where he carried out his instructional duties from May 1814 to April 1815. During this period, Clay was in England most of the time as a member of the U. S. Commission, which negotiated the Treaty of Ghent; the remainder of the period he was busy in Washington in the House of Representatives.[12] Mrs. Clay brought Kendall into Kentucky society life where he acquired additional polish.

While living in the Clay household, Kendall was granted a license to practice law in Kentucky. He also developed somewhat of a cynical view of politics and the manipulation of opinion: "I have, I think, learnt the way to be popular in Kentucky, but do not as yet put it in practice. Drink whiskey and talk loud, with the fullest confidence, and you will hardly fail of being called a clever fellow."

Along about this time, Kendall was called up to do what he was perhaps his first bit of ghostwriting. A local citizen, apparently one of prominence,

---

[11]*Ibid.* p. 75.
[12]It was not until May 1816 that Kendall met Clay for the first time. He "found him a very agreeable man, and was familiarly acquainted with him in half an hour." *Ibid.* p. 172.

asked Kendall to write for him a Fourth of July oration. That such an intelligent man would ask such a thing surprised Kendall, but he consented. A note of disdain for his first brush with such activity is evident in his comment that "I am sure I would never depend for my reputation on the talents or exertions of another."

Toward the end of his stay with the Clays, news reached Kentucky that Major General Andrew Jackson had won the Battle of New Orleans.

After leaving the Clay household, Kendall spent several months looking for a promising pursuit. He considered going back to teaching only as a last resort. A corporation that was to deal in land speculation in Indiana held his interest for a time, but he finally declined to participate because he was not satisfied with some provisions of the charter. His law practice, which he treated somewhat as a sideline, attracted only a few clients. Finally in 1815, through a series of complicated promissory arrangements, he became postmaster at Georgetown, KY., and the half owner and editor of a small newspaper, the *Minerva Press.* Shortly thereafter, a mortgage and other debts against the paper came to light, and it folded in a few weeks. There is no indication that Kendall was ever again caught short in a business deal; no doubt he learned his lesson with this experience. He spent January 1816 traveling around the area trying to collect back subscription fees from readers of the late paper. In his conversations with the people, he found that they had liked little about the paper and presumably Kendall formed definite ideas as to what they would like and what would be effective on them.

In April 1816, Kendall and two other men began publishing the *Georgetown Patriot.* Though he owned no part of the paper—in fact, he didn't want to—Kendall was the editor. But he was determined to be an "independent one." This attitude was fortunate because an independent editorial course was necessary to gain the needed support from all parties in the county; this full support was essential if the paper was to exist. In the Congressional campaign later in the year, Kendall seemed to be successful in keeping all the candidates in a state of "half mad and half pleased." His chief editorial efforts on the *Patriot* dealt with discussion on the problems of currency and with demands on the banks to resume specie payments that had been suspended during the War of 1812. This was the genesis of Kendall's attitude toward banks that came to be reflected in Jackson's battle with Nicholas Biddle.

In September 1816, while Kendall was on a trip to Frankfurt, William Gerard, one of the editors of the state paper, the *Argus of Western America,* proposed that he buy half interest in the paper and become its editor. Gerard even arranged for the necessary loan of $2,000 from the Bank of Kentucky. Kendall accepted and assumed his new duties in October. When the general assembly convened that winter, Kendall received permission to sit in the House and report the speeches and proceedings. The legislators were pleased with the results. Also "it gave an importance to our paper which brought it many subscribers, and made the representatives in some measure dependent on me."

KENDALL WAGES FIRST CAMPAIGN

Soon after connecting with the *Argus*, Kendall undertook an apparently hopeless campaign. The governor had recently died, soon after taking office. Kendall was convinced that the Kentucky constitution implied that a new election should take place. An overwhelming majority of the general assembly opposed such an election. Kendall began the campaign with a series of persuasive, reasoned articles in the *Argus*. Then he wrote acquaintances throughout the state to take action to get his articles republished, which they did. This was Kendall's first effort on creating public opinion on a sizeable scale. But he was not through. To his delight, several papers opposed his stand; he clearly and decisively rebutted their arguments. He also published a 39-page pamphlet and several handbills to add to his campaign. Candidates for the state House of Representatives made the proposal for a gubernatorial election the prime issue. In the spring election, a large majority favoring the issue was elected to the House. Thus, Kendall waged and won his first political campaign.[13]

While editing the *Argus*, Kendall successfully withstood oral, written, and physical attacks by editorial and political opponents. His most potent weapon, which he invoked whenever possible, was public ridicule. For example, after Moses A. Bledsoe, a Federalist editor, had bodily assaulted him, a friend gave Kendall a pocket pistol for protection. The pistol was out of order, but before Kendall could get it repaired, he encountered Bledsoe and another large man on a lonely road. They obviously were preparing to horsewhip Kendall, but he scared them off with the broken pistol. Kendall overcame his initial impulse to get the pistol fixed and shoot Bledsoe on sight. Instead he hurried back to Frankfurt and told of the incident. The story spread rapidly, and Bledsoe's cowardly attack and inglorious flight became the subject of laughter and ridicule. Bledsoe finally abandoned his paper and left the state.[14]

Early in his editorship, Kendall developed a code of conduct that would be a credit to today's editors. Stickney's summary of his rules is:

> He would never knowingly assert an untruth about men, measures, or things;
> that if betrayed into one by misinformation or mistake, he would, as soon as

---

[13]*Ibid.* pp. 186–189.
[14]*Ibid.* pp. 195–196.

correctly informed, retract it, whether requested by an injured party to do so or not; that no threats or violence should induce him to retract any statement which he believed to be true; that if insulted, he would return the insult in kind; that if assaulted, he would defend himself by any means at hand, if necessary by taking the life of the assailant, but would sooner take a whipping than run when attacked.[15]

For the next few years, Kendall and the *Argus* were engrossed in the welfare and politics of Kentucky. He carried on a running campaign for a public school system, pointing out how Kentucky was lagging behind the Eastern states. His editorials constantly needled the people to develop manufacturing and stop depending on goods manufactured elsewhere. Castigating the wealthy and the politicians for being "clothed from head to foot in the drapery of England," Kendall suggested this could be changed if the "great and influential men should set the example." In addition, "associations might be formed, extended over the whole country, the great object of which should be the *wearing* of domestic manufactures."

Kendall's most important campaign began in 1813 and ended in the late 1830s. It was against the Bank of the United States, which was chartered by Congress in 1816. Kendall's first assault was a series of 11 scholarly, persuasive, and readable articles that argued that the Bank was unconstitutional. Some of the same ideas in these articles were to appear again in Jackson's famous veto message 14 years later, one mainly written by Kendall.

In 1818 Kendall, then 29, married Mary B. Woolfolk of nearby Jefferson County. Their marriage was happy, fruitful, but short-lived. Mary died in 1823, leaving Kendall with four small children.

In January 1823, Kendall and A. G. Meriweather became the sole owners of the *Argus*. In their initial statement as owners, which no doubt was written by Kendall, the political philosophy of the *Argus* and Kendall was clearly reflected: "The only charge we have lately heard against the *Argus* is, that it is too *democratic*. If we err at all, we prefer erring on that side, because it is the safest. The people had better have too much power than too little, because it is very easy to delegate power to our rulers, but not so easy to resume it."

After his wife's death, Kendall devoted his time almost exclusively to the *Argus*. In the words of Stickney: "National and State politics, education, morality, and religion constituted fields in which his mind delighted to range. His lucid and terse style, his cogent reasoning, and his exhaustive arguments, attracted attention, and soon won for their author a national reputation. Few journalists have so suddenly become famous. His appeals were to the intellect; he sought to convince men by force of argument."[16]

---

[15] *Ibid.* p. 196.
[16] *Ibid.* p. 269.

Kendall went on to become a leading "relief" man in Kentucky politics and a director in the Bank of the Commonwealth. Though he supported Clay in the 1824 election, Kendall's increasing advocacy for relief to benefit the "common" man finally brought about his break with Clay in 1826. This break, together with his strong support for Andrew Jackson in the 1828 election, "was the bridge over which he walked to his public service career."[17]

Kendall's second marriage, in 1826, was to Jane Kyle of Georgetown. She was 20 years his junior. Though she was to live a full and fairly long life, Amos was to outlive her by several years.

KENDALL EMERGES AS LEADER IN KENTUCKY'S RELIEF WAR

In the view of one Kentucky historian, "The Kentucky Relief War of the early 1820s gave Kentuckians one of their most inflammatory political conflicts and provided newspaperman Amos Kendall a training ground for studying the controversial banking system, developing persuasive editorial argument, and understanding the public mind."[18] The nub of the controversy arose when heavily indebted Kentucky citizens sought state legislation to make it easier for them to pay off their debts. Kendall emerged as Kentucky's leading "relief man" and in so doing honed the arguments he used later to destroy the Second Bank of the United States.

Kendall had a strong personal stake in getting debt relief. Although he was making money with his Frankfort newspaper, Kendall found himself heavily in debt for property purchases, which included a paper mill, a saw mill, grist mill, dwelling house, and 50 acres of land. Sometime in 1825, he had borrowed $1500 from Henry Clay; 2 years later he wrote an urgent note to Martin Van Buren seeking a loan of $3000. Kendall was not alone in his financial troubles. A sufficient number of Kentuckians were in the same boat to develop pressure on the state legislature to vote them relief. In December 1821 and again in December 1822, the legislature passed bills of replevin that were aimed at protecting debtors' property from forced sales and to enable them to pay off their debts with depreciated paper currency. Now it was the creditors who felt oppressed so they took their case to the courts. In late 1822, the creditors' grievance culminated with the Anti-Relief Party appeal of two test cases to the Kentucky Court of Appeals. Hardin wrote, "Alarmed by this action Kendall rallied to the Relief cause."

---

[17]Leonard D. White, *The Jacksonians: A Study in Administrative History 1829–1861*. New York: Macmillan, 1954.

[18]Billie J. Hardin, "Amos Kendall and the 1825 Relief Controversy," *The Register*, Kentucky Historical Society, Vol. 64, July, 1966, pp. 196–208.

Determined to check "ursupation," Kendall launched a series of impassioned editorials devoting his persuasive skills to the problem of enforcing the sovereign will of the people. Beginning in late 1823, Kendall argued the constitutionality of relief legislation, led the assault on the Court of Appeals, rallied the debt-ridden voters to action, and on Christmas Day 1824, saw his ends achieved when the Relief Party organized a New Court, invalidated the Old Court, and tossed the Anti-Relief judges off their benches.[19]

The state legislature's ousting of the Old Court cannot solely be attributed to Kendall's vigorous campaign that struck a responsive chord in the people. Nonetheless, his voice had emerged as one of the most powerful ones in the state. Hardin concluded that "Kendall became valuable to Jackson's Administration, especially during the Bank War, chiefly because he was able to draw upon the persuasive skills and political knowledge developed during the Kentucky Relief War." Kendall had learned the public mind and ways to mold it.

KENDALL BREAKS WITH CLAY

Henry Clay, whose wife took Kendall into the Clay home as a tutor when he had arrived in Kentucky jobless, had a long career as a Whig politician. He was a candidate for the Presidency six times but was never elected. He served from 1806 in the Kentucky legislature, in Congress, and in the U. S. Senate. Prior to the 1824 election, Kendall, then a Clay man, was doing political writing for Clay in 1822, which was under cover. As Kendall suggested, his own hand was well known, so the material should be copied before it was sent out on Clay's behalf. Later, Kendall asserted that Clay employed him to write a series of letters signed "Wayne" attacking John Quincy Adams and accusing him of being hostile to the West and internal improvements and that Clay had these letters distributed in Ohio that year. Further, testimony was given in the Kentucky legislature in 1828 that Clay had paid $100 dollars to William Tanner, a printer, for the republication of letters by Kendall that attacked Adams on the Ghent negotiations.[20] Van Dusen concluded that Clay did not comprehend the significance of the democratic movement that was making Jackson its idol. Given his pivotal role in the 1824 Relief War and his own troubles with debt and banks, Kendall did.

Two unpublished letters in the archives of the State of Tennessee reveal that Kendall introduced himself in a letter to Jackson on August 22, 1827. "Although I have never had the pleasure of a personal acquaintance with you, there are some circumstances of a peculiar nature which induce me now to address you." In another letter on August 27, Kendall followed up his

---

[19]*Ibid.* p. 198.

[20]Glyndon G. Van Dusen, *The Life of Henry Clay*. Boston: Little Brown, 1937.

discussion of a political situation in Kentucky with a formal invitation to Jackson to attend a dinner in his honor in Frankfurt. Jackson did not attend, but some 4,000 Jacksonians did, in contrast to the 2,000 who turned out for Clay."[21]

Kendall took on the tasks of not only promoting Andrew Jackson's candidacy for the Presidency in 1828 through his paper but also worked tirelessly in many other ways to put Kentucky's votes in the Jackson column, as the previous letters suggest. In seeking to build broad voter support for Jackson, Kendall was not only promoting his candidate, he was participating in the building of the nation's second two-party system.

THE JACKSON CAMPAIGN

President James Monroe's peaceful Era of Good Feelings government ended abruptly with the bitter Andrew Jackson–John Quincy Adams Presidential contest in 1824. Although there was revival of Presidential contests that year the campaign did not extend widely nor arouse much interest in the public at large—a fact made plain by a total vote of 350,000 in a population of nearly 11 million persons. This reflects not only low interest in the outcome but the fact that the voting franchise was still narrowly held in 1824. In only six states did more than one third of the eligible voters to the polls. This all changeed with the innovative lively Jackson campaign of 1828. The 1824 contest was among four candidates—Adams, Jackson, Henry Clay, and William H. Crawford and wound up in the House of Representatives where Adams was elected even though Jackson had polled far more votes in the popular election. The 1824 election marked the break up of what little was left to the nation's first two-party system, described in the previous chapter. Explaining the apathy that characterized the 1824 campaign, McCormick wrote:[22] "In most states both political leaders and the voters were so heavily predisposed toward one candidate as to foreclose any real competition. Where genuine rivalry developed, there was commonly too little time available to construct elaborate campaign organizations. Moreover, the voters had not been accustomed to participating in contests for the presidency."

Understandably, Jackson felt that he had been cheated out of the presidency in 1824 and resolved that this would not happen again. His 1828 campaign brought, according to Bishop, "the modern Presidential campaign, with its organized uproar, great parades, innumerable mass meetings, often vigorous exchange of vituperation and personal abuse, and the use of cari-

---

[21]Stuart Gerry Brown, *The American Presidency*. New York: Macmillan, 1966.

[22]Richard P. McCormick, *The Second American Party System*. Chapel Hill: University of North Carolina Press, 1966, p. 332.

cature as a weapon of attack."[23] Seeking to capitalize on his aura of a war hero as a result of his leading the winning battle for New Orleans on January 8, 1815, Jackson opened his 1828 campaign with a flourish never before seen in U.S. politics. Delegations were invited from all parts of the country, and they responded in large numbers. A steamer was sent from New Orleans, with a reception committee aboard, to meet the General at Natchez and escort him down the river. A procession, a banquet, and a ball were staged in his honor at Natchez. A fleet of steamers went out from New Orleans to greet the General's *Pocahontas*. Bishop wrote:[24] "Jackson landed on the levee amid a great throng of people, conspicuous among them many of his brother soldiers. Four days of high festival followed, with enthusiastic speeches of congratulation from the visiting delegations and stirring responses from the General, the echoes of which floated over the land and stirred it to unwonted excitement."

This kicked off a bitter, scurrilous campaign between the forces of General Jackson and President Adams. Schlesinger noted: "Hardly an issue of policy figured in the campaign." Then, as now, the contest centered on personalities more than substantive issues. The enlarged band of voters were voting for a man, not deciding issues. The Jacksonians made it appear as a contest between rich and poor, the few and the many, the plowholders versus the bondholders, thus establishing a basic theme that has threaded its way through most of subsequent Presidential campaigns, a theme that was dominant in U.S. politics as late as the 1992 campaign between President George Bush and then Governor William Clinton.

By 1828, the Jacksonians had put together an elaborate political organization, the Democratic Party. The Democrats in Congress set about creating a nationwide newspaper system that would enable them to carry the Jackson message to the people. Kendall was an important cog in this new machine in Kentucky. The 1828 contest stimulated the formation of political parties in virtually all of the states. Of this development, Remini wrote:[25] "The initiative and drive for this enterprise came from Congressmen, but the work was aided by governors, state legislators, county leaders, and politicians of every rank. Together, they strove to paper the country with enough propaganda to wrap the Coalitionists in defeat." By 1828, there were an estimated 600 newspapers in the United States, 50 of them dailies, 150 semiweeklies, and 400 weeklies.

In Remini's words: "Each month a raft of publications flooded the reading market in all forms: newspapers, books, pamphlets, addresses, biographies,

---

[23]Joseph Bucklin Bishop, *Our Political Drama*. New York: Scott Thaw Co, 1904, Chap. 1: "The Advent of Gen. Jackson."

[24]*Ibid.* p. 99.

[25]Robert V. Remini, *The Election of Andrew Jackson*. Philadelphia: J. B. Lippencott, 1963, p. 76.

and throwaways." The some 375 printing offices in the United States as of 1810 had increased to three times that number by 1825, and in roughly the same period publication of books had increased by 10%. As the late Edwin Emery noted: "The press was more and more counted upon to supply the information, inspiration, agitation, and education of a society often unable to keep up with its need for schools." These pressures for popular rule were mounting, and the press provided the forum for the demands and debates of the people.

State committees learned, asserted Remini, the power of emotional appeals to the unsophisticated and "shamelessly exploited it." "By linking organization and the ballyhoo of entertainment behind an appealing candidate who supposedly represented the common man, politicians were able to stir the people from their lethargy to a fleeting interest in national politics.[26] Adams carried all but two states in the North; Jackson won every state in the South and West. He had also won the hearts of the frontiersmen. In sharp contrast to the 1824 vote, 1,150,000 votes were cast in 1828 in a population grown to 12,240,000 people. Little wonder that Amos Kendall proclaimed that Inauguration Day "was a proud day for the people." Surely it was a boisterous one, as the Jackson supporters took over the White House and had themselves a party.

The election of Jackson marked the beginning of the practices and procedures that have remained as distinguishing features of the U.S. political system—spirited competition between the two major parties carried on through the press and platform utilizing the skills of publicists. In Remini's view, the election "did provide the ordinary citizen with an elaborate party machine through which he could more effectively control the operation of government and shape public policy.[27] Not only did Jackson closely identify with the plain people and talk incessantly of their rights, but his lieutenants did likewise. Chief among these was Martin Van Buren, who, Schlesinger said, "was the first national leader really to take advantage of the growing demand of the people for more active participation in the decisions of government."[28] Van Buren, early in his career, said: "Those who have wrought great changes in the world never succeeded by gaining over chiefs; but always by exciting the multitude."

KENDALL GOES TO WASHINGTON

Burdened by considerable debt, Kendall set about after Jackson's victory to share in the excitement and spoils of Old Hickory's administration. He garnered the task of delivering Kentucky's electoral vote to the Electoral

[26]*Ibid.* p. 192.

[27]*Ibid.* p. 203.

[28]Arthur M. Schlesinger, Jr., *The Age of Jackson.* Boston: Little, Brown, 1945, p. 50.

College in Washington. Thus, January 1829 found Amos Kendall in Washington seeking a political appointment that would pay him somewhere between $2,000 and $3,000 a year. Over and above such income, Kendall expected to make an additional $1,000 writing for others. He got started quickly on this sideline, for in the weeks before Jackson's inauguration, he wrote a number of circulars for Congressmen. One week, according to Stickney's *Autobiography*, he pocketed $50. It was in Washington that Amos Kendall found power, national fame, and the wealth that eluded him in Kentucky.

With the coming of Jackson's administration, "the prospect of wholesale removals brought protests from some of the prominent men in the party. The appointment of editors brought the loudest protest. Editors [had] worked as hard in the canvass as political speakers and asked for the same rewards."[29] Jackson complied with their requests, showing his favor for the profession by appointing several of them to jobs, including Amos Kendall as Fourth Auditor in the Treasury Department.

Kendall's chief supporter for a post in the Jackson Administration was Martin Van Buren, Jackson's staunch ally from New York. Van Buren, regarded as shrewd judge of men, urged Kendall's appointment because of his demonstrated editorial talent and as a reward for his work for Jackson's victory in Kentucky. Van Buren understood that the day of a party press and popular elections required a Presidential publicist. As one of Jackson's rivals, Henry A. Wise, later commented that Kendall became "the President's thinking machine, his writing machine, and his lying machine, chief reporter, amanuensis, scribe, accountant, general man of all work," as quoted in Schlesinger's *Age of Jackson*.[30]

Kendall held the post of Fourth Auditor for 5 years—until 1835. "He brought no experience to qualify him" for the job, other than "a broad education, training in law, interest in political movements, and character and integrity." Any shortcomings were not apparent as he proceeded to do a highly efficient job and at the same time, to inject into the Treasury an element of morality and honesty that had been lacking. But that job was only his left hand at work. His right hand was aiding Jackson as an adviser, fact finder, and publicist.

Kendall quickly won Jackson's favor when he uncovered large frauds in the accounts of his predecessor, Tobias Watkins, a close friend of the defeated President John Quincy Adams. Kendall's exposé gave Jackson justification for the spoils system that he brought to the federal government. Little wonder Adams later bitterly complained, not without reason, of Jackson and Van Buren: "Both have been for twelve years the tool of Amos Kendall,

---

[29]John Spencer Bassett, *The Life of Andrew Jackson*. New York: Macmillan, 1981, p. 449.
[30]Schlesinger, 1945, pp. 72–73.

the ruling mind of their dominion." The previous Fourth Auditor did not even wait for Kendall to arrive; he departed without offering any assistance. Kendall found a loose-run organization, with many of its practices verging on the illegal. He stopped disbursing money that was not clearly authorized by law, even though such disbursements had been made "for many years." He stopped his office from handling letters of private citizens, the practice of which had been to avoid payment of postage. He stopped at least 20 newspapers his predecessor had been taking at public expense. In addition, he called a halt to payroll padding. On April 4, he wrote: "Discharged my assistant messenger. I did not know I had one until the 1st inst., when he presented an account as *laborer* for three months' services." As soon as he could get to it, Kendall put in writing for the 16 clerks in his office a code of ethics and conduct. There can be little doubt that a new broom had swept through the office of the Fourth Auditor.[31]

A small group of men, none of whom was a cabinet member, advised Jackson from the beginning. The group was tabbed the "Kitchen Cabinet" by Jackson's opponents. Membership varied, but Kendall, W. B. Lewis, and A. J. Donelson, the Pesident's private secretary, were generally in it. The influence of this group was believed to be great. Jackson might have been sensitive on the point, because it tended to belittle him. "However this possibility never seemed to diminish his use of the group." Some evaluations have placed Kendall as "the cleverest, most audacious, and powerful member of the Kitchen Cabinet" and have even described him as "more powerful than any Cabinet Minister in the determination of Jacksonian policies."

The Kitchen Cabinet did meet sporadically, but Richard P. Longaker said it never became an institutionalized entity because it "seldom met as a group." He added: "If there was a first position in the hierarchy of influence, it probably belonged to Kendall for his influence was the most pervasive and his talents the most widely used by the President." For example, Kendall assisted in the writing or wrote at least 10 Jackson messages to the Congress. Kendall always worked in collaboration with Jackson on these messages. Surely President Jackson was not the captive of the Kitchen Cabinet as his enemies liked to jibe. Old Hickory was always very much his own man.[32] Lynn Marshall thought the Kitchen Cabinet was more the forerunner of the Democratic National Committee than a subcabinet.

Because there is no record of the innerworkings of the Kitchen Cabinet, we do not know exactly how it functioned. But function it did. Also, that Kendall had great influence on some of the big names in the administration, there can be little doubt. The major unsolved mystery seems to center on the extent to

---

[31]Kendall, *Autobiography*, pp. 303–318.

[32]Richard P. Longaker, "Was Jackson's Kitchen Cabinet a Cabinet?" *Mississippi Valley Historical Review, 94*, pp. 94–108.

which Kendall wrote Jackson's major papers. Professor Anderson gave the most authoritative answer:[33] "That he at least wrote quite a number of them I found was abundantly clear, for the originals, now among the Jackson papers in the Library of Congress, were in Kendall's handwriting." Specifically, "Kendall had a large share in the preparation of at least five of the annual messages he was the principal author of the message vetoing the bill to recharter the Bank . . . and he wrote Jackson's well-known letter of June 26, 1833, to [Secretary of the Treasury] Duane foreshadowing the removal of the deposits." Anderson pointed out, however, that though Kendall's service to Jackson was of the highest importance, "its extent and character were often exaggerated at the time by rumor and by hostile critics."[34]

Stickney must have also wondered about Kendall's contributions to Jackson, for years later, a few days before Kendall's death, Stickney asked him if he wrote much of Jackson's messages. "No," Kendall replied, "the old hero wrote the most of his own messages. I wrote nearly all of those portions of his messages connected with the Indians." Perhaps Kendall's strong devotion to Old Hickory caused him to remain loyal to the end.

Early in Jackson's administration, the lack of a completely faithful administration newspaper caused some concern. The *United States Telegraph*, edited by General Duff Green, supposedly served this purpose. Green was not necessarily dependent on the administration, as he was the public printer for the Senate and later also for the House. Some of Jackson's friends, Kendall among them, doubted the faith of Green and the *Telegraph* and quietly made arrangements to start another paper. Kendall induced Francis P. Blair of Kentucky to come to Washington as editor. Blair, as a contributor to the *Argus*, had done good work for Jackson since 1827. In addition to his journalistic duties, Blair was added to the Kitchen Cabinet as a full-fledged member.[35]

The Washington *Globe* appeared December 7, 1830. However it was not the formal organ of the administration until a short time later when a difference of opinion developed between Jackson and Vice President John C. Calhoun. Jackson's views were upheld by the *Globe* and Calhoun's by the *Telegraph*. Thereafter, the *Globe* was Jackson's spokesman. Stickney rejected the allegations that the *Globe* was started at the suggestion of Jackson or of Van Buren. "It originated with those friends of General Jackson who regarded

---

[33]Frank Meloy Anderson, *The Mystery of a Public Man*. Minneapolis: University of Minneapolis Press, 1948, p. 48.

[34]Frank Meloy Anderson, "Amos Kendall," *Dictionary of American Biography*, Vol. X. New York: Charles Scribner's Sons, 1933, pp. 325–327.

[35]The notion has crept into some histories that Blair was the editor of the *Argus*; Emery and Smith in their *Press and America* even gave the impression that Kendall and Blair were co-editors of the *Argus*. The evidence suggests that some of Blair's writings appeared in the *Argus*, but that he was never the editor. See Kendall's *Autobiography*, p. 372.

measures more than men, and desired his re-election for another four years, not so much for his own sake as to effect reforms in the government which no other man was capable of bringing about."

By 1831, knowledge of the existence of the Kitchen Cabinet must have been widespread, undoubtedly made so by the opposition press. Alfred Balch, a Tennessee Jacksonian, wrote quite plainly but with some alarm that the feeling is general that in Washington there is "a power behind the throne greater than the throne itself. It is my most decided opinion that Major Lewis should set up an establishment for himself—should disconnect himself from you. It is also my opinion that Mr. Kendall should attend only to the duties of his office and let you wholly alone."[36] Surely not because of such criticism, but the Kitchen Cabinet did undergo some change in 1831. Some turnover in personnel made the group more homogeneous; and with Jackson men well ensconced, it left patronage more to Congress and devoted more time to administrative policies and party principles.

KENDALL EMERGES AS JACKSON'S PUBLICIST AND STRATEGIST

Amos Kendall emerged early in the Jackson Administration as the President's most influential adviser, publicist, and political strategist. Kendall achieved his proximity to Presidential power on the basis of his keen mind and skilled pen, not on the basis of personality. Frank Anderson wrote of Kendall: "it is clear that Kendall was among the most potent [of the Kitchen Cabinet members]; that his influence steadily increased, especially after 1831; and that in the war on the Bank of the United States his influence was the most powerful." Anderson added: "As an administrator Kendall was the most capable and successful of the Jackson appointees."[37]

That Amos Kendall emerged as the White House's first press counselor is amazing indeed given the popular stereotype of a public relations counselor as handsome, smooth, and personable—say a David Gergen who for a year played Kendall's role in the Presidency of Bill Clinton. Lynn Marshall depicted Kendall as "sallow, tubercular, painfully shy," and "entirely lacking in the figure and presence that could attract voters." In short, he was the antithesis of the public relations serotype.

As a youth, he had been shy and by many thought priggish. In Washington, he thought the "ladies laced too tightly" and the men "drank too much." Because of his frequent illnesses and his adverse reaction to Washington social gatherings, Kendall participated little in Washington's social

---

[36]Bassett, p. 457.
[37]Anderson, "Amos Kendall."

life. This lent an aura of mystery to his role in Jackson's Administration. In his appearance and in his New England taciturnity, Amos Kendall was a poor fit for the public relations stereotype of today. But Jackson's public relations counselor he was—truly, the David Gergen of his day.

Early in his administration, President Jackson turned more and more to Kendall for help in writing his messages, first on the troublesome Indian question and then on other issues. In a short time, Kendall's ability to interpret and verbalize Jackson's policies made him indispensable to the President. "The President would lie on his bed beneath the picture of his Rachel, smoking away and pour out his ideas in vigorous, but imprecise language, which Kendall would smooth out and then read it back. Revisions would take place until "Old Hickory" was satisfied, and "Kendall himself would be surprised at the full force of the point."[38] Other work for the President included answering his letters, preparing addresses, and providing press releases for the *Globe* and other newspapers—in short, all the tasks performed by today's White House large, high-powered public relations staff.

Certainly Kendall played an influential role in the administrations of Jackson and his successor, Martin Van Buren, whom Kendall helped elect. Officially he served the first 6 year's in the auditor's post at Treasury, then for 5 years as postmaster General. The twelfth year, he served as editor of *The Extra Globe* to work for Van Buren's re-election. Clearly in Jackson's two terms, Kendall was the chief figure in the Kitchen Cabinet. Claude G. Bowers evaluated Kendall as the "cleverest, most audacious, and powerful member of the Kitchen Cabinet."

The central theme of Jackson's two terms in the White House was opposition to the Bank of the United States. This "Bank War" has been evaluated by Remini as "the most single important event during the entire middle period of American history." The war was a fiercely fought, shrewdly waged battle for public opinion with both sides utilizing every channel of communication and persuasion open to them. The Bank War marked the first all-out public relations battle between Big Business and the U. S. Government, the first of countless ones to follow in the next 2 centuries. In this war, Amos Kendall was the General of the Jackson forces. The Bank War is the subject of the next chapter. In this saga, we shall see Kendall's skills as a propagandist and strategist succeed.

---

[38]Schlesinger, p. 70.

The Jackson–Biddle Public Relations War

The central theme of President Jackson's two terms was his fierce, unyielding opposition to the Bank of the United States and his determination to kill it, which he finally did with the skilled help of Amos Kendall and Francis Blair, who shared Jackson's hatred of the Bank. In various letters and places Jackson described the Bank as "a monster, a monster equipped with horns, hoofs, tail" and so dangerous "that it imperils the morals of our people." He once charged that the Bank had "bought up members of Congress by the Dozzen." Another time he ranted that the Bank sought "to destroy our Republican institutions." Robert V. Remini concluded that "at first he only intended to chain the beast to keep it from inflicting further harm, but soon found himself locked in a death struggle with the monster. Andrew Jackson destroyed the Second Bank of the United States. Reverberations from that clash echoed for over a hundred years."[1]

The war against Biddle's Bank was equally significant as a milepost in public relations. The Bank War was an intense struggle for public opinion with both sides employing skilled publicists who utilized every channel of communication available to them. At Jackson's side were Kendall and Blair, both embittered by their experiences with debt and their part in the Kentucky Relief War. Directing the propaganda campaign for Nicholas Biddle was Mathew St. Clair Clarke, perhaps the first publicist to be employed by a bank or business.

Bray Hammond delineated these forces acting against the Bank:[2]

---

[1]*Andrew Jackson and the Bank War.* New York: W. W. Norton, 1967, p. 15.
[2]*Bank and Politics in America.* Princeton, NJ: Princeton University Press, 1957, p. 329.

The Jacksonians were unconventional and skillful in their politics. In their assault on the Bank they united five important elements, which, incongruities notwithstanding, comprised an effective combination. These were Wall Street's jealousy of Chestnut Street, the business man's dislike of the federal Bank's restraint upon bank credit, the politician's resentment at the Bank's interference in states' rights, popular identification of the Bank with the aristocracy of business and the direction of agrarian antipathy away from banks in general to the federal Bank in particular.

Schlesinger saw the root causes of antagonism against the Bank somewhat differently. He wrote in *The Age of Jackson*: "The war against the Bank enlisted the enthusiastic support of two basically antagonistic groups: on the one hand, debtor interests of the West and local banking interests of the East; on the other, eastern working men and champions of the radical Jefferson tradition." The President and his comrades-in-arms, Kendall and Blair, exploited all these antagonisms in their battle with Biddle.

Biddle, the able, but arrogant head of the Bank, at first hoped to win Jackson over, but Old Hickory was determined to attack the Bank in his first message to Congress. Many members of the President's Cabinet opposed this move, but Jackson and Kendall were undaunted. The "news leak," now a standard public relations technique in Washington and elsewhere, was first used by Kendall to leak news of Jackson's decision. Late in November, Kendall wrote Mordecai M. Noah, editorial associate of James Watson Webb and James Gordon Bennett of the New York *Courier and Enquirer* to tell him what the President planned. The next day, most of Kendall's letter "with a head and tail stuck to it," was published as an editorial in the *Courier and Enquirer*. This was the first shot in the war.[3]

Drawing on techniques he had developed in the Relief War in Kentucky, Kendall wrote many letters to friendly editors around the country to prepare them and their readers for the forthcoming attack on the Bank. It appeared to Kendall that the public would support Jackson's move against the Bank. Remini noted "When President Andrew Jackson summoned popular support for his War against the Bank, men from all classes joined him."

ISSUE JOINED IN 1832

The battle over the Bank was fully joined in July 1832, when Congress passed a bill-chartering it as of 1836, a move that had been requested by Biddle the previous January. Wilburn speculated that Biddle acted to get a new charter well ahead of time because he thought Jackson might sign the

---

[3]Claude G. Bowers, *The Party Battles of the Jackson Period*. Boston: Houghton Mifflin, 1922, p. 204.

new charter if presented to him prior to the election, "but wouldn't once re-elected."[4] In Remini's view, this was an "incredible blunder" on Biddle's part:[5] Despite the repeated warnings of (Louis) McLane and others not to bait Jackson in an election year and despite the President's obvious gesture toward compromise, Biddle dismissed it all and plunged ahead with a request to Congress to re-charter in 1832, four years before the date of expiration. By this single calculated, foolish act, Biddle wrecked all hope for a peaceful solution to the issue and forever doomed his institution.

Jackson called his Cabinet together and announced his intention of an uncompromising veto. None of the Cabinet supported him, so Jackson dismissed the meeting and called in Kendall to work on the veto message. Attorney General Roger Taney was asked to assist. Others were involved in early discussions and drafts of the famed Veto Message but the final work was Amos Kendall's, a fact in dispute until recent years. Lynn Marshall found:[6]

> Of the three Library of Congress drafts, two in the handwriting of Andrew Jackson Donelson are incomplete, and the other, the only complete draft and obviously the principal one, is entirely in the hand of Kendall. The patchwork of deletions and interlineations, plus a few insertions on separate sheets, which make up the Kendall draft is essentially the final message ... only about four sentences in the final veto message do not appear in this Kendall draft.

In writing his historic and effective message, Kendall, in Marshall's opinion, "did not try to set forth logically consistent doctrine *per se*; rather he probed for the popular mind, as he had learned in Kentucky in the 1820s." Kendall had a fairly accurate sense of the popular mind on this issue. Although the Biddle Bank had widespread support in the states and in Congress, it was killed when it could not muster enough votes to override Jackson's veto, described by Remini as "the most important presidential veto in American History." Some 150 years later this seems hyperbole. Jackson and Kendall had carried the day against considerable odds and a crafty opponent.

Lynn Marshall concluded his study of the Veto Message with this observation:[7] "Might not historians now more profitably turn their attention from the veto's ideological content, which has been well explored, to investigation

---

[4]Jean Alexander Wilburn, *Biddle's Bank.* New York: Columbia University Press, 1967, p. 5.

[5]Remini, p. 75.

[6]"The Authorship of Jackson's Bank Veto Message," *Mississippi Valley Historical Review*, 50 (1963), pp. 466–477.

[7]*Ibid.*

of the general values and aspirations of the people to whom it was addressed?"

Donald C. Lord, reviewing Remini's *Andrew Jackson*, said of the Bank Veto: "The Bank Veto is correctly analyzed as economically ignorant document but a masterpiece of political propaganda." Kendall was indeed a master propagandist!

President Jackson was obviously pleased with the public reaction to his veto of the Bank's rechartering. He wrote Kendall on July 23, 1832: "My Dear Sir. I am off this morn; the veto works well. I wish you to look at the Harbor Bill, and compare it with my veto message on the Mayville Road Bill, and my message to Congress in 1830. I am determined in my message to put an end to this waste of public money, in short to stop this corrupt, log-rolling system of legislation." This note illustrates Kendall's key role as "Jackson's thinking machine."

1832 ELECTION SETS PATTERN
FOR TWO-PARTY SYSTEM

The 1832 Presidential election formally initiated this nation's two-party political system that endures to this day. The new party system began when the Democrats held their first national party convention in Baltimore in 1831 to nominate Andrew Jackson for a second term and Martin Van Buren for Vice President. The National Republicans (to become the Whig Party in time) gathered in Baltimore in December 1831 and nominated Henry Clay for President and John Sergeant of Pennsylvania for Vice President. The Republican convention issued a national address that has been proclaimed as the first major party call to battle. The convention urged each state to go home and issue an address of its own. These conventions, a first, demonstrated that the combination of political organization and popular participations then coming to characterize U.S. politics was effective. This was the sort of politics Jackson, Kendall, Blair, and Van Buren reveled in and were so good at.

Latner gave this account of the Kendall Blair public relations campaign:[8] Blair and Kendall used all their organizational and editorial skills to aid the Democratic ticket. The *Globe* made sharp thrusts at the National Republicans, their candidate Clay, and, especially the Bank. Like the *Telegraph* in 1828, the *Globe* became the focal point of a national network of Democratic newspapers, feeding information to other papers and collecting news of

---

[8]Richard B. Latner, *The Presidency of Andrew Jackson.* Athens, GA, University of Georgia Press, 1979, p. 138.

local events for distribution throughout the country. Blair and Kendall also issued a special campaign *Extra Globe* designed "to be circulated and *read in every neighborhood.*" In order to assure extended circulation local Jackson politicians to give him the name "of good honest whole hog Jackson man" at each post office. "Every neighborhood must be reached to meet the slanders of our adversaries," he declared. 'We have to war to the knife and the knife to the hilt.'

Kendall also encouraged the formation of a chain of Hickory Clubs and through its committees of correspondence, the Central Hickory Club became a central channel of communication between local and national politicians and was useful in circulating campaign material. A page out of Sam Adams' book! The result of this intense campaign was, in Claude G. Bowers' view, to arouse as never before "that class consciousness to which politicians have since appealed," adding "it gave dignity to demagogy, and made it pay."[9] Bowers added:

> It [the 1832 campaign] marked the beginning of active participation of powerful corporations, as such, in the politics of the country, witnessed the adoption of methods of intimidation and coercion, of systematic propaganda, of the subsidization of disreputable newspapers. From that day on, the powerful corporations have been an anathema to the masses, monopoly has been a red flag, and the contest between capital and labor has been a reality.

Explaining the intensive publicity and organization efforts that the Democrats and Whigs both put in the 1832 campaign, Bone said, "The great emphasis in campaigning for the presidency undoubtedly grew in part from the growing realization that the office offered tremendous opportunities for patronage and for furthering the interests of Populism."[10] Certainly development of the two-party system, extension of the electoral franchises, and the intensive political publicity efforts all served to extend the people's interest and participation in their government. In this significant development, Amos Kendall played a key role.

As the 1832 Presidential election approached, Kendall realized that Jackson had to appeal strongly to the masses in order to succeed against the opposition of Clay and the Whigs. "He therefore conceived the idea of inaugurating the campaign with a more solemn and dignified appeal to the more intellectual element. The result was a carefully prepared campaign document reviewing . . . with a master hand . . . the work of the first three years of Jackson's administration." This document, the first of its kind, was disseminated around the country for use by the Jacksonian editors. The

---

[9]Bowers, p. 368.

[10]Hugh A. Bone, *American Politics and the American Party System.* New York: McGraw-Hill, 1949, p. 278–79.

effect was as Kendall expected; the Jacksonians again became unified and more militant.[11]

With the influentials behind the campaign, attention now turned to the masses. The *Globe* of course served as the mouthpiece in the campaign; it also was the center of the Democratic organization. Many of its columns were filled with the writings of Blair and Kendall. Blair wrote the hard-hitting, vitriolic articles and editorials with the average man in mind. "The longer and more sustained argumentative articles were written by the more brilliant Kendall." In addition, Kendall worked far into the nights "preparing articles and editorials laudatory of the Jackson policies, denunciatory of the opposition, and these, sent to editors all over the country, were printed as their own." The Jackson campaign, one of the best conceived in U.S. political history, won decisively over Henry Clay.[12]

With the passage of Biddle's requested early rechartering of the Second Bank of the United States and President Jackson's veto in the strident language of Amos Kendall, the Bank became the central and overriding issue of the fall Presidential campaign. Biddle's forces were supporting Henry Clay and the Whigs with publicity, pamphlets, and money in unprecedented dimensions. Of Clay's campaign, Nichols wrote:[13]

Clay and his associates did their best. They had learned some of the arts of organization. There was a flood of literature, pamphlets and press notices. There was a Clay campaign biography extolling his talents and achievements. There were Clay clubs, Clay balls, Clay barbecues, and Clay banquets with their unending toasts. Clay had, likewise, a campaign manager in the person of Josiah S. Johnston, a fellow Senator from Louisiana. Clay's campaign literature charged Jackson with being a dictator, a violator of pledges, and an extravagant spender of government money. He had corrupted the civil service, he was attacking the economy by his veto of the Bank bill. He had mishandled foreign affairs and lied about his Acts. He was even putting the Supreme Court to defiance.

These charges seem to have a contemporary ring today!

As the campaign to re-elect Jackson headed for a victorious climax, a few members of his Administration began a campaign to carry out the mandate of the people to destroy the Bank. Kendall and Blair were active in this campaign, although some historians attribute Kendall with being the "guiding light." The objective of the campaign centered on removing government deposits from the Bank and placing them in state banks.

---

[11]Stickney's *Autobiography of Amos Kendall* carries full text of this campaign document.
[12]Bowers, pp. 242–243.
[13]Roy E. Nichols, *The Invention of the American Political Parties.* New York: Macmillan, 1967, p. 312.

Though Jackson hated the Bank with a passion, he doubted he could carry out the removal in face of Congressional opposition. Kendall overcame this obstacle by suggesting that the removal be well-timed and that the public be prepared for it. He asked Jackson "to give us several months to defend the measure in the *Globe*, and we will bring up the people to sustain you with a power which Congress dare not resist." Kendall's experience as a journalist, campaigner, and political strategist had taught him well that public opinion moves more like a glacier than lightning, thus it would take time to bring public opinion to acceptance of taking Government funds out of the Bank of the United States. Kendall was sustained in his unrelenting fight against the Bank and his other political campaigns by an abiding faith in the public. As he wrote President Jackson on March 20, 1833, urging action against the Bank: "We have no right to destrust the purity and intelligence of the people."

BANK WAR STARTS IN EARNEST

Once re-elected, Jackson and his aides decided to move on the Bank by withdrawing the government's deposits. Remini reasoned that this move was promoted by Jackson's fear that Biddle would use the 3 remaining years of the charter to upset the verdict of the 1832 election. Also, Remini wrote: "By escalating the War, Jackson could force greater control over the direction and operation of the government, and thereby strengthen his position as President." He was encouraged in this by Blair who told the President that Biddle was spending public funds to frustrate the people's will, referring to the public relations campaign that had been mounted by the Bank. When Blair later told Jackson that most of his Cabinet were against the move, the President replied: "My mind is made up on the matter. Biddle shan't have the public money to break down the public administration with. It's settled."

Jackson's firm views were reinforced by a letter from Kendall to him dated March 20, 1833, in which Kendall was responding to the President's request for his views of the Bank of the United States. Kendall, wrote, in part:[14]

> The conduct of the managers of the present Bank; their interference with the payment of the public debt; the subterfuges and falsehoods resorted to by them to palliate their own illegal conduct; their base attempt to make the government responsible for their acts; their notorious corruption of the press and of public men; the part taken by them in the political conflicts of the country; the extravagant and mischievous extension of their loans, particularly

---

[14]John Spencer Bassett, *Correspondence of Andrew Jackson*. Washington, DC: Carnegie Institution, 1931, Vol. 42, pp. 41–44.

in the West, prior to the late presidential election, and the character of the debts there contracted; the exclusion of the government directors from all committees and consequently from all participation in the principal business of the Bank; constitute irresistible mass of evidence proving those who control the institution to be destitute of just principle, of prudence and truth, and consequently unworthy to be trusted with the money of the people. At the commencement of the late session of Congress, you expressed doubts of the safety of the public deposits in their hands; and so far from being removed, those doubts must have been strengthened and confirmed by developments since made.

Secretary of the Treasury McLane, who would have to take the action of removing the deposits, strongly disagreed with Jackson with the result Jackson shifted McLane to Secretary of State and appointed William J. Duane, a leading opponent of the Bank, to Secretary of the Treasury. In March, Kendall saw an acute political need for action. In a letter to McLane, dated March 16, 1833, Kendall argued that the President must act while the President's deep-rooted popularity could offset the Bank's power and that this action was necessary to perpetuate the Democratic party. Kendall wrote Secretary McLane: "The president's friends are presently in a state of doubt, hesitation, and discouragement." He thought these friends "needed some decisive act to reunite and inspirit them." The internal debate continued into early summer with the President at the vortex of conflicting counsel from his appointed Cabinet and the Kitchen Cabinet.

Growing impatient, Jackson on July 20 instructed Secretary Duane to appoint Amos Kendall as special agent for the purpose of finding suitable state banks capable of receiving the government's money. Reluctantly, Duane complied. This order provided a cover for what Kendall had recommended to the President—that before the funds are removed from the U. S. Bank, he must be certain that the act has the backing of other bankers.

KENDALL INTRODUCES FACT-FINDING
TO THE WHITE HOUSE

As soon as he received his appointment, Kendall immediately began his fact-finding mission with planned stops in Baltimore, Philadelphia, New York City, and Boston, the nation's financial centers of that period. In undertaking the assignment he had urged on the President, Amos Kendall had brought another dimension to White House public relations—fact-finding research before an action is planned and executed. Kendall's purpose was not only to find banks willing to take the government's money but to find those who qualified as loyal Jacksonians. This Kendall made plain in a letter to John Niles seeking his opinion on banks to be used in the New England area. Kendall wrote: "With equal capital and character, those which are in hand politically friendly will be preferred; but if there are none such we must take those which are in control of opposition men whose feelings are liberal."[15]

Typical of Kendall's reports back to the President on this fact-finding mission was his letter from Baltimore dated August 2, 1833. The nub of the report is found in this paragraph:[16]

> I have addressed to the three Banks which have signified their desire to undertake the agency, a letter making specific propositions, first after the plan set forth in my instructions, and secondly upon the supposition that the government may prefer to make its arrangements with each bank respectively. The plan laid down in my instructions will be found to be impracticable from want of legal power in the Banks to enter into the requisite obligations. The Bank of Maryland is probably the only one here which possesses the power under its charter, and that Bank is willing to enter into the arrangement. The Union Bank accedes fully to the propositions made by me for a separate arrangement, as does the Bank of Maryland, also, and both are ready to give ample security in public stocks or otherwise for the safety of the public deposits and the performance of every service for the government now rendered by the Bank of the United States. They are also willing to furnish Exchange on London *at cost* whenever the government may require it.

Then on August 14, Kendall reported to the President from New York City that "of the nine banks here from which I have received an answer eight have signified their willingness to undertake the public service. I have a good prospect of inducing some of them to offer the personal responsibility of their Directors in addition to that of their Banks as security for the government. This would have a conclusive effect on public opinion." Then Kendall added:[17]

> The only *certain* course, it seems to me, is to make up an issue at once; but if they will give assurances of support on which reliance can be placed, it may be better, for the purpose of avoiding other difficulties, to take the step suggested.

> Excuse me for making these suggestions. They arise solely from a desire to see the removal take place in such a way as to be sustained. The whole cabinet acting with you in good faith, can sustain it in the House of Representatives, and that result, if attainable, is devoutly to be wished. But to make delay expedient, it seems to me, that the dispositions of those gentlemen in the respect, should be *undoubted*.

---

[15]Letter dated October 2, 1833, in *John M. Niles Papers*, Connecticut Historical Society.
[16]Bassett, p. 145.
[17]*Ibid.*

This evening I leave for Boston.

Upon completion of his fact-finding mission in Boston in late September, Kendall had found a large number of state banks in favor of receiving the U. S. Government deposits. However, his investigation in Boston found a much different response than he had found in Baltimore, Philadelphia, and New York City. The U. S. Bank had learned of Kendall's mission and had applied pressure to the state banks in Boston. However, the Bank was too late; Kendall already had a true picture of the state banks' opinions.

KENDALL'S REPORT TIPS THE SCALES

Kendall's report to Jackson probably was the major factor in tipping the scales. Jackson made his decision and announced it to his Cabinet on September 18, 1833. Beginning October 1, all public funds received would be deposited in state banks. At the same time, withdrawals from the U. S. Bank would be made over a period of time. Thus, the Bank was doomed.

The Bank's adherents, led by Clay, made a desperate, last-ditch stand to save it. The Whig press whipped up considerable public enthusiasm; mass meetings were held around the country; petitions were forwarded to Washington. But Jackson's hold on the masses, buttressed by the actions of Kendall, Blair, and others, survived these attacks. A Senate resolution criticized Jackson, but the Senate took no other action. A House resolution actually sustained the removal. After this, the question of rechartering the Bank was never seriously considered and the existing charter expired in 1836. This is, in part, the lasting legacy of the first White House press counselor!

NICHOLAS BIDDLE RESPONDS WITH A PUBLIC RELATIONS CAMPAIGN

Nicholas Biddle and his associates were fully alert to the ways and importance of influencing public opinion. In fact, banks were the first business interests to use the press to mold opinion. The banks, by loans to editors and by placement of advertisements, influenced many newspapers and silenced some. John C. Calhoun asserted as early as 1816 that the banks had, "in great measure, control over the press." The charge has been made many times that Biddle bribed or subsidized the press in his fight against Jackson and Kendall. The Bank was in the business of lending money and did so to many newspaper editors, both pro and anti-Jackson editors. One historian who examined this charge against Biddle concluded: "In most cases the loans from the Bank had no pronounced effect on the political opinions of the editors; the newspapers of these men either supported or opposed the Bank as they had before the loans were granted."[18] There were two exceptions perhaps—Duff Green's *Telegraph* and Webb and Noah's *Courier and Enquirer*—both of which got loans from the Bank and subsequently changed from opposition to support of the Bank. Crouthamel concluded that the flat charge of bribery could not be proved in either case and thus remains "a matter of doubt." Nonetheless, banks were among the business interests that early made use of the newspapers, according to a study of early 19th century journalism made by Elwyn Burns Robinson. He added: "Since these financial institutions operated under charters given them by the state, they were interested in maintaining a favorable public opinion toward their activities."[19] Another author wrote of this period: "The banks, by loans to newspaper editors and also the dependence of journalists upon the banking interests for advertising, effectively silenced the press, and the evils of bank note money were not often ventilated in the newspapers."[20]

UNPRECEDENTED PROPAGANDA CAMPAIGN

Nicholas Biddle's main thrust against the Jackson forces was to launch a propaganda campaign unprecedented for its time spending what for that day was very large sums on press releases, pamphlets, friendly Congressional reports, and other media to argue the Bank's case with the public. Made aware of this all-out campaign to save the Bank by Kendall, President Jackson wrote a letter to three directors of the Bank on August 3, 1833, demanding an accounting of the expences [sic] for such purposes. The President wrote: "Mr. Walsh [Robert Walsh, who in 1819 established the *National Gazette*] admits that his publisher had received about $1000, for printing newspapers calculated to operate in the elections, which leads me to think, and believe, that a considerable sum of expences [sic] of the Bank have been incurred in this way." The Bank directors responded to Jackson's request on August 19, 1933, and spelled out in the detail the expenditures for "Printing and Stationery" that went into the Mathew St. Clair Clarke-directed propaganda campaign. Their justification for the campaign was a resolution by the Bank's board on March 11, 1831, in support of Biddle's recommendation that reports favorable to the Bank be "widely disseminated through the United States."

[18]James L. Crouthamel, "Did the Second Bank of the United States Bribe the Press?" *Journalism Quarterly*, 36, 1959, p. 35.

[19]Elwyn Burns Robinson, "The Dynamics of American Journalism From 1787 to 1865," *Pennsylvania Magazine of History and Biography*, LXI, 1937, pp. 425–445.

[20]William M. Gouge, *The Curse of Paper Money and Banking*. London: 1833, Printed by Mills, Jowett, and Mills.

Distribute the Gallatin pamphlets and the Congressional reports widely Mathew St. Clair Clarke and his staff did! The Bank's expenditure for these items and other propaganda jumped to $29,970.92 for the first half of 1831, an "enormous sum" by the Bank's own admission in its report to President Jackson. This propaganda output, spectacular for its time, also included a favorable article by a Professor George Tucker of the University of Virginia. (Perhaps the first time an academic had been brought into a battle as a spokesman for a special interest—but far from the last!)

The growing intensity of the public war between Biddle and the Jacksonians is reflected in the Bank's own figures. In the last 6 months of 1829, the Bank spent $3,765.94 for "Stationery and Printing," then in the first 6 months of 1830, the expenditures increased to $7,131.27 and to $6,950.20 during the last half year. We must remember that these were dear dollars in 1830. The bulk of the $7,000 spent in the last half of 1830 was for the reprinting a House Report by a Whig Congressman, McDuffie, and Albert Gallatin's* pamphlet "Article on Banks and Currency" published in the *American Quarterly Review* that was favorable to the Bank. Biddle's publicists reprinted the article as a pamphlet and distributed it widely in "the expediency of making the views of the author more extensively known to the public, than they can be by means of a subscription list." The March 18th minutes of the Bank's board recorded: "The President stated to the Board, that, in consequence of the general desire expressed by the Directors, measures had been taken by him, in the course of the last year for printing numerous copies of the reports of General Smith and Mr. McDuffie on the subject of this Bank." (General Smith was a U. S. Senator supporting the Bank.) His report was Senate Document No. 104.)[21]

In the first half of 1832 as the Jackson–Kendall War against Biddle's Bank intensified, the Bank's publicity expenditures totaled $12,134.16 plus $18,000 paid to Mathew St. Clair Clarke for "300 copies of Clarke and Halls Bank Book." This was the payoff to Clarke who, with D. A. Hall, wrote a propaganda tract defending the Bank. It was entitled *Legislative and Documentary History of the Bank of the United States*, published in Washington in 1832.

The Bank's directors at the end of their report to President Jackson wrote, incredibly: "Having made the examination of the Expense Account, we were struck with the large sum that had been expended under the head of Stationery and Printing, in the two years to which you refer." The Bank's report

---

*Albert Gallatin was revered as Jefferson's Secretary of the Treasury. McDuffie was Rep. George McDuffie from South Carolina who served as chairman of the House Ways and Means Committee until 1834 when he resigned to become governor of South Carolina. He would later returned to Congress as a U. S. Senator.

[21]"The Government Bank Directors to Jackson," dated August 19, 1833. Bassett, *op cit.* pp. 160–165.

to the President was signed by Directors H. D. Gilpin, John T. Sullivan, and Peter Wager.[22]

Other Public Relations expenditures by the Bank included:

> Gales and Seaton $1300 for distributing the Gallatin's pamphlet.
>
> William Fry for Garden and Thompson $1675.75 for 5000 copies of General Smith's and Mr. McDuffie's reports.
>
> To Jesper Harding $440 for 100 extra papers.
>
> To the *American Sentinel* $125.74 for printing, folding, and postage of 3000 extras.
>
> To William Fry $1830.27 for upwards of 5000 copies of the *Gazette* and Supplements, containing addresses to members of the State Legislature, review of Mr. Benton's speech, abstract of Mr. Gallatin's project of a Treasury Bank.
>
> To James Wilson $1447.75 for 25000 copies of the address to members of State Legislatures.
>
> To Carey and Lee $2850 for 1000 copies of Gallatin on Banking, and 2000 copies of Professor Tucker's article.

BIDDLE'S PUBLICISTS CREATE
THE DAVY CROCKETT LEGEND

Another tactic Biddle's publicists developed in an effort to blunt Jackson's moves against the Bank was to co-opt a brash, loud-talking Tennessee Congressman, the colorful Colonel Davy Crockett and build him up as a frontier hero to counter Old Hickory's appeal to the frontiersmen. "When the name of any person is accounted of sufficient importance to be conferred on negroes, dogs, horses, steamboats, omnibuses, and locomotive engines, he may be considered a pretty certainly on the road to immortality. This now the case with Colonel David Crockett, whose go-a-head name, with great propriety, has been or is about to be conferred on the locomotive engines on the Boston and Lowell Rail Road."[23]

The Davy Crockett legend, manufactured mainly by Nicholas Biddle's publicists in their battle with Jackson–Kendall forces in the Bank War, was born of the second great "shirt stuffing" campaign in the history of public relations. The first, as recounted in chapter 1, was that of John Filson, a Kentucky land promoter, who used the legend of frontier hero Daniel Boone to boom the sale of his book extolling the glories of Kentucky.[24]

---

[22]Bassett, *Ibid.*

[23]The *Boston Evening Transcript*, August 1, 1834.

[24]See J. Winston Coleman's Introduction to John Walton's *John Filson of Kentucke.* Lexington, KY, 1956. Also John Mack Farragher, *Daniel Boone, the Life and Legend of a Pioneer,* New York, 1992.

The transmogrification of Davy Crockett from a boorish, backwoods boob into a colorful frontier statesman was the work of several ghostwriters and press agents, not just one as in Boone's case. The purpose in Crockett's case was to forge a Whig political weapon to use against Andrew Jackson. The big "buildup" of Crockett as a folk hero was largely financed by Biddle. The Davy Crockett legend was given an intensive if short-lived revival in the 1950s when Walt Disney featured that "yeller flower of the forest" in movies, television programs, books, and records. Disney did not create the Crockett mythology; he embellished it and cashed in on it.

Wecter wrote in his *The Hero in America* that "out of the War of 1812 and Andrew Jackson's campaign leaped the braggart of the canebreaks"— personified by Davy Crockett. In 1818, Crockett was living near Shoal Creek, Tennessee, as a frontier squatter when his neighbors made him justice of the peace. At this time Crockett had, to use his language, "suffered only four days of schooling." In those days, Davy was a lazy, easy-going, slovenly squatter, one of the most peaceable men in "The Shakes," his region of Tennessee. His press agents later pictured him a fighter who when challenged to fight, would "jump into the air and crack his heels and crow like a rooster, and neigh like a stallion." With his election as justice of the peace, Davy's career was launched. Throughout his political service, he relied, to use words supposedly written by him, "on natural born sense, not on law learning," because, as he wrote, "I never read a page in a law book in all my life." Crockett became a militia colonel and taught himself to read and write in these years. Next he was elected to the state legislature. After one term, he accepted a dare to run for Congress in 1824. Amazingly, he won.[25]

Vernon Parrington recorded that Davy, who went to Washington in John Quincy Adams' administration, "spent four years loafing and boasting at the Congressional bar."[26] He rarely spoke on the floor of the House but frequently at the bar. He was known more for his marksmanship, which enabled him to trim the wick of a candle with his bullet at a distance of several hundred feet, than for his statesmanship. He went to Washington a Jacksonian but his understandable sympathy with land squatters led to a break with Jackson whom Crockett accused of siding with the land speculators. Until he broke with Jackson, his political influence was inconsequential. The break with Andy Jackson was the beginning of the Crockett buildup that resulted in today's legendary figure. Old Hickory's enemies—the Whigs—saw in Crockett a means of wooing the frontier vote, a growing bloc of voters the Whigs had unwisely neglected. They pictured Crockett as a "real frontiersman," who boasted that he wore "no collar labelled My Dog—Andrew Jackson."

---

[25]Dixon Wecter, *The Hero in America*. New York: 1972, pp. 189–193.

[26]Vernon Parrington, *Main Currents in American Thought*, (Originally copyrighted in 1927, republished by University of Oklahoma Press, 1987) Vol. II, pp. 175–178.

The Whigs went to work in earnest to create the public image of Crockett as the bold, courageous coonskin-cap frontier democrat with a lusty pioneer spirit.

James A Shackford, a historian who has made a thorough study of Crockett, both man and legend, said "It is highly probable that Crockett made a deal with Eastern interests against Jackson in favor of bills which his West Tennessee squatters wanted in the summer of 1828."[27] This was well before the hotly-contested 1828 Presidential election that Jackson won. The "Eastern interests" were, in fact, Nicholas Biddle and his associates in the United States Bank. That summer Biddle sent his friend and associate, Mathew St. Clair Clarke, to visit Crockett in his backwoods home to make the deal. When Davy returned to Congress in December, the Biddle forces began supplying him with speeches that were quite superior in style to his own writings and ways of speaking. They also issued Circular Letters in his name to be sent to the press, letters quite different from his own poorly-written personal letters. The political ghost writer is not as modern a phenomenon as one may think.

One of these ghost writers was Clarke; another was Thomas Chilton, Kentucky Whig, who served in the House from 1827 to 1831 and again from 1833 to 1835. Chilton was a lawyer and a Baptist preacher as well as a Crockett ghost writer. From 1828 on, Davy and Chilton were seen increasingly in one another's company, and they were commonly found supporting or opposing the same measures in Congress. That Chilton was doing Davy's writing may be seen in a Circular Letter issued on February 1829 by Crockett that followed by one day a remarkably similar letter Chilton sent to his constituents. Shackford said, "They were too much alike not to have been written in collaboration." The probability is that Chilton wrote both in a meat-axe attack on Jackson's extravagance, cruelty to Indians, opposition to internal improvements, appointment of Congressmen to high office, and for his plans to run for re-election.

The next step in the big buildup of Crockett the Congressman came with the publication of a book purportedly written by him entitled *Sketches and Eccentricities of Colonel David Crockett*. The book was written by Mathew St. Clair Clarke. It was probably intended for use in the 1832 campaign but was not copyrighted until January 1833. Shackford said Clarke finished the book in 1832. The information supposedly came from Crockett and the narrative itself describes a visit by the author to Davy's home. The book was suitably flavored with Whig bias. It is interesting to note that *Niles'*

---

[27]*David Crockett, The Man and The Legend.* (Chapel Hill) University of North Carolina: 123. The most recent book on the Crockett legend, *Davy Crockett: Legend, The Legacy,* by Michael A. Loforo (Knoxville, TN: The University of Tennessee Press, 1985), neglects the role of Biddle's publicists in the build-up of Crockett as a ploy against the Jacksonians. Focuses more on the contemporary exploitation of the Crockett legend. Or should we say myth?

Register first takes note of Davy at precisely this time and publicizes the fact that the Second United States Bank had already lent the free-spending Crockett money. This suggests that there may have been a connection between the loan and Crockett's willingness to have Clarke write the book. That Davy pretended not to know the book's quite obviously Whig author is understandable. Davy couldn't publicly admit having a part in the Biddle efforts to elect him.

The buildup continued. A "Crockett March" was composed in his honor. James Kircke Paulding wrote two plays with Davy as the central figure—*The Lion of the West* and *The Kentuckian*. Wecter recorded: "Before a wildly cheering audience, the real Crockett in store clothes, and Colonel Nimrod Wildfire in buckskins on the stage, bowed to each other."[28] The Whigs, stressing Davy's eccentricities, his humananity, and his frontier spirit, were endeavoring to make him a popular vote-getter. Davy soon found himself much talked about, and he loved it. He was inflated to hear his rugged Western honesty applauded, his shrewd backwoods intelligence praised, and his frontier humor brushed up.

Parrington said "Davy was vastly surprised and pleased with his sudden rise to fame." His fame had become such by 1831 that note of him was taken by Alexis de Tocqueville, during his tour of the United States. During his journey to Memphis, the astute French observer noted: "When voting rights are universal, and deputies are paid by the State, it is a strange thing how low the people's [sic] choice can descend and how far it can be mistaken. Two years ago the inhabitants of the district of which Memphis is the capital, sent to the House of Representatives of Congress an individual called David Crockett, who had received no education, could read only with difficulty, had no property, no fixed dwelling, but spent his time hunting, selling his game for a living, and spending his whole life in the woods. His competitor, who failed, was a fairly rich and able man."[29] Perhaps De Tocqueville saw in Davy his preconceived stereotype of the ignorant, crude, semi-literate U.S. frontiersman. He was this—life size.

Next the Whigs arranged an Eastern tour for their now-inflated frontier politician, ostensibly to promote an "autobiography," but patently for political purposes. This triumphant journey was later recorded in another ghost written book carrying Davy's name as author. The book, entitled simply *An Account of Colonel Crockett's Tour to the North and Down East*, was published in 1835 and was the result of the collaborative efforts of Pennsylvania's Representative William Clark, a Biddle supporter, the ghost writer Mathew St. Clair Clarke, and the Philadelphia publishers Carey and Hart. A letter of

---

[28]Wecter, p. 190.
[29]de Tocqueville's *Journey to America*. New Haven: Yale University Press, 1960, p. 254. Entry from Memphis, 20th December, 1831.

Davy's dated January 8, 1835, to the publishers reads: "I was with Mr. Clark this morning and he red me what he has finished of the Book and I have no doubt of its filling your expectation it must sell." Hero Davy probably referred to the Congressman, not the publicist.

In the book, much is made of the cheering throngs and Davy's diffidence thereto. Davy supposedly wrote: "This is all very well, but I most think I'd rather be in the wilderness with my gun and my dogs than to be attracting all this fuss."

For the tour, the Whigs arranged everything carefully beforehand in the best public relations fashion. News was sent ahead that Davy was coming to build his crowds; ghost written speeches—not the ones he gave—were printed and distributed widely; Davy was paraded at meetings with Daniel Webster, given fancy dinners, enthusiastically applauded for his rustic wit and homespun honesty. Philadelphia Whigs gave him a gold watch and a fine rifle; New York reportedly "cheered itself hoarse"; in Boston, he was toasted at rallies, "The champagne foaming up as if you were supping fog out of speaking trumpets." He made many speeches lambasting his one-time hero, President Jackson. How much the Tennessean realized he was being used by the Whigs can only be surmised. Certainly, "the Whigs had never had a more obliging puppet." He proved to be worth just that.

In 1834—the same year the tour was made—another autobiography was written for him and published by the Whig interests, this one entitled *A Narrative of the Life of David Crockett, of the State of Tennessee.* This autobiography was written by Thomas Chilton, the Kentucky Whig. One piece of evidence is a letter written to the publishers instructing them to pay half the royalties to Chilton. Shackford reproduced a letter supposedly written by Crockett to his publisher but one that reads in Chilton's style, not in Crockett's halting prose. In 1835, the same year the none-too-learned Crockett was supposedly writing the account of his *Tour to the North and Down East,* he also supposedly wrote a political biography of Martin Van Buren in a futile effort to tear down Jackson's chosen successor. The fly leaf of this book, purportedly written by Davy, reads: "The Life of Martin Van Buren Heir-Apparent to the Government, and the Appointed Successor of General Andrew Jackson containing Every Authentic Particular by Which His Extraordinary Character Has Been Formed. With a concise history of the events that have occasioned his unparalleled elevation; together with a review of his policy as a statesman." Next comes a little poem and the author's name, David Crockett. Not so coincidently the book was published in the Philadelphia by a Robert Wright, thought to be a "front" name for Carey and Hart. The preface reveals the flavor and purpose of the book. It says, in part: "Statesmen gamesters, and people are the cards they play with. I have gone for enough on this book to show what I mean; the people are tricked and cheated, and what is worse, they are satisfied to stay so." The author of the vitriolic attack on Van Buren is thought to have been Judge Augustin Smith Clayton of Georgia. This is not an established fact.[30]

The voters of Tennessee weren't tricked by the Biddle buildup of their Congressman. In 1836, they repudiated Davy at the polls.

As usually happens with publicity-made public figures, by 1836 Davy had begun to take himself seriously. For a while Tennessee's great "bar-hunter" even expected to be nominated for the Presidency. Instead he went down to political defeat in his home territory. Angered, he told his constituents they could all go to hell and off he went to Texas. He fought in the battle of the Alamo and there was killed. This put a dramatic finish to his colorful, if greatly exaggerated career. Subsequent to his death, a book entitled *Colonel Crockett's Exploits and Adventures in Texas* was published, but Shackford rejected this one as completely spurious with no connection to Davy. Death on the barricades of the Alamo provided an appropriate claim for the legend of Davy Crockett, which, like that of Daniel Boone, lives in history and in the dreams of each succeeding generation of American boys.

---

[30]Shackleford, p. 123.

Amos Kendall: Postmaster, Promoter, Philanthropist

By 1835, the U. S. Post Office was heavily in debt and increasingly the subject of Congressional investigations and attacks on President Jackson. Again, demonstrating his confidence in Amos Kendall's ability and integrity, President Jackson persuaded Kendall to accept appointment as Postmaster General as of June 1, 1835. Thus, Kendall became the only member of the Kitchen Cabinet to achieve full Cabinet status. Jackson confidently turned to Kendall barely in time to avert a scandal from Major William Barry's "amiable and innocent mismanagement."[1] Kendall did not blame Barry as he might have; he felt that one "who knew his amiable disposition and his want of business habits, could readily comprehend how he might have been misled by corrupt men about him."

By is his own account, Kendall was reluctant to accept appointment as head of the Post Office Department. For one reason he was sure that with the "Whig Party in the ascendancy in the Senate" his nomination would be rejected. Also he told the President "I had made arrangements to resign the office that I held and go into private business." Nonetheless, the President insisted, telling Kendall that he knew he would put everything right in the department then in disarray.

The onetime postmaster of Georgetown, KY, proceeded to do to the Post Office Department what he had done with the Fourth Auditor's office; he turned it upside down and gave it a few hard shakes. He completely reorganized the department, overhauled all of its financial procedures, applied

---

[1]Marquis James. *Andrew Jackson—Portrait of a President.* New York: Bobbs-Merrill, 1937, p. 400.

without favor the laws concerning the lowest bidders among carriers, levied fines on carriers when mail delivery was late, and instituted needed qualifications for jobs of postmasters.[2]

As with most things he touched, Kendall elevated the department's ethical standards.[3] Putting an end to payola was one example: "I announced to my subordinates that the acceptance of any present of value from any mail contractor, or a free ride in stage lines, steamboats, or railroad cars carrying the mails, would be cause for instant dismissal, and that the rule prescribed to them I adopted for my own guidance."

At the time that Kendall assumed office, the post office debt was $600,000, an extraordinary amount for the time. Ten months later, on April 1, 1836, he reported the department was free of debt. And by the end of Jackson's reign in 1837, the department had a surplus of $800,000.

As Postmaster General, Kendall noted the difficulty that postmasters and agents had in drawing the line between their rights as citizens and their political activity as officeholders. His advice was "to keep as clear from the excitement of political strife as possible—to shun mere political meetings, or if present to avoid taking any part in the proceedings. To decline acting as members of political committees of conventions and to take especial care to treat all men alike in their official intercourse."[4]

Apparently Kendall hewed to the line of his own instructions. There is no indication in his *Autobiography* that he took an active role in the 1836 Presidential election that brought his longtime ally, Martin Van Buren to the Presidency in 1837. The Democrats, under President Jackson's leadership, called a national political convention to be held in Baltimore in May 1835, nearly a year and a half ahead of the 1836 election. "The Jacksonians wanted to strengthen the colorless Van Buren by nominating for Vice President a western hero, Colonel Richard Mentor Johnson, who had slain Tecumseh in the War of 1812, even though Johnson was unpopular in the South."[5] Kendall's adherence to his edict that Post Office Department employees not take part in politics is further confirmed by the fact that he resigned as Postmaster General in 1840 so that he could take an active part in the campaign to re-elect Martin Van Buren.

The Democrats issued an address to the voters claiming among other things that their Whig opponents were working to make the rich grow richer and the poor grow poorer by establishing the Bank, exacting exorbitant tariffs, and by taxing one part of the country to build roads and canals in another. A campaign theme has echoed down through the years and was

---

[2]Kendall, *Autobiography*, pp. 338–342.

[3]White, *The Jacksonians*, p. 274.

[4]*Ibid.* p. 338.

[5]Roy F. Nichols, *The Invention of American Political Parties.* New York: Macmillan, 1967, pp. 332–333.

heard again in the 1992 Presidential campaign that elected Democrat Bill Clinton. The Whig Party was badly divided and not as well organized as the Democrats with the result that Van Buren won, although not by a wide margin. Nichols observed:[6] "In fact there had been a larger percentage of voter participation in state elections than ever before had developed in the Jacksonian contests. But there had as yet appeared no real counterorganization." He added: "Jackson's machine, now better oiled, had functioned with relative smoothness." Kendall surely had played a major role in developing this machine even though he apparently sat out this election.

KENDALL SETS ABOUT PUTTING POST OFFICE DEPARTMENT IN ORDER

One of the actions that helped the department get of out debt was Kendall's refusal to approve payments that he considered excessive and consequently in his eyes, illegal. His practice was to approve reasonable and just amounts. One of his early actions, which was to plague him for many years, was to disapprove a payment of $120,000 to Stockton and Stokes, longtime carriers of the mail between Philadelphia, Baltimore, and Washington and between Baltimore and Wheeling.

Stockton and Stokes had great influence in government circles, some of it surely coming from their extensive practice of transporting at no charge Congressmen, judges, members of the executive branch, and influential private citizens. Even while Kendall was initially checking on the legality of the payment, an attempt was made through his wife to bribe him. This, of course, was futile. But Stockton and Stokes had little difficulty getting a bill for their relief through Congress. When they filed the necessary papers to collect the awarded amount, their claim contained an additional $40,000. Kendall refused to pay the extra amount. By this time, the action had stretched into the Van Buren Administration. Stockton and Stokes next turned to the courts where they, in time, collected the $40,000. But they were not satisfied.

In the early 1840s, after Kendall had retired from public office, they brought a private suit against Kendall for damages. They won, and when Kendall's counsel obtained a new trial, they won that also. Kendall, who by this time was debt-ridden and had little income, carried the case to the Supreme Court. He won a reversal; in addition Stockton and Stokes were required to pay costs, and Congress, without a dissenting vote, passed an act of relief for Kendall.[7]

Kendall's inflexible moral character in fighting Stockton and Stokes was the single factor that shaped the rest of his life. The court battles kept Kendall

---

[6]*Ibid.*

[7]Kendall, *Autobiography,* pp. 350–360.

in Washington, whereas he had made previous arrangements to move to New York and enter the newspaper field. But by remaining in Washington, Kendall came to know Samuel F. B. Morse and his telegraph. Little did Kendall know the part the telegraph would play in his life when earlier, on February 31, 1838, he, along with President Van Buren and other members of the Cabinet, witnessed Morse demonstrate the telegraph. But the telegraph story was still to come.

Most contemporary word pictures of Kendall as Postmaster General were painted by opponents of the Jackson and Van Buren administrations. Some commentators attributed Kendall with greatness; others pictured him as the epitome of evil. In the opinion of John Quincy Adams, both Van Buren and Jackson were "Kendall's tools."[8] Admiration shown through some descriptions, whether the writer intended it or not; in 1856, Colonel Claiborne recalled: "When I first saw him, he had a whooping voice, an asthmatic cough, with a stooping frame. Yet this little whiffet of a man, whom the hoosiers would not call even an individual, was the Atlas that bore on his shoulders the weight Jackson's administration. He originated, or was consulted in advance, upon every great measure, and what the prompt decision and indomitable will of the illustrious chief resolved upon, the subtle and discriminating intellect of Kendall elaborated and upheld.*"[9]

Perhaps the closest thing to an objective description of Kendall and his place in the intrigue of Washington politics comes to us from Harriet Martineau,** an English traveler and writer who spent 2 years touring the United States in the mid-1830s. She observed:[10]

I was fortunate enough once to catch a glimpse of the invisible Amos Kendall, one of the most remarkable men in America. He is supposed to be the moving spring of the whole administration: the thinker, planner, and doer; but is all in the dark. Documents are issued of an excellence which prevents their being attributed to persons who take the responsibility of them; a correspondence is kept up all over the country for which no one seems to be answerable; work is done, of goblin extent and with goblin speed, which makes men look about them with a superstitious wonder; and the invisible Amos Kendall has the credit for it all. President Jackson's *Letters to His Cabinet* are said to be Kendall's; the *Report on Sunday Mails* is attributed to Kendall; the letters sent from Washington to appear in remote country newspapers, whence they are collected and published in the *Globe* as demonstrations of public opinion, are pronounced to be written by Kendall. Every mysterious paragraph in

---

[8]Robert Gray Gundeson, *The Log-Cabin Campaign*. Lexington: University of Kentucky Press, 1957, p. 84.

[9]Frederic Hudson, *Journalism in the United States from 1690 to 1872*. New York: Harper Brothers, 1873, p. 243.

[10]Harriett Martineau, "Life at the Capital in 1835," *America Through British Eyes*. Allan Nevins, ed. New York: Oxford University Press, 1948, pp. 150–151.

opposition newspapers relates to Kendall; and it is some relief to the timid that his having now the office of postmaster-general affords opportunity for open attacks upon this twilight personage, who is proved, by the faults in the post-office administration not to be able to do quite everything well.*** But he is undoubtedly a great genius. He unites with his "great talent for silence" a splendid audacity. (p. 150)

*From this description, it would appear that Kendall was a small man. That his frame was slender and his shoulders stooped, there is no doubt, but Anderson has also established that he was a "tall man."
**That Martineau was acutely aware of contrasting interpretations of everything connected with American politics is indicated by this quotation from the same writing that described Kendall: "We amused ourselves with the different versions given by the *Globe* and *Intelligencer*—the administration and opposition papers—to speeches and proceedings at which we had been present the day before." (p. 142)
***The writer was premature here in her judgment; Kendall had only recently become Postmaster General.

It is clear that he could not do the work he does (incredible in amount anyway) if he went into society like other men. He did, however, one evening; I think it was at the Attorney-General's. The moment I went in, intimations reached me from all quarters, and nods and winks, "Kendall is here." "That is he." I saw at once that his plea for seclusion (bad health) is no false one. The extreme sallowness of his complexion, and hair of perfect whiteness as is rarely seen in a man of middle age, testified to disease. His countenance does not help the superstitious to throw off their dread of him. He probably does not desire this superstition to melt away; for there is no calculating how much influence was given to Jackson's administration by the universal belief that there was a concealed eye and hand behind the machinery of government, by which everything could be foreseen, and the hardest deeds done. A member of Congress told me this night that he had watched through four sessions for a sight of Kendall, and had never obtained it till now. Kendall was leaning on a chair, with his head bent down, and eye glancing up at a member of Congress with whom he was in earnest conversation, and in a few minutes he was gone.

Kendall wanted to resign as Postmaster General in 1838 because of poor health but remained at the urging of Van Buren. Kendall, who often suffered attacks of indisposition brought on by his administration of the Post Office Department, wrote President Van Buren in August, 1838, to which the President replied:[11] "I have read the account of your state of health with great pain. Your retirement from a post for which you are so eminently qualified

---

[11]Kendall, p. 434.

would be a positive and great detriment to the public service, and to be regretted on every account."

Kendall, finding his health improved over the next few weeks, yielded to the President's wishes and continued to perform the duties of his office until May 1840. Finally, because of recurring poor health, the demanding duties of the office, and the upcoming Presidential campaign to which he wanted to devote himself exclusively, Kendall resigned May 9, 1840.

WHIGS WIN WITH LOG CABINS AND HARD CIDER

In 1840 the Democrats in their national convention renominated Martin Van Buren for a second term but failed to dump Vice President Richard M. Johnson, who had proved a great embarrassment to the Democrats with his African-American mistress and his ineptness in presiding over the Senate. Instead, the Democrats left the Vice-Presidential slot to "the decision of Republican-Democrat fellow citizens in the several states." Earlier, the Whigs had gotten the jump on the Democrats by nominating William Henry Harrison and John Tyler to head the Whig ticket. The Whigs trumpeted the slogan, "Tippecanoe and Tyler, Too" in their log-cabin and hard-cider campaign. Nichols described it as a "frolicsome campaign of song and smear, with seldom an idea or issue. Not only were there log cabins galore and hogsheads of cider, but other zany devices were used." The Whigs successfully portrayed General Harrison as the hero of the battle of Tippecanoe and as one who had been born in a log cabin. The latter appeal was used in future elections. The upshot was that Harrison and Tyler were elected, thus ending the long Democratic reign.

Kendall had resigned as head of the Post Office Department so that he would work in the campaign for Van Buren, long a strong ally. He worked with Francis Blair to publicize the virtues of Van Buren and the Democratic Party.[12] He edited the *Extra Globe*, which was published throughout the campaign. Blair, who was paid $60,000 to do the government's printing, subsidized the *Extra Globe*. Sensing the Democrats' lack of attention to campaign organization, Kendall put out a circular on how to organize the campaign. He advised party leaders on how to prepare and distribute propaganda, how to collect funds to pay for officeholders and others. The Democrats did take advantage of the fact that 1840 was a census year, and many census takers were used as party workers. Other papers were set up for the campaign—*The Rough Hewer* in Albany, New York, *The Old Hickory* in Illinois, and others. But this time the propaganda efforts failed to stem the rising Whig tide. This marked the end of Kendall's public career.

---

[12]Gunderson, p. 84.

Following a short rest after the election, Kendall began publishing in February, 1841, a small, biweekly newspaper, *Kendall's Expositor*. The purpose of the sheet was primarily to give him an income while he fought Stockton and Stokes in the courts. He built a house on a 100-acre farm on the northeast edge of Washington and settled down to editing and farming. The *Expositor*, which was largely a sheet of commentary, was a financial success its first year but thereafter went downhill rapidly.

With the decline of income from the *Expositor*, the building of the new house was put off for a time. Kendall was finding great difficulty in meeting his payments on the farm, but a timely loan of $2,000 saved the place and "gave grateful relief to Mr. Kendall and family." The incomparable publicist then turned to farming and editing." "Kendall Green," the name of his homestead, and the *Expositor* kept him fully occupied for a while. Kendall continued publication until late 1844, at which time he gave it up because it afforded a "meagre income."

ANOTHER CHALLENGE—THE TELEGRAPH

In 1844, Samuel Morse placed the first telegraph line in operation; it ran from Baltimore to Washington. He then tried to obtain government aid to extend the line on to New York. It was about this time that he and Amos Kendall became well acquainted. When Morse failed to get a government appropriation, he turned to Kendall and interested him in becoming his business agent.[13] The Morse patents were owned by Morse and three other men, and two of them joined with Morse to constitute Kendall as their attorney and to commit their telegraph interests to his control. The contract making Kendall agent for three fourths of the patent rights was signed March 10, 1845. He was to receive 10% on any sum that the proprietors might receive from the government or any other purchaser. If Morse's interest of 9/16 should be sold for over $100,000, Kendall would receive half of all over that amount.[14]

Perhaps Kendall did not press the sale of the patents to the government very hard for he thought from the beginning that the telegraph had a bright future as a private enterprise. Aside from the sending of private messages, Kendall visualized that the telegraph would cause the demise of the national circulations of such big newspapers as the *National Intelligencer* and the *Journal of Commerce*. He believed they would be limited to the area in which published because newspapers in every other locality would already have received news by telegraph before the big city newspapers arrived by train.[15]

---

[13]Kendall, p. 527, and Samuel Irenaeus Prime, *The Life of Samuel F. B. Morse, LL.D.* New York: D. Appleton and Co., 1875, p. 513.

[14]Kendall, p. 538.

[15]Carlton Mabee, *The American Leonardo—A Life of Samuel F. B. Morse.* New York: Alfred A. Knopf, 1943, p. 286.

As Kendall, Morse, and the others set about to extend the line northward, it became apparent that a more businesslike arrangement was necessary. In May, the Magnetic Telegraph Company, the first successful telegraph company, was formed. Kendall was its president. In the months that followed, one company after another was formed for the purpose of constructing specific lines; the owners of the patents received about one half the stock of each company.[16] Thus, Kendall made a good beginning in the business world.

He did not, however, abandon his earlier experience; rather, he carried over into the business world those techniques and practices that would be useful. To announce the new telegraph line from New York to Philadelphia, he placed advertisements in the leading newspapers of the two cities and sent out a letter to prospective customers announcing the arrangements and rates (25 cents for a 10-word message). Receipts for the first 4 days of operation were $100; this indicated success and with the rapid growth that followed, Kendall's faith in private enterprise proved correct.

Beginning with the initial success of the telegraph, Morse and the other patent owners were harassed for years by lawsuits in which various plaintiffs usually claimed to be inventors of the telegraph; other suits involved patent infringements. Kendall's governmental experience and legal training stood him in good stead, for he successfully masterminded the legal actions on behalf of his clients.[17]

"For the first seven or eight years Kendall's labors in the telegraphic field brought only meager and very uncertain returns. But by about the 1853 the initial difficulties had been so far overcome that both Morse and Kendall had become rich men, as wealth was reckoned in those days."[18] The extent of Kendall's wealth is not exactly known but there is no question that he made an "ample fortune" in his words.

The problems encountered by Kendall were not all legal and financial. Some of them involved people, as indicated by his account in a letter to Stickney in 1855:[19]

> The North Alabamians continue to cut down the telegraph almost every day. At first it was under the pretext that it produced the dry weather; but as they have had abundant rains, it seems now to be the mere spirit of mischief or ambition to carry a point. It is said they were encouraged by a preacher who proclaimed from the pulpit that God had sent the dry weather to punish the world because man had got to be "too smart" in reducing his lightning to human uses.

Kendall was touring the South at the time; whether he did anything to straighten out the situation is not recorded.

---

[16]*Ibid.* 287–288.

[17]*Ibid.* pp. 296–317.

[18]Anderson, *Dictionary of American Biography*, p. 50.

[19]Kendall, p. 552.

A rising band of young capitalists, led by Cyrus W. Field, set out in the late 1850s to wrest control of the Telegraph from the pioneers, Kendall and Morse. But the old boys, led by Magnetic telegraph and Amos Kendall, successfully out-maneuvered the American Telegraph Company and Field who were trying to create a monopoly. Kendall's opponents, tabbing him "Amos the pious," made a concerted effort to rid the industry of him, but Kendall, then approaching 70, was not ready to go. Finally in October 1859, the competing companies, whose lines collectively stretched from New Foundland to New Orleans, declared peace and merged into the American Telegraph Company. This occurred, however, according to the basic terms established by Kendall and Morse. In addition, they were on the new board of directors, along with Field and Abram S. Hewitt.[20]

Kendall's moral scruples, which had dictated so many actions during his life, came to the fore again in 1860 when the New York Associated Press (AP) tried to get preferential treatment from the telegraph company. Kendall felt that the AP should pay the same rates for long messages as anyone else, including any competing news services. The controversy reached major proportions. Harking back to some of his Jacksonian days, Kendall got out a pamphlet attacking the leader of the AP's interests that began by asking, "Who is this D. H. Craig?" He then proceeded to answer it. "In the first place, he is a VULGAR BLACKGUARD, wholly unapproachable by any gentleman. The country abounds with evidence of this," and then Kendall presented some of it.[21]

In a few months however, peace was made with the AP and a new contract was drawn up "by which the rights of the public, of the telegraph, and of the press were fully recognized." Kendall was satisfied with the result.

In the years that followed, Kendall became less active but he carried on a spirited correspondence with Morse and the business leaders in the industry. His and Morse's satisfaction of the results of their labors in the previous 21 years are best summarized in a letter by Morse to Kendall, dated March 19, 1866. "Our telegraph interests," Morse wrote, "are now very much as you and I wished them to be at the outset, not cut up . . . into irresponsible parts, but making one great whole like the Post Office system. It is becoming, doubtless, a monopoly, but no more so than the Post Office system, and its unity is in reality a public advantage if properly and uprightly managed."[22]

KENDALL AS A PHILANTHROPIST

It is inconceivable that a man like Amos Kendall could cut himself off from other activities once he became associated with the telegraph. And Amos Kendall did not.

---

[20]Robert Luther Thompson, *Wiring a Continent—The History of the Telegraph Industry in the United States*. Princeton, NJ: Princeton University Press, 1947, pp. 331–333.

[21]*Ibid.* pp. 337–339.

[22]*Ibid.* p. 426.

About 1855, he was attracted by the activities of a man who was touring the country exhibiting deaf-mute children. It developed that the man was raising money for their education, but Kendall found out that little of it ended up to their benefit. This moved him, along with some other citizens, to found an institution for the deaf and dumb. Kendall's gift of a house and two acres of land was instrumental in the success of the school. Kendall and the other trustees persuaded Congress to charter the school in 1857 and to contribute to its support. Initially named the Columbia Institution for the Deaf and Dumb, its name was later changed to Gallaudet College. For many years, it was the only college for deaf-mutes in the world.[23] Kendall was its first president, and he held a deep interest in the school the rest of his life.

Despite his telegraphic battles and his philanthropic activities, Kendall did not stand apart form the course of events that were leading up to the Civil War. As early as 1832, he adopted the philosophy that the "Federal Union must be preserved."

In a political address in 1832, the far-sighted Kendall foresaw the strife that would come less than 3 decades later. He said: "Men are beginning to think too lightly of the Union of these States. Some maintain that its value to the South is overbalanced by the evils of the present protecting system. Others insist that the system be abandoned because it is of no value to the North. Both are wrong yet there advantages in *Union* which transcend them all."[24] His basic message in that speech was the Union must be preserved at all costs. He stepped up his writings deploring any thought of secession as the fateful period approached. At the outset of Buchanan's administration in 1857, Kendall beseeched him to "let the public mind be led to have faith in procuring remedies of all existing evils *within* the Union and not out of it." His last great effort to stave off secession was a brilliant series of 12 articles published in the Washington *Evening Star* in November and December 1860. Drawing on 50 years of study and experience in dealing with public opinion, the law and the Constitution, and politics, Kendall set forth a reasoned and persuasive argument to settle differences within the Union.

Typical of his arguments in this letter printed in the *Washington Evening Star* of November 16, 1860, headed by "Washington News and Gossip," is the *Star's* prefatory note disclaiming a position of its own:

Amos Kendall upon Secession—Below we print a letter from the Hon. Amos Kendall, followed by a paper from his able pen address to the People of the South; the first of a series designed to combat the current doctrine of secession. We accord space to this communication as we shall to those to follow it, without there designating to commit the *Star* to the correctness of the positions that distinguished writer may assume. If there lives a man entitled to be heard

---

[23]Mabee, p. 358.
[24]Kendall, pp. 429–430.

attentatively and respectfully upon such a subject by the Democratic Party, that man is surely Amos Kendall, the right-hand man of Andrew Jackson in times as trying to the party and the country as those upon us now. In those times, next to Jackson's his mind was the controlling one in the government of the Confederacy, stamping the impress on its patriotism and will more indelibly upon the future of the United States, than those of all the rest of Jackson's constitutional advisers. Long since, entirely disconnected from politics, and now at a very advanced age, if any man can approach the discussion of such a subject in such times unbiased by any other than the purest considerations, that man is Amos Kendall.

Kendall's letter, dated November 16, 1860, follows:

The annexed article was prepared for the [Atlanta] *Constitution*, but its editor, avowing himself a secessionist, closes his columns against friend of the Union! The writers for his paper denounce as no true democrat all would deny the new doctrine of secession, thus setting up a new test of democracy.

From boyhood, I have considered myself a democrat, reared in the school of Jefferson, in those words or acts I challenge any one to find the trace of a thought giving color to this doctrine. I have some claim to be heard by Southern people. Like hundreds of others in the Border States, I have suffered by abolition thieves. When at the head of the Post Office Department, I incurred violent denunciations by denying the right of abolitionists to distribute their incendiary papers and documents in the Southern States through the United States mails and postmasters, by justifying the postmaster at New York for refusing to mail them to Charleston, and the people of Charleston for seizing and burning them in the street. Moreover, I am an old man, whose political race is run, who has no motive of ambition or gain to influence him, nor any inducement to take up his pen but such as are common to all who have property to lose or families to leave them behind.

Amos Kendall

His final article, "Secession No: XII," was published Friday, December 28, 1860. His articles taking to task "the Southern disunionists" were in vain. South Carolina seceded before the final article was written and published.

During the war years, Kendall was active in public affairs primarily as a letter writer. He communicated with many government officials and prominent citizens. His consistent theme was to save the Federal Union and the Constitution. Even though he felt that Lincoln had at times received poor advice, he urged the Democrats to support the war effort. Kendall's feeling for political parties in those years is summarized in these words:[25] "Being now and forever a Democrat of the Jackson school, I have no affinity for those who, under that honored name, cry for peace by the sacrifice of the

---

[25]Kendall, p. 649.

Union, and quite as little with those who seek to save the Union by the destruction of the Constitution. When the Democratic party becomes a secession party, and the Republican party becomes an abolition party, I shall seek for new political affinities, or remain *a party by myself.*"

Kendall's second wife died June 25, 1864, of typhoid fever. She had been an active member of the Cavalry Baptist Church in Washington. Her death, which left a void in Kendall's life, together with Kendall's diminishing business and political activities, probably caused the intensification of Kendall's interest in religion. Though he had been a religious man and a student of the Bible since boyhood, he had never formally associated himself with any single religion or church. He did, however, teach a Sunday School class in Frankfurt when he was editor of the *Argus.* His interest in religion began picking up about the time he "retired" in 1860, but he found "little *practical Christianity* among professing Christians." Finally however, in 1865 at the age of 75, he was baptized in the Cavalry Baptist Church.

Characteristically, he approached his church life almost as if it were another career. He attended all meetings, was a devoted Sunday School teacher, and became an outstanding lay leader. When the congregation set out to build a new church, Kendall was chairman of the building committee. He contributed more than $100,000 himself* and was indeed a proud man when the building was dedicated in June 1866.

For the next 15 months, Kendall, accompanied by his daughter and son-in-law (Stickney), toured Europe and the Biblical lands. The trip was taken in an effort to improve Kendall's health and to satisfy his desire to see Palestine. A few months after he returned from Europe, the new church was gutted by fire. Kendall believed the fire was a "chastisement for the overweening pride of the members of the church in their beautiful edifice." But he again took the lead, and the church was rebuilt and rededicated in July 1869.[26]

There is little evidence that Amos Kendall was ever given to humor, but he does seem to have mellowed in his late years. In 1868, he wrote, "My poor walking machine is wearing out by constant use and must soon tumble to pieces." Of a mild illness in the last year of his life, he observed, "I apprehend my disease is incurable, being *old age.*"

From the time Jackson left the White House until Kendall's death, Kendall rose to challenge any criticism of the Old Hero. He never tired of straightening out editors. Among his last reactions to criticism of Jackson was one that lacked his usual reasoned explanations, but rather exhibited somewhat of a modern quality: "Editors of the *National Intelligencer*: Please discontinue your paper sent to my address at 443 11th Street. I know of no more fitting

---

*Kendall's large gift also prompted Morse to contribute to the building fund, even though Morse was living in Poughkeepsie in retirement. This, however, indicates the close relationship of the two men.

[26]*Ibid.* pp. 652–84.

way to express my indignation at your infamous attack upon the character of General Jackson in this day's issue. Can no degree of integrity, patriotism, and public service save the memory of the illustrious dead from the jackals of a licentious press?"

Kendall was correct early in 1869; old age was his difficulty. It became apparent in August that Kendall did not have long to live. He methodically wound up his affairs, sent a final message to the Columbia Institution, earmarked $25,000 for mission Sunday School work, and even discussed his funeral arrangements. With his family around him, he watched the sun rise on the morning of November 12 and faintly whispered, "How beautiful, how beautiful," and calmly died.[27]

IN RETROSPECT

No authoritative evaluation has been made of Amos Kendall as a whole, primarily because no one has studied his life as an entity. Journalism historians have lifted out those segments appropriate for their purposes; political historians have described Kendall's influence to fit their interpretations of the Jacksonian period; and histories of the telegraph and biographies of Morse seem to consider business enterprise as Kendall's main accomplishment. The evidence is overwhelming that Kendall became a master of journalist without exhausting his abilities, and for the other periods of his life, perhaps Bowers was correct in asserting that he was "a man who made history that historians have written and ascribed to others."[28] Professor Anderson also suggested that there is considerable untold and unevaluated about Kendall when he wrote: "From my study of Kendall I found him a man of great interest, quite a different person from that depicted in the usually accepted estimates."[29]

Recalling the great Americans of the 19th century, one is struck by the fact that they all seem to have concentrated on one or possibly two careers. Jackson was a soldier and a politician, as was U. S. Grant; Lee, Sherman, and Thomas Jackson were soldiers; Van Buren, Clay, Calhoun, and Lincoln all owe their fame to politics; Morse, Carnegie, Biddle, Field, and Cooke left their marks in finance and private enterprise; Bennett, Greeley, and Raymond are recorded as great journalists.

Perhaps it can be said that Amos Kendall, with three major careers and numerous other activities, spread himself too thin. Looking back over his life, we see him as a teacher, a postmaster, a lawyer, a journalist, a publicist, a presidential adviser, a Cabinet member, a publisher, a business agent, a

---

[27]*Ibid.* p. 690.
[28]Bowers, p. 151.
[29]Anderson, p. 66.

corporation president, a philanthropist, a college president, and a church leader.

Given the significance of the Jackson Administration in enlarging the power of the Presidency, in banking reform, and in promoting formation of the nation's two-party system, *The Washington Star's* 1860 evaluation of Kendall—"In those times next to Jackson's, his mind was the controlling one in the government." Beyond that Kendall demonstrated the vital role public relations plays in a democratic government, in politics, and in the promotion of business. Kendall left a legacy that those who follow in his footsteps today can take pride in.

A BIBLIOGRAPHIC NOTE

Perhaps because Amos Kendall was a supporting actor in The Age of Jackson, there is quite a bit of inaccuracy in accounts of his public life as well as the lack of a definitive biography of this remarkable man. John Spencer Bassett, for example, included this phrase about Kendall: "in 1842, when he had lost the auditorship to which his patron appointed him" (Bassett, p. vi). The fact is that Kendall had left the Fourth Auditor's office 7 years earlier to become Postmaster General. Leonard D. White, in his *The Jacksonians*, made the statement that "Professor Frank M. Anderson has written a convincing demonstration that Kendall was the mysterious author of *The Diary of a Public Man*" and cited Anderson's *The Mystery of Public Man* as the source (p. 274). The facts are that Anderson originally delivered a paper to the American Historical Society in 1928 that tentatively proved that Kendall was the author of the *Diary* (first published in 1879 in the *North American Review*). As a Lincoln document, the *Diary* is important because Lincoln scholars have depended on it for well-known sayings of Lincoln. Extensive investigation by Professor Anderson finally disclosed that Kendall was in Washington on that date and the writer of the *Diary* was in New York City. Anderson further concluded that the author was Sam Ward, but that the *Diary* as published was a fabricated, semifictional work that "ought not be regarded as history."

Another glaring misstatement about Kendall was printed in *The Encyclopedia Americana* in its 1945 edition that stated that Kendall was a "man of low moral perceptions, and, as a politician, was the incarnation of the worst evils of the American system." (Vol. 16, p. 463) and proceeds to cite James Parton as its authority. Parton published his 3-volume *Life of Andrew Jackson* in 1860. It is a slanted, opinionated collection of "chapters" that read like the vindictive and irresponsible editorials of the 19th century. The fact is that Amos Kendall was a highly moral person who repeatedly demonstrated integrity in his public actions, although he was highly partisan in a highly partisan age.

A WORD ON KENDALL'S PAPERS

The papers of Amos Kendall have not come down to us, save in very small part. At his death in 1869 they passed into the hands of his son-in-law. The papers appear to have been destroyed in a warehouse fire about 1891, though occasionally a document turns up; which at one time was among the Kendall papers. Before the fire, some of the papers, "it is not possible to say how many, came into the hands of W. G. Terrell, a Washington newspaper man, who disposed of them in various ways. Some were published in the Cincinnati *Commercial*, February 4, 5, and 10 1879. These were sixty-nine letters from Jackson to Kendall and cover the period from September 4, 1827, to May 20, 1845, and entire acquaintance of the two men." Jackson's daughter, Mrs. Rachel J. Lawrence, obtained other papers in 1909 that had been in Terrell's possession. The most important were published in the Nashville *Tennesseean*, April 18 and 25, 1909.

Actually a great many of Kendall's letters are in existence; they are scattered among the papers of dozens of prominent men who lived during this time. The diffusion of his letters is magnified by the fact that many of the collections are quite large. For example, the Henry O'Rielly Manuscript Collection (New York Historical Society Library), which includes a number of Kendall's letters, contains "about 100 vols. of manuscript and printed material."

In other words, a study of Kendall would be a daunting endeavor but a worthwhile one.

"The First Public War"

Amos Kendall's effort to stem the rising tide of secession of the Southern states was in vain. Stanley Elkins and Eric McKitrick, in their recent book, *The Age of Federalism* asserted that the partisan divisions of the Founding Fathers—encapsulated in the enmity between Alexander Hamilton and Thomas Jefferson as recounted in chapters 3 and 4—brought the nation to the brink of political collapse in the time of the French-ignited struggle in Europe. Yet despite all the machinations and maneuvering on each side in the Federalist–Republican battle for power, the Constitution survived and endured intact for another half century. Then a different kind of struggle ensued—this one based on sectional conflicts. This time the conflict was resolved by war, a war that has been called "the single most transforming and defining force in American History." A war that was fought on the fields of public opinion as well as on the battlefields—the first public war.

Vernon Parrington once wrote that it is but a step "from the sword of the spirit to musket and ball," yet it took a 30-year intensive propaganda campaign by the militant abolitionists to bring this young nation to the point that the South would declare "those who oppose us will smell powder and feel Southern steel."[1] The abolitionists' campaign came in the context of a United States enfeebled by weak political leadership.

The antislavery crusade was led by the flinty firebrand, William Lloyd Garrison, properly desribed by one biographer as "the great publicist of the movement," who "deserved primary credit for bringing the problem of slav-

---

[1]Jefferson Davis, *His Letters, Papers, and Speeches.* Dunbar Rowland, ed., Jackson, MS: 1923, p. 48.

ery to the nation's attention."[2] It was Garrison who, more than any other person, through his tireless writing drew the cleaving issue between the equalitarian, industrializing North and the libertarian, cotton-based South. Garrison was able to force Southerners to defend slavery in a "full-blown rejection of much they once held inviolate."

Garrison, son of an immigrant family, was abandoned early by a shiftless father. After a troublesome childhood, he found his first happiness, significantly, working at the printer's case. "Chance threw in his way the job of village editor, and inclination plunged him into politics." On January 1, 1831, he launched his own paper, *The Liberator*, an unimpressive four-page paper, nonetheless, a "little paper that was to make a mighty stir in the world during a long period of hand-to-mouth existence."[3] Garrison stoutly proclaimed in his first issue, "I will be heard." He was. He single-mindedly propagandized the wrongs of human slavery and marshaled the forces of discontent of his generation, using "no other weapon than the sword of the spirit." Merrill concluded:[4]

> The malcontented Newbury Port boy had traveled far since the days of his apprenticeship. There had been a long struggle against wind and tide, with passionate, self-righteous sometimes indiscriminate exhortation and abuse. But for a generation, as central publicist, as Liberator of the reform movement, he had been the leading abolitionist, the universal reformer. The name of William Lloyd Garrison had become a symbol of the prophetic New England conscience. The unsubstantial dream of evil overthrown had become the fabric of reality.

Equally effective in arousing the emotions of the North against the slavery of the South was Harriet Beecher Stowe whose *Uncle Tom's Cabin* stands as one of the powerful propaganda tracts of all time. Hers was a Puritan mind, nurtured in an environment of preaching; she was the daughter of a minister, wife of a minister, and mother of ministers. Parrington described her as "a child of her own romantic generation as well as a daughter of Puritanism." Her famed novel was originally published serially in the *National Era*, an antislavery newspaper in Washington, DC. *Uncle Tom* was published March 20, 1852, and quickly swept the country, mobilizing emotions against the brutality and injustice of slavery. By mid-1853, some 1,200,000 copies had been sold. It was soon converted into a stage play, and this form greatly extended its impact. Her novel, inspired by the Fugitive Slave Act of 1850, laid bare slavery's elementary injustice. The nation got the message.

Aiding and abetting Garrison and Mrs. Stowe in arousing the public against slavery and thus against the South was the equally effective, if not so noisy,

---

[2]Walter M. Merrill, *Against the Wind and Tide, a Biography of William Lloyd Garrison.* Cambridge, MA: Harvard University Press, 1963, Preface.

[3]Vernon Parrington, *Main Currents of American Thought.* New York: 1927, Vol. III, p. 353.

[4]Merrill, pp. 330–331.

Wendell Phillips who used the platform rather than the press or stage to carry his message to the people. A superb speaker, Phillips in his effort to free the slaves also freed oratory from the old formalities in which it had been bound by such giants as Daniel Webster and Edward Everett. In a calm, modulated voice, without histrionics, Phillips reasoned with each person in his audience instead of shouting and screaming.

He traveled the length and breadth of the land with his message until he "knew every locomotive, every conductor and the depth of mud on every road in the United States." In 1837, the lawyer's eloquent protest on the assassination of the abolitionist editor, Elijah P. Lovejoy, marked the beginning of a long career in which Phillips felt driven by the need to "educate, arouse, and mature a public opinion which shall compel the administration to adopt and support it in pursuing the policy I can aid."[5]

Phillips was fully conscious of the power of public opinion and the role of press, pulpit, and platform in molding it. In a speech on public opinion, the abolitionist campaigner said:[6] "The man who launches a sound argument, who sets on two feet a startling fact and bids it travel from Maine to Georgia, is just as certain that in the end he will change the government, as if, to destroy the capitol, he had placed gunpowder under the Senate chamber." In the same speech, he argued that the penny papers of New York did more to govern the United States than the White House in Washington. Phillips argued: "We live under of a government of men and morning newspapers." Given the nation's weak Presidents prior to the Civil War this was not all hyperbole. Fully cognizant of public opinion's power, this eloquent Harvard-trained lawyer worked tirelessly to mobilize it against slavery—and the South.

Goaded by such effective propagandists in a nation crippled by weak political leadership, civil war came to the United States of America. The Civil War was the first major war to be fought on the public opinion field as well as on the battle field. This was a war in which winning public support was paramount. As one historian accurately noted:[7] "It is not surprising that the Civil War became largely a war of opinion, a war to win people's approval, a truly public war. Victory might well go to the people who responded first with the fullest national effort."

Fortunately, for the preservation and future of the United States, the Union had an astute student of public opinion and a most gifted writer in Abraham Lincoln. Of Lincoln, Alfred Kazin wrote:[8] "A self-educated child of the primitive frontier, brought up, he said, 'on extreme experiences,' turned out—as

---

[5] *Wendell Phillips, Speeches, Lectures, and Letters, First Series.* Boston, 1863.

[6] Oscar Sherwin, *Prophet of Liberty.* New York: Bookman Associates, 1958, pp. 258–260.

[7] Frank E. Vandiver, "The First Public War, 1861–1865." Lecture published by Public Relations Society of America. 1962.

[8] Review of two volumes of Lincoln's speeches, letters, and writings (The Library of America) in *The New York Times Book Review,* December 10, 1989, p. 3.

the fires of war burned away everything inessential—to have the brains, the will, the conviction and (not least) the rhetorical force and grace that would ultimately bind his people to him forever. He gave America back its soul." The simple eloquence of Lincoln's Gettysburg Address and its profound impact on the course of American history is a monument to his skill as a communicator and rhetorician.

Lincoln stands as the greatest writer of all our Presidents. Moreover, much of his skill in leading the United States through its greatest ordeal flowed from his keen appreciation of the power of public opinion in shaping public decisions. One historian praised him as "perhaps the most effective fashioner of public opinion in American history." Many have paid homage to the power of public opinion, but none has stated it more vigorously than did Lincoln with his classic statement, made during his debates with Stephen A. Douglas: "Public sentiment is everything; with public sentiment, nothing can fail; without it nothing can succeed. He who molds opinion is greater that he who enacts laws." Though there were no White House publicists and press conferences in Lincoln's time, the important uses of publicity were understood and utilized by him. J. G. Randall offered this example:[9]

> Thought was given to public pronouncements and to their timing. When, after Gettysburg and Vicksburg, the fall of Port Hudson was expected, thus opening the entire Mississippi River, Halleck wrote Grant: "The Prest, will then issue a genl order congratulating the armies of the east & west on their recent victories. This consideration has prevented me from issueing [sic] one myself for your army. I prefer that it should come from the Prest."

Lincoln knew well the importance of keeping a sensitive finger on the public's pulse. He once advised a friend: "Keep close to the people—they are always right and will mislead no one." Lincoln sincerely believed this and imaginatively devised ways of keeping "close to the people."

Carl Sandberg, Lincoln's great biographer, told how the President, twice each week, set aside a period of his valuable time for conversations with ordinary folk, the housewives, farmers, merchants, and pension-seekers—"the stream of thousands who wore the thresholds of the White House, nicked its banisters, smoothed the doorknobs, and spoke their wants and errands."

In this time, the War Department had recruited an officer from the ranks of journalism whose duties approximated those of today's Pentagon information officer. He was Charles G. Halpine, a colorful Irishman who worked on the New York *Herald* and the New York *Tribune*. Halpine, who became a brevet brigadier general on General David P. Hunter's staff, once told the

---

[9]J. G. Randall and Richard N. Current, *Lincoln the President*, New York: Dodd, Mead, 1955, p. 45.

President that he was wasting his time on these unimportant people. Lincoln gently rebuked him, saying:[10]

> I feel, though the tax on my time is heavy, that no hours of my day are better employed than those which bring me again within the direct contact and atmosphere of the average of our whole people.
>
> I tell you Major that I call those receptions my *public opinion baths*—for I have little time to read the papers and gather public opinion that way; and though they may not be pleasant in all particulars, the effect, as a whole, is renovating and invigorating.

In the words of Ida Tarbell, Lincoln's "eyes and ears were always strained to catch the winds of the people's thinking" and he had "rare skill . . . in gauging their strength and velocity." Miss Tarbell recorded the story of Lincoln's fact-finder in the closing months of the war, Henry Wing. As the bloody struggle neared its climax in the summer of 1864, Lincoln was fairly confident that he knew the mind of the North but as to the crucial factor of the mind of the Army of the Potomac, he was uncertain. He needed an astute observer to go among the soldiers and report back to him. He found his man in a plucky cub reporter for the *New York Tribune* who had turned to journalism after being wounded as a Union soldier.

Wing had come to the President's attention when Lincoln learned at the War Department telegraph room, where he had gone in desperate search of word on General Grant's "lost Army," that young Wing had word on the Army of the Potomac but refused to divulge it until he could first send his "scoop" to his paper. Because Wing had refused to comply with Secretary of War Stanton's order to give him information on Grant's whereabouts, Stanton had ordered him shot as a spy. The wiser Lincoln, instead, had him brought from Union Mills, Virginia, where he was being held, to Washington to give a full report to the President and his Cabinet.[11]

After Wing was through with his story, the President told him of his need for a personal news gatherer in the Army and that he wanted the young man to serve him in this way. "You are to see me whenever you come to Washington, Henry," Lincoln told the 19-year-old reporter as the latter prepared to return to Grant's headquarters in the Wilderness. Three weeks later, after the bloody battle of Cold Harbor, when Wing returned to the Capital with his dispatches, Lincoln immediately sent for him and from the crippled, war-wracked correspondent heard firsthand the information he needed to know but could not get through official reports. "For Mr. Lincoln it was like riding at the youth's side; for the young man told a score of incidents—what

---

[10]Carl Sandburg, *Abraham Lincoln, The War Years*, Vol. II, New York: Harcourt Brace, 1939, pp. 236–237.

[11]Ida Tarbell, *A Reporter for Lincoln*. New York: Macmillan, 1927, pp. 1–15.

had happened, what he had seen or heard there, the unreported, the officially unimportant."[12] Throughout that a crucial summer and fall, Henry Wing made his personal, graphic reports to the President who, through Wing, came to know "the mind of the Army of the Potomac." President Lincoln had no intelligence apparatus or White House pollsters to keep him informed on the progress of the war or on the changing state of public opinion in the armies and in the public. These are administrative essentials in today's organizations, essentials provided by public relations professionals.

Lincoln was equally sensitive to good press relations as a means of influencing public opinion. Early in his career, he perceived the value of publicity. In June 1836, when the Sangamon (IL) *Journal* called for candidates for a minor office to declare themselves, Lincoln responded with a letter to Simeon Francis, the editor. Lincoln became a frequent contributor to newspapers, writing unsigned editorials, news letters, and articles resembling today's news release. Pollard wrote:[13]

> From the very beginning of his public career, Lincoln was keenly aware of the importance of public opinion. He deliberately cultivated the press, especially that of his own neighborhood and party. He was familiar with the ways of publicity and appreciated its uses. In nearly thirty years of public life, newspaper writers and editors were among his correspondents, his advisers, and his confidants. When he came to power he knew how to deal with them.

Lincoln and his associates needed all the skill they could muster to deal with a lively, aggressive press. As the tensions that split the Union had mounted, so had the public's demand for news. "The public wanted to know what had happened yesterday rather than some man's opinion on what happened last week," Elmer Davis once wrote. To meet the demand for news, new rotary presses were fed by news gathered by a growing army of mobile reporters. The lengthening railroads fostered the spread of postal service and the Pony Express filled in the gaps. By 1861, the "magnetic" telegraph's metallic web had reached the Pacific Coast. On the eve of the Civil War, there were 386 daily newspapers with a circulation of 1,475,500 to serve a nation of 31 million. There were more than 3,000 weekly papers. These papers played an important role, North and South, in the titanic struggle.

Lincoln fully agreed with the noted orator, Edward Everett, that "the newspaper press of the United States is, for good or evil, the most powerful influence that acts on the public mind." In dealing with the press, Lincoln was denied one powerful weapon when the Government Printing Office was established in 1861. Prior to that time, Presidents had used the patronage

---

[12]*Ibid.*, pp. 54–55.

[13]James E. Pollard, *The Presidents and the Press.* New York: Macmillan, 1947, p. 312.

of government printing as a lever on newspapers; but Lincoln still had the power of political patronage, and this he used to the full. A Baltimore newspaper noted at the beginning of the Lincoln administration:[14] "Editors seem to be in very great favor with the party in power—a larger number of the fraternity having received appointments . . . than probably under any previous Administration." It is doubtful whether Lincoln made more such appointments than were made in the Andrew Jackson administration, as indicated in chapter 5. Surely, Lincoln was the first President since Jackson to be so astute in the ways of winning public support.

The way he used patience and patronage to bring James Gordon Bennett, long a thorn in the Lincoln flesh, to his side in the 1864 campaign is but one example. Bennett's New York *Herald* was a bitter critic of the President. In the autumn of 1861, Lincoln "wrote personally to Bennett to apologize when the Navy Department held up a pass for a *Herald* reporter to go aboard one of its ships." The following spring, he again took trouble to smooth the paper's feathers, explaining in his own hand to Bennett that the proclamation of an overzealous Union Commander, General David P. Hunter, had not been gotten up with Secretary Stanton's connivance.[15] Near the end of the war, Lincoln offered Bennett the ambassadorship to France, but Bennett declined. Similarly, Horace Greeley's "erratic enthusiasms were a matter of concern to the President, for the *Tribune* stood high in favor among the Republican elect, and its popular circulation was impressive."[16]

LINCOLN RECOGNIZES GROWING POWER OF PRESS

One of Lincoln's most effective ways in utilizing the press was his use of the open letter, which Randall praised as "the fine art of correspondence with a public purpose." When Lincoln saw the need to present a view or matter to the public, in lieu of a speech, he would write a carefully phrased letter to the appropriate person or group, fully intending it for the voters. His "save the Union" letter of August 22, 1862, to Horace Greeley is a prime example. Randall wrote: "It is in these occasional letters that one finds some of Lincoln's best turned passages of eloquent but unprovocative appeal to public sentiment."[17]

Lincoln broke new ground in Presidential press relations and played a not insignificant part in the news revolution that came with the war. Starr noted:[18] From the beginning of political parties in the United States, succes-

---

[14]The Baltimore *Evening Patriot* quoted in Randall and Current, pp. 40–41.

[15]Bernard Weisberger, *Reporters for the Union*. Boston, 1953, pp. 129–130.

[16]*Ibid.*, p. 174.

[17]Randall and Current, pp. 46–47.

[18]Louis M. Starr, *The Bohemian Brigade*. New York: Knopf, 1954. pp. 152–153.

sive administrations had used pet newspapers as organs for the release of news and quasi-official expressions of policy. Lincoln upset this precedent from the outset, he would have no organ. "The collection of news in Washington became the free-for-all it has remained ever since." Starr failed to explain that the reason Lincoln had no government subsidized newspaper to propagate his views and support his policies was the establishment of the Government Printing Office in 1861, thus depriving Lincoln of this propaganda asset. It seems reasonable to conclude that this policy of Lincoln was born of his conscious effort to muster support in every quarter he could. Generally speaking, reporters were well received at the White House, and they had easy access to Lincoln's secretary, William O. Stoddard.

Despite Lincoln's considerable effort to woo and placate editors and reporters, the President, his Cabinet, and the generals of the Union Army had an abundance of troubles with the increasingly aggressive and vitriolic press of that day. Nelson observed:[19]

> Tolerance on the part of government and people were great but exhaustible. Lincoln reluctantly ordered newspapers closed and editors jailed. Military commanders of Northern districts did the same with far less reluctance and forbade entry of mailed "Copperheadism" into their districts. The postmaster general barred some newspapers from the mail. One grand jury investigated "Copperhead" newspapers and hoped they would be punished; another indicted anti-Union editors.

PAMPHLETS AGAIN BECOME WEAPON OF WAR

The pamphlet, which had been so effectively used in the American Revolution, was once again utilized as a weapon of political and psychological war by both sides, particularly by competing political factions of the North. Pamphlets poured from the presses in unprecedented numbers, and in Frank Freidel's opinion,[20] they "may well have found proportionately more readers than those appearing in either earlier or later crises." For one thing, this was the first war fought when there was general literacy in the United States. Civil War pamphlets were many in number and varied in purpose; some appeared simplistically to the mass of voters or soldiers, whereas others were aimed at the influential opinion makers. In these pamphlets can be found many of the ideas that went into the making of public opinion of the 1860s, thus providing windows to the fierce debates of this tumultuous time.

---

[19]Harold L. Nelson, ed., *Freedom of the Press from Hamilton to the Warren Court.* Indianapolis, IN: Bobbs-Merrill, 1967, p. XXVI.

[20]Frank B. Freidel, ed., *Union Pamphlets of the Civil War, 1861–1865.* Cambridge, MA: Belknap Press of Harvard University Press, 1967.

Also, as Freidel observed, "They record something of the response to the shock of the war."

Organization of publication societies in support of President Lincoln in the dark days of 1863 to counter the discouragement of soldiers and civilians alike gave great impetus to Civil War pamphleteering in the North. Propamphlets quickly begat antipamphlets in the propaganda war. Harvard Historian Frank Freidel in his *Union Pamphlets in the Civil War* wrote: "The Republican societies tried to bolster morale, or in the case of the Democratic one, to capitalize upon the depressed state of opinion, by utilizing techniques long since developed by political campaign organizations, anti-slavery societies, and religious groups. All of these had long engaged in organized production of pamphlets." The American Tract Society, a religious organization organized a generation earlier, provided the pattern for the war-born pamphleteering groups such as the Board of Publications of the Philadelphia Union League, the New England Loyal Publication Society, and the New York City-based Loyal Publication Society. Most active of these was the Philadelphia Union League that boasted: "There is scarcely a post-town, from Maine to California, that has not received a package of our publications."

Public relations skill always has been and always will be part and parcel of leadership. These President Lincoln had in "full measure."

JEFFERSON DAVIS PROVED INEPT IN PUBLIC RELATIONS

In sharp contrast to Lincoln's sensitivity and astuteness in dealing with the press and public stood the ineptitude of President Jefferson Davis of the Confederate States. Davis tended to try to keep most matters secret, and for this, he was sharply criticized by many Southern newspapers. Roland wrote:[21] "The President often failed to take Congress and the people into his confidence, and Congress frequently debated and enacted important legislation behind closed doors. Long after Davis had sent agents to Europe for the purchase of military supplies he was attacked in *The Charleston Mercury* for failing to do so. It had not occurred to him to inform the country of such measures." One analyst of Davis' character wrote that a "fireside chat" by him would have been inconceivable. Nonetheless, he gave many speeches.

The Charleston Mercury was especially critical of Davis and his presidency and did much to trouble him during his leadership of the Confederacy. There was a reason for this. The paper was published by the son of Robert Barnwell Rhett, who had wanted the Confederate States of America (CSA)

[21]Charles P. Roland, *The Confederacy*. Chicago: University of Chicago Press, 1960. p. 108.

presidency and was hurt by Davis' refusal to include him in the new government. At first Rhett's attacks were with little effect, but with the reverses in 1862 "popular confidence in the government faltered sharply at these reverses and many who had been Davis' staunchest supporters fell away. Editors of the Richmond *Examiner*, Edward A. Pollard and John M. Daniel, now joined the chorus against Davis. Pollard possessed Rhett's power of vituperations."[22] "Other papers in the Confederacy followed suit, attacking Davis on such issues of conscription, tax in kind, and impressment of private property. It is to his credit that he permitted a free press to flourish in the South." Jefferson Davis was a constitutionalist and his support of a free press despite its aggravations stands in sharp contrast to the actions of Lincoln and his generals who closed newspapers, suspended the writ of habeas corpus, and had a reporter ridden out of military camps with the sign "Libeller" around his neck.

Davis knew full well the importance of ascertaining and molding public opinion but was untutored in dealing with the public and inept in the ways of public relations. Vandiver wrote:[23]

> The Confederate president worked to sustain morale by using accepted methods of public appeal. Often he spoke to Congress, outlining policy and fostering cooperation. Increasingly it grew difficult for him to persuade and cajole as the cause faded on the battlefield; increasingly he preached and demanded.

> When the press turned against the government, Davis fell back on more speeches himself and requests to governors for appeals to their own citizens. He sought, too, approval from the pulpit—long a standard method of reaching large segments of the populace.

Davis also realized the need to win support for his cause in nations abroad, particularly Great Britain. In the opinion of most historians, the South was more adroit with its overseas propaganda than it was at home. Eaton, for example wrote:[24] "Although the Confederate government spent much money and effort in foreign propaganda, it gave light consideration to domestic propaganda, to buoy up the sinking spirits of the people."

Once the war started, the Confederate States quickly turned to Great Britain for support of its cause. Southern leaders knew well the role France had played in helping the States win their independence from Britain; they placed their hopes on getting England as an ally on the latter's dependence on the South's cotton. The Confederacy also sought to win the British to its side with an organized propaganda campaign. It soon hired James Spence,

---

[22]*Ibid.*, pp. 52–55.
[23]Vandiver, pp. 8–9.
[24]Clement Eaton, *A History of the Southern Confederacy.* New York: The Free Press, 1956, p. 261.

described by Roland as "one of the most influential British propagandists." In 1862, Spence published a book—one that he had been at work on for some months—called *The American Union*, which was more a Southern polemic than a history of the United States. Spence "upheld the constitutionality of secession and emphasized the superiority of Southern culture over that of the North."[25] Spence's obvious purpose was to persuade England that it would benefit from a division of the United States. Whether this was Spence's honest view or one bought with Confederate dollars is not known.

HENRY HOTZE, CONFEDERATE PROPAGANDIST

The Confederacy's main propagandist in England was Henry Hotze, described by Roland as a man "with winning ways, a keen mind, and an unerring editorial instinct." Born in Zurich, Switzerland, in 1834, Hotze came to the United States as a child and was naturalized as a citizen on his twenty-first birthday in Mobile, AL. In 1859, after serving briefly in the U. S. legation in Brussels, Hotze got a job on the Mobile *Register*. When the war broke in 1861, he joined the Mobile Cadets and marched off to fight. Because of his newspaper training, Hotze was given a job on the regimental staff and there caught the approving eye of superior officers. CSA Secretary of War Leroy P. Walker sent Hotze on an intelligence mission to London in the summer of 1861. Soon after his return to the South later that summer, Hotze was appointed "commercial agent" for the Confederacy to lay the South's cause before the British people.

Hotze arrived in London with little money but with great public relations skill. Roland observed: "He quickly gained the confidence of the leading editors of England, and presently was contributing articles on the war to the newspapers of both British political parties."[26] Hotze's methods included paying professional free-lance "leader" writers from 2 to 10 guineas. "Hotze presented his articles to these free lancers who would sell them to the London papers. Thus, Hotze got his material in the English press without open evidence of Confederate inspiration, the professional writers got their 2 to 10 guineas, and the papers got their leaders."[27]

Hotze knew the importance of blandishments in winning the press. He referred in his accounts to "little personal compliments" consisting of Cuban cigars, American whiskey, and other articles scarce in London.[28] Hotze's job was made easier by the pro-Confederacy sympathies of much of the British

---

[25]*Ibid.*

[26]*Ibid.*, p. 109.

[27]Richard B. Harwell, "The Creed of a Propagandist," *Journalism Quarterly, 28*, 1951, pp. 213–218.

[28]R. F. Durden, *The Index*, unpublished master's thesis, Emory University, 1948.

press and public. The London *Times*, the mighty Thunderer, and the Manchester *Guardian*, spokesman of England's industrial north country, both favored the South. "Many other newspapers were of like persuasion, and they opened their columns to Southern views on secession and Southern accounts from the battlefield."[29]

Despite his success in getting the Confederate version of the war planted in the British press, Hotze decided that he needed a journal to represent the South in all things. Thus, in May, 1862, he established the weekly *Index*, a journal of news and comment on the Confederacy and the war. Hotze explained the need for the *Index* to act as a "machine for collecting, comparing, and bringing before the public with proper comments the vast amount of important information which is received in Europe through private channels."[30] Hotze shrewdly realized that he should target his message to the influential leaders of British thought—newspaper editors, members of Parliament, and the ministers of the government. He did not concern himself with a mass circulation. Also, this indefatigable propagandist gave the *Index* a tone of dignity and reasonableness, not one of shrill vituperation. He knew his British audience. Harwell thought "the Index was successful out of all proportion to the success of Confederate arms" and "should have insured for Hotze a lasting reputation as a propagandist." It didn't. Eaton explained the value of Hotze's *Index*:[31] "The *Index* was an admirable propaganda paper. Prior to its establishment the European public in general received its news of the Civil War through Northern newspapers, whose accounts were branded by Confederate agents as 'mendacious.' Typical of the propaganda carried in the *Index* was an "Address to Christians Throughout the World" in the June 11, 1863, issue, an appeal signed by a long list of Southern ministers. The *Index* ceased publication August 12, 1865.

To influence French public opinion, the Confederacy sent Edwin De Leon, a former consul general in Egypt, to Paris, but he soon got into quarrels with other Southern agents. "Early in February, 1864 de Leon was dismissed, and Hotze took charge of manipulating the French press. Hotze had a rare piece of good fortune in being able to persuade the Havas agency, the press agency for distributing news to Europe, to accept him as the supplier of reliable news from the South and concerning the American war, which it disseminated without excessive *Abonnements*."[32] de Leon had more directly bought French writers, "to manufacture a favorable public opinion" for the South. The collapse of the Confederacy brought the eclipse of Hotze, who

---

[29]Roland, p. 108.

[30]Quoted in Harwell.

[31]Eaton, Also see Charles Cullop, *Confederate Propaganda in Europe. 1861–1865*. Coral Gables, FL: University of Miami Press, 1969.

[32]Eaton, p. 76.

never returned to the United States. After a postwar career as a publicist in England and France, he died at Zug, Switzerland, in 1887.

THE UNION ALSO SOUGHT SUPPORT ABROAD

Lincoln and his wartime associates, also, knew the importance of building support for the Union cause in Great Britain and other European countries. Admittedly theirs was the easier task of simply preventing English interference in the Civil War whereas the South, on the other hand, had to try to stimulate action on the part of the British "at a time when no British interests urgently required that anything be done for them." As historians noted:[33] "The North held the interior lines, the forts of formal diplomatic conversations, which the South had to force." Consequently, as these authors observed, "Northern propaganda was a less vigorous growth [in England] than that of the South." The Union had no counterpart to Hotze in England, but John Bigelow, representing the North in Paris, did have a somewhat similar task. Occasionally, Bigelow extended his efforts to England but only in a spasmodic, ineffectual way. Charles Francis Adams, the representative in Great Britain, devoted little energy to "acting on the public mind."

The Union forces—acting at Lincoln's direction—sent more than 1,750,000 booklets and more than 100 lecturers to England during the war in an effort to maintain British abstention from the fratricidal conflict on this side of the Atlantic.[34] One of these lecturers was the famed preacher and orator, Henry Ward Beecher, who was sent to England in 1863 to preach the righteousness of the Northern cause. He was sent abroad not by the U. S. government, but by the Emancipation Society. "Beecher's speeches were made in rapid succession in October in the largest towns of the kingdom, where they rallied the 'American Party' in tremendous numbers."[35] There was also a Union counterpart to Hotze's *Index*—the *London American*—founded prior to the outbreak of the war and lasted until 1863. Managed and edited by J. A. Knight and A. Bostwick, the paper met with little success.

The Union also sought support from the antislavery forces in Europe. Robert Sorensen in his *The Word War* recorded that "in 1863 a group of laborers in Manchester sent President Lincoln a resolution supporting his Emancipation Proclamation, expressing a view contrary to much influential opinion in England. Lincoln replied an open letter that created some excitement, for the disregard of diplomatic precedent he spoke directly to the people of another country." This was long before the time major nations

---

[33]Donaldson Jordan and Edward J. Pratt, *Europe and the Civil War*. Boston, MA: Houghton Mifflin, 1931, p. 165.

[34]Edward W. Barrett, *Truth is Our Weapon*. New York: Funk and Wagnalls, 1953, p. 21.

[35]Jordan and Pratt, p. 165.

used radio and television to go to the people of other countries in 20th Century propaganda wars. Lincoln wrote the laborers:[36] "I have understood well the duty of self-preservation rests solely with the American people, but I have at the same time been aware that the favor or disfavor of foreign nations might have a material influence in enlarging or prolonging the struggle." The "favor of nations" Lincoln needed, and the United States has needed to win the favor of nations in every crisis and conflict it has been involved in since that time of "the first public war."

Fortunately for the fate of this nation, the Union's efforts in winning support at home and abroad were more effective than those of the Confederacy. As Frank Vandiver concluded: "Fate gave the North a leader whose language would echo down to history with timeless luster, a leader whose vision of freedom and whose conception of the Union transcended the moment to capture the future; it gave the Confederacy a leader whose wisdom none could doubt but whose appeal was muffled in legalistic phrase. It may well be that in selecting voices so aptly tuned to each cause, fate foredoomed one and evoked the other."[37]

THE MILITARY WAS ILL-EQUIPPED
IN DEALING WITH THE PRESS

The Civil War presented public relations problems to the military which it was not equipped to handle. Censorship of military information became a major consideration in its treatment of the press, yet effective censorship in a civil war is virtually impossible. The dissemination of news had been speeded up by the telegraph, and the larger daily papers could afford to send reporters to the front in this domestic war, fought in the front yard of Eastern metropolitan papers. Most correspondents roamed the battlefront at will. The government was still reporting to the people through Congress, by proclamations, or by occasional dispatches to newspapers. The amount of information that reached the public by this means was not in proportion to the sacrifice the public was being asked to make. Much of the press was filled with criticism of the military throughout the war. The military commanders on both sides had no prior experience in dealing with what was now a lively and aggressive band of war reporters. Neither army had an organized way of assisting these reporters confronted with a difficult news gathering task. Consequently, the military leaders showed little eptitude in their press relations.

On one occasion, for example, General George Meade ordered a reporter, Edward Grapsey, expelled from his camp but only after he had been paraded

---

[36]Thomas C. Sorenson *The Word War: The Story of American Propaganda.* New York: Harper & Row, 1968, p. 2.
[37]Vandiver Lecture.

through camp with a placard reading "Libeller of the Press" hung around his neck. The press repaid the general with a conspiracy of silence. The experiences of Union Generals Meade, Ulysses S. Grant, and William T. Sherman were strangely parallel. Each of them had been vilified by the press each of them had occasion to discipline reporters, and, in the end, each of them learned to live with the war correspondents.

The tense nation got most of its news of battle from the hurried, brief, and generally none-too-accurate reports of the correspondents and from letters sent home by soldiers, many of which were printed in local papers. Official reports, thought often printed, were usually so much delayed that they had little news interest. The short, telegraphic reports that arrived early did not tell much. The longer official reports were too long in seeing print. The military, and the nation, suffered by the lack of public relations program in the armed forces.

To partially fill the information vacuum, U. S. Secretary of War Stanton began publishing an official *Army and Navy Gazette* in July 1863, and it appeared weekly for 2 years. The journal, slow in printing news, never had a high readership. The last one, number 208, was issued June 27, 1865. General Halleck, in his new role as Chief of Staff, began the practice of issuing Official Bulletins that were a compilation of reports from the field, the first of which was issued May 4, 1864. These were made available to the press but did not provide much beyond orders, letters, and telegrams, material that had been released to the press all along.[38]

NAVY TAKES INFORMATIONAL STEPS IN SELF-DEFENSE

One naval historian, F. Donald Scovel, found that it was in the Civil War that the Navy took its first halting steps to provide the public with information about its actions. Mainly, news of the Navy throughout the war was dependent on battle reports. Secretary of the Navy Gideon Welles, himself a former newspaper editor, handed communiques from the Navy ships to reporters in Washington.[39] Exceptions were made—many were not released to protect military security. Then as now the military sought to hide its failures. News of failures of the Union Navy's monitors in the 1863 attempt to capture Fort Sumter and Charleston harbor was stricken from the reports by Welles. According to the published diary of Secretary Welles, he thought "it did not appear wise to make any deficiencies in those vessels prominent in the official reports which were to be published if monitors are weak in

---

[38]Col. Bennett Jackson, unpublished thesis, "The History of Army Public Relations," University of Wisconsin, 1968.

[39]Richard S. West, "The Navy and the Press During the Civil War," *Naval Institute Proceedings, 63* (1937), p. 38.

any part, there was no necessity for us to proclaim that weakness to our enemies." For the military, this has been official doctrine from that day to the day of the Gulf War of 1991.

Also interservice rivalry, which has sparked the public affairs programs of the four services, played its part in prompting the Navy to release news of naval actions. On several occasions Welles was distressed to find the Army getting a major share of the limelight for actions that depended on naval forces. Welles instructed Admiral Porter to make certain his battle reports were in ahead of those of the military commanders. Porter responded at his next opportunity and scooped the Army on the news of the Battle of Vicksburg. On July 7, 1863, Welles wrote, "Admiral Porter's brief dispatch to me was promptly transmitted over the whole country. I am told, however that [Secretary of War] Stanton is excessively angry because Admiral Porter heralded the news to me in advance of General Grant to the War Department. He craves to announce all important information."

The Navy was at a disadvantage in this interservice rivalry. It was common practice for correspondents to travel with both Union and Confederate armies, whereas, news directly from reporters with the ships was rare. The difficulty of communicating with their papers was the main reason for the high disparity between news from the front and the lack of it from blockade and river squadrons. A notable exception was when a New York reporter, B. S. Osbon, accompanied the abortive relief expedition to Fort Sumter. Osbon became what might be called the Navy's first public information officer. Through some connections he had, he got from Admiral Farragut a combination job as signal clerk and secretary of the Flagship Hartford. From that vantage point, he witnessed the battle with the forts and the capture of New Orleans. He sent the story to the New York papers. By the summer of 1864, Osbon had compiled a handbook on the Civil War histories of ships in the Union Navy, which provided a useful reference for reporters and commentators. By that time, Osbon had established himself as a clearing house for news about the Navy. He wrote Sunday articles, which he sold to a group of 18 newspapers. Osbon boasted of thus having established the first news syndicate in the United States.

One of these reports got Osbon in hot water with the Navy brass. When the Powder Boat Expedition against Fort Fisher was being prepared, Osbon wrote an advance story that he embargoed until the operation was completed. On hearing a rumor that the attack had taken place, a Philadelphia editor printed the story. This provided the Confederates with abundant information prior to the attack. The editor was arrested, and the paper closed. Such was "freedom of the press" on the Union side in the Civil War. And following the successful attack more than a month later, Osbon was arrested and put in the old Capitol prison in Washington until nearly the end of the war. Such was the fate of the Navy's first information officer!

Then as now the military high commands fought the battle of leaks. The most successful of the Confederacy's commerce raiders, the *CSS Alabama*, captured a merchantman, *SS Manchester*, bound from New York to Liverpool. Captain Soammes found a batch of newspapers on board and wrote: "I learned from them where all the enemy's gun boats were, and what they were doing. Perhaps this was the only war in which the newspapers explained, beforehand, all the movements of armies and fleets to the enemy." This history has repeated itself many times to the despair of the military.

Correspondents were not the only source of news leaks. Naval officers corresponding with the press caused Flag Officer S. F. DuPont to issue an order prohibiting such correspondence to his South Atlantic Blockading Squadron. On several occasions he was forced to take disciplinary action against his officers. Admiral Porter also found it necessary to issue a similar order. Information leaks in the Charleston Campaign caused Admiral John Dahlgren to complain to Secretary Welles "There are probably no means upon which the enemy has so relied for information as this insane propensity for making public the most valuable items."

A lesson learned in this war but too often forgotten by later commanders and chief executives of the nation was that an aroused but ill-informed public opinion can have its ill effect on naval strategy. The depredations of the Confederate commerce raiders, coupled with the threat of completion in England of the Confederate ironclads, brought near panic to the Eastern seaboard. The demand for warships to defend the harbors, to chase the raiders, and to patrol the fishing grounds brought intense pressures on Secretary Welles and President Lincoln. Metropolitan editors, shipowners, mayors of port cities, governors of seaboard states, and members of Congress exhorted for a departure from sound naval strategy of firm and unrelenting blockade in favor of helter-skelter pursuit of private and individual interests. The Navy and its commanders failed to heed President Lincoln's famous dictum of the importance of the power of public opinion: "With it nothing can fail; without it, nothing can succeed."[40]

WAR BRINGS FIRST HIGH PRESSURE FUND DRIVE

Fighting long, expensive wars requires more funds that can be raised with tax revenues. The First Public War brought the nation's first high pressure war bond drive, one that would set the pattern for the war bond drives of World War I and World War II. This pattern-setting model of a war bond

---

[40]This section is largely based on F. Donald Scovel's master's thesis, *History of the Development of the Public Affairs Function in the United States Navy, 1861–1941*, The University of Wisconsin, 1968.

drive was put together by a wealthy financier, Jay Cooke. Parrington called Cooke the first modern American, "the first to understand the psychology of mass salesmanship." Cooke was largely responsible for the financing of the Union cause through the sale of government bonds to the public on a hitherto unprecedented scale. He pulled out all the emotional stops to "sell patriotism" to the North with thorough organization and effective publicity that pounded hard the theme that the soldier at the front must be supported at the rear.

Parrington described the Cooke-directed sales appeal:[41]

> It was every loyal American's war, and patriotism demanded that idle dollars—in greenbacks—should be lent to the boys in blue, and a grateful government would return them, both principal and interest, in gold. To induce slacker dollars to become fighting dollars he placed his agents in every neighborhood, in newspaper offices, in banks, in pulpits—patriotic forerunners of the "one-minute men" of later drives. They also served their country, he pointed out, who sold government bonds on commission. He subsidized the press with a lavish hand, not only the metropolitan dailies but the obscurest country weeklies. He employed an army of hack writers to prepare syndicate matter and he scattered paying copy broadcast.

The "lavish hand" he extended to the press is illustrated by Weisberger:[42] "Cooke knew the quarter from which blow the breezes that stirred public opinion. From his home in Toledo, he proceeded to ship several lots of wine, ducks, and fish to a number of gratified editors and correspondents." Parrington also wrote that "cases of wine flowed in an endless stream to strategic publicity points." Cooke's agent visited newspaper editors and correspondents to push the loan drive. Some writers were given a chance to profit by speculation in government securities, which their efforts might enhance. Congressmen of this era were used to such blandishments, "But newspapermen, whose calling had generally been thought of as less elevated, were not usually subject to such pleasant persuasions."[43]

Illustrative of the publicity that Cooke and his agents obtained is an editorial in the Philadelphia *Evening Bulletin* urging people to subscribe for the bonds:[44]

> It is most gratifying to see not only the large accumulations of the capitalist, but the little, hard-won earnings of the artisan and the laborer, and the modest savings of the widow, are trustingly confided to the use of that Government

---

[41]Parrington, p. 36.

[42]Weisberger, p. 3.

[43]Elwyn B. Robinson, "The Dynamics of American Journalism from 1787 to 1865," *Pennsylvania Magazine of History and Biography, 61,* 1937, p. 444.

[44]Issue of September 23, 1861.

which alike protects the rights, and redresses the wrongs of the rich and the poor.

Robinson found that "the staid *North American* likewise persistently filled its broad editorial columns with arguments to prove the soundness of the government credit, the iniquity of gold speculators, the wisdom of Secretary of Treasury Chase, and the extraordinary advantages of investing in the government loan."

The Philadelphia *Daily News* was not to be outdone by its rivals in promoting Cooke's loan drive. That newspaper editorialized:[45]

It is safe; that no loyal man or woman will dispute. It pays well; no other permanent investment will yield, at the present time, nearly seven and one-half percent. The mechanic, or laboring man, who, by industry and economy has accumulated a small store for the hour of need, can avail himself of this loan, only fifty dollars being necessary to secure a note.

Little wonder that Robinson concluded that for this period of our history "the hidden springs of editorial policy" lay in the dependence of party machines and business enterprises on public favor.

IN CONCLUSION

These fragments of history clearly demonstrate that in the "first public war," the battle for public support was recognized as essential although the methods of gaining it were still somewhat primitive. What stands out about this bloody civil was President Abraham Lincoln's great power in mobilizing public opinion for the Union cause. Lincoln's ability to muster public and military support for the Union cause with his skill in public relations had no small part in the ultimate triumph. But he did more than this with his oratory of elegant simplicity. In Gary Wills' studied opinion Lincoln in his Gettysburg address "called up a new nation out of the blood and trauma." Wills wrote of that historic moment:[46] "Lincoln doesn't not argue law or history, as Daniel Webster did. He *makes* history. He does not come to present a theory, but to impose a symbol, one tested in experience and appealing to national values, with an emotional urgency entirely expressed in calm abstractions (fire on ice). He came to change the world, to effect an intellectual revolution. No other words could have done it. The miracle is that these words did."

---

[45]Issues of September 27, 1861, and March 11, 1863, as quoted in Robinson.

[46]Gary Wills, *Lincoln at Gettysburg*. New York: Simon and Schuster, 1992, pp. 174–175.

CHAPTER NINE

Publicity Moves
America West

*We are beginning to find that he who buildeth a railroad West of the
Mississippi must also find a population and build up business. We wish
to blow as loud a trumpet as the merits of our position warrants.*
—Charles Russell Lowell, Burlington publicist (1859)

The lure of the West, painted in romantic colors, that sped the development
of the continental United States and its aura that today provides vicarious
adventure for millions of Americans through books, motion pictures, and
television is deeply embedded in U.S. thought and culture. Westward expansion was both a practical and symbolic expression of the United States'
Romantic Movement in the opinion of J. Valerie Fifer, a historian. A *New
York Times* writer observed as late as 1993:[1] "The West has been redefined
many times. It is perhaps an inverted testament to the vast landscape, where
the clouds seem close enough to touch, that it has managed to serve as a
chalkboard on which myth after myth has been created, erased, and rewrit-
ten." Publicists, sung and unsung, played a vital role in creating these myths
to lure settlers and tourists West, thus creating the romantic aura that still
hovers over that part of the nation west of the Mississippi.

Ray Allen Billington, scholar of the Westward movement, confirmed this:[2]
"the migrations that peopled California and the Oregon country in the 1840s

---

[1]Sam How Verhovek, "Myths Die With Their Boots On," *New York Times*, Oct. 24, 1993,
Week in Review, p. 1.

[2]*Words That Won the West*. New York: Foundation for Public Relations Research and
Education, 1963, p. 6.

were induced not only by the usual impulses governing folk movements—hope of gain, thirst for adventure, a desire to escape an uncongenial homeland—but by one of the most effective promotional campaigns in history." Kevin Starr affirmed this generalization in his *Inventing the Dream* when he wrote that the railroads settled Southern California—the Southern Pacific coming down from San Francisco in 1876 the Atchison, Topeka, & Santa Fe coming in across the desserts in 1865. Even before the Southern Pacific arrived in Los Angeles, it had hired as a publicist, Charles Nordhoff, a reporter on the *New York Evening Post,* to promote Southern California. His book, *California for Health, Wealth and Residence,* published in 1872, brought thousands to that region in search of health, wealth, and residence, and in Starr's words, "transplanting their notions of gentility and self-improvement."[3]

More recently Fifer summed up the elements in the settlement of the West this way:[4] "Together the transport, tourist, and information industries played a crucial role in Western development. . . . All brought new settlement and investment into the West, demanded a new awareness of the environment, helped to define the new word 'transcontinental' and stimulated the growth of a new spirit of American nationalism." In sum, we again find the unseen power wielded by publicists working in the shadows of large enterprises having a profound influence on the United States' economic, social, and cultural fabric.

The romantic picture painted in roseate hues by the publicists to lure settlers and tourists west created a distorted canvas that plagues us to this day. No where in their publicity releases or tourist guides will you find the hardships of Nannie Alderson who in 1883 married, left her home in Virginia, to travel to a new life on a ranch in Montana. There she found "Everyone in the country lived out of cans and you would see a great heap of them outside every little shack." Patricia Nelson Limerick made a thorough study of this dichotomy of the romantic West and the West of reality. She has written:[5] "The conquest of Western America shapes the present as dramatically—and sometimes as perilously—as the old mines of Colorado shape the mountainsides. In the popular imagination, the reality of conquest dissolved into stereotypes of noble savages and noble pioneers struggling quaintly in the wilderness. In Western paintings, novels, movies, and television shows, those stereotypes were valued precisely because they offered an escape from modern troubles."

---

[3] *Inventing the Dream: California Through the Progressive Era.* New York: Oxford University Press, 1985, pp. 40–41.

[4] J. Valerie Fifer. *American Progress: The Growth of the Transport, Tourist and Information Industries in the Nineteenth-Century West.* Chester, CT: Globe Pequot Press, 1988, p. 2.

[5] *The Legacy of Conquest: The Unbroken Past of the American West.* New York: Norton, 1987, p. 18.

RAILROADS PIONEERED IN PUBLIC RELATIONS

The United States' railroads, the nation's first major industry, pioneered in the practice of public relations out of necessity. In the some 170-year history of railroads in this nation, the industry and its executives were compelled to confront innumerable problems involving relations with the public. In the early days, one of the principal problems was that of persuading a skeptical public of the feasibility of railroads and the superiority of rail travel over canals and turnpikes. There was much public opposition to this new means of travel, strange as that may seem today. When the railroad was about to enter Philadelphia, fearful citizens covered the town with a scare poster: "MOTHERS LOOK OUT FOR YOUR CHILDREN! Artisans, Mechanics, Citizens! When you leave your family in health must you be hurried home to mourn a DREADFUL CASUALTY. Philadelphians, your rights are being invaded!"

But by 1850, much of the opposition to railroads had disappeared, and the period from 1850 to 1870 was an era of good feeling. With few exceptions, the press and people were friendly and enthusiastic as the railroads pushed west. Edward Hungerford wrote in his history of the Baltimore & Ohio Railroad: "It was an age of ceremonials. Public oratory today seems to be a well developed and fairly flourishing art; but it is nothing when one compares it with its heyday in the middle of the last century. It was a fact patent from the outset that, in addition to the inevitable dinner, there must be an excursion." One such celebration of a new rail line will suffice—the arrival of the Baltimore & Ohio in Cincinnati in June 1857.[6]

> The trains began arriving at the station of the Little Miami Railroad at a little before one o'clock and were greeted by vast numbers of people. Not only the fire companies, but the militia were out, and there was a super abundance of band music. More speeches and then the entire party sweeping into great rotunda of Burns House, where there were still more speeches. It was esti- mated that twenty thousand came by rail from afar for the celebration; and the entertaining of them was no easy matter for the town.

Obviously the arrival of a new rail line by the 1850s was big news and a cause for celebration. But the railroads were facing more fundamental problems that brought them to adopt public relations programs. Early railway promoters and builders of necessity had extensive dealings with property owners, investors, and public authorities in the selection of routes and the raising of funds to build the lines. The investing public, still a bit skeptical, had to be persuaded of the worth of the new railroad. All these called for

---

[6]Edward Hungerford, *The Story of the Baltimore & Ohio Railroad* (Vol. 10). New York: G. P. Putnam's Sons, 1928, p. 309.

a public relations effort of a high order. Carlton J. Corliss recalled in a speech in 1956:[7] "Methods employed were mainly in the nature of personal contacts, pamphlets, newspaper articles, and railroad meetings and conventions which drew the most influential men of the day and often took on the fervor of old-fashioned revival meetings or political conventions." Another communications tool used early by the railroads was newspaper advertising.

But Alan Raucher insisted that much of their work was secret. He asserted:[8] "Railroads early in their history had begun efforts to win friends by hiring lobbyists and secret press agents. Offering passes for free transportation to reporters and editors, railroads had successfully influenced newspaper opinion during the nineteenth century." As early as 1880, *Railway Age*, a trade journal, established a Bureau of Information "for the purpose of educating the press, legislators and the public, as to the true relations of the railway interest to the public welfare." Because of the pressures to win routes, raise money, and generate freight and passenger traffic, most railroad executives were sensitive to influencing public opinion. For example, William K. Ackerman, president of Illinois Central, straightforwardly argued that increasing public attacks made it necessary for the railroads to "manufacture public opinion." Ackerman and Charles E. Perkins, vice-president of the Burlington line, cooperated in paying for favorable books and articles that would be published as supposedly independent analysis and scholarship. They also had their staff write articles for periodicals and give wide circulation to the executives' speeches. They and other railroads provided funds to send reprints of one favorable magazine article to 2,000 newspapers throughout the country and to 30,000 other influential individuals in the United States and abroad.[9] Perkins early on understood the two-step opinion process many practitioners would follow in the 20th century—"get the elite on your side and the rest will follow."

RAILROADS: PRINCIPAL PROMOTERS
OF THE MOVE WEST

The railroad executives and their staffs were experienced in the ways of public relations and promotion when free or cheap lands opened up beyond the Mississippi and thus were able to capitalize on this great opportunity to

[7]In speech to Fourth Annual Meeting of the Railroad Public Relations Association, French Lick, Indiana, June 14, 1956. In Library of American Association of Railroads, Washington, DC.

[8]*Public Relations and Business 1900–1929*. Baltimore: Johns Hopkins University Press, 1968, p. 33.

[9]Letter from Ackerman to a previous Illinois Central president, William Osburn, quoted in Marvin N. Olasky, "Origins of the Independent Agency Form," Corporate Issue Analysis series, March 27, 1980, p. 7.

expand and prosper. The railroads with lands to sell and legislation to influence, were the principal promoters of the Westward movement. Early in the 19th century as seekers of land grants and capital as well as settlers and tourists for their expanding lines, the railroads had learned the value of publicity.

When the Whigs came to power in 1841 after defeating the forces of Martin Van Buren and Amos Kendall, good land was available in the Mississippi Valley at $1.25 an acre in a time when much of the present Midwest was still unpopulated. Louisiana, Arkansas, and Missouri were relatively new states. Thus, there seemed to be little economic pressure for people to move on to a West largely unknown and thought to be mostly barren wasteland and peopled by hostile Indians. Yet, during the next decade nearly 100,000 Americans pushed to the Pacific's shores to settle California and Oregon. Billington concluded: "This miracle was the product of many forces, not the least of which was an effective publicity campaign which revealed how well its proponents gauged the popular psychology."[10] This migration was the product of many forces. This chapter focuses on one of those forces—the railroads' intense promotional programs to lure settlers and tourists to the West.

The nation's railroads, which beginning in the late 1840s, carried on a steady campaign of publicity and promotion to sell their government-given lands and thus generate freight and passenger revenues—an organized publicity effort that continued well into the 20th century. The railroads were confronted with public relations problems from the start. Canal and river carriers, stagecoach lines, and wagoners fought the coming of the railroads as the railroads later fought the highway truck and the airplane. Articles appeared in the press arguing against the need for railroads, recounting the perils involved in their operation, and prophesying that the new system of travel by steam would do away with the market for horses and put stage drivers out of work.

Railroads, along with the circuses and the patent medicine companies, were the first to use advertising. From 1830, when the columns of Baltimore newspapers carried Baltimore & Ohio train schedules, the daily and weekly press were used by the railroads as a means of reaching the public and encouraging it to travel by rail. The excursion was employed by railroads almost from the start to promote travel, to generate publicity, and to advertise the lands along their routes. The *American Railroad Journal* commented July 25, 1846: "The fashion of making 'excursions' is one of the novelties introduced by the modern facilities in traveling, they are perfectly in accordance with the genius of our people."

Guidebooks were a prime medium in the early campaigns to urge settlers westward. These guidebooks extravagantly proclaimed the opportunity for

---

[10]Billington, *Words That Won the West*, p. 6.

riches and adventure. Those stimulating the Gold Rush of 1849 minimized the investment needed to reach California, minimized the hardships of travel overland, and exaggerated the riches awaiting at the end of the journey. Most of them were shoddy pamphlets, a few pages in length, and cheaply printed. Many were unabashedly fraudulent. The guidebooks that were written to promote the Gold Rush of 1849 to Colorado were of better quality, a bit more honest. Billington said that these can be "categorized as 'Books That Won the West.' "[11]

THE GOLD RUSHES AND LAND PROMOTION ALSO PLAY A PART

The railroads were greatly aided in their promotions by the pioneer settlers who reached the slopes of the Pacific in the 1820s and 1830s. Their purpose was much the same as that which prompted John Filson to write of the glories of Kentucky a century earlier—to sell land and/or to sell goods to the arriving settlers. This was particularly true in the case of California, which was first boomed by John Marsh, who in 1836 established himself on a 50,000 acre ranch in the San Joaquin Valley, and John A. Sutter, a Swiss adventurer, who got a large land grant from Mexico in the Sacramento Valley. Billington said: "Both men were eager to attract settlers to their unpopulated lands; both wrote endless letters to Eastern newspapers that glorified the delights of California life and even detailed travel routes from the Mississippi Valley."

Or take a later example of such promotion: Charles Nordhoff, now employed by General Edward Fitzgerald Beale, a feudal lord in Southern California, wrote:[12] "To one who likes a free, outdoor life, I think nothing can be more delightful than the life of a farmer of sheep or cattle in Southern California. The weather is almost always fine; neither heat nor cold ever goes to extremes; you ride everywhere across the country, for there are no fences, game is abundant in season." Nordhoff was promoting Beale's land in Tejon country. By contrast, Oregon's first promoters were missionaries, determined to enlighten the spiritually starved—in their opinion—Indians. Both states were promoted by an increasing flow of letters to newspapers in the East, by books written by travelers, and articles sent to magazines such as the *Whig Review* and *Hunt's Merchants Magazine* boosting the West. "As this shower of words descended on the East the image of the Far West began to take shape in the minds of Americans that was compelling as it was attractive."[13]

---

[11]"Books That Won the West," *The American West*, 4, 1967, p. 25.
[12]Starr, pp. 26–27.
[13]Billington, *Words That Won the West*, p. 8.

News also played a powerful role in encouraging the westward movement. This was dramatically demonstrated in the story of the discovery of
gold in California. Gold was first discovered in the Sierra foothills on January
24, 1848, but the find created no excitement because it went unpublicized.
It was 2 months before a San Francisco newspaper casually reported this
momentous news, a story that caused some prospectors to set out in search
of riches. As late as April 1848, one San Francisco editor branded the growing
rumors of great wealth as "a fantastic a take-in as we ever got up to guzzle
the gullible."

The United States' historic Gold Rush didn't really get started until President Polk in his message to Congress on December 5, 1848, publicized and
authenticated the discovery at Sutter's Mill in an effort to justify his war
against Mexico. The United States' historic Gold Rush of 1849 followed—
spurred by an increasing band of promoters. Typical was Sam Brannan, a
Mormon landowner and merchant, who had a store near Sutter's Fort. To
promote his business, he took a quinine bottle filled with gold dust and
went to San Francisco where he ran through the streets waving his hat and
shouting at the top of his lungs, "Gold! Gold! Gold!" By the end of 1849, it
was estimated that California's population had increased by 100,000 persons.

The Colorado rush was first boomed when a trader washed out a sackful
of earth on the streets of Kansas City and got 25 cents of gold per panful.
Once again the press spread the news of easy riches to be had on West.
Guidebook authors were quick to seize on this new market in an effort to
lure the prospectors for Pike's Peak through a particular outfitting town.
"Every author tried to minimize the distance and exaggerate the case of his
favored route while magnifying the length and stressing the hardships of all
others." Many of these misleading guidebooks brought angry reactions when
their exaggerations and untruths were exposed through bitter experience.
Yet of these guidebooks then flooding populated areas, Fifer wrote:[14] "Guidebooks setting out to capture the spirit and purpose of this new age had to
bring the West into perspective. As well as being guides for the road, they
had also to be travel books in the old and best American tradition. The role
of the new Western guidebooks was thus to provide light and shade in the
great physical and mental transformation scene that marked the opening of
the West."

Frontier newspapers also were used to promote settlement to the west
in the United States. These pioneer editors had a vested interest in building
up their towns and lavishly extolled the virtues of their new territory. For
example, James M. Goodhue, publisher of the *Minnesota Pioneer*, first paper
published in Minnesota, wrote: "For producing wheat, oats, and potatoes,
Minnesota may safely challenge the world. Every word of this is true; but

---

[14]Fifer, p. 13.

not a newspaper in all New England or New York will copy it, for fear of turning the attention of people there to the free, fertile, healthful Northwest." Little wonder George Hage observed:[15] "The similarity of the frontier editor to the modern chamber of commerce did not stop with initiating good news of his or minimizing the bad," but also consisted of answering queries from prospective settlers in luring terms. Most editors on the edge of the frontier edited their papers as though Easterners were looking over their shoulders, and thus said nothing that would discourage migration.

RAILROADS MOVE STEADILY WEST

The railroads reached their first main objectives in the 1850s. Eastern lines were extended to the Ohio River and to the Great Lakes as the Erie, the Pennsylvania, the Grand Trunk, New York Central, and Baltimore & Ohio crossed the Appalachians. Similarly, lines extending westward from Chicago began to reach the Mississippi. Rail transportation was needed even more urgently in the Mid West and Far West where distances were great.

These sparsely populated lands, settled mostly by farmers, could not generate sufficient capital and revenues to make railroads financially feasible. This led to railroad-generated lobbying for government subsidy of railroad construction as public improvements. Westerners quickly responded to suggestions to pressure Congress and state legislatures for subsidies. Iowa was the only state in the first tier of states west of the Mississippi not to aid the railroads in any substantial fashion. "Starting with the Illinois Central grant of 1850 other states received similar gifts until all of the first tier of trans-Mississippi states had been aided, while other grants were made to specific important projects farther west. Texas made its own grants. The last of the railroad grants was made in the early '70s as a result of anti-railroad sentiment spurred by the Granger Movement."[16] The construction of railroads west of the Mississippi began in the 1850s. Albert Fishlow believed that the primary contribution of the railroad to growth before the Civil War was its inducement of the expansion of settlement and agriculture. The railroads' success depended on early settlement of their lands by an industrious population and by the establishment of cities with industries.

Most of these Western railroads launched widespread publicity campaigns to make known the agricultural and industrial advantages of their particular territories. One land-grant railroad built up a staff of 30 persons to prepare and distribute advertisements, pamphlets, newspaper stories, and magazine

---

[15]George Hage, *Newspapers on the Minnesota Frontier 1849–1860*. St. Paul, MN: Minnesota Historical Society, 1967, p. 12.

[16]Robert Riegel, *America Moves West*. New York: Holt, 1930, p. 431.

articles to sing the praises of the resources of their lands. This promotional pattern was utilized by nearly every large railroad that received a federal land grant as they pushed Westward. Many extended these campaigns to Western Europe.

By one of the most extensive advertising campaigns in railway history, James J. Hill, the "Empire Builder," made his Great Northern Railroad a household word throughout the world. He advertised in newspapers, magazines, on billboards, in circulars, and in other ways. When he gave a blooded bull to every big farmer in Montana to promote high-grade cattle production, the press carried the story around the world. Hill was a big and persistent advertiser.[17]

BURLINGTON CAMPAIGN FASHIONS MODEL CAMPAIGN

Illustrative of the role railroad publicity programs played in the settlement and development of the Mid West and West is the story of the Burlington Railroad. Between 1852 and 1864 the Burlington system received more than 3,500,000 acres of public land from the federal government to promote railroad construction and development of the West. To encourage settlement on this land, mainly in Iowa and Nebraska, the Burlington developed a promotion program as intensive and costly as many of today's promotional ventures. The cost of advertising and "similar expenses" for the Burlington's Iowa and Nebraska lands was placed at $969,500 by a Burlington official in the 1880s.[18]

The Burlington system was put together between 1852 and 1856 by a group of Boston financiers. Its promotional program was initiated by President Edward Baker, headquartered in Boston, and by his right-hand man in Iowa, Charles Russell Lowell. Lowell, nephew of the famous poet, was appointed assistant treasurer and land agent for the Burlington in 1858, shortly after graduating from Harvard at the head of his class. He arrived at the railroad's headquarters in Burlington, Iowa, on a hot, sultry day in August of that year. A week later, the local weekly, the *Hawk-Eye*, advised Lowell "the first and greatest want of immigrants is cheap lands and not railroads." Early in October, President Baker wrote Lowell that the time had come to prepare a pamphlet of some 10 to 20 pages "cracking up Iowa." He suggested to Lowell that it be something like those already being issued by the Illinois Central and the Hannibal and St. Joseph, only on a smaller scale. As earlier indicated, the Illinois Central, starting in the early 1850s, was the first railroad to embark on a large-scale promotion program.

---

[17]Paraphrased from Carlton J. Corliss.

[18]C. J. Ernst, "The Railroad as a Creator of Wealth in the Development of a Community," *Nebraska History and Record of Pioneer Days, 7, 1924,* p. 20.

Lowell took to his task with alacrity. He wrote to various friends and farmers in Iowa for information on crops, climate, and other facts about the area. As he wrote one friend, Charles Mason, a year later: "We are beginning to find that he who buildeth a railroad west of the Mississippi must also find a population and build up business. We wish to blow as loud a trumpet as the merits of our position warrants."[19]

The Illinois Central and Hannibal and St. Joseph programs, to which Baker had referred, provided both guidance and an incentive of the Burlington promotion. As Lowell noted in a letter November 2, 1859: "It is by giving wide circulation to facts & suggestions of this sort that the Illinois Central Railroad has turned so much of the emigration to that state: we wish to trumpet the prairies of southern Iowa, & we think we have as great or greater advantages & inducements to offer, but we must have our facts from the old settlers."[20] The Hannibal and St. Joseph, in northern Missouri, was already putting into effect the type of advertising Lowell had in mind. Late in 1859, there appeared a 60-page booklet booming that company's 600,000 acres and providing useful information for the prospective settler. A full-page map showed the country's main trunk lines, a smaller map of Northern Missouri showed the location of the land grant. The pamphlet was enlivened by several lithographs showing a Missouri farmer's home, typical landscapes, and the cities of Hannibal and St. Joseph. The format of this pamphlet followed closely the earlier one put out by Illinois Central. Lowell in his Burlington pamphlet tried to improve on both.

Simultaneously Lowell worked to build a good community relationships for the railroad in Burlington and to cultivate goodwill among the Iowa farmers. Lowell wrote one agent: "Keep it constantly before the farmers that we are a *railroad* company & not a *land* company—that settlers are more important to us than a high price for our land."[21] In October 1860, Lowell resigned to take a job in Maryland and his assistant, Charles E. Perkins, took over the task. Perkins, who held this position until 1866, eventually rose to the presidency in 1881. During the Perkins' years as land agent, the Burlington attempted to sell only small sections of land. The company did not launch any publicity of its own but supported other projects advertising Iowa and Nebraska. In 1864, the Burlington received its biggest grant— 2½ million acres in eastern Nebraska. This generated a renewed and much more intensive promotional effort 2 years later.

Then, 1866, Perkins was named chief officer of the Burlington and Missouri in Iowa, and Colonel J. W. Ames took over the land department. Three years later, Ames and A. E. Touzalin, general ticket agent in Iowa, produced

---

[19]Richard C. Overton, *Burlington West*. Cambridge, MA: Harvard University Press, 1941, pp. 153–159.

[20]*Ibid.* p. 161.

[21]*Ibid.* p. 150.

the Burlington and Missouri's first publicity news sheet. Called the *Southern Iowa Land and Railroad Gazette,* the paper boomed 75,000 acres of land near Des Moines in a candid and informative manner. More than 15,000 copies were distributed. Articles included information on farming, churches, schools, climate, history, and prices. Results of this broadside were termed "prompt and gratifying." Ames did much to build goodwill for the company among government officials, settlers, and land agents. But in November, 1869, he quit when it became apparent to him that the railroad's directors had tired of his lack of initiative. Overton summed up the conflict:[22] "Conscientious, courteous, and unimaginative, he [Ames] had felt that his most important task was to preserve and build up goodwill. . . . The confidence born of this policy was . . . invaluable. On the other hand, his haphazard pricing policy and his lack of initiative would have been a serious handicap when the time came for the company to sell the bulk of its grants."

That time was at hand, and to direct the campaign the directors brought in George S. Harris, head of the Hannibal and St. Joseph land department. Harris had a monumental task ahead of him, because he would be in charge of more than 250 land agents, direct European and U.S. advertising campaigns, develop agricultural programs to make the lands productive of freight revenues, and all the myriad of problems involved in promoting settlement of 3 million acres of land. A few weeks later, Harris hired J. D. Butler, a native of Wisconsin who was well known as a lecturer, world traveler, and newspaper correspondent, to be "advertising correspondent" for the Burlington lands in Nebraska and Iowa. His salary was set at $2,500 per annum. As with many publicists of that day—and this—Butler's connection with the company was to be kept secret. Approving Butler's continuing his public lectures while on the Burlington payroll, Harris wrote:[23] "This will not injure but rather help your usefulness to the B. & M. RR's Land Dept. by giving yourself and them a profitable notoriety, as you will of course tuck in Iowa & Nebraska Lands in such a way as to advertise them, & people not know the motives, either in lecture rooms or in the columns of the numerous periodicals to which you gain access."

In explaining this arrangement to President Brooks of the firm, Harris said that his idea was to popularize Iowa and Nebraska lands through Butler's widely published "entertaining and practical letters," and by means of "well-concocted circulars, posters & a judicious amount of advertising," which he was certain, would produce a "big stampede of immigrants for these favored lands."

Butler's colorful prose, on the platform and in the press, quickly focused on the West, particularly Iowa and Nebraska. Though his accuracy might

---

[22]*Ibid.* p. 271.
[23]*Ibid.* p. 299.

be questioned, his letters and pamphlets made interesting reading. In one of his pamphlets, he wrote of the United States: "It is latitudinarian that it is said to be bounded on the north by the aurora borealis and on the south by the Day of Judgment." In the same pamphlet, he wrote that those who tried to stop westward migration fared as King Canute when he "forbade the billows of the advancing tide to wet his sacred feet."

Harris knew better than Butler the value of unvarnished practical information. He wrote the "professor," as Butler was called:[24] "I . . . deem it very important for you to spend enough time in Iowa (and Nebraska too by & by) to become thoroughly posted in all items of local interest by seeing the country with your own eyes & coming in personal contact with Tom, Dick, and Harry and learning to word-paint current moving interests better than you can by reading all the books, pamphlets, & papers published. . . . Besides, there will be [more] . . . freshness, originality, vigor and snap to your plain Anglo-Saxon words than can be possible if you quote all the finest things said or written by the best authors."

Burlington officials decided that the first large block of land, 300,000 acres, would be put on sale April 1, 1870. Thus by the end of March, the promotion campaign was under full steam. Hundreds of thousands of advertising pamphlets printed in English, German, French, Welsh, Bohemian, Norwegian, and Swedish were circulated in the East and abroad, distributed mainly through the ocean transportation companies. Land offices were opened in England, Scotland, Sweden, Germany, and most of the Eastern states in the United States.[25] Harris and other Burlington officials looked to Europe, and particularly Great Britain, as an important source of settlers for their Iowa lands. Many promotion and publicity schemes were undertaken to lure Europeans to these Midwest lands.

Butler used letters to the editor that Cornelius Schaller, Burlington's European representative, successfully planted in British papers. Schaller arranged for rooms in Liverpool for whole boat loads of emigrants who paid for their night's lodging by attending a meeting where they heard sung the glories of Iowa and Nebraska. Harris and Butler placed most of their promotional chips on pamphlets widely distributed in Europe and in the Eastern United States. These pamphlets not only provided basic information on the territory but also featured success stories of European settlers who found their fortunes in Iowa and Nebraska—for example the story of Jonas Sugden, a Yorkshire mechanic who acquired a prairie farm, orchard, and honey business in Nebraska in less than 3 years.[26] By 1872, the railroad has spent nearly a half million dollars on European immigration.

---

[24]*Ibid.* p. 299.

[25]Richard C. Overton, *Milepost 100*, Burlington Railroad pamphlet, 1949, p. 47.

[26]*Nebraska, Burlington and Missouri Railroad Lines*, Burlington pamphlet, 1878. In Archives of the State Historical Society of Wisconsin, Madison.

Based on his experience in Hannibal, Harris had great faith in the power of pamphlets, and "since they were to carry complete information, he saw no reason for long and involved columns of expensive newspaper advertisements such as the Illinois Central had used. He preferred rather very brief notices merely stating that the pamphlets were available to anyone interested; such squibs had brought hundreds of inquiries a day to the Hannibal and St. Joseph."[27] In addition to pamphlets, the Burlington used bulletin boards, car posters, handbills, and circulars. These, like the newspaper items, carried only headline information designed to arouse interest in obtaining the pamphlet.

Burlington's publicists used no opinion survey techniques, but they were keenly aware of popular stereotypes. One of these was the notion that land west of the Missouri was part of "The Great American Desert." To combat this impression, the Burlington spent vast sums on agricultural development programs and in displaying Nebraska crop samples to prospective settlers. One of Professor Butler's pamphlets argued emphatically that Nebraska was not a desert and that Nebraska soil was even better than Iowa or Illinois soil.

Another unfavorable image that Butler and other Burlington publicists fought was that of Nebraska and Iowa as primitive and uncultured areas. Burlington's promotional literature stressed the area's educational facilities, churches and its many "cultured citizens." One of the early Burlington news sheets said:[28] "Come from where you may, you will find Nebraskans who have traveled as far as you—and those no whit your inferiors in culture, gained either in schools or in the discipline of adventurous lives, men who will prove your match on any arena where you meet them." Harris also worked hard to encourage education in this Burlington territory. Burlington advertising and pamphlets also tried to discourage the opinion that the West was only for farmers. Mechanics, shopkeepers, and single women got special appeals. The news sheet quoted above also carried this line: "When a daughter of the east is once beyond the Missouri, she rarely recrosses it except on a bridal tour."

Harris was not only concerned with luring settlers in the early 1870s; he worked equally hard to maintain the goodwill of the settlers already in Iowa and Nebraska. These efforts included sidetracking a coach each Sunday at various towns for use as a chapel, carrying seed and various possessions of settlers free of charge, and seeking the friendship of Iowa and Nebraska weekly editors. When the Burlington introduced a new dining car, "the flying dining palace St. Charles," in September 1872, editors from Omaha and Council Bluffs were invited for a lavish dinner and drinks, followed by free Havana cigars. The Omaha *Bee*, in its September 2, 1872, issue said: "The 'Favorite Route East' will never be forgotten by us. Travelers would hardly

---

[27]Overton, *Burlington West*, pp. 300–301.

[28]*Railroad Lands in Southern Iowa and Nebraska*, Burlington news sheet, 1870. In Archives of State Historical Society of Wisconsin.

think that they were taking their meals while going at the rate of 25 miles an hour."

In the same year, the Burlington helped some Nebraskans get through the winter by hauling 700 pounds of pork and two tons of meal to Harvard to be distributed to needy families free of freight charge and with payments deferred until later. The Burlington constantly endeavored to identify its interests with the region's interests. To counteract the scarcity of timber, the Burlington planted 560,000 trees along 120 miles of right-of-way in 1872 and 1873—a project that brought much praise in the press. "It is not to be supposed that railroad companies surpass all men in disinterested benevolence, but it is beyond question that they know their own interest and so will take some pains to help you earn a dollar whenever they can, and thus make two for themselves."[29]

Throughout the early 1870s, Burlington press releases and Professor Butler's "entertaining and practical letters" continued to pour into newspaper offices. News releases from Harris were accompanied by this notice:[30] "As the matter is one in which we are all materially interested, will you give the notice one or two insertions and oblige." Generally the editors obliged. Sometimes Butler's long literary efforts would anger an editor. For example, in April, 1872, the Ashland, NE, *Times* admitted that the Burlington was "the best line in the West," but said of Butler: "The truth is a certain literary deadbeat, who like the rest of his species is barefooted on top where his brains ought to be and wears sandstone goggles to keep him from seeing anything useful, . . . this peripatetic old sardine, one Prof. Butler, spends his time riding on the road on a free pass and annoying the press with effete details of his wandering jew excursions. We've got a stack of his truck over 14 feet high."

Despite such criticisms, Butler continued writing his letters and traveling through Iowa and Nebraska. One of his other duties included organizing trips to the area for newsmen and other interested parties from the East. In June 1871, he arranged an "Indiana Editorial Excursion" for newsmen from 16 towns to tour the Burlington and Missouri lands. The trip resulted in a great deal of free publicity in Indiana papers, and it was probably no coincidence that a group of Indiana businessmen bought $25,000 worth of land near Lincoln a month later.

BURLINGTON USES 'UNOFFICIAL' SPOKESMEN

Harris also saw the value of using testimonials from "unofficial spokesmen" to praise the railroad with an air of objectivity and the use of settlers' personal success stories. One of the unofficial spokesmen was a Rev. Darius Jones,

---

[29]*Ibid.*

[30]Overton, *Burlington West*, p. 370.

who helped establish colonies and who sent letters to papers around the country, citing success stories and defending Burlington policies. The personal success stories in one pamphlet included those of a man who had made a fortune of $10,000 in 7 years, and the story of "Edward Jones whose Nebraska farm had paid for itself by its produce during the first year."[31]

Butler tells of similar success stories in his pamphlets. In an 1877 pamphlet, for example, he tells of a Mr. Hoover who "being 68 years old when he came into the country from Ohio in 1873, thought best to buy a farm near the station already improved by a pre-emptor. He reckons it today worth 4-fold what he paid for it." Success stories also appeared in letters written by Burlington settlers to hometown papers. It seems quite likely that at least some were inspired by Burlington's agents. Most praised the Burlington's land policy in some way.

Another promotional medium used by the Burlington was the handbill, which could be printed quickly to communicate the latest land information, offer special inducements, or combat a current criticism. Some of the special inducements offered in these circulars were free room and board for families on their way to new land, free transportation for purchasers and for their domestic goods, and 10 years' credit or a 20% discount for cash for the land purchase. Some of these handbills overflowed with superlatives, for example: "This road has the best crops, best settlers, best lands, most successful farmers, and offers longest credits, lowest interest, and cheapest fare and freights." Despite such occasional exaggerations, most of the Burlington pamphlets and advertisements were fairly objective. Much helpful information, such as guidance on agriculture, was disseminated through these media. Many of the news sheets and pamphlets candidly warned settlers not to go West without enough capital for emergencies and supplies—a contrast to the fraudulent promotions of the California and Colorado gold rushes.

The financial panic of 1873 brought Burlington's land sales to a near halt for the next 4 years. There was a corresponding drop in westward migration. Early in 1874, Harris resigned his post because of ill health. A few months later, the job was given to E. A. Touzalin, who had helped Colonel Ames publish Burlington's first news sheet in 1869. In the late 1870s, Burlington's pamphlets showed a renewed sense of excitement about westward migration. A 31-page Butler pamphlet printed in 1877 describes the growth of the region the past few years and says:[32] "Among a millon and a half acres of Burlington and Missouri lands, no farm is now removed a full mile from lands on which some settler has erected his dwelling." This renewed spirit of promotion in the late 1870s sold much land. From 1870 to 1880, the

---

[31] *Views and Descriptions of Burlington and Missouri Railroad Lands*, Burlington pamphlet, 1872. In Archives of the State Historical Society of Wisconsin.

[32] J. D. Butler, *A September Scamper*, Burlington pamphlet, 1877. In Archives of the State Historical Society of Wisconsin.

Burlington disposed of over three fourths of its Iowa and Nebraska grants by selling some 2 million acres to more than 20,000 buyers.[33] The settlement of the West is more than a story of adventure, gold rushes, and railroads; it is also the story of some of our earliest public relations and promotional campaigns. The Burlington story is one of these.

NORTHERN PACIFIC PROMOTES
THE "WHOOP UP COUNTRY"

Settlement of Minnesota and states along the Canadian Border, the "whoop-up country," was first promoted by an old hand at such things—Jay Cooke, and by the Northern Pacific (NP) Railroad. Cooke, a noted Philadelphia banker, had earlier promoted the Union's war-bond drives with spectacular results. The Northern Pacific was chartered in 1864 but did not begin construction until Cooke came into the enterprise in 1869. The NP's first section track—229 miles across Minnesota—was completed in 1871. The year before, Cooke told an immigration convention in Indianapolis that it was the purpose of the Northern Pacific "to promote, so far as possible, immigration by colonies, so that neighbors in Fatherland may be neighbors in the new West."

In the early 1870s, competition for settlers became quite keen. The NP hired John S. Loomis from the Kansas Pacific railroad to head its land committee. In February 1871, Loomis submitted a plan that contained detailed suggestions for the promotion of immigration to NP's lands, a plan largely built on the successful efforts of the railroads in the Midwest. Under Loomis' plan, the NP organized a land department to sell its government grant lands and an emigration department to speed settlement of them. The departments started work early in 1872 and worked aggressively at the task until 1874 when sales and migration ground to a halt as the result of the Panic of 1873, a financial crisis brought on by the failure of the Jay Cooke firm. He lost control of the NP in his fall. NP resumed its promotional efforts in 1879.

Unlike the Burlington, Cooke and his Northern Pacific associates concentrated more on colonization than on the sale of land to individual settlers through publicity and advertising. The colonies took promotion nonetheless. Maps and pamphlets descriptive of the railroad and the lands along its route were published in many languages for distribution in the East and in Europe. "Friendly business relations were to be maintained with the U.S. and European press, and every effort was to be made to enlist the sympathy and active support, not only of professional and public men, but also of humane and benevolent societies and religious organizations of both continents, in the work of settling the lands of the Northern Pacific country."[34]

---

[33]Overton, *Milepost 100*, p. 49.

[34]James B. Hedges, "The Colonization Work of the Northern Pacific Railroad," *Mississippi Valley Historical Review, 13*, 1926, p. 325.

One of the first Northern Pacific colonies to be promoted was that at Detroit Lake planned for veterans of the Civil War. In 1871, the NP organized a bureau of immigration for soldiers and sailors in the wake of a Congressional act granting homesteads to veterans. In November, 1871, this bureau, headquartered in New York, issued a pamphlet suggesting organization of colonies. It urged such colonies to send committees "to secure the most favorable locations" before migration started. The railroad offered to provide transportation at reduced rates, to build reception houses, and to sell building materials at wholesale rates. The NP further aided these colony organizations by assisting with their promotion.[35] George B. Hibbard headed the bureau. By December 1871, the NP was promoting the Detroit Lake settlement by sending printed matter to all post commanders of the New England Bureau of Migration in Massachusetts and by running one-inch ads in a number of weekly papers for 4 weeks. "The New England Bureau of Migration continued to spread information about the colony through the winter of 1874."[36]

Another such enterprise was the Red River colony settled at Glyndon, Minnesota. This one was promoted by L. H. Tenney and D. R. Haynes of the Northwestern Land Agency of Duluth, Minnesota, under a contract with the NP. The railroad agreed to help promote sale of the land and to advertise the colony. By the middle of March, 1873, the land firm was engaged in an extensive advertising campaign, an effort that was producing some 30 to 40 queries a day at its peak. The promoters published the *Red River Gazette* and distributed this paper throughout the East. Tenney and his associates also used paid newspaper space. Ads were published in newspapers in New York, Boston, Chicago, Cincinnati, Hartford, Toledo, St. Louis, and Philadelphia. Ads were also placed in some 850 weekly papers and in two Swedish papers. Soon a newspaper was started at Glyndon, and its columns were used to sing the glories of the community. The promoters asked the NP to buy 100 copies a week for distribution in the East. Simultaneously the railroad was working to advertise the Minnesota territory here and abroad. "The advertising material published . . . was for the most part, a rather bare statement of facts and figures. At the same time there was enough of the advertiser's license in some of the statements. To the climate of Minnesota and Montana was ascribed, the power of healing almost any malady.[37] But the railroad did not rely solely on its promotional advertising. It established a general European agency in London with branch agencies in Liverpool, in Germany, Holland, and the Scandinavian countries. Special agents were

---

[35]George B. Hibbard, *Land Department of the Northern Pacific Railroad Company*, Bureau of Immigration for Soldiers and Sailors. New York, 1871.

[36]Harold F. Peterson, "Some Colonization Projects of the Northern Pacific Railroad," *Minnesota History, 10*, 1929, p. 135.

[37]Hedges, p. 315.

often sent abroad to recruit settlers. With them went pamphlets, circulars, and folders to promote the attractions of the "New Northwest."

Typical is a pamphlet, *Guide to the Lands of the Northern Pacific railroad in Minnesota*, published in 1872 to promote the one million acres of NP lands surveyed and ready for sale. The basic appeals were the fertility of the soil, the cheapness of land, and low transportation rates made possible by the Northern Pacific's connection to the Great Lakes. This one reads:

> The Boston colonists who are rearing their homes on the shores of beautiful Detroit Lake in Minnesota can ship their grain to market at as low rates as the farmers who live in Dubuque, 188 miles from Chicago. The colonists who have settled in the Red River Valley are receiving as much per bushel for their wheat as the farmers around Davenport, the largest city of Iowa. With cheap transportation, with soil as fertile as the most favored sections of the Western state there must be a corresponding increase in the value of land, and the settler who secures a farm of 160 acres now may be sure of an advance of several hundred per cent for his investment a few years hence.[38]

In this same period, the Chicago and Northwestern Railroad was promoting the sale of a million acres of land in Southern Minnesota, along the route of the Winona and St. Peter Railroad with the same methods, same appeals, same adjectives. A *Guide to an Unsurpassed Farming Region in Southern Minnesota and Eastern Dakota* proclaimed:[39] "The Winona & St. Peter Railroad Company now offers to all persons who wish to obtain cheap and productive farms in a healthful and beautiful country, a selection from more than one million . . . acres of the best located and most fertile lands in the midwest."

As indicated earlier, missionaries were the first to promote settlement in the Oregon country. In the 1860s, the mineral wealth of Montana and Idaho became known, and there was a rush of population to the land east of the Cascades. To counter this loss of population—and customers—Portland, in 1869, created a Board of Statistics, Immigration, and Labor Exchange. Little came of this effort. In 1874, a State Board of Immigration was organized that was supported, not by state funds, but by funds donated by Portland businessmen. This board sent out agents, issued publicity, and answered queries about the advantages of life in Oregon. Its efforts did not prove fruitful and here "as in some other sections of the country, local efforts toward stimulating immigration yielded to the superior efficiency of the railroads."[40]

---

[38]In Archives of the State Historical Society of Wisconsin.

[39]*Guide to an Unsurpassed Farming Region in Southern Minnesota and Eastern Dakota.* Archives of the State Historical Society of Wisconsin. Undated.

[40]James B. Hedges, "Promotion of Immigration to the Pacific Northwest by the Railroads," *Mississippi Valley Historical Review, 15,* 1928, p. 184.

Henry Villard, first sent to the Northwest by German bondholders in an effort to salvage the Oregon and California Railroad, was the prime promoter of the Northwest in the 1870s and early 1880s, first to promote the Oregon–California line, later the Northern Pacific. Villard secretly obtained control of the Northern Pacific in 1881 and from then until 1883, he headed all transportation companies in the Pacific Northwest. In 1874, he directed the Oregon and California Railroad to open a land office in Portland to promote sale of railroad grant lands. To lure settlers to the Northwest, two immigration bureaus were established, one in Portland and one in Boston. Boston was selected because it was an important port city and farming in that area was proving unprofitable. The Boston NP bureau became, in fact, the eastern bureau of the Oregon State Board of Immigration. These immigration agencies were soon provided with a variety of printed material boosting the scenic and agricultural riches of the Oregon country. Late in the first year of this promotional campaign two additional bureaus were established—one in Omaha and one in Topeka—in an effort to divert westward migration from California to the Northwest.

Hedges described the promotional efforts this way:[41] A booklet presenting the popular form the physiographic, agricultural, commercial, and industrial features of the Northwest Coast, was printed in English and was accompanied by a short circular designed for a more extended circulation. Brief reading notices were inserted in the more influential English, German, Norwegian, and Swedish newspapers. Samples and specimens of products of the Northwest were secured for display at the bureaus. . . . Within a short time inquiries from German and Scandinavian sources, prompted by newspaper advertisements, became so numerous that the printing of the booklet in those languages became necessary. The work of the Boston bureau grew so rapidly as to require an increase in the personnel and budget.

The basic promotional document in these campaigns to promote settlement in the West was the guidebook, usually longer on adjectives than on facts. Illustrative is the *Northern Pacific Guidebook* that Villard directed be prepared shortly after he got control of the NP. Another *Guidebook and itinerary for the use of tourists and travellers over the lines of the Northern Pacific Railroad*, was written by Henry J. Wisner and published in 1883 by G. P. Putnam's Sons. Typical prose found in such promotional books: "The Great Northwest has already become famous for the prodigality of its cereal productions; the salubrity of its climate is an accepted fact; the extent and variety of its mineral deposits and the value of its grant forests are everywhere acknowledged, while the marked diversity and extraordinary attraction of its scenery are recognized as not the least prominent of its features."

---

[41]*Ibid.* p. 186.

The Wisner-written guidebook comprehensively covered the NP line from Wisconsin to the Northwest. It was liberally illustrated with sketches by A. von Schilling and by photographs by F. Jay Haynes and others. Also illustrative is a pamphlet on *The Climate, Soil and Resources of the Yellowstone Valley* which the Northern Pacific published in 1882 and distributed in large numbers to promote both tourist excursions and settlement in Montana territory. These promotional efforts were highly productive if one takes their contents at face value. In the Yellowstone pamphlet, we read that the foreign immigration "has recently grown to such unheard-of proportions that now every few months time throws upon our shores a swarm of people which is sufficient to thickly populate a new state." Beneath the purple prose was the appeal to self-betterment by urging Easterners to move to "the newly opened regions where public lands lay for the taking." These pamphlets and the publicity hammered away in the effort to create "this restless desire for new and more prosperous homes—for better surroundings in which to struggle for competence and fortune."[42] Yet a prefatory note in the Yellowstone pamphlet insists: "What follows presents a fair and unexaggerated account of the Yellowstone country." Have not promoters always spoken thus?

Encouraged by the results obtained in the promotional campaign in 1875, the Oregon and California stepped up its publicity program the next year. In addition to distribution of pamphlets, circulars, advertising in newspapers, and maintenance of a large flow of correspondence, the immigration department sent a special representative to the Philadelphia Centennial Exposition in 1876. A total of $24,000 was spent in the Portland and Boston offices in 1876, but no material increase in immigration resulted. Those in charge explained that this was due to "the quite unusually bad weather that afflicted our country principally in winter and spring." The next year, bad weather hit the crops in the rival territory of California, and Villard's executives quickly directed publicity to those settlers. Advertising was placed in several California papers touting the climate and soil of Oregon. Assessment of the effects of publicity campaigns was even more difficult then than it is today. Hedges admitted that accurate estimates on the number of settlers attracted to the Northwest by this promotional campaign is not possible but logically concluded that these "efforts gave a powerful impetus to the ultimate development of the Northwest."

UNION PACIFIC CREATES
A TRANSCONTINENTAL NATION

As railroads slowly extended westward in the 1840s and 1850s men began to dream of a railroad linking the Pacific Ocean to the Atlantic seaboard. Congress, though preoccupied with the grim problems of the Civil War, in

---

[42]In Archives of the State Historical Society of Wisconsin. Undated.

June 1862, passed the Pacific Railroad Act to create the Union Pacific (UP) Railroad and finance its construction with land grants and loans. The big dreamer and prime promoter of the legislation was Theodore Judah of the Central Pacific (CP) Railroad who envisioned the UP linking up with the CP to create a continental rail bond for the nation. Judah, who gave the best years of his life to this dream, was squeezed out by the financial tycoons before the UP became a reality. He was no match for Collis P. Huntington and his crowd. President Lincoln signed the bill July 1, 1862, and construction began late the next year. The historic legislation went little reported in the press of the day, smothered by the more dramatic news of war.

The Union Pacific's controlling group were wise in the ways of promotion as well as shrewd in the ways of finance. The UP was started with a public relations flourish in a ground-breaking ceremony at Omaha December 2, 1863. The territorial governor of Nebraska turned the first shovelful of earth, Lincoln telegraphed his good wishes, and there was oratory aplenty. McCague suggested "The affair . . . did not differ markedly from the Central Pacific's ground-breaking almost a year earlier" at Sacramento. The modest celebration that followed used up all the company's money and no construction was undertaken in almost a year. The ground breaking, too, went virtually unnoticed in the nation's press. UP's next chance to celebrate came when its track reached the hundredth meridian—set forth in the Congressional Act—in October 1866, a year ahead of the government's requirements.

The milestone was celebrated with the Great Pacific Railway Excursion, carried out with all the fanfare of a present-day airline junket. Described at the time by a *New York Times* writer as a "novel undertaking," the excursion was widely publicized in the newspapers of New York, Chicago, and other major cities beforehand as "celebrating the attainment of the 100th meridian, at the 247 mile post, in 182 working days." The railroad invited 100 or so VIPs. President Andrew Johnson and his cabinet, the ambassador of every important foreign country, high Army and Navy officers, and leading capitalists and railroad executives. The President sent his regrets. The main party started from New York October 15 and was joined at Chicago with another group. The combined party was then split into two groups that took different routes to Omaha, one finishing the trip by stage, the other by steamer. Omaha gave the guests a great ball and a tour to emphasize the growth of this onetime frontier town. The Omaha *Herald* reported with pride that the excursionists expressed amazement at finding themselves "after a week's journeying westward from New York, still among people of wealth, refinement, and enterprise." Tuesday, October 23, the UP's guests, now totaling 200, left Omaha on a special bunting-bedecked train to travel along the new rail line. The special train carried two bands and a "refreshment saloon." *The Railway Pioneer*, a newspaper, was especially issued by UP's promoters to chronicle this gala occasion. Many publishers, including Joseph Medill of

Chicago, and correspondents were included, thus assuring UP of considerable publicity.[43] Wrote one reporter of UP:[44] "No railroad excursion of similar character and magnitude had ever been projected in this, or any other country; and the parties most interested were, of course, untiring in their efforts to make it a complete success."

PUBLICITY SETTLES THE WEST

As the railroad neared completion, its managers decided to publicize this fact by setting another excursion, this one for the press exclusively. This junket was staged by Peaslee and Company, advertising agents for the road. On July 14, 1868, a party of "editorial gentlemen" left New York City for a tour over the UP's line. Included were newsmen from New York, Boston, Philadelphia, Baltimore, Pittsburgh, and Chicago. Charles Dana of the New York *Sun* was in the group. Once more Omaha generously entertained the UP's excursion group, and there the reporters were told the line would be completed to Salt Lake by January 1, 1869. The trip on to the end of the UP's track brought a "full measure of commendation" and made the Union Pacific "very real" through the pens of these newsmen. To assure these desired results, "Peaslee and Company had been hired to see to it that the men had a good time on the tour."[45]

The excursion had become a standard item in railroad promotion and in building passenger revenues. Newsmen taken on these excursions waxed eloquent with their praise and induced others "brought to curiosity's edge," to follow. Noted Springfield editor Samuel Bowles, after a railroad junket in 1869, wrote:[46] "We fear the early travellers by the new pathway of iron will be appalled by the variety of entertainment to which we here invite them. But if they start with the protest that we have promised too much, they will return with the confession that half was not told to them." Important leaders in Eastern and Midwestern communities were taken on these excursions as guests, the UP knowing that their letters and their tales upon their return home would promote travel and migration. Typical is a letter of July 26, 1869, by Lucien Hanks of Madison, WI, written from Salt Lake City. Hanks wrote that he was one of a list of persons who had received free passes from the UP and that "we have special car of Pullman's palace coaches

---

[43]For full account, see James McCague, *Moguls and Iron Men*. New York: Harper & Row, 1964, pp. 131–136.

[44]Silas Seymour, *Incidents of a Trip Through the Great Platte Valley to the Rocky Mountains and Laramie Plains*. New York: van Nostrand, 1867, p. 73.

[45]Levi O. Leonard and Jack T. Johnson, *A Railroad to the Sea*. Iowa City, 1939, p. 180.

[46]*The Pacific Railroad Open*. Boston: Fields, Osgood, 1869, p. 116.

which roll over the road like a boat upon water," adding "Eating stations furnishing good meals and well cooked along the entire route."[47]

Completion of the Union Pacific called for another flamboyantly staged event—the driving of the Golden Spike May 10, 1869, near Ogden, Utah, linking the Union and Central Pacific lines to make the United States a continental nation. Special trains brought the owners, executives, and a host of VIPs from each line to Promontory Point, where the lines were linked. A Union Pacific news release described its train as "the most elegant in equipment with the largest number of passengers ever to travel over the UP." One observer recorded that "there were lots of newspapermen and plenty of champagne there for the occasion." The Ogden train brought a band from that city newly equipped with instruments costing $1,200. McCague said there were some 20 or more correspondents present, including reporters from California, New York, Omaha, Springfield, MA, Chicago, and from the Associated Press. Flashing of the news bulletin at 2:27 p.m., Eastern Time, set off excitement and celebration across the land. This time Union Pacific news did not go unnoticed. Executives wise in the ways of publicity saw to that. One participant, Alexander Toponce, recalled "I do not remember what any of the speakers said now, but I do remember that there was a great abundance of champagne."

GEORGE A. CROFUTT ANOTHER PIONEER PUBLICIST

George Andrews Crofutt, was another of those pioneering promoters of the Westward Movement. Fifer described him as "one of the most prolific and widely-read authors on the American West in the last half of the nineteenth century." He wrote countless guidebooks and published a periodical, *Crofutt's Western World.* He was born in Danbury, CT, in 1827. In his youth, he left that small town to seek opportunities first in New York City, then in Philadelphia as an editor, publisher, and advertising agent. Crofutt was bankrupted by the Financial Panic of 1857, so he joined the Gold Rush to Pike's Peak, reaching Colorado in 1860. In Fifer's words, "Crofutt found no gold, instead discovered the West." For the next 10 years, he became a long-haul freighter and then turned to his role as publicist and editor of guidebooks. It was the Great Event at Promontory, UT, that brought Crofutt back to his first love, journalism. He called the Gold Spike ceremony "the most thrilling scene he had ever witnessed."

During the next 25 years, he promoted the West through his guidebooks, his periodical, extensive correspondence with prospective settlers, and his personal contacts with editors, railroad agents, and publishers. In Fifer's

---

[47]In *Lucien Hanks Papers,* State Historical Society of Wisconsin, Madison.

judgment, Crofutt did much "to satisfy the huge demand for reliable information about the West." She continued:[48] "It was largely as a result of Crofutt's efforts that the word *transcontinental* was suddenly and widely adopted throughout the United States. Chosen as the title for his first guidebook in 1869, the word *transcontinental* stressed both the physical and mental connection of the West's new Union Pacific-Central Pacific Railroad with the rest of the United States.

Next came the task of settling the UP's vast territory with settlers who would provide it with freight and passenger revenues. McCague wrote:[49] "By the time the railroad was completed this company had its agents busy by the hundreds in Eastern and Midwestern cities and towns. Gaudy posters and glowing prose promised fertile lands, salubrious climate and opportunity unlimited for farmer, mechanic, and artisan alike. Soon the agents numbered in the thousands, many of them working out of offices set up in populous centers across the Atlantic." The Central Pacific joined in; to all intents and purposes, in fact, both companies operated as one in the promotion of their land-grant holdings, and the organization grew fantastically efficient.

The widespread publicity campaigns of the nation's railroads to sell their lucrative land grants and thus carry the nation Westward reached their crescendo as the new century and the Age of the Automobile neared. All told, the nation's railroads were given 155,504,994 acres of land by the U.S. Government—an area almost equivalent to the state of Texas. Western states also granted the Western roads another 49 million acres of land. Most, but not all, of this land was sold by the railroads to finance their construction and to enrich their promoters.

By 1880, the Burlington Railroad campaign had resulted in the sale of more than three quarters of Burlington's Iowa and Nebraska grants by selling more than 2 million acres to more than 20,000 buyers.[50] In 1880, first year of this period, the Burlington spent $39,411.07 in promoting land sales. The sale campaign continued until 1905 when the Nebraska grant was closed out. The final balance sheet showed that the Burlington had cleared nearly $17 million dollars from land sales, after taxes and expenses. This income more than paid for the construction of the main line from Burlington, IA, to Kearney Junction, NE, completed in 1872.

Its sales job three quarters done, Burlington's promoters began to shift their focus to viewing the newcomer as a future shipper and receiver and only incidentally as a buyer of land. This shift is seen in the gradual transfer of the "general immigration work" from the land commissioner to the passenger traffic department. In 1882, the railroad issued a pamphlet, *The Heart*

---

[48]Fifer, p. 344.
[49]McCague, p. 344.
[50]Overton, *Milepost 100*, p. 49.

of the Continent: an Historical and Descriptive Treatise for Business Men, Home Seekers and Tourists, of the Advantages, Resources and Scenery of the Great West. Burlington's publicists hadn't learned the value of brevity in pamphlet titles! The 64-page text included descriptive and statistical material concerning Burlington's territory; the pamphlet was copiously illustrated.[51] Burlington's most elaborate advertising effort of this period was *The Corn Belt*, a newspaper first published in Chicago in December, 1895. Edited by the passenger department, the first issue indicated that 20,000 copies were printed—12,000 to go to farmers in Illinois, Indiana, Ohio, and Michigan; 4,000 to ticket agents east of the Mississippi River; and 4,000 to Burlington passenger and land agents. The publication's primary purpose was to promote Nebraska. "This paper appeared regularly each month through November, 1902, and its average circulation for the seven years was approximately 27,000."[52] By 1896, the Burlington had so little good land left to sell that any considerable expenditure for advertising was not deemed warranted. Burlington's promotional campaign had virtually achieved its goal by the end of the century.

ROBERT STRAHORN—MASTER PUBLICIST

One of the most successful and colorful of this little-sung band of railroad publicists who promoted the Westward movement was Robert Edmund Strahorn. Born in Pennsylvania in 1852 and reared in Northern Illinois, Strahorn migrated West to Denver, and there in 1870 he got a job as reporter and editor. From that year until 1877 he worked on a Denver paper and served as correspondent for the Indian wars for *The New York Times* and *Chicago Tribune*. In these years, he also did some publicity on the side for the Denver and Rio Grande Railroad. "When he was eighteen, Strahorn was advised by a physician to move to the Rockies for his health. In 1870 he went west, became a tramp printer, and for the next seven years crowded into his life the many experiences which made him a knowledgeable Westerner. He worked at the case, desk, and circulation counter for newspapers in Denver, Greeley, Cheyenne, Central City, and Black Hawk."[53]

Toward the end of his period in Denver, Strahorn wrote and published a book extolling the scenery and resources of Wyoming. In his unpublished biography, Strahorn recalled that he had then "sensed the oncoming tide of settlers and capital" in deciding to write the book on Wyoming.[54]

---

[51]Overton, *Burlington West*, p. 469.

[52]*Ibid.* p. 472.

[53]Oliver H. Knight, "Robert E. Strahorn, Propagandist for the West," *Pacific Northwest Quarterly, 59*, 1968, p. 33.

[54]"Ninety Years of Boyhood," typescript autobiography in the Strahorn Memorial Library, College of Idaho, p. 257. (Available on microfilm from Idaho State Historical Society.)

A copy of the Wyoming book fell into the hands of Jay Gould, then energetically promoting his Union Pacific railroad, which had rails running from Omaha to Ogden and Salt Lake City. The upshot of this happenstance event was that Gould hired Strahorn to promote the Union Pacific. The offer came 1 week after his marriage to Carrie Adell. She told it this way:[55]

> The fancy seized Mr. Gould to have Mr. Strahorn create a literary bureau and advertising department for the Union Pacific Railway Company, and to write a similar book on all Western States and Territories. It was a new departure for a railroad company, but as the scheme was discussed its scope broadened until it seemed to be without limit. The offer came within a week after our marriage. It was a career so suited to his capabilities and his liking that I determined not to be a stumbling block at the very threshold of our new life. It meant going the length of nearly every stage road across our great frontier many times over.

One of Strahorn's first moves was to start a monthly magazine, *The New West Illustrated*, to promote settlement along the UP line. "Pard"—as Mrs. Strahorn called him—was "a veritable Corliss engine at pumping up statistics of the various products and prospects of every foot of land. The periodical *New West Illustrated* came out with astonishing regularity and filled to the brim with just such information as the emigrants were searching for in view of new homes."[56] Strahorn supplemented his inviting travel books, pamphlets, and the magazine with a steady stream of letters to Eastern newspapers touting the lands in UP country. Mrs. Strahorn helped him a great deal. She wrote that she had written "more than 45 columns in *The Omaha Republican* one summer." From 1877 to 1884, Strahorn managed the publicity bureaus of the Union Pacific and Kansas Pacific in Denver and Omaha, and also did some confidential fact finding for Gould. Strahorn's publicity function served to camouflage his economic intelligence work.

Strahorn was a publicist with a message—the message that the Wild West of Wild Bill Hickok and General Custer was gone and that the day of the empire builder was at hand. Knight evaluated Strahorn's work thus:

> Strahorn's emphasis on guidebooks differentiated him from other publicists. His job was not to publicize the Union Pacific but the entire West, not to sell Union Pacific lands but to attract settlers who would create freight tonnages and passenger revenues. This is not to imply that he was unique because of the guidebooks, for western railroads used a variety of publicity techniques, including guidebooks. His propaganda, however, was the kind that contrib-

---

[55]Carrie Adell Strahorn, *Fifteen Thousand Miles by Stage.* New York: G. P. Putnam's Sons, 1911, p. vi.

[56]*Ibid.* p. 96.

uted to the urbanization and industrialization through which the developing West was absorbed into the economic nationalization of America.

From 1884 to 1890, Strahorn carried on townsite and irrigation enterprises in Oregon, Washington, and Idaho. The latter year he returned to the East to sell municipal bonds and develop an investment business. In 1891, he located in Boston and there, from an office in the Equitable Building on Milk Street, ran his investment business. In these years, the Strahorns "explored the East as we had the West but with entirely different motives and in most luxurious ways." Strahorn's work as a UP publicist had made him well-to-do.

But the lure of the West and more money pulled him Westward once more—"in 1898 he came to Spokane to develop waterworks, electric plants, and irrigation schemes, and in 1905 he blossomed forth as the promoter of the North Coast Railroad to bring Spokane and Walla Walla closer to Portland, Tacoma, and Seattle."[57] Strahorn quickly started buying up land in Spokane, built tracks, organized the Spokane Union Terminal project, and paid for everything with his personal check. His promotional genius and foresight paid off when he induced the Chicago, Milwaukee, and St. Paul Railroad, which had intended to pass 40 miles south, to come into his scheme, thus connecting the Milwaukee and the Union Pacific at Spokane. Strahorn was both rich and "the toast of Spokane when, September 14, 1914, he wielded silver hammer to drive home the last spike which connected the two railroad systems."[58] Few publicists profited from their promotional efforts as Strahorn did.

SEATTLE SHOWS THE WAY FOR CITIES

Erastus Brainerd is another publicist promoter whose exploits deserve to be noted and whose methods tell us much of the practice in this era. Seattle, was a small city of 42,837 population when gold was discovered in the Alaskan Klondike in 1896, a discovery that fired the same get-rich-quick frenzy that sparked the 1849 Gold Rush to California. Seattle saw its opportunity and quickly sent out the following press release:[59]

> The news that the telegraph is bringing the past few days of the wonderful things of Klondike in the land of the midnight sun has opened the flood gates, and a stream of humanity is pouring through Seattle and on to the Golden Mecca of the North. It is a crowd at once strange, weird, and pictur-

---

[57]*Ibid.* p. 96. Glenn C. Quiett, *They Built the West.* New York: 1934, pp. 537–538.
[58]*Ibid.* p. 538.
[59]*Ibid.* p. 471.

esque. The good ship *Portland*, which recently brought a million and a half of treasure to this port, sails for Alaska tomorrow at noon. She will carry every passenger and every pound of cargo that she has the ability to transport.

Shortly after this release was put on the news wires, a meeting of business men was called to consider advertising Seattle as the principal outfitting point to offset the promotional efforts of other Northwest cities. "Four days later a committee reported in favor of a heavy schedule of paid advertising and propaganda, to be under the direction of its chairman, Erastus Brainerd." A three-quarter page ad was taken in the *New York Sunday Journal* to dwarf the smaller ads of Portland and Victoria. Other ads were placed in *Munsey's, McClure's, Cosmopolitan, Century,* and *Scribner's*. But publicity was used as the main weapon to channel the gold seekers through Seattle:[60]

> Brainerd soon proved his genius as a ballyhoo artist by laying down such a barrage of magazine and newspaper articles and advertisements that no other city had a chance to be heard, as a result of which it was soon reported that Seattle was getting five times as much publicity as any other outfitting point. Brainerd then sent the following crafty telegraphic news despatch:
> "As a result of the Klondike excitement, which has overwhelmed the city with inquiries from all parts of the world as to routes of transportation and costs of outfitting, there has been established under the auspices of the Chamber of Commerce a public Bureau of Information."

Thus, one of the first, if not the first, municipal promotion programs was born. Thus bureau promoted Seattle in many ways—by sending a Klondike edition of the Seattle *Post-Intelligencer* to each of the nation's 70,000 postmasters, public libraries, and mayors of cities; placing advertisements in rural newspapers with a circulation totaling nearly 10 million, and by getting new settlers in Seattle to write glowing letters back to their hometown newspapers. The bureau provided the written letter stamped and addressed, needing only the signature of the new resident. Brainerd kept up a steady barrage of advertisements, publicity releases, and letters stressing that Seattle was the point of departure for the Klondike. Quiett said: "Brainerd might well have called himself even in those simple times a public relations counsel." Seattle's population, 42,837 in 1890, had nearly doubled by 1900 to 80,671 persons. As late as 1880, it had been a small Pacific outpost village of 3,533 adventuresome souls.

One of the last and most spectacular of the railroad land promotion campaigns was that put on by the Northern Pacific (NP) Railway Company between 1896 and 1902, which resulted in the sale of more than 17,000,000 acres of the railroad's land in the states along the Canadian border from

---

[60]*Ibid.* p. 472.

Minnesota to the Pacific. The NP's campaign was put under the direction of F. W. Wilsey, who had the title of Eastern land agent, and his assistant, Willis Drummond. Most of the effort was pitched at populating the unsettled sections of Minnesota and North Dakota. According to Sigfried Mickelson, who made a thorough study of this campaign:[61]

> It was Wilsey's theory that the best medium for reaching prospective migrants was the country press. In order to use that medium to the fullest possible extent he embarked on a program on January 1, 1897, that embraced advertisements paid for in cash, advertisements paid for in transportation, readers' press handouts, letters to the press from apparently disinterested sources, land seeker's excursions, exhibit cars and widespread use of solicitors and agents. Every paid advertisement was used as a key to unlock page forms, thus permitting the infiltration of free publicity.
>
> Whenever it was possible, Wilsey preferred to pay for his advertising in transportation due-bills. He explained that the use of this method would cut down the cash outlay . . . and thus make it possible to use more papers; it would permit publishers to travel to points of interest, including Yellowstone National Park; and finally, every publisher favored with transportation would undoubtedly record in the columns of his paper the experiences of his trip, thereby, benefitting the passenger as well as the land department.

Wilsey's carefully planned program of publicity was aimed mainly at the rural populations of Iowa, Minnesota, Nebraska, South Dakota, Wisconsin, Illinois, and New York. The publicity was kept at low key during the summer months because Wilsey and Drummond knew that most farmers were too busy with crops to read or to travel. Wilsey insisted that his advertisements be placed on local pages; he had a great aversion to having them placed alongside boiler plate or legal notices. Mickelson recorded:[62] "Through 1897 and 1898 the weekly papers, primarily in Iowa, kept up a running series of interviews praising Northern Pacific lands in Minnesota and North Dakota. Most of these interviews came from residents of the towns in which the stories were printed and described excursions to points on the Northern Pacific line." That these came from the NP publicity office is seen in the fact that all these interviews were similar and in many cases whole paragraphs were exactly alike.

Willis Drummond kept busy writing news stories and sending out "letters to the editor." In November 1897, he wrote the Superior, Wisconsin *Evening Telegram* that he was submitting an article about the development of the country near Superior, and in 1889, he wrote the Primghar (Iowa) *Democrat* that he was enclosing an article for the *Democrat's* special Red River Valley

---

[61]Sigfried Mickelson, "Promotional Activities of the Northern Pacific's Land Department," *Journalism Quarterly, 17,* 1940, pp. 324–334.

[62]*Ibid.* pp. 327–328.

edition, "A Good Start in Timber." Mickelson found that a "constant barrage of newspaper articles left the St. Paul office (of Northern Pacific) during this period," and, in that author's opinion, most of it "was as skillfully conceived as was the selection of vehicles for its dissemination."[63]

The payoff for the Wilsey Drummond publicity advertising campaign is seen in the fact that the railroad sold more than 17,000,000 acres of land in 6 years—between July 1, 1897 and July 1, 1903—and that Minnesota's population of 1,301,826 in 1890 had climbed to 2,075,708 by the 1910 census.

Publicity, advertisements, paid readers, and press junkets were also proving their value for businesses with goods and services to sell and cities and railroads with land populate.

Just as the story of the Westward movement is a story of railroads, Indian fighting, and adventure, so it is a story of some of the United States' earliest and most successful promotional campaigns. It is a fact writ large in U.S. history that these unsung promoters of land and settlement in the West played an influential role in speeding the nation's settlement and in weaving in irresistible magic around the words, *The West*, a magic that today's publicists in the hire of motion picture and television producers, publishers, and the National Rifle Association exploit to the hilt.

---

[63]*Ibid.* p. 333.

CHAPTER TEN

Press Agentry, Promotion, Advertising Flower in 19th Century

The U.S. railroads promotion of the Westward movement was but part of the rapidly expanding fields of press agentry, promotion, and advertising that flowered in the 19th century. These fields, which often meld into one another, have the common purpose of attracting the public's attention for an entertainment or a product or a service. Consequently they all run together in the public's mind. Today our world is stuffed with the cascading messages of the press agent, the promoter, and the advertiser. Early in that century the commercial value of publicity to sell books, circuses, stage shows, and patent medicines was discovered and put to wide and imaginative use.

For example, author Washington Irving used a clever press-agent gimmick to promote his *Knickerbocker's History of New York*. On October 26, 1809, Irving inserted a paid notice in the New York *Evening Post* headed, "Distressing," which told of the disappearance of a Diedrich Knickerbocker from his lodgings. Subsequent notices reaffirmed the man's disappearance and further publicized the story. A few days later, the Columbian Hotel announced that Knickerbocker had left the hotel, leaving behind "a very curious kind of written book." The hotel threatened to sell the book to cover the man's unpaid hotel bill. Then, on November 28, a month after the final notice, Innskeep and Bradford announced that they would publish the book, authored by Washington Irving.[1] This may have been the first instance of a gimmick being used to promote a book—but surely it was not the last.

---

[1]Alfred McClung Lee, *The Daily Newspaper in America*. New York: Macmillan, 1939, p. 429.

170

A fabulous development of the United States 19th century—the circus—did much to stimulate the growth of press agentry and display advertising. In 1993, the circus celebrated its 200th birthday, still providing spectacular entertainment for the young and old. The earliest U. S. circuses—for example, Rickett's Circus and the Boston Circus—were permanently located and relied on the advertising practices of the day—use of small agate type in classified ads. All this changed when Hackaliah Bailey, whose name lives on in the greatest circus of them all—Barnum & Bailey and Ringling Brothers—began a tour of New England with his elephant, "Old Bet" in 1815. Bailey soon realized that he must publicize his coming in advance or else by the time the people wanted to see the first elephant ever brought to the United States, he would have to move on to the next town. He knew he had to arouse the public's curiosity before his exhibit got to town. Bailey came up with advertisements that displayed an eye-catching drawing of an elephant and curiosity-creating blurbs about the creature from far-away exotic lands. A circus historian, the late Robert Parkinson, asserted:[2] "It was clearly the circus which originated and developed newspaper display advertising. . . . It started with the very first traveling menagerie, Hackaliah Bailey's tour of 'Old Bet,' and grew with the industry. The first press agent, the first advertising agencies; first regular and specialized use of cuts and mats, press releases, free publicity . . . all came at the hands of the circus."

P. T. BARNUM SHOWS THE WAY

Today's patterns of promotion and press agentry in the world of show business were drawn, cut, and stitched by the greatest showman and press agent of all time—that "Prince of Humbug," that mightiest of mountebanks, Phineas Taylor Barnum. One writer termed him "the first great advertising genius and the greatest publicity exploiter the world has ever seen."[3] The beloved William Lyon Phelps of Yale said Barnum was "the greatest psychologist who ever lived . . . the Shakespeare of Advertising." In 1926, the playwright, Robert E. Sherwood, later a propagandist in World War II, thought Barnum "the greatest genius that ever conducted an amusement enterprise in this country; a man of superlative imagination, indomitable pluck and artistic temperament." The spectacular Barnum and glowing adjectives go hand-in-glove. He can only be described in such terms.

A later biographer, Irving Wallace, believed that "a new age—the age of showmanship" began in August 1835, when young Barnum put on display "the greatest natural and national curiosity in the world, Joice Heth, nurse

---

[2]"The Circus and the Press," *Bandwagon*, 7, 1963, pp. 3–9.

[3]Frank Presbey, *The History and Development of Advertising.* Garden City, NY: Doubleday, Doran, 1929, p. 211.

to General George Washington, the father of our country."[4] Joice Heth, Barnum's first exhibition, was reputedly a slave of George Washington's father and alleged to be 160 years old as proved by a bogus bill of sale executed in 1727. Though the woman was partially paralyzed, blind, and had no teeth, Barnum taught her to talk freely to the crowds about "dear little George." Barnum paid $1,000 for Joice and first put her on display in New York City. Barnum printed posters and placed advertisements in the newspapers, both written by himself. He hired an assistant to help with the display and the publicity—Levi Lyman, described by Barnum as "a shrewd, sociable, and somewhat indolent Yankee Lawyer." Barnum directed Lyman to write a memoir of Joice Heth. The widely promoted exhibit was soon grossing $1,500 a week. Next he took Joice to Boston and there promoted attendance by writing a letter to a newspaper asserting that Joice Heth was a humbug, made of Indian rubber, whalebone, and springs, and that her exhibitor was a ventriloquist. From that day on, fostering controversy in the press was a much-used tactic of Barnum's. The exploitation of Joice Heth was a pioneering piece of press agentry.

Phineas Taylor Barnum was born July 5, 1810, in Bethel, CT, near Danbury, the son of a none-too-successful small storekeeper, and died 81 years later, near the end of the century, a world renowned showman, multimillionaire, and a legend, much of which he had manufactured himself. His life span covered a period of great importance in the evolution of public relations, and he contributed significantly to that evolution. Barnum was a great innovator and knew it. He did much to cast the patterns and stimulate the development of press agentry, advertising, and product promotion. He was in no sense a public relations pioneer; his interest was in building box office not in earning understanding and support. Nonetheless, his imaginative publicity methods are frequently used by today's practitioners. Wallace said of him:[5] "Barnum's showmanship was evident not only in a canny instinct that enabled him to give the masses what they wanted, but also in his ability to dictate to them a desire for what he thought they should want."

"I thoroughly understand the art of advertising," Barnum once wrote, "not merely by means of printer's ink, which I have always used freely and to which I confess myself so much indebted for my success, but by turning ever possible circumstance to my account." On another occasion, Barnum said: "Advertising is like learning—a little is a dangerous thing."

He placed an even higher value on publicity. Another time he said that the value of an advertisement was far below that of an editorial line or two,

---

[4]Irving Wallace, *The Fabulous Showman, the Life and Times of P. T. Barnum* (New York: 1959), pp. 3–5. For another example of Barnum's genius see W. Porter Ware and Thaddeus C. Lockwood, Jr., *P. T. Barnum Presents Jenny Lind.* Baton Rouge: Louisiana State University Press, 1980.

[5]*Ibid.* p. 75.

paragraph, or column, which an incident, invention, or individual compels the newspaper to give publicity. He added that: "If a man says, or does, or proposes something which is noteworthy enough to get into the newspapers *as news*—something worth reading, hearing, and telling—at once the thing and the man, both together, are talked about all through the country and, if of sufficient importance, all over the world."[6] Barnum's most notable successes were in the buildup of Tom Thumb, the midget; the U.S. tour of Jenny Lind, "The Swedish Nightingale"; and the circus that still carries his name. He contributed the word Jumbo to our language.

Before going into show business, Barnum had a brief fling at journalism. When Barnum was 21, New England was swept by a wave of religious fanaticism that reached a feverish pitch in Bethel. When Barnum's letters of protest to the nearby Danbury papers were not printed, he started his own paper, *The Herald of Freedom*, a weekly. The vigor and boldness with which Barnum conducted his newspaper caused the circulation to soar but involved the young editor in three libel suits, the last being pressed by a deacon whom Barnum had accused of "taking usury of an orphan boy." Barnum was found guilty, sentenced to 60 days in jail, and fined $100.[7]

PRESS PROVIDES WIND FOR BARNUM'S SAILS

He continued to blast the religious fanatics from his Danbury jail cell. Barnum aroused such fervent support that when he was released from jail he was honored with a parade, including a band, 40 horsemen, a long line of carriages, an ode, and a banquet. This event taught Barnum the power of publicity. At the age of 24, he gave up journalism and moved to New York City.

A year later, he was launched into show business with his Joice Heth exploit. His next successful venture was the New York Museum in the heart of lower Manhattan, at Broadway and Ann Street. Wallace wrote:[8] "His publicity began with the Museum itself. One morning it was a hulking, drab, marble building, and lo, the next, it was a breath-taking rainbow, a kaleidoscope of color and curiosity. Overnight Barnum mounted monstrous oval oil paintings of outlandish 'birds, beasts, and creeping things' around the fourth story of his building." Barnum also had a band play from the balcony. He cleverly used publicity to get control the museum derogatorily by publicizing a group of stock speculators who were seeking to get the museum, and then to attract attention to its exhibits. He made frequent trips to the nearby New York newspapers, often after the editors had gone home so that he could give his flamboyant copy to the composing room foreman.

---

[6]Harvey W. Root, *The Unknown Barnum*. New York: Harper & Brothers, 1927, p. 205.
[7]James S. Hamilton, *Barnum*.
[8]Wallace, p. 76.

Barnum did not exaggerate when he wrote:[9] "If I am ever profoundly thankful for any instrumentalities, it is for the editor and his paper. They furnish the wind for my sails." He also knew the publicity value of stunts and faked events and used both with great abandon.

Barnum's innovative and successful publicity devices were quickly copied by others, especially his competitors. For example, Harry Bennett, who owned a competing museum, created publicity for his business by parodying Barnum's attractions. When Barnum was showing his faked "Fejee Mermaid," Bennett countered by advertising a "Fudg-ee Mermaid." Barnum ultimately bought out Bennett and hired him to continue his parodying because it created publicity for the American Museum.

In the mid-1850s, the Hackaliah Bailey style of advertising began to fade as circus owners took more space and used more cuts to hawk their shows and relied more and more on press agentry. More white space and more varieties of types were also used. Parkinson asserted, "The circus was the first to inject artistic ingenuity into newsprint," and develop "true display advertising." The style of circus ads was soon being copied by the makers of patent medicines and farm implements. In the early 1870s, circus ads blossomed into grandly decorated and profusely worded advertisements of two or three-column displays. The transition from wagon shows to railroad circuses and increased competition caused a sharp step-up in number and size of ads and in amount of press agentry. Fiercely competing in the 1870s were the circuses of Barnum, Sells, Great London, Forepaugh, Coup, and W. W. Cole. Circus advertising of these giants was eye-catching and gaudy. By 1880, the ornamental, colorful circus wagon and the street parade had been developed as another means of promoting "The Greatest Show on Earth"—and all were no less than that.

The earliest known use of the title, "press agent," is found in the 1868 roster of John Robinson's Circus and Menagerie that listed "W. W. Duran, Press Agent," as the circus' third top executive. Press agentry was that important in show business. It may be presumed that Robinson's competitors used press agents, possibly before he did, and that they were fairly common even at that early date. Their number today is legion. The showman led the way, and others followed in an ever-increasing number.

THE SUPER PRESS AGENT HIRES PRESS AGENTS

Although he was the most imaginative of press agents, Barnum hired press agents to beat his circus drums. The first of these was Rufus Wilmot Griswold, described by Wallace as "the most unsavory character in Barnum's circle." It is thought that Griswold wrote most of the autobiography, first published

---

[9]Hamilton, p. 55.

in 1855 by J. S. Redfield. This was the opinion of Charles Godfrey Leland, who had been editor of Barnum's ill-fated *Illustrated News* and who declined the task. Barnum's 404-page account of his first 45 years was advertised as "the success story of a self-made man and a guidebook to riches." The critics criticized it harshly, but it got Barnum publicity, always his goal.[10]

Best known of the Barnum press agents was Richard F. "Tody" Hamilton. Hamilton, described by a press agent of more recent time, Dexter Fellows, as "press agent plenipotentiary for Phineas Taylor Barnum." Fellows added: "Showmen of the wagon days made capital of the veneration of our forefathers for exaggeration, but the man who developed it into a fine art was Richard F. Hamilton, better known among newspapermen in the eighties and nineties as Tody." Chary as Barnum was of giving credit to anyone but himself, he has been quoted as saying that "he owed more of his success to Tody Hamilton than to any other man." A contemporary newspaperman praised Hamilton as "the world's greatest press agent." This writer continued:[11]

> As a propagandist he has never been equalled. Napolean's proclamations seem petty and hopelessly amateurish in comparison to Tody's many-syllabled announcements. . . . As a newspaper reporter he had early demonstrated a gift for dramatic expression. . . . Mr. Barnum tempted him from the straight and unremunerative path of literature, put him into a gilded band wagon, paid him a vast honorarium coupled with a Byzantine expense account and so forever robbed legitimate literature.

Hamilton joined the circus shortly after Barnum and Bailey formed their partnership and quit the show shortly after the death of the surviving partner, Hackaliah Bailey, in 1902. "Tody" Hamilton, who died in Baltimore, MD, in 1916 at the age of 69, set the pattern for today's press agent with the firm belief that "to state a fact in ordinary language is to permit a doubt concerning the statement." Dexter Fellows, who would eventually outshine Hamilton as the Prince of Hyperbole, got his start as a circus press agent with Colonel William F. Cody, idolized by generations of young boys as the incomparable "Buffalo Bill." Fellows later became known to every news room in the United States as the press agent for the Barnum & Bailey Circus.

BUFFALO BILL—ANOTHER HERO MADE BY PRESS AGENTS

"Buffalo Bill" Cody, an intensively publicized showman of this era, has long since become firmly embedded in the folklore of U.S. culture as a brave and

---

[10]A condensed version of Barnum's 1855 "autobiography" can be found in Waldo R. Browne, *Barnum's Own Story.*

[11]Ralph D. Blumenfeld, *R. D. B's Procession.* New York: Macmillan, 1935, p. 55.

heroic figure of the Western Frontier—a tribute more to the skill of his several press agents than to any great deeds. Cody was probably not the greatest scout to ride the Western plains, nor did he take part in the really important Indian battles of his time. But, as Dixon Wecter pointed out: "Two immense advantages were his. He looked every inch the hero, and his publicity men were by far the best."[12] Another historian, Marshall Fishwick, observed:[13]

> Cody's principal hero-makers were Ned Buntline, Prentiss Ingraham, and John Burke. Also helpful were Nate Salesbury, Texas Jack Omohundro, Dexter Fellows, Courtney Ryley Cooper, and Johnnie Baker. To them belongs the credit for making Buffalo Bill the most highly publicized figure in Western history. What they did was not easy; no one should underestimate their endeavors. More spectacular men had to be outdistanced. Mountains had to be made out of molehills.

Early in his career as a scout and buffalo hunter, Cody had shown a flair and thirst for publicity, but less concern about facts. He was discovered and brought to national attention by Ned Buntline, a writer of lurid fiction whose real name was E. Z. C. Judson, described by Wecter as "a battered customer who had weathered adventures as fantastic as his own novels." After a scouting trip with Cody on the Western plains in 1869, Buntline returned to the East to tell tall tales of Cody's prowess and to make him the hero of a dime novel, *Buffalo Bill King of the Border Men*. Soon the New York *Herald* was referring to Cody as "the beau ideal of the plains." Buntline, who popularized but didn't originate the memorable nickname, Buffalo Bill, persuaded Cody to go on the stage in 1872. Buffalo Bill earned $6,000 for the season but thought this sum too little, he blamed his failure to earn more on Buntline's publicity that had been plentiful and florid. They split, and then Cody hired John Burke who was his press agent and devoted aide for life, through good years and bad.

JOHN BURKE MAKES CODY A HERO

Burke got his preparation for his role as press agent in travel, as an actor in a stock company, as an acrobatic troupe manager, and as a freelance journalist. As Burke recounted many times later, meeting Cody changed his life. "I have met a god." The colorful, lovable Burke set about to spread Cody's fame by turning out stories, providing interviews, and inventing new myths about the scout. Henry Nash Smith, in *Virgin land*, wrote:[14] "To Burke

---

[12]Dixon Wecter, *The Hero in America*. New York: Scribner, 1972, p. 359.

[13]*American Heroes: Myth and Reality*. Washington, DC: Public Affairs Press, 1954, p. 100.

[14]Henry Nash Smith, *Virginland: The American West as Symbol and Myth*. New York: Vintage Books, 1950.

belongs the credit for carrying through the major revision of the character of Buffalo Bill as Buntline had originally conceived it." In Fishwick's view: "Burke so wedded fact and fancy that no completely reliable biography of Cody has yet been, or ever will be written."

The rotund, affable Burke, who dubbed himself as "Arizona John," could open all doors and was welcomed in newsrooms and theatrical offices. Even when editors doubted his embellished tales of Cody's heroism, they printed them. Major, as his associates called him, was not an Indian fighter, but he dressed to give that impression and in many a barroom he told epic tales of his Indian battles.

Typical of the way in which Burke publicized Cody is the story of the much-told, much-exaggerated tale of Buffalo Bill's duel with young Chief Yellow Hand. Although he found show business lucrative and exciting, Cody was shrewd enough not to lose his identification with the West that had nourished him. In the early summer of 1876, the nation had been excited by the epic story of Custer's Last Stand on the Little Big Horn. The death of the flamboyant and bumbling general had set the whites on the warpath. Cody joined the chase. Wecter told it this way:[15] "In one of the minor skirmishes of 1876, Buffalo Bill fought his much publicized duel with young Chief Yellow Hand. The scout advanced upon his foe wearing a Mexican suit of black velvet, with silver buttons and lace and scarlet slashing. First he shot the brave, then drove a knife into his heart: 'Jerking his war bonnet off, I scientifically scalped him in about five seconds and shouted, "The first scalp for Custer!"' "

Cody's press agent, Major Burke, immediately put the story on the press wires. The New York *Herald* gave the duel nearly a column. The episode was exploited by Burke for years to come and was re-enacted a thousand times in Cody's Wild West shows.

The lengths to which Cody would go to promote himself as the frontier hero, "for the small part I have taken in redeeming the West from savagery," is seen in a 766-page book that he purportedly authored in the 1880s to link himself with earlier frontier heroes—Daniel Boone, Davy Crockett, and Kit Carson. The book, *Story of the Wild West and Camp Fire Chats*, is billed on the title page as "A Full and Complete History of the Renowned Pioneer Quartette" and as "Replete with Graphic Descriptions of Wild Life and Thrilling Adventures by Famous Heroes of the Frontier." The book was first copyrighted in 1888 by H. S. Smith, then again in 1891 by the Historical Publishing Co. of Philadelphia, the publisher.

Cody, in the preface, said; "The task of writing the lives of the three greatest pioneers of western settlement has been assumed by me with no little diffidence, surrounded as the work has been with many hard disad-

---

[15]Wecter, p. 359.

vantages, and obstacles of no ordinary character." He said the task was made difficult by his "disadvantage of poor literacy qualification" and by "the fact that the several biographers of Boone, Crockett, and Carson have generally made quite as much use of fiction as of actual, verified incident in making up their history of these three prominent characters." This book compounds rather than corrects the fiction born of the press agentry for Daniel Boone, Davy Crockett, and Buffalo Bill. Who actually wrote it is not known, but it is more likely that it was Cody's press agents seeking to cloak him in the aura of Boone, Crockett, and Carson than it was the flamboyant showman himself. The fabrication of the Boone and Crockett myths have already been recounted in this volume. Of such press agentry history is made.

Prentiss Ingraham, "a Southern colonel with slouch hat and walrus mustache," was not a hired Cody press agent but with his dime novels probably did more than either Buntline or Burke to glorify the colorful Cody. Ingraham wrote more than 200 dime novels with Buffalo Bill as the hero with such titles as *Buffalo Bill at Bay*. Ingraham, perhaps the most popular of all the dime novelists, wrote these from about 1876 to 1883.

John Burke became the mentor of Dexter Fellows in the ways of the press agent, or as Fellows put it, "in the humanities." Fellows, who at the peak of his career was crowned "the dean of press agents," was hired by Burke, now general manager of the Buffalo Bill Wild West and Congress of Rough Riders of the World, in 1895. Fellows was born in Boston in July 1871 and grew up in Fitchburg, Massachusetts, where he was known as "a wild lad who loved to play pranks." In April 1893, Pawnee Bill's Historic Wild West played in Fitchburg and young Fellows was enthralled by it. He talked Pawnee Bill into a job, but 2 years later the show went broke, and Fellows then signed on with Buffalo Bill. Fellows worked under Burke's tutelage for 9 years, then went back to Pawnee Bill's Historic Wild West for one season. In 1905, he got a job as press agent for the Barnum & Bailey Circus. When Barnum & Bailey and Ringling Brothers combined, Fellows remained as the Ringling Brothers' press agent as "minister plenipotentiary of the greatest show on earth." One writer dubbed him "public relations counselor of the circus." Press agent he was. As *The New York Times* wrote of Fellows: "In the gentle art of inducing hard-boiled city editors not only to accept but to clamor for news copy of that variety, Dexter Fellows, dean of the circus press agents, was extremely successful." Fellows' success begat wide imitation. Thus, were the ways and wiles of the pioneering circus press agent carried from the 1880s down to modern day United States. Fellows described the transition:[16]

---

[16]Dexter Fellows and Andrew Freeman, *This Way to the Big Show*. New York: Viking Press, 1938, p. 16. Also see Obituary, *The New York Times*, November 27, 1937, p. 20.

My life has been a fantasia. . . . "Bigger and Better" has been its motif, floridly embellished with flights through the looking glass and with interludes wherein I turned from a synthetic wonderland and became an ordinary human being.

To begin with it was a simple melody in which I played an insignificant part. The orchestra then was brass, without the softening and insidious influence of reeds, woodwinds, and strings. The story was a straightforward one, and it was loudly and lustily told.

It was not until the turn of the century, when my name began to appear in the public prints, that the orchestration became more complex.

THE PRESS AGENT'S WORK BECOMES PERVASIVE

Not only was the orchestration becoming more complex, the practice of press agentry was becoming more pervasive. Near the end of 1898, *The Fourth Estate* reported:[17]

Press agents have become a necessary adjunct to nearly all commercial enterprises. It was not so very long ago when those energetic purveyors of publicity were confined in their efforts to the circus, theatrical and operatic fields. But business methods have changed materially during the last few years. Advertising and plenty of it is now essential to the success of almost any undertaking that depends on a large public patronage. Merchants and manufacturers have found that newspaper writers can put advertising into a more readable shape than any other class of men. . . . The press agents who do this kind of work are alert, wide-awake body of young men who endeavor in one way or another to keep the name and business of their employers continually in the public eye. Press agents are now employed by public men, insurance, railway, and telegraph companies, by wholesale and retail dry goods houses, by young cities, summer and winter resorts, lecturers and entertainers, racing associations, hotels and athletic clubs.

ENTER PAID AND UNPAID ADVERTISING

In Will Irwin's language, press agentry "was mere fluff on the surface of national journalism, part of the showmanship that has always gone with the amusement business." In this period, the expanding number of business firms, borrowing a leaf from the showman's notebook, began to use publicity and advertising to promote products and services in an aggressive fashion. Advertising and product promotion, today intertwined and often confused, have their roots in the post-Civil War industrialization of the United States.

---

[17]Issue of December 22, 1898.

With introduction of mass production methods, more and more businesses needed regional or national distribution of their mass-produced soaps, foods, and other products. For example, as Ginger noted: "To break down consumer bias against eating meat that had been slaughtered weeks earlier and half a continent away, Swift turned to advertising."[18] The result was the appearance of the advertising agent and the extension of press agentry to the business world. By 1879, advertising revenue in newspapers totaled $21,000,000.

The advertising agency was born at the end of the Civil War and became a vital part of business and communication in the great expansion of industry and business that took place after the war and before the turn of the century. The oldest agency, J. Walter Thompson, was started in 1864, and N. W. Ayer & Son was founded in 1869. In March 1877, Albert Frank opened a one-room, two-man agency in lower Manhattan—an event that created no great stir in the Wall Street community. Today it survives as Albert Frank Gunter Law—as do the Thompson and Ayer agencies. Other agencies started in these years have long since disappeared.

THE PRESS AGENT MULTIPLIES—"A SNEAK AND A SPONGE"

As the United States moved toward the new century, the press agent, "an expert in crashing the editorial gate," appeared in increasing numbers. The press agent, born in show business, is still mainly associated with enterprises depending on "box office" for financial success. It is an over simplification to assert baldly that public relations has evolved from press agentry, but such a statement has much truth in it.

Will Irwin recounted:[19] "When the road company was the standard amusement for the 'provinces,' he [the press agent] traveled ahead of the actors, his pockets stuffed with passes, his mouth with humor, repartee and anecdote. Arrived in town, he mingled with his old friends, the newspapermen, spilling stories calculated to dress up the news columns and to spread the word that the show was coming. He was a harmless, picturesque and privileged liar."

Later in the century, press agentry was coming to be widely used by the proliferating number of circuses, fashionable spas, and the burgeoning theater late in the century. By 1880, for example, there were 250 touring companies in the legitimate theater business. This brought tough competition,

---

[18]Ray Ginger, *The Age of Excess*. New York: Macmillan, 1965, p. 25.
[19]*Propaganda and the News*. New York: 1936. p. 110.

and the competitors turned more and more to press agentry to gain an edge. By the 1880s, book publishers, resorts, and railroads had begun to hire publicity men to get "free advertising" in the growing number of newspapers and magazines. Publicity getting had reached sufficient volume to cause some editors to cry out against space stealing and to provide a market for a clipping bureau. Burrelle's Press Clipping Bureau, still in business, was born on January 24, 1888, when Mr. and Mrs. Frank Burrelle started clipping newspapers on their kitchen table. They initially sold the clippings for a penny apiece. From a few hundred clippings a week for a few shows and celebrities, Burrelle's grew to be the largest firm of its kind in the United States.[20] The *Journalist*, in its October 18, 1884, issue carried an article criticizing both business and the press for abuse of the press pass, which it saw as getting out of hand. Years earlier Horace Greeley had denounced the press agent as both "a sneak and a sponge."

The strident exaggeration of press agentry of the 1880s can be seen in this paid reader booming Sells Brothers' Circus for its Springfield, IL, showing April 28, 1880:[21]

> The totally unparalleled magnitude of our stupendous confederation of eminent entertainments demands proportionate employment of printers' ink in almost every pictorial, lithographic, illustrative and typographical form, in order that even passing attention may be directed to the incomputable feast of rarest features and phenomenal feats which we have provided to sate the public palate for amusement.

Lest a skeptical reader doubt these polysyllabic claims another paid reader is headed:

> $100 Reward.
> For the especial benefit of those who may deem it necessary to discredit the authenticity or genuineness of the above notices, we hereby promise, upon honor, to pay any person the sum of $100, as compensation for his time and trouble, in every instance where he shall be able to prove any notice anywhere published by us to be either a forgery, or in language and purpose different than as originally published.

Much of the early advertising was bought to promote patent medicines sold to cure every ailment under the sun. James Harvey Young, in *The Toadstool Millionaires*, asserted the well-greased engines of advertising and public relations that dominate Madison Avenue today had pretty humble beginnings in the late 19th century in the promotion of pills and potions guaranteed to cure everything from corns to senility. By 1871, the patent

---

[20]"Burrelle, 75, Snips 300,000,000 Clip," *Editor & Publisher*, Vol. 96, 1963, p. 44. Burrelle in 1993 was still in business, providing video reports as well as newspaper clippings.

[21]Springfield *Sangamon Monitor*, April 1, 1880.

medicine hawker had become a successful and wealthy business man, at least in the view of the *American Newspaper Reporter*.[22] "Twenty years ago the patent medicine man had no business status; they were few in number . . . and were regarded as a class of adventurers. . . . Now, their ranks include a large number of the most capable, successful, and wealthy business men of the day." Such were the mores of the business world.

Native nostrum production commenced in the era of the Revolution and reached its flood tide in the late 19th century, according to Young. Grotesque, misleading advertisements for these pills and potions provided much of the press revenue of this period. In Wood's view:[23]

> The advertising of, roughly, 1885 to 1905 reflected a world of bold enterprise and unrestricted commercial competition. This advertising was brash and full-bodied. There was no sense yet that the world had cracked, was cracking or was going to crack wide open. The idea prevailed without serious question that it was legitimate and laudable to make money, as much as possible, in business, and certainly in advertising. Advertising was vigorous, and it was fun. The men who plied it plied it lustily.

PAID ADVERTISING BEGINS TO FLOURISH IN 1890s

The advertising boom in the 1890s was brought about largely through the ambition and industry of the advertising agents whom Wood described as "gadflies stinging the timid or torpid businessman into advertising." Most of these were buyers, sellers, and procurers of space and offered the advertiser no assistance, no expertise. The man who changed all this, Albert D. Lasker, arrived in Chicago in 1898, to join Lord & Thomas, then one of the three major agencies though it had less than 1,000,000 dollars in billings. Lasker soon made his firm the dominant force in building modern advertising. In those days, advertising was a pretty much hit-and-miss business, and the agency business was chaotic. Lasker, often termed the father of modern advertising, never successfully developed a publicity department in his agency. Nonetheless, he made many important public relations contributions in his public services. One of the two leading agencies of that day was successful in using publicity to augment its advertising.[24]

The Ayer agency entered the field of public relations about 1900 when it began to handle the advertising of such large firms as the National Biscuit

---

[22]"The American Patent Medicine Man," February 20, 1871, p. 125. .

[23]James Playsted Wood, *The Story of Advertising*. New York: The Ronald Press, 1958, p. 500.

[24]John Gunther, *Taken at the Flood, The Story of Albert D. Lasker*. New York: Harper, 1960, pp. 42–43.

Company (NBC) and the Standard Oil Company because "it soon had to take account of the attitude of the public toward these 'big business' institutions." The agency set out to build goodwill mainly by the use of advertising, but inevitably "it was compelled to prepare publicity material as part of its regular work and also to prepare news releases."[25]

The National Biscuit Company, with Ayer's assistance, introduced the packaged cracker, Uneeda Biscuit, that was to revolutionize marketing and to bring Ayer into public relations. This firm was the first of the modern marketers. "It bought its raw materials as cheaply as possible in huge quantities. It centralized its manufacturing. . . . It improved plant layout and production processes. It stopped selling in bulk to wholesalers, and began selling small packages under brand names directly to retailers. And it launched a big advertising program to build demand for its Uneeda Biscuit brands."[26] The homier word *biscuit* was used to get away from the old-fashioned word, cracker, and the popular symbol of the Boy in the Yellow Slicker was used to give Uneeda an identifiable image. When NBC took the cracker out of the barrel and put it in a sanitary package, it changed the course of U.S. life and commerce.

PRESS AGENTRY SPANS THE ATLANTIC

The practice of press agentry apparently spanned the Atlantic in these years. In 1899, John Beaufoy Lane, London correspondent of several U.S. newspapers, was sued for a dressmaker's bill. He contended in court that the bill, contracted by his wife, Annie Morton Lane, was to be paid for "by puffs" in their letters published in the U.S. papers. Mrs. Lane was correspondent for the New York *Mail* and *Express* at the time.

This revelation caused *The Fourth Estate* to editorialize:[27] "This is not the first time that foreign correspondents have been caught using the columns of the newspapers for advertising purposes. . . . The proper place for advertising is in the advertising columns. The reading columns should be kept free from advertising matter unless it is marked in the usual manner. Such matters are as much out of place in a London letter as they would be in an obituary."

The newspapers themselves transgressed by accepting paid advertising matter to be published as news matter without its being labeled as advertising. The early advertising agencies started paying periodicals to publish advertisements as news, and this soon extended to the practice of paying publications to publish news releases and editorials to advance a political

---

[25]Ralph M. Hower, *The History of an Advertising Agency*. Cambridge, MA: Harvard University Press, 1939, pp. 297–298.

[26]Ginger, p. 213.

[27]Issue of March 16, 1899, p. 4.

or business cause. Some periodicals rebelled, but most went along in the 1880s and 1890s. In 1883, the *Railroad Gazette* firmly announced that it would "entertain no proposition to publish anything in this journal for pay, except in the advertising columns."[28]

One of the first to employ this shady practice was the Mutual Life Insurance Company, which established a "species of literary bureau" in 1888 under the direction of Charles J. Smith who, in due time, became known as "$ a Line Smith" for obvious reasons. Another large firm that was exposed for buying news space was Standard Oil Company.

Mutual's payment for publication of news releases dates back to at least 1878. *The New York Times* on December 18, 1878, published an article supposedly clipped from the *Hudson River Chronicle* that attacked Elizur Wright, Massachusetts' first insurance commissioner and often referred to as the father of life insurance. Wright found that the story was a paid ad from the Mutual Life Insurance Company. The president heatedly wrote Wright that the "executive officers of this company did not procure, pay for, or approve the article." Wright reported that when he showed the president's letter to *The New York Times* editors, "they broke into a guffaw."[29] According to Burton J. Hendrick, Wright "showed that Mutual Life subsidized by ads about 30 life insurance papers and had also largely muzzled the daily press." Hendrick also wrote that Wright exposed the dollar-a-line rate in 1870.[30] There was an investigation of the insurance business in New York in 1870, but the report was copyrighted and suppressed by Mutual.

In Wood's opinion, "Part of the impulse and impetus behind the force which burst into the eruption of advertising in the United States in the 1890s sprang from England."[31] Much of this impetus came from Thomas Lipton, a canny Scotsman with a great flair for publicity and a strong believer in advertising of all kinds. The world-renowned merchant used every publicity and advertising trick his inventive mind could dream up. He paraded freshly scrubbed pigs through the streets of Glasgow; he always arranged loud advance publicity each time he opened a new store; he issued thousands of Lipton one-pound notes, redeemable in his shops; he hired balloons to drop advertising telegrams; he imported a huge jumbo cheese from New York state filled with gold sovereigns, and raced his various Shamrocks for the American Cup. Four times he failed to win the yachting cup; but each time he got invaluable publicity as a cheerful loser. Lipton taught businessmen on both sides of the Atlantic the value of promotion.[32]

---

[28]Vol. *15* (1883), p. 8.

[29]Phillip Green Wright and Elizabeth Q. Wright, *Elizur Wright, the Father of Life Insurance.* Chicago, 1937, pp. 261–262.

[30]"The Story of Life Insurance," *McClure's Magazine, 27,* 1906, p. 169.

[31]Wood, p. 217.

[32]*Ibid.* pp. 218–222.

In this "dawn of national advertising," the value of the public personality endorsement was soon discovered. An ad of the period shows the President of the United States, Rutherford B. Hayes, and Mrs. Hayes plugging a clothes iron, the "Cold Handle Sad Iron." Lucy Hayes is shown telling the President, "We cannot leave until we visit the Enterprise Mfg. Col. and order some of Mrs. Potts' Cold Handle Sad Irons like this." The President replies, "But my dear they are for sale by all hardware stores in this country."[33]

STAGED OR PSEUDO-EVENT COMES INTO PLAY

The staged event as a means of promoting products was being used increasingly as the United States moved toward the new century. In 1892, for example, the manufacturers of Sapolio Soap sent a 14-foot sailing sloop to Spain to commemorate the fourth centennial of Columbus' voyage of discovery. Obviously, the object was more to sell soap than glorify Columbus. To promote its circulation and the new-fangled automobile, the Chicago *Times Herald* staged a highly publicized race in Chicago November 28, 1895. The race was won by a two-cylinder Duryea car driven by J. Frank Duryea. He plowed through icy streets to complete the 55-mile course at an average speed of 5 miles an hour 7½ miles an hour when time for repairs was deducted![34]

Racing was used as a prime means of popularizing the newly-invented automobile. Rae dates the beginning of commercial production of the motor car in the United States from 1897. Henry Ford who early broke out of the pack of the makers of motor cars, used racing to publicize his car but that story belongs in the 20th Century.

C. B. Knox was one of the early businessmen to take a leaf out of Barnum's book on getting publicity be creating controversy. During the McKinley Bryan campaign of 1896, Knox organized and made himself president of the American Voter's League. Using this paper organization as a front, Knox got permission to stretch a large political banner across Fifth Avenue in New York City. For 4 days this banner displayed pictures of Bryan and McKinley flanking a large picture of a Knox Gelatine package. The banner read: "Each Candidate Hopes to Win but Knox Gelatine Will Win." Alfred McClung Lee recounted: "Four days of denunciation in the press compelled Knox to remove the banner, but Knox Gelatine won. Knox repeated the gag in many other cities with similar results."[35]

---

[33]Stephen Birmingham, *Our Crowd*. New York: Harper and Row, 1967, p. 234.
[34]John B. Rae, *The American Automobile*. Chicago: University of Chicago Press, 1965, p. 9.
[35]Lee, p. 443.

COLUMBIAN EXPOSITION USES PUBLICITY

One enterprise that quickly discovered this new truth that publicity was now essential for "any undertaking that depends on a large public patronage" was the World's Columbian Exposition staged in Chicago in 1893. Exposition authorities decided to organize a Department of Publicity and Promotion in November 1890, because the newspapers were either ignoring or ridiculing the exposition. The new department was headed by Moses P. Handy, a journalist from Pennsylvania. He hired as assistants: Robert E. A. Dorr of New York City; H. E. O. Heineman, who handled the German press; L. H. Ayme, who handled French, Spanish, Italian, and Portuguese publicity; William M. Knox and James P. Holland. The main job of this publicity effort, at least in the early stages, was to raise funds from states and from trade associations. The Exposition's new department issued its first publicity release February 1, 1891, one sent to newspapers around the world.

The Exposition's publicity effort was stepped up gradually from that date until the Exposition opened in 1893. Handy and his aides developed mailing lists, prepared brochures, and catalogs preparatory to the opening of this U.S.-staged world's fair. All told, the department mailed out 161,200 pieces of publicity and promotion, distributed 4,875 colored lithographs, 31,687 printed pictures, and 168 electrotypes. In his final report, Handy recorded that he issued 106,919 press passes during the exposition. A crude evaluation of this gigantic effort—for its time—based on newspaper clippings claimed a total of 4,616,620 words printed in papers and periodicals of the world about the Exposition. The report indicated that in accomplishing all this, that the publicity department had spent only $190,000 of the $300,000 budgeted for publicity and promotion. In any event, this was a publicity campaign of unusual magnitude for its time.[36]

What *The Nation* derisively termed "The Itch for Publicity" was coming to afflict most segments of society as this century neared its end. "It is probably useless to look for any speedy abatement of the itch for publicity on the part of many of our fellow citizens," wrote a *Nation* editorialist. "The politician will not soon give up his reporter, nor the eminent citizen and general oracle his typewritten impromptu."[37] This writer was particularly caustic about the efforts of literary men to publicize themselves and thought this attributable "to the same cause as the impertinence and coarseness of modern journalism—the jingle of the guinea." To this *Harper's Weekly* retorted: "This is the age of publicity and we have reason to rejoice at it." Whether it was a matter for rejoicing or not, the fact was that "the age of publicity" was dawning.

---

[36]The foregoing based on Rossiter Johnson, ed. *A History of the World's Columbian Exposition in Chicago in 1893*. Vol. II, New York: Appleton, 1897, pp. 1–35.

[37]*The Nation, 56*, p. 249.

CHAPTER ELEVEN

"The Public Be Damned"

The last two decades of the 19th century brought discernible beginnings of today's public relations practice in the United States. It is here that we find the roots of a vocation that were to flower in the Seedbed Years of 1900–1917 and beyond. The fundamental force in setting the stage of public relations in the 20th century was the wild, frenzied, and bold development of industry, railroads, utilities in the United States' post-Civil War years. In the 25 years from 1875 to 1900, the United States doubled its population, a population fed by waves of immigrants, jammed its people into cities, enthroned the machine and mass production, spanned the nation with rail and wire communications, developed the mass media of press and popular magazine, saw the princes of industry in the North seize power from the war-ravaged Southern plantation baron, and replaced the versatile frontiersman with the specialized factory hand. This quarter-century saw the passing of the frontier that did so much to influence the values and mores of the nation, then and now. It also witnessed cruel exploitation of human labor and ruthless exploitation of the nation's abundant resources.

Contemporary public relations, as a practice and as a management concept, was to emerge out of the melee of the opposing forces in this period of the nation's rapid growth. Goldman, in his brief history of public relations observed:[1] "Shouldering aside agriculture, large-scale commerce and industry became dominant over the life of the nation. Big Business was committed to the doctrine that the less the public knew of its operations, the more

---

[1] Eric F. Goldman, *Public Relations and the Progressive Surge, 1898–1917.* New York: Foundation for Public Relations Research and Education, 1966, p. 4.

efficient and profitable—even the more socially useful—operations would be." It was a day of business arrogance toward employee and citizen alike; a day when railroad magnate E. H. Harriman boasted, "I don't want anything on this railroad that I cannot control"; a day when merchant Marshall Field made $600 dollars an hour each day while his clerks earned a maximum of 12 dollars a week for a 59 hour week. It was a period of weak and corrupt government, a period of government that the dour Yankee, Henry Adams, described as "poor in purpose and barren in results." Wrote Henry George in his *Progress and Poverty*: "Get money—honestly if you can, but at any rate get money! This is the lesson that society is daily and hourly dinning into the ears of its members."

In this era of bustle and building—the era between the fall of the aristocracy of wealth and the emergence of middle-class revolt in the early 1900s—the United States was, in the liberal language of Vernon Parrington:[2]

> little more than a welter of crude energy, a raw unlovely society where the strife of competition with its prodigal waste testified to the shortcomings of an age in transition. The spirit of the frontier was to flare up in a huge buccaneering orgy. Having swept across the continent to the Pacific coast like a visitation of locusts, the frontier spirit turned back upon its course to conquer the East, infecting the new industrialism with a crude individualism, fouling the halls of Congress, despoiling the public domain, and indulging in a huge national barbecue.

It was truly the era of "The Public Be Damned," epitomized in the unforgettable phrase of William Henry Vanderbilt, son of the buccaneering Commodore Cornelius Vanderbilt and his successor as head of the New York Central Railroad. Vanderbilt made the remark, if indeed he did make it, in an interview with a Chicago freelance reporter in 1882. Vanderbilt would later heatedly deny having uttered this historic phrase. His denials mattered little then or since—the phrase has lived through the years to characterize one kind of response to the power of public opinion. The quote stuck because it accurately reflected the attitude of the business giants of that day—men whom Charles Francis Adams described as "a course, realistic, bargaining crowd."

The circumstances of that historic interview are these: Vanderbilt and a party of New York Central officials were enroute to Chicago Sunday, October 8, 1882, when two newspaper reporters boarded his special train at Michigan City, IN. One was from the *Chicago Tribune*, the other a freelancer working for space rates. Of him, Melville Stone, editor of the *Chicago Daily News* and later general manager of the Associated Press, wrote:[3] "Clarence Dresser

---

[2]Vernon Louis Parrington, *Main Currents in American Thought*. Vol. III, New York: Harcourt, Brace, 1930, pp. 4–5.

[3]*Fifty Years a Journalist*. New York: Doubleday, Page, 1921, pp. 116–117.

... was one of the offensively, aggressive type—one of those wrens who make prey where eagles dare not tread.... Dresser had, because of his audacity, proved a failure as a news gatherer and had been employed and speedily dismissed by all the papers." (Stone insisted that Dresser boarded Vanderbilt's private car when it was parked in the Michigan Central yards.) Another account states that the two reporters discussed several matters with Mr. Vanderbilt enroute to Chicago. One was the possibility that he might take off the New York Central's express train from New York to Chicago. *The New York Times'* version of the interview read like this:[4]

"Does your limited express pay?"

"No, not a bit of it. We only run it because we are forced to do so by the activities of the Pennsylvania Road. It doesn't pay expenses. We would abandon it if it was not for our competitor keeping its train on."

"But don't you run if for the public benefit?"

"The public be———. What does the public care for railroads except to get as much out of them for as small a consideration as possible. I don't take any stock in this silly nonsense about working for anybody's good but our own because we are not. When we make a move we do it because it is in our interest to do so, not because we expect to do somebody else some good. Of course we like to do everything possible for the benefit of humanity in general, but when we do we first see that we are benefiting ourselves."

The *Chicago Tribune's* account of this part of the interview reads thus:[5]

"Do your limited express trains pay or do you run these for the accommodation of the public?"

"Accommodation of the public! Nonsense, and they do not pay either. We have tried again and again to get the different roads to give them up; but they will run them, and, of course, as long as they run them, we must do the same."

Considerable furor churned in the wake of the magnate's quoted remark; in an interview in Denver, CO, Vanderbilt denied making it. According to the *Chicago Tribune* of October 12, 1882, he told the press:

The reporter talked to me about making rates to suit the public, and he printed my answer to the effect that the public might be damned for all I cared for it. This was telegraphed to New York and printed in the *Times*, which paper, so I am advised by telegram ..., recommended the people go to my house and tack placards on it bearing, "Damn the public." This is an injustice to me.

---

[4] *The New York Times*, October 9, 1882, p. 1, cols. 3–4.

[5] *Chicago Tribune*, October 9, 1882, p. 8, cols. 3–4.

What I did tell the interviewer was that the management of a railroad owed its first duty to its stockholders.

Melville Stone's account differs and goes this way. Dresser boarded Vanderbilt's car and demanded an interview.

"Well, sit down at the other end of the car until I have finished dinner, and I will talk to you. . . ."
   "But it is late and I will not reach office in time. The public—" This was too much for the infuriated Vanderbilt, who interrupted his tormentor with the ejaculation: "The public be damned; you get out of here."

Stone concluded that Dresser first offered his story to *The Daily News* where it was rejected, he then carried it to the *Chicago Tribune*, which published it.

When Vanderbilt returned to New York October 17, he told the *New York Tribune*: "You ask me about the expression—'the public be d——d' which has been put in my mouth. . . . I never used it, and that is all there is about it."

The first strong protest movement against this "public be damned" arrogance on the part of the railroads and the Robber Barons of finance came from the National Grange, an obscure secret order known first as "Patrons of Husbandry." This spearhead of the agrarian revolt was largely responsible for passage of the Interstate Commerce Act of 1887, the first Granger regulatory law designed to curb the excess of the new industrial era. Eventually, this Act was influential in inducing public relations programs in public utilities and common carriers. After this peak of influence, the Grange slowly receded in influence. Its protest strength flowed into other groups, such as the Farmers' Alliance, the Greenbackers, and the Populist Party. The people were on the march against the excessive abuses of Big Business and its "huge buccaneering orgy." These rumbles of protest in the late 19th century became a loud roar after the turn of the century, bringing Theodore Roosevelt's Square Deal and the Age of Reform.

MOGULS LEARN TO USE THE PRESS

Expressed or not, Vanderbilt's remark reflected the attitude of the great majority of industrialists and financiers who thought nothing beyond purchase for their selfish ends—the nation's resources, lawmakers, and press. They also knew the power of publicity as was demonstrated by the railroads in their push West. When Jay Gould and Jim Fisk were attempting to corner the nation's gold, Gould subsidized financial writers to plant stories that the U. S. Treasury would not sell gold in an effort to influence President U. S. Grant. Then Gould got A. R. Corbin, the President's brother-in-law, to write an editorial that Gould then persuaded James McHenry, a British capitalist, to plant with John Bigelow, *The New York Times* editor. *The Times*, according to later testimony by Gould, ran the editorial with only slight changes. Frederick Hudson in his *Journalism in the United States* mistakenly referred to McHenry as Gould's "press representative."

When the notorious Gould decided to take over the Manhattan Elevated Railway Company, he first filed legal suits over certain unauthorized stock issues and then began a vigorous publicity campaign against the worth of the company in the *New York World*, which he owned.[6] After he drove the stock down to $15.50 a share within a few months, Gould bought in and then used publicity to boost the stock to $55 a share in another few months.

The Tweed political ring used the press in similar ways. According to James Parton, writing in *Harper's Monthly* for July 1874, the Tweed Ring had 89 newspapers on the payroll, "of which twenty-seven so depended on this plunder for subsistence that when the ring was broken, they gasped and died."[7]

James I. C. Clarke, the first publicity man to be hired by Standard Oil Company in 1906, in his memoirs described George Crouch as Jim Fisk's "publicity man." Crouch was a reporter on the *New York Herald* but apparently was also on Fisk's payroll. He too was used in the gold market fix.

INSURANCE COMPANIES USE PUBLICITY TO BOOST SALES

In this period, publicity was being used in the competition for business, especially in the brawling young insurance field. A historian of Mutual Life Insurance Company, describing this period wrote:[8]

> To facilitate the labors of the sales force, the Mutual Life, like all similar institutions, endeavored to establish in the public mind not only its name, but also a favorable impression of its operations. Its chief vehicles of advertising were the insurance press and pamphlet literature. In the former the Company not only inserted bona fide advertisements, but it also paid editors to run its message as news articles or editorials. For the campaign against Jacob L. Greene of the Connecticut Mutual, the Mutual, along with the Equitable and the New York Life, hired the services of C. C. Hine, editor of the *Insurance Monitor*, Stephen English of the *Insurance Times*, and Charles J. (Dollar-a-Line) Smith of the *Insurance Record*. The editor of the *Insurance Monitor* had a

---

[6]Robert T. Warshow, *Jay Gould, the Story of a Fortune*. New York, 1928. p. 160 ff.

[7]Quoted in Frank Luther Mott, *American Journalism* (3rd ed.). New York: Macmillan, 1962, p. 383.

[8]Shepard B. Clough, *A Century of American Life Insurance*. New York: Columbia University Press, 1946, pp. 168–169.

fixed price for his Connecticut Mutual extras of $50 a thousand and boasted that he sold them "by the ton."

This obvious purchase of editorial content in these trade journals was expensive and had its risks. These mercenaries were available for hire to all sides. English, for example, served the Equitable's cause so well in a campaign against Mutual that the latter firm hired him away from Equitable. Even though these battles to tear down the competitors served more to undermine public confidence in life insurance than to build sales, "they continued with more or less vigor throughout this period of managerial domination."

Mutual's establishment of "a species of literary bureau" and the activities of its Charles J. "$ a Line" Smith were told in chapter 10.

The lack of business morality and the crude, heavy-handed ways of dealing with public opinion in this period were accurately mirrored in this insurance brawling and bribing. English was typical. Labeled by one writer as a "wild Irish adventurer," English, in the opinion of one muckraker, "ranked far ahead of the venal blackmailer who then so largely infested the insurance press. In a few years he became the terror of the insurance world. When not pounding away at solvent concerns, he was singing the praises of dishonest ones."[9] These companies also bought their way into the daily press. For instance, Joe Howard, Jr., a correspondent for several New York, Boston, and Washington papers, was on the payroll of both Mutual and Equitable for $2,500 a year. He was paid $5,000 to suppress a series of unfavorable articles on one occasion.[10] It should be remembered that in this era of U.S. journalism reporters were paid on space rates and poorly paid at that.

Yet amidst all this bribing and blackmailing, some sounder public relations practices got started. In 1885, Mutual Life began a publication, *The Weekly Statement*, to inform and inspire its agents—one of the nation's first house organs. Clough said the internal publication was "relatively free from aspersions on other companies." Massey Harris launched its *Triphammer*, an employees' magazine, the same year. There were earlier ones. The first known company publication was the *Lowell Offering*, put out by the Lowell, MA. cotton mills in 1840 as a literary magazine of sorts. *The Locomotive*, was started in 1867 by the Hartford Steam Boiler Inspection and Insurance Company. The Travelers Insurance Company started an internal publication, *Traveler*, in 1865, but the name has been changed and publication halted several times. Aetna Life Insurance Company started an employee magazine in 1868, and the National Cash Register started one in 1891.

---

[9]Burton J. Hendrick, "The Story of Life Insurance," *McClure's, 27* (1906), p. 542.
[10]*Ibid.* p. 665.

ROCKEFELLER MAKES GRUDGING RESPONSE
TO PUBLIC OPINION

Big Business' response to the swelling protests of an increasingly articulate public in this pre-20th century era is reflected in the changing posture and tactics of John D. Rockefeller's Standard Oil Trust. "Between 1872 and 1892 the Standard Oil combination came to stand before the bar of public opinion as the epitome of the evils of Big Business. The Trust was pictured as bloated in size, as a creation of railroad rate discriminations, and as a menace to free enterprise in the United States."[11]

At first Rockefeller and his associates ignored their critics and gave the public no information as they went about their business of getting a strangle hold on the petroleum industry. As criticism mounted, Standard Oil began to respond with apologia and subsidies for organs of opinion. Toward the end of this period it resorted to the purchase of advertising space and paid but unmarked editorial readers. None of these tactics proved effective in staying public demand that this Goliath be brought under control.

During the 1870s and early 1880s, Rockefeller and his associates generally kept silent when attacked by such powerful critics as Henry Demarest Lloyd and Joseph Pulitzer. A trade publication, the *Oil Paint & Drug Reporter* for January 9, 1884, printed this biting criticism: "The Standard Company not only owns and runs Cleveland but it also holds a first mortgage on the bodies and souls of the Cleveland people." The first public defense of Standard Oil's actions was made by one of its lackeys, United States Senator J. N. Camden of West Virginia, in a published debate with J. C. Welch. The opposing views were published in the *North American Review* for February 1883. Rockefeller, seeking to protect his oil interests in West Virginia, bought control of the State Legislature so that it would appoint Camden to the United States Senate and there Camden dutifully sought to protect the interests of Standard Oil. Typically, Camden tried to justify Standard's plan to corner the oil business as simply an effort to curb the speculation, waste, and overproduction in crude oil and in the manufacture of petroleum products. The Hidys observed: "Camden's defense of the combination was really an exception to the general Standard Oil rule of unobtrusive action in public relations."

Most of Standard's efforts to mollify the public were less obvious. During the 1880s Standard officials maintained financial ties with some newspapers. In 1881, Ohio Standard carried on its books $10,000 in stock of the Cleveland *Herald*, originally acquired 2 years earlier. There is good evidence that Standard controlled, through subsidy, the Oil City, PA, *Derrick*, which vo-

---

[11]Ralph W. and Muriel E. Hidy, *History of the Standard Oil Company (New Jersey) Pioneering in Big Business 1882–1911.* New York: Harper, 1955, p. 201.

ciferously supported its machinations. Its publisher, Patrick Boyle, was widely regarded as an apologist for Standard. Quiet pressure was also brought to bear on newspapers. "When the policies of prominent newspapers conflicted or threatened to conflict with those of Standard Oil, either top managers or their friends tried to learn the facts and to persuade editors and owners to adopt a more reasonable course."[12] By 1887, the Standard managers began to show some signs of adjusting their public relations policies to prevailing conditions. Standard began to give out some information and to cooperate in industry movements. Indicative was Standard's decision not to oppose the 1887 bill to regulate interstate commerce, by creating the Interstate Commerce Commission. The bill was too mild to pose a serious threat to either Standard or the railroads.

S. C. T. Dodd of Standard's legal staff appears to have taken the lead in altering the trust's public relations policies. He encouraged a franker, less evasive response to inquiries of the New York Senate and a House of Representatives committee in 1888. Later that year, Dodd published his testimony in the pamphlet, *Combinations: Their Uses and Abuses, with a History of the Standard Oil Trust*, a strong defense of the right of combination. Dodd was in the vanguard of lawyers who, in time, endeavored to argue their employer's case in the court of public opinion as well as in courts of law.

"During the late eighties officials among the Standard Oil group began to show more appreciation of the power of the press and attempt to utilize it. Dodd was frequently called upon for comments in connection with reports circulating in the newspapers. . . . During these years the apostle of silence himself, John D. Rockefeller, began to turn a more favorable face to the press than he had turned earlier."[13]

When the fiery Dr. Washington Gladden, Congregational minister, began his attacks on Standard, the trust engaged George Gunton to rebut the criticisms. Gunton, an English-trained economist, was given an annual subsidy of $15,000 or more to support his work in adult education and to publish *Gunton's Magazine*. "Gunton criticized emotional pulpit economists and sensational newspapers which flourished on prejudice." Standard Oil quit supporting Gunton in 1904 in order to "avoid a public scandal."[14] The Hidys found that while Standard did provide financial support to several newspapers, it did not subsidize as many as its critics of that time asserted. As the firm began to develop some experience in dealing with the public and press, it began to turn to paid advertising and paid but unlabeled readers inserted in a large number of newspapers. This dishonest practice of buying editorial space came in response to strong newspaper attacks growing out

---

[12]*Ibid.* p. 213.
[13]*Ibid.* p. 217.
[14]*Ibid.* p. 660.

of the State of Ohio's efforts to void Standard's Trust Agreement. As criticism of Standard's monopolistic practices swelled, the company employed, through Henry Apthorp, newspaperman and lobbyist, the Malcolm Jennings News Bureau and Advertising Agency, headquartered in Cleveland. On behalf of Standard, Jennings made contracts with about 150 journals in Ohio and Indiana for publication of what came to be termed *tainted news.*

Ohio Attorney General Frank S. Monnett, when he had Standard on trial for contempt of court in 1898, brought out a typical contract that included this clause:[15] "The publisher agrees to reprint on news or editorial pages of said newspaper such notices, set in the body type of said paper and bearing no mark to indicate advertising, as are furnished from time to time by said Jennings Agency at the rate of—per line, and to furnish such agency extra copies of paper containing such notes at four cents a copy." Examples of articles published under this arrangement—all them in high praise of Standard Oil—were offered in testimony. Years later Standard Oil used the same tactics in the "oil war" in Kansas of 1905. Some of these articles were copies from other newspapers and some were written by Jennings. The general nature of items inserted by the agency is indicated by this item from the Lima, OH, *Times–Democrat,* introduced as Exhibit A at the time the relationship of Jennings and Standard Oil was being aired in court:[16]

> Whether the Standard Oil Company of Ohio is in trust or out of a trust is a question for the courts to decide, and whether the consumers of oil are getting a better quality at less cost, and handled with greater safety than formerly, is a question for the people to decide. In the commercial affairs of life it is things, not words, that count in making up the balance sheet of loss or gain, of benefit, or injury. Monopoly and octopus, combines and trusts are haughty words, but the best goods at lower prices are beneficial things. It is much easier to say harsh words than it is to make things cheap.

According to the Hidys: "At about the same time that the arrangement was made with the Jennings Agency, Standard Oil quit giving financial aid directly to any newspapers. It is a sad commentary on the press of that day that many an editor would come hat in hand to 26 Broadway—Standard Oil's New York headquarters—begging for financial assistance and promising support of Standard in return. The directors of Standard decided 'for self protection' that they could not discriminate between supplicant journals and started turning down these requests. This decision appears to have been reached about 1898 and was firmly established five years later."

Yet in 1903, Senator J. B. Foraker of Ohio received $50,000 from John D. Archbold, Standard vice-president, to be used to purchase part interest in the *Ohio State Journal,* published in Ohio's capital city. Later when Foraker

---

[15]"Manufacturing Public Opinion," *McClure's, 26,* 1906, p. 451.

[16]Hidy and Hidy, fn. 60, p. 802.

was unable to make the purchase, he returned the money to Archbold.[17] Archbold's correspondence indicates that after he took control of Standard Oil, "the Pittsburgh *Times, The Manufacturer's Record, The Southern Farm Magazine,* and *Gunton's Magazine* were all assisted." *Gunton's Magazine* folded shortly after Standard Oil's subsidy was cut off.

In subsequent years, Archbold subsidized books and universities to spread a favorable image of John D. Rockefeller and his company. One example: In the words of its newly hired publicist, James I. C. Clarke, Archbold, to get "an authenticated history of the Standard Oil," to counter Ida Tarbell's critical two-volume *The History of Standard Oil,* published in 1904, found his man in Chancellor James R. Day of Syracuse University. Once described as a "booming flagellant of sinners and worshiped for his sense of justice," Chancellor Day answered Tarbell with his *The Raid on Prosperity.* As Day's reward, coincidentally of course, John D. Archbold provided the university with a stadium, a gymnasium, and a dormitory, Sims Hall. Understandably, such coincidences gave credence to the muckraker charge that Rockefeller and other millionaires were seeking to buy good reputations with their philanthropies. In 1911, the Standard Oil Trust was broken up in a decree issued by Judge Kenesaw Mountain Landis in response to the U. S. Government Anti-Trust lawsuit.

NOT ALL NEWSPAPERMEN COULD BE BOUGHT

Fortunately for the public weal not all newspapermen could be bought by the plunderers and plungers. One was the *Railroad Gazette,* which announced in 1883 that it would "entertain no proposition to publish anything in its journal for pay, except in the advertising columns."[18] Another was Josephus Daniels, North Carolina's distinguished editor and Democratic Party stalwart. Daniels later served in the administrations of Woodrow Wilson and Franklin D. Roosevelt. He started his newspaper career in 1885 on the Raleigh (NC) State *Chronicle,* a weekly started 2 years earlier by Walter Hines Page. Page, later Wilson's ambassador to Great Britain, was the father of Arthur W. Page, a man who would make public relations history in the 20th Century. In 1895, Daniels was able to buy the Raleigh *News and Observer,* which he built into one of the South's leading newspapers. In his editorials, Daniels fought the railroads' abuse of the public interest and took on the "tobacco trust" after it was put together in 1890 by the Duke family.

Typical of business' way of dealing with editorial opposition was the approach the vice-president of the Southern Railway made to Daniels in

---

[17]William Kittle, "The Making of Public Opinion," *Arena, 41,* 1909, p. 442.

[18]*Railroad Gazette, 15,* 1883, p. 8.

1889. The railroad executive offered to help Daniels buy the *News and Observer* provided the young editor would not support creation of a Railroad Commission, adding:[19] "From time to time I would send you extracts from other papers about railroad and industrial matters that would develop the South and ask you to print them, of course, without committing yourself to the approval of the views of the editor quoted in your paper. Most of the articles I would furnish would be about railroad expansion."

When the railroads and the tobacco trust found that they could not buy Daniels' support, they next tried to put another paper in the field against him, but it failed.[20] The day of the bought publication or the company owned newspaper, with a few exceptions—such as Anacoda Copper's Montana newspapers—was fading by the end of the century. Other ways had to be found to get a message into the common carriers of public information. Hence, the demand for the publicist would grow.

THEODORE N. VAIL SEES A MORE ENLIGHTENED WAY

There was at least one rising young business executive in this public-be-damned era who saw the long-term profit in accommodating the public interest and providing information about business to the news media. Understandably his views went unheeded in this day of raw exploitation and extravagance. He was Theodore Newton Vail, who in the next century, fashioned the public relations policies that were to save the American Telephone and Telegraph Company and set the pattern for more enlightened corporate public reactions practices.

Vail was born July 16, 1845, in Carroll County, OH, but grew up in Morristown, NJ. He moved with his family to a farm near Waterloo, IA, in 1866, but soon found farm life boring and took a telegrapher's job with the Union Pacific Railroad in 1868. He was assigned as night operator in Pine Bluffs, WY. Restless and ambitious young Vail was not long content with his telegrapher's job. He applied for and got a job in the U. S. Railway Mail Service at the age of 24. Vail soon introduced a new plan for distribution of the mail on trains that won him the attention of the Postmaster General's Office. His drive and his intelligence took Vail from the job of telegrapher in Pine Bluffs to the superintendency of the U. S. Railway Mail Service in less than 8 years. Vail at once set out to reform the U. S. mail service and speeded mail delivery to the nation.

---

[19]Josephus Daniels, *The Story of a Tarheel Editor.* Chapel Hill: University of North Carolina Press, 1939, p. 407.

[20]Edwin Emery, *The Press and America* (2nd ed.). Englewood Cliffs, NJ: Prentice-Hall, 1962, p. 472.

In 1878, 2 years after Vail had become superintendent of railway mails, Alexander Graham Bell's father-in-law asked Vail if he would become general manager of the Bell Telephone Company, then only 9 months old. *Fortune* records:[21]

> Vail took the risk because he was a leader; he responded to Bell's vision of a great national telephone network, and he was moved to bring the vision to pass. In the next eight years Vail established the form, a strategy, character, and direction of the Bell System as a "natural monopoly." He foresaw that the system could hold its dominant position by (a) licensing hundreds of local telephone companies; (b) controlling them through a network of long lines connecting every exchange; (c) controlling all new telephone developments through operations of a manufacturing affiliate.

Vail saw that for the company to flourish and for it to be accepted as a "natural monopoly," that it would have to earn the goodwill of the public—a most revolutionary idea in the business world of the 1880s. In his early experience in the communication fields with telegraph and mail services, he had seen the power of an aroused public opinion. As early as 1879, only 1 year after he joined the Bell Company, Vail wrote a New York Telephone company official stressing the need to adopt the best system possible. Four years later, he wrote the head of the Iowa Union Telegraph and Telephone Company a letter that reflected Vail's concern over whether the service rates were satisfactory, whether these rates could be reduced, and whether relationships between the public and company could not be improved. This historic letter is reproduced on page 199. These were rare concerns indeed in those years.

As the telephone business grew rapidly, Vail kept urging the Boston capitalists who owned the Bell Company to take smaller dividends and put more money into research and into improving the telephone service—most unorthodox thoughts for this time. But the owners, caught up in the mood of the time to get rich while the getting was good, ignored Vail's advice. By 1887, he had had enough: "My present position in the company is not such as I had hoped to attain, and is also in some ways embarrassing and unpleasant." He resigned and spent the next 15 years traveling widely. But in 1902, he responded to J. P. Morgan's call to help save AT&T, then suffering sorely from overexpansion, poor public relations, and tough competition from a proliferating number of independent companies. Five years later, Vail was named president of AT&T and given a free hand to run it, and in this position he made public relations and business history. In the late 19th century Vail's voice was a feeble one in the roar of the great barbecue.

---

[21]Perrin Stryker, "The Rarest Man in Business," *Fortune, 59,* 1959, p. 120.

Subject: **re information as to service, rates &c.**

Wм R DRIVER Treasurer

FORBES President   **THE AMERICAN BELL TELEPHONE CO.**   [illegible] General Manager

№ 95 MILK STREET

P O DRAWER 2

W. A. Leary, Esq.   *Boston* Dec. 28th, 1883.
Iowa Union Tel. & Tel. Co.
Davenport, Iowa.   *In reply to yours*

Dear Sir : -

     Now that the Telephone business has passed its ex-
perimental stage, I would like to get your opinion upon points giv-
en below. This opinion to be based upon our existing relations,
and upon your own and your associates observation and experience
in your particular field : -

     Is the Telephone service as it is now being furnish-
ed, satisfactory to the public.
     Are the prices satisfactory to the public, consider-
ing the facilities and service that is given.
     Would it be advantageous to furnish the same ser-
vice now being furnished at any lower rate provided it could
be done.
     Is it possible in view of the contingencies of storm,
under ground legislation &c., to make any lower rate to the
public for same classes of service.
     Is it desirable, and what would be the most practi-
cable way, to provide a service at a rate which would be within the reach of families. etc,.
     Is it practicable to give different classes of ser-
vice within the same Exchange.
     What has been the tendency of the relationship be-
tween the public and the local Co's., for the past year ie.,
are the relations between the public and the Co's. improving.
     Where there has been any conflict between the local
Exchange and the public, what has been the cause of the dif -
ficulties, and what has been the result.

     A full and detailed reply from you by the 8th, of
January, would be of great service to me. Trusting that I am not
asking too much,

     I am,

         Very respectfully, &c.

         Theo N Vail

         Courtesy AT&T Archives.

WESTINGHOUSE PIONEERS CORPORATE PUBLIC
RELATIONS—OF NECESSITY

One of the nation's oldest corporate public relations programs, that of Westinghouse Electric Company, had its origins in a bruising, gutter-level business battle that took place in the infant electrical industry in the late 1880s.
This struggle, which came to be known as "The Battle of the Currents,"

ensued when George Westinghouse developed generation of an alternating electrical current (AC) in 1886 to compete with Thomas A. Edison's direct current systems already on the market. In this fight, Edison had the assistance of his secretary, the youthful and astute Samuel Insull who in later years, wrote public utilities relations on his own. When Westinghouse put his new AC system on the market, Edison decided to fight change rather than adopt it, contrary to Insull's advice. According to Insull's biographer:[22]

> Insull, who readily perceived the competitive disadvantage at which Washington's a.c. system was placing the Edison central stations, urged Edison to work on alternating current apparatus. Edison reluctantly agreed. . . . But in exchange for his agreement to fight Westinghouse fairly, Edison demanded that it be fought unfairly as well, to which Insull agreed . . . it was the unfair fight that was waged in earnest. Edison G. E. attempted to prevent the development of alternating current by unscrupulous political action and by even less savory promotional tactics.

Edison and his associates used scare tactics to frighten the public from acceptance of the new AC system and there is circumstantial evidence indicating that Edison was involved in promoting the electric chair for capital punishment as part of this scare campaign. "Their only hope of being successful in this attempt was that the whole of the electric art was new at that time; and while the general public was beginning to enjoy some of the fruits of this development it was not yet educated to an understanding of any of the scientific facts which were responsible for these accomplishments, which seemed to be almost miraculous."[23]

According to Matthew Josephson, the Edison laboratory at West Orange, NJ, was the principal source of "scientific" evidence purportedly demonstrating the dangers of AC. There, on any day in 1887, one might have found Edison and his assistants electrocuting stray cats and dogs by means of high-tension AC currents. "In the presence of newspaper reporters and other invited guests Edison . . . would edge a little dog onto a sheet of tin to which were attached wires from an AC generator supplying current at 1,000 volts."[24]

A bitter press battle ensued. The publicity campaign against the Westinghouse system was launched by the publication of a booklet, A Warning—bound in red—put out by the Edison firm in February 1888. This booklet contained many pages that recounted the dangers of alternating current and an appendix listed the names of individuals killed by it. "The Edison viewpoint was that alternating current endangered the lives of all members of a

---

[22]Forrest McDonald, *Insull*. Chicago: University of Chicago Press, 1962, pp. 44–45.

[23]Malcolm MacLaren, *The Rise of the Electrical Industry During the Nineteenth Century*. Princeton University Press, Princeton, NJ, 1943, p. 177.

[24]Matthew Josephson, *Edison*. New York: McGraw-Hill, 1959, p. 347.

community where it was present. . . . The strategy of the Edison Company was to educate public opinion to the view that AC was an intolerable menace to the American people, fostered upon it by a selfish and profit seeking corporation."[25] Whether Edison directly involved himself in promotion of the electric chair as part of his anti-AC campaign is not known. On this point McDonald asserted, on somewhat questionable evidence, that:[26]

> The promotional activity was a series of spectacular stunts aimed at dramatizing the deadlines of high voltage alternating current, the most sensational being the development and promotion of the electric chair as a means executing criminals. The state of New York adopted this innovation in 1888 after a gruesome promotional campaign, conceived by Insull, Johnson, and Edison, and carried out by a German-American named Thruington and H. P. Brown, one of Edison's former lab assistants.

After asserting that Edison did not invent the chair, a friendly biographer explained Edison's connection with the grim idea this way:[27]

> When the apparatus was being installed at Auburn, he visited the prison and inspected the interesting instrument whereby murderers who commit their crimes in the State of New York are sometimes shocked out of existence. Moreover, when experiments were being conducted to decide whether or not electrocution should be adopted as the capital sentence in lieu of hanging, Edison placed his Menlo Park laboratory at the disposal of the investigators and allowed some of his electricians to assist in the work of investigation.

Engineer Harold P. Brown, a former Edison employee, conducted the experiments and these were well publicized by Edison who "bombarded the press with letters on the dangers of alternating current."[28]

New York's adoption of electrocution in 1888 was thought to be a great victory of the advocates of direct current, but MacLaren thought that "it really had no bearing at all upon the relative safety of the two systems of distribution." An exhaustive search of available records does not show whether Edison was or was not the originator of the electrical chair. At the least he assisted and encouraged its development. It is depressing to contemplate the origins of this barbarous instrument.

Westinghouse was slow to respond to the Edison–Insull propaganda campaign. He had expected that the superiority of his system to prevail over

---

[25]Harold C. Passer, *The Electrical Manufacturers 1875–1900*. Cambridge, MA: Harvard University Press, p. 167.

[26]McDonald, p. 45.

[27]Francis Arthur Jones, *Thomas Alva Edison: Sixty Years of an Inventor's Life*. New York: Thomas Y. Crowell, 1908, p. 203.

[28]Mary Childs Nerney, *Thomas A. Edison: A Modern Olympian*. New York, 1934, p. 123.

Edison's locally bound system. MacLaren suggested "The literature of the period indicates that the Westinghouse Company made little attempt to answer these false accusations directly, but they gave many descriptions of new and successful plants which they were installing throughout the country."[29] For a time, Westinghouse considered suing Edison but finally decided to fight fire with fire; thus historic public relations battle was joined. The Westinghouse firm published a booklet, *Safety of the Alternating System of Electrical Distribution,* in October of 1889, intended to refute Brown's assertions about the lethal nature of the AC system. More importantly, Westinghouse realized his need to tell his story to the public through the press. Like many a businessman since, he hired a newspaper person.

In the latter part of October 1889, Westinghouse phoned Ernest H. Heinrichs, a reporter for the Pittsburgh *Chronicle Telegraph,* whom he had known for some time, and asked the newsman to come to see him. Heinrichs went to see Westinghouse expecting to get a news story but got a job instead. The conversation went this way:[30]

> "Heinrichs, how would you like to work for me?"
> The question was so unexpected that the caller was for a moment unable to form a reply, but after a while he managed to answer in a somewhat hesitating manner:
> "I should be very glad to work for you, if there is anything that I can do."
> "The work I have in mind," replied Mr. Westinghouse, "I believe you will be able to do very well."

In this case, it was the businessman who saw the need for the trained communicator to carry his message to the public rather than having to be sold the idea by one seeking a public relations job. Heinrichs reported for work November 1 and was placed under the direction of H. M. Byllesby, vice-president and general manager. The former reporter served Westinghouse until the latter's death in March 1914. When Heinrichs started work, Westinghouse, reflecting an understanding of public relations rare for that day, personally instructed him:[31]

> I wish you success, and I feel that the papers should cooperate with you in what you are trying to do. I do not want any free publicity. Advertising is one of the chief revenues of the papers and all advertising matter should be paid for. But the Westinghouse Companies produce achievements almost daily which the papers may legitimately publish as news because they are accomplishments which reflect with credit upon the city, and they will help to

---

[29]MacLaren, p. 180.

[30]E. H. Heinrichs, "George Westinghouse as an Employer," unpublished memoir, November 1935, in Westinghouse Company archives.

[31]*Ibid.*

advertise . . . Pittsburgh. As to general news about my companies or my personal affairs, all I want is to see that the papers print it accurately. The truth hurts nobody, but misleading, garbled statements invariably do, and I want you to prevent any misrepresentation whenever you can.

Heinrich suggested that Westinghouse thought "all this opposition to the Alternating Current system by our competitors is doing our business a great deal of good" and that the manufacturer didn't want to play the other fellow's game. The new press relations man for Westinghouse moved quickly to meet the Edison–Insull campaign of misrepresentation by ghosting a reply to articles by Edison and Brown that had been published in the *North American Review* the month Heinrichs went to work. In an article, "The Dangers of Electric Lighting," Edison asserted: "There is a record of nearly one hundred deaths, which furnishes an unanswerable argument in support of these statements [against the AC system]."[32]

Concluding his reply to Mr. Edison, George Westinghouse, Jr. wrote:[33]

It is worthy of note that for three years past the purchasers of apparatus for electric lighting, who are at perfect liberty to buy from any company have, for the most part, preferred to use the alternating current system, so that to day the extension of that system for incandescent lighting is at least five times as great as that of direct current. If the opinion of these persons, who can have no interest except to purchase what they believe to be the best, is of any value, then the alternating system has been demonstrated to be the one which can give the public that which they so much desire—a safe, cheap, efficient and universally-applicable system of incandescent electric lighting.

The Edison–Insull propaganda scare campaign didn't pay off, and the merits of the Westinghouse AC system eventually won public acceptance demonstrating that performance and merit are the foundation stones of effective public relations. But Heinrichs soon came to realize that it took publicity and advertising as well as good products to meet the stiffening competition in this new market.

In 1893, after his duties had been broadened to include advertising, Heinrichs advised businessmen that it was now necessary to "promulgate" their distinctive advantages through advertising. In an article, he wisely saw the need for writing and publishing advertisements for specific audiences, a lesson some practitioners have yet to learn. Thus begun the corporate practice of telling its story to the public via the expanding carriers of public information by means of press releases and paid advertisements. Like many

---

[32]See Harold P. Brown, "The New Instrument of Execution," *North American Review*, CXLIX, 1889, p. 586.

[33]*Ibid.* p. 653.

a corporate public relations department born later, the Westinghouse public relations program had its beginnings in the need for communication in a public battle. Alan Raucher hailed Heinrichs as "the nation's first industrial press agent."

THIS WAS A DAY OF UNION BUSTING

The prevailing hard-bitten attitudes of businessmen toward people—be they employees, customers, or voters—in this era was epitomized in the brutal methods used by Henry Clay Frick to crush a labor union in the Carnegie–Frick Steel Company's Homestead, PA, plant in 1892. Callous, tough Henry Frick directed the struggle while Carnegie calmly viewed events from afar in his Scottish castle, seemingly unperturbed by the brutality and killings Frick directed. This strike broke out early in July 1892 and lasted 143 days. Frick's first move was to hire the notorious Pinkerton Agency, which at that time was in the lucrative business of furnishing private guards to strikebound plants.

On a misty morning, July 6, a pair of barges bearing some 300 company-hired Pinkerton guards were towed to Carnegie–Frick steel plant at Homestead, on the Monongahela River just south of Pittsburgh. Thousands of strikers threw a barrage of bullets, dynamite, and cannonballs (these duds) at the barges. The Pinkerton strikebreakers, who had not been told their mission when they were signed up in New York and Chicago, fired back and the battle was on. In all, some 35 guards and strikers were killed and hundreds were wounded in this bloody battle between Americans—hired strikebreakers and striking workers.

The strike was ultimately broken and the union destroyed by the use of Pennsylvania state militia. In view of one who wrote a concise account of this struggle:[34]

> Carnegie's triumph in the crucial western Pennsylvania region, coupled with the severe depression of 1893–1897 and its attendant slashing of wages and employment in the metal trades, crippled the Amalgamated [Union] and proved that even the world's strongest craft union could not cope with a modern, multimillion-dollar industrial giant reinforced by state military power.

Cold-blooded might won this battle. The employees eventually won the war in the 1930s. Much of public relations history—constructive and de-structive—is woven into this unending struggle between employer and em-

---

[34]Leon Wolff, *Lockout.* New York: Harper & Row, 1965, p. 228.

ployee that today is fought with publicists, not Pinkertons. Later chapters of the unending struggle are told in *The Unseen Power—Public Relations.*[35]

ATTITUDES BEGIN TO SHIFT
AS NEW CENTURY APPROACHES

As the fires of protest burned stronger in the 1890s, other individuals and industries became somewhat aware of the need to dampen the flames of criticism and the opportunity to use publicity in promoting land sales and new businesses. Historian Merle Curti wrote, of this period: "Corporations gradually began to realize the importance of combating hostility and courting public favor. The expert in the field of public relations was an inevitable phenomenon in the view of the need for the services he could provide."

One of those mentioned by Curti was George Harvey, newspaperman, magazine editor, publicist, and political fixer from the 1890s to the 1920s. Harvey, then managing editor of the *New York World*, worked with William C. Whitney in promoting the election of President Grover Cleveland. In 1893, he left the *World* to become a freelance publicist and promoter for Whitney and Thomas Fortune Ryan.

"Whitney employed Harvey in a confidential capacity of much importance. . . . He not only performed his duties with efficiency and discretion, but also greatly magnified his work, until he became little less than his employer's indispensable *alter ego.*"[36] Whitney at this time was engaged in exploitation of New York City's street transportation system. Thomas Fortune Ryan was an associate in this enterprise. Through these connections, Harvey was able to make enough money to buy the *North American Review* in 1899. He became president of the J. P. Morgan-controlled Harper Bros. publishing firm in 1900 and editor of *Harper's Weekly* in 1901. He used these positions to advance enterprises of the entrenched Wall Street community. Harvey was among the early promoters of Woodrow Wilson's Presidential candidacy until Wilson shucked him off. Harvey later presided over the "smoke-filled room" in which Warren G. Harding was handed the GOP nomination in 1920. Harvey was more a fixer and promoter than a public relations man in the modern sense. Nonetheless, he had a definite flair for publicity. He quickly put publicity to work to rehabilitate the fortunes of the sadly disorganized House of Harper soon after he took over for the Morgan interests—the prime creditors of the hard-up firm.

---

[35]Scott M. Cutlip, *The Unseen Power: Public Relations. A History.* Hillsdale, NJ: Lawrence Erlbaum Associates, 1994.

[36]Willis Fletcher Johnson, *George Harvey, Passionate Patriot.* Boston: Houghton Mifflin, 1929, p. 62.

J. Henry Harper recounted:[37] "he proceeded to invent and execute his own series of publicity stunts. The first gun in the campaign was the House dinner at Delmonico's, a gathering of one hundred and fifty men representing the several executive, editorial, business, and mechanical departments. It was a notable turnout which included cabs, full dress coats, top-hats, and white ties. . . . New York had never seen anything quite like it." Harper said that prior to Harvey's coming, "the *Harper's* had shrunk from ordinary journalistic publicity." Harvey left Harper's in 1915 and sold his *Review* in 1926 to work on a biography of Henry Clay Frick. He was obviously a man of conservative, if flexible convictions.

RAILROADS AND UTILITIES FIRST
TO FEEL HEAT FROM FIRST OF PROTEST

Railroads and local utilities were among the first businesses to feel the searing heat of an aroused citizenry; thus, it was logical that these enterprises were among the first to take steps to placate their critics though some of these efforts were obvious.

The railroads were not as indifferent to public opinion in the 1870s and 1880s as some of the machinations indicated. Early the railroads employed the free pass, the letter to the editor, and contributions as means of gaining public goodwill as recounted in chapter 9. Free passes for the press, politicians, clergy, and other influential groups were common though the value of these was debated. Railroader James M. Walker once wrote: "I think the grant of a free pass to make one friend creates half a dozen enemies," whereas another executive George Watrous, wished "it were a capital offense to ask or give free transportation." Typical of the opposite point of view was the executive who directed a subordinate to issue a pass to a clergyman by saying: "I think it is as good a use of so much value as our company can possibly make to it. We want friends of this sort in Iowa."[38]

Railroad executives relied heavily on the letters to influential citizens as a means of stifling criticism and heading off regulation. Cochran termed this "an important type of public relations." These letters argued that regulation would injure all industry in the state and discourage outside investors. Typical was James C. Clarke's letter stating that the Illinois Central would not "entertain the idea of building a railroad anywhere in the North West, nor indeed in any other locality, with the present outlook and hostile legislation, both state and nation, threatening railroad interests." [39]

---

[37]*I Remember.* New York: Harper, 1934, p. 103.

[38]Quotes are from Thomas C. Cochran, *Railroad Leaders, 1845–1890.* Cambridge, MA: Harvard University Press, 1953, p. 188.

[39]*Ibid.*

Cochran noted:[40] "In addition to influencing politicians, editors, clergy-men, and other prominent citizens by favors or argument, railroad entre-preneurs were generally careful to make use of special opportunities to improve or sustain public relations." As examples, he cited gifts to soldiers' funds, aid in epidemics, transportation of delegates to conventions, beauti-fication of new towns, and contributions to county fairs. One of the early leaders, Charles E. Perkins, president of the Burlington, "wanted to introduce a sound economics text in the grammar schools of Chicago," in 1885, which indicates the businessman's zeal to teach the nation's youth "sound eco-nomics" is not exactly new, a business tactic oft-repeated in the 20th century.

The Boston (Massachusetts) Elevated Railway pioneered among local transportation companies in setting up a publicity department. In 1897, the utility hired J. Harvey White because of William A. Gaston's conviction that "the public, which furnished the patronage and the dividends of the com-pany, really had some rights in addition to that of riding a certain distance for 5 cents."[41] In this same period in Chicago, the crusty Charles T. Yerkes, Chicago's leading utility magnate until Insull took over, was showing only contempt for the public. When a group of commuters asked Yerkes to put on more cars during the rush hours, he testily replied: "Preposterous. It is the straphanger who pays the dividends."[42] There were more Yerkes than Gastons in the utility business then.

Public relations pioneer White also suggested a more practical reason for Colonel Gaston's decision to hire a publicity man. "Another important con-sideration was that the time of the president was too valuable to be infringed upon very extensively even by newspaper men; and this was probably the determining reason for establishing the bureau." The economy for a top executive in having an aide to deal with the press, troublesome correspond-ence, and to write messages, and speeches, and so forth is too often over-looked as a factor in public relation's development. As pressure on executives mounted in the 20th century, such an aide became ever more necessary. White and others asserted that Gaston fully recognized the public's right to legitimate information in a day when most businessmen thought this heresy.

White was selected for this new task even though he had not had news-paper experience and "knew as little as the company about what was wanted." "There were no manuals of procedures for pioneers. Nevertheless, he broke into the work with the general understanding that he was to experiment in regard to securing better relations between the company and the public."[43] At first White devoted only a part of his time to public relations,

[40]*Ibid.* pp. 188–189.
[41]J. Harvey White, "A Department of Publicity," *Street Railway Journal, 30,* 1907, p. 874.
[42]McDonald, p. 876.
[43]"Publicity Among the Bostonese," *Electric Railway Journal, 50* (December 8, 1917), p. 1034.

but with the growth of the system and the increasing demand for his services by the Boston press, he was soon giving full time to public relations. In a few years, he had his own office, an assistant, and a secretary.

Ten years after starting the department, White described his task as "not to advertise the company, except as that may come in incidentally to his regular work, but to save the time of President Bancroft—one of the busiest men in New England—and to aid the newspapers in getting authentic news reports about the company, be it changes in policy, accidents, appointment of officials, additions of new rolling stock, or what not."[44] This article was written in the third person but carried White's byline, suggesting that it may have been prepared by him to be published without the byline to promote White and his firm.

From the start, White eschewed the flamboyant methods of press agentry and gained rapport with the Boston press by trying to meet reporters' needs. He preferred to go "along, day after day, with reporters good, bad and indifferent, giving out what they know they want or he [White] knows has a public interest. The papers get what they want, and they get it when they want it."[45]

In 10 short years after starting a department from scratch with no prior experience to guide him, White arrived at a remarkably mature concept of public relations. In the 1907 article, he wrote: "The problems involved in the public relations of large corporations today are quite as important as, in many cases more complicated than, those involved in the operation. It is in the general field of public relations that a department of publicity finds its principal usefulness and performs its most valuable service. Its function is to enable the public to know the corporation as it really is." This concept stands today. Little wonder that the function and department grew in size and stature under his leadership.

The railroad and local traction companies, early employers of publicists, came rather quickly to using the term, *public relations*. One of the earliest uses of this term—one for which in later years several would take credit—was *Railway Age*. That publication's annual *Year Book of Railway Literature* for 1897 stated: "The object of the publishers of the *Year Book of Railway Literature* is to put annually in permanent form all papers or addresses on the public relations of railways, appearing or being delivered during the year, which seem to have enduring value."

Railroads and utilities saw not only the value of publicity as a defensive measure, but much earlier had discovered its value in generating traffic and in selling land. Local streetcar companies, for example, were given this

---

[44]White, p. 876.
[45]"Publicity Among the Bostonese," p. 1034.

advice in 1898:[46] The personal acquaintance of all city editors and local railroad reporters is the first essential move. This preliminary call should be accompanied by an explanation that the management is desirous of catering to the public by giving more efficient service with better equipment than has ever been offered before, and that he desires their good will and assistance rather than their enmity and antagonism. This establishes congenial relations between the management and the press with the result that "news items" sent in are generally given space. This attention with the paid advertisements . . . cements, relations that are very valuable to railroad companies. Were it that simple, then or now!

Kennedy noted in his article that "the trunk line railroads find this item [dealing with the press] so important as to maintain a press agent and staff, at considerable cost, to handle the press." Indeed, the railroads from the middle of the 19th century on had used the press to promote settlement along their new tracks Westward, to generate freight and passenger traffic, to silence criticism, and to win public support for their land grabs in Congress, as described in chapter 9.

Back in the more settled parts of the country, railroads were beginning to pay some attention to public relations, at least in some superficial ways, as the farmers' protests against high freight rates began to be heard in the land. Here, from the records of the Wisconsin Press Association, is an account of the association's 33rd convention at Marinette, WI:

> The 33rd convention of the Wisconsin Press Association met at Marinette, Wis., on Tuesday, August 17, 1886. On Monday afternoon, a large number of editors with their wives and daughters gathered in Milwaukee.
> A special train of Pullman cars had been provided which was to bear us over the charming route of the Milwaukee & Northern Railway. Promptly at 2 p.m. the Association boarded the train at the Union depot in Milwaukee with Superintendent Kelly in charge. The Milwaukee & Northern R. R. had generously tendered the use of an engine, and the service of a special run over their new road by daylight, agreeing to land us in Marinette, 186 miles, in five hours. When well aboard we found that this was not all. . . . The Association was tendered a profusion of exquisite bouquets and fragrant Havanas. The substantial as well as graceful courtesy tendered the Association by the Milwaukee & Northern Ry. Co. will long be remembered by the editorial fraternity of Wisconsin.

Thus, the crunch of events and the growing strength of public opinion—as exemplified in the Granger Movement—were planting the seeds of reform and public relations that flowered in the seedbed years of 1900–1917.

---

[46]H. Milton Kennedy, "Methods of Developing New Traffic on Street Railways," *Street Railway Journal*, 14, 1898, pp. 647–648.

The Genesis of National Political Campaigns and Government Information

The modern political campaign employing the talents of campaign consultants, publicists, poll takers, electronic mail experts, video producers and writers, had its genesis in the last 2 decades of the 19th century. The newspersons who worked the political literary bureaus of the 1880s and 1890s bear little resemblance to today's highly skilled and experienced political handlers. But progenitors of today's professionals they were! The rise of these political literary bureaus is told in the section on "The Genesis of National Political Campaigns" in this chapter. Employment of publicists by government to win public and Congressional support for the incumbent administration also got its start in the waning years of the 19th century. This development is described in the section on "The Genesis of Government Public Relations."

The political campaign fashioned by Amos Kendall, Martin Van Buren, and others in the Jacksonian Era of the 1820s and 1830s had remained little changed with the rise of democracy, enlargement of the voting franchise for men, and the spread of the public schools until the 1880s.

The Republican Party, which had dominated the nation's politics and the Presidency since the Civil War, got a rude jolt in the Rutherford Hayes–Samuel Tilden squeaker of 1876. Republican leaders came to realize that they could no longer take victory for granted by waving "The Bloody Shirt"; Democrats were inspired to increased effort by their near success. More systematic efforts to carry the party message to the growing number of voters were developed in time for the 1880 Presidential campaign. Such plans were given impetus by improved printing presses, the reduced cost of printing paper, a growing awareness of the power of newspaper publicity, and the spread of public schools. The nation's expanding industrialization had brought more foreign workers to the nation and both parties set out to "educate" these first-time voters. The political literary bureau and an increased output of campaign literature were the result.

By the turn of the century, a writer for *Munsey's Magazine* observed:[1]

> Expert and experienced political managers give their closest attention to this [campaign literature] detail. Men who are learned as regard to the issues at stake, and who have that requisite of the successful politician which might be termed a knowledge of applied psychology, hold the blue pencil. Paragraphs, sentences and words are weighed with reference to their effect on the mind of the reader. What will be of advantage to one part of the country may be useless or possibly harmful in other parts.

The "Burchard Episode" in the Blaine–Cleveland campaign of 1884 surely impressed party managers with the necessity of having a system of controlled publicity. Responding to a Republican newspaper advertisement, a group of New York Protestant clergymen, described by Allan Nevins as "obscure," called upon James G. Blaine the morning of October 29, just a week before the election, to pledge their support. Their spokesman, the Reverend Samuel Burchard, labeled by Muzzey as "dull witted," told Blaine they were supporting him because "we don't propose to identify ourselves with the party whose antecedents have been rum, Romanism, and rebellion. We are loyal to our flag. We are loyal to you."[2] Accounts vary as to whether Blaine caught the remark at the time or whether he didn't sense its explosiveness. In any event, he didn't repudiate it on the spot, and when he did disavow it on November 1, it was too late. The damage had been done.

There were no reporters present at the hotel meeting, but the Democratic Party had a shorthand reporter shadowing Blaine. When the "reporter" returned to party headquarters, Colonel John Tracy, director of the Democrats' literary bureau, saw immediately the slip's importance as campaign issue and "hurried the phrase into 'manifold copy,' making it a vital part of a news story which every paper in the country hostile to Blaine published under big headlines within twenty-four hours."[3] From October 29 until election day, Democratic publicists and newspapers dinned the phrase "Rum, Romanism, and Rebellion" into the minds of voters. This classic blunder did much to enable Grover Cleveland carry his own state of New York by a narrow margin and thus become the first Democratic president since Buchanan. Little wonder that Blaine later referred to Reverend Burchard as "an ass in the shape of a preacher."

---

[1] Luther B. Little, "The Printing Press in Politics," *23*, 1900, pp. 740–741.
[2] *New York World*, October 30, 1884, p. F1.
[3] Little, p. 3.

The Republicans had learned their lesson. Their next campaign to defeat Grover Cleveland—this time with Benjamin Harrison, grandson of President William Henry Harrison—was a more carefully controlled one. The GOP campaign of 1888 was the first of three so-called "front porch" campaigns—1888, 1896, and 1920.

The GOP strategists decided that New York, home of Cleveland, and Indiana, home of Harrison, were the crucial states, and the Republicans made an intensive campaign in both states. For example, "more than 10,000 political speeches, delivered by 2,500 orators—they were orators in those days—filled the crisp October air in Indiana. Battalions of 5,000 even 10,000 enthusiastic citizens assembled in little crossroad villages on 2 or 3 days notice to watch the floats and parades and listen to the bands and the speakers and to picnic and politick. A man could scarcely escape the tumult."

Harrison stuck to his front porch. "From mid-July to the eve of the election, Harrison on the front porch of his Indianapolis home welcomed 110 delegations of well wishers, nearly 200,000 persons. He shook hands with them and had a few words for each. Most came from Indiana, but many came from Illinois and Ohio." To avoid another Burchard fiasco, Harrison and his staff read and edited advance texts of the visitors' statements. The 1888 front porch campaign worked smoothly and successfully.

GEORGE F. PARKER—PUBLICIST
FOR GROVER CLEVELAND

One of the political publicists to emerge in this period was Col. George F. Parker, who in partnership with Ivy Lee, later organized one of the nation's early public relations firms. Parker was born December 30, 1847, in Indiana, went to school in Iowa, and gradually worked his way to New York, where he lived the latter half of his life and died at the age of 80 in 1928. When he was 26, Parker left his father's Iowa farm and jumped into both journalism and politics by founding the *Indianola (Iowa) Tribune*, a Democratic weekly. After 3 years, the young editor sold his weekly and then worked on several other newspapers and spent 2 years (1877–1878) studying in Germany. In the 1880 campaign, Parker worked for the Democratic National Committee in Indiana and later with succeeding Democratic National Committees in 1884, 1888, 1892, and 1904. It was their work in the 1904 Democratic campaign that brought Parker and Ivy Lee together.[4] As a plum for his work in Pennsylvania during Cleveland's 1884 campaign, Parker was given the assistant postmastership of Philadelphia, a job he held from 1885 to 1887.

---

[4]*National Cyclopedia of American Biography*, Vol. 24. New York, 1935, pp. 24–49.

Parker was chosen by President Cleveland early in July of 1888 to prepare the Democratic campaign book for that year. Parker had known Cleveland in a casual way previously, but from this time on, he served the conservative Democrat in many important ways as a public relations aide. The campaign book was a history of the accomplishments of the Democratic administration and of the little-understood personality behind it. After 7 weeks of secretive, intensive work in the White House, the book was completed, and Parker was transferred to the Democratic Party's national headquarters in New York. He worked there in the publicity department until the end of the campaign, which Cleveland lost to Benjamin Harrison.[5] Parker later said the 1888 campaign was incompetently managed and that much effort was wasted.[6]

George Parker resolved to see Cleveland win in 1892—and did. To appreciate Parker's accomplishments in turning public sentiment toward Cleveland around about 180 degrees over the next 4 years, one must understand Cleveland's attitude toward politicians and the press. Grover Cleveland was a rugged, blunt man with strong convictions, an iron will, and high ideals. He usually acted with little regard for public opinion. In the view of one biographer, "He seemed unable to crusade successfully for anything that required him to build an effective following among the politicians and the voters."[7] Cleveland's relations with the press were incredibly bad because he disliked the press, refused to seek publicity, or to curry favor. Pollard believed that Cleveland suffered more from the newspapers than any other President.[8]

Parker worked hard to change all this in the years 1889–1891 when he was editor of the weekly New York *Saturday Globe*. Cleveland's political comeback began with a speech in Boston in November 1889, which Parker helped write and then disseminated widely. This was Cleveland's first formal address since leaving the Presidency and his former secretary, Colonel Daniel S. Lamont, who had entered private business, asked Parker to lend a hand, explaining that he had handled this sort of thing for the President in the past and that Cleveland knew nothing of how to go about it.

After Cleveland and Parker had worked out the speech, an argument developed over its distribution. Cleveland, fearful of the press, insisted that the speech be mailed no more than 5 days in advance and only to a select list of newspapers. Parker insisted on at least 7 days to allow enough mailing time for copies to reach newspapers in all parts of the country. Parker stuck

---

[5]See George F. Parker, "Cleveland the Man," *McClure's Magazine, 32,* 1909, pp. 338–342; George F. Parker, "How Grover Cleveland Was Nominated and Elected President," *Saturday Evening Post, 192,* 1920, p. 173.

[6]George F. Parker, "Cleveland the Man."

[7]Horace Samuel Merrill, *Bourbon Leader: Grover Cleveland and the Democratic Party,* Seattle: University of Washington Press, 1967, p. 91.

[8]James E. Pollard, *The Presidents and the Press.* New York: Macmillan, 1947, p. 499.

by his guns.[9] "This understanding between presidential candidate and press representative was a crucial one for Parker. The rapport he established with Cleveland was to last throughout the latter's life," although "Parker never became an indispensable part of Cleveland's staff." This speech was the opening gun in the Presidential campaign of 1892. This long-term campaign for Cleveland, wrote Parker:[10]

> . . . was so conducted as to be almost unsuspected, even by the newspapers themselves, but from 1889 to 1893 his smallest utterance was echoed from end to end of the country with a success never seen before or since [written in 1924]. But even this outward graciousness, whatever its motive or effect, was powerless to change [Clevelands'] attitude toward the press as a whole. Nothing could remove the feeling of distrust which had taken such a firm hold upon him.

During 1891–1892 Parker's small office at 57 Broadway served as the unofficial campaign headquarters for a rising tide of Cleveland supporters for a third Democratic nomination, a tide that eventually became strong enough to get Cleveland to agree to accept nomination.[11] Once the campaign was under way, even Cleveland became enthusiastic; his passive mood of 1888 was now replaced by a vital desire to succeed. Assisted by Parker's counsel and tireless publicity efforts, he did, winning a decisive majority in both electoral and popular votes. For his efforts, Parker was given a foreign service assignment. Had Cleveland taken Parker to the White House with him as a press secretary his second administration our history might have turned out far differently. And George Parker's name would not have faded from the pages of the nation's history.

1896 CAMPAIGN SETS NEW PATTERN

George Parker took no part in the epochal 1896 Presidential campaign that was to shape the format of national election contests for the next half century. This dramatic, hard-fought campaign between the conservative William McKinley and the Populist-leaning William Jennings Bryan brought a stepped-up emphasis on publicity and campaign management. The lines of

---

[9]Gordon A. Moon, "George F. Parker: 'A Near Miss' as First White House Press Chief," *Journalism Quarterly, 41* (1964), p. 186.

[10]George F. Parker, "Grover Cleveland: Estimate of His Character and Work," *Saturday Evening Post, 197,* 1924, p. 121.

[11]Moon, p. 187.

this significant struggle were unmistakably drawn when the Republicans, at their St. Louis convention in June, nominated McKinley, who believed in high tariffs and hard money, and the Democrats, at their convention in Chicago in July, chose the silver-tongued orator from Nebraska who believed in free silver as the key to prosperity.

The first move for both parties was to move the center of their campaign operations to Chicago where previously they had been in New York City. Both sides realized that the Midwest would be the crucial battleground in this time of intense economic and political unrest. William McKinley more than Mark Hanna set the McKinley strategy for the Republicans. He told Hanna, Charles G. Dawes, and other members of the Republican Executive Committee at the McKinley home in Canton, Ohio, July 16, of his firm decision to stick to front-porch campaigning. He was sure, he said, Bryan would plead poverty and try to capitalize on the plea. Dawes, who was to take charge of the main campaign headquarters in Chicago, agreed with the nominee; the others did not.[12] McKinley's combination front porch–massive publicity plan was implemented by large campaign staffs in Canton, New York, and Chicago, which overlooked no detail, spared no expense. Bryan, on the other hand, possessing a rare oratorical talent and having little money was forced to rely on cross-country tours that took him to as many voters as time and funds permitted. "It was upon Bryan . . . that the chief burden and the major hope of the Democratic campaign were centered."[13]

Early in July, "the Republicans began operations to 'educate' the voters through literary and other channels that would eclipse all previous efforts of this kind in our political history."[14] The Bureau of Publications and Printing of the Republican National Committee, directed by Perry Heath, began operations in Chicago almost as soon as the committee was established. It started sending out news releases, canned editorials, and editorial reprints, but its main purpose was the publication and distribution of literature. More than 275 pamphlets and leaflets, a series of posters, sheets of cartoons, and other campaign material were produced at a feverish pace over the next few months. These went flooding out to state and local GOP campaign workers, often in carload lots. Some 20,000 express packages were sent out, some 50,000 freight shipments made, and about half a million packages went by mail. Heath, a reporter on the Cincinnati *Commercial Gazette*, had

---

[12]Bascom Timmons, *Portrait of an American: Charles G. Dawes.* New York: Holt, 1953, p. 56.

[13]Stanley L. Jones, *The Presidential Election of 1896.* Madison: University of Wisconsin Press, 1964, p. 302.

[14]W. B. Shaw, "Methods and Tactics of the Campaign," *Review of Reviews, 14,* 1896, pp. 552–559.

been hired by McKinley early in June to handle his public relations at the GOP convention. Dawes, in a letter dated August 22, 1896, described Heath as "a very capable and experienced newspaper writer and editor."

The scope of Heath's output can be seen in the total of $469,079 spent for printing, a sum that assuredly bought several hundred millon pamphlets in that day of low printing costs. These large sums paid for bales of partisan publicity sent to daily and weekly newspapers in plate, ready-print, and news release form in an unending torrent and for tons of pamphlets and posters. McKinley, who guided his campaign more than has been generally acknowledged, was an avid newspaper reader and a strong believer in publicity. An article written in 1902 commenting on the fact that President Theodore Roosevelt was "not much of a reader of the newspapers," said this of McKinley:[15] "President McKinley . . . was a perfect glutton for reading the newspapers. He not only perused the principal Republican papers of the country, but he also read the Democratic sheets. He never depended upon his subordinates or associates in office for his information as to what the people of the country, through their newspapers, thought of his administrative actions." McKinley's concern for public opinion caused House czar Joseph Cannon to quip that McKinley kept his ear so close to the ground that he got it full of grasshoppers.

Just how much the Republicans spent all told on the campaign is not known, but they spent freely knowing full well that the nation's businessmen would foot the bill. The only record of what was spent is found in Dawes' carefully kept books for the Chicago headquarters. Dawes, writing in his diary September 9, said, in something of an understatement: "The disbursements for National Committee for printing and expenses are very large." The preservation of the gold standard and desire for high tariffs spurred the business interests to give heavily to the GOP. The Armstrong investigation of the insurance business in 1905 brought out, for example, the fact that Mutual Life Insurance gave $15,000, New York Life probably $50,000, Metropolitan Life contributed $7,500, Prudential $6,000—big contributions in those days.[16]

Ginger asserted that:[17] "by frying the fat out of men who feared that free silver would lead to depreciation of their investments, Hanna collected at least $3,500,000," but Mrs. Henry Cabot Lodge set the figure at twice that sum.

---

[15]"President Roosevelt Not a Newspaper Reader," *The Fourth Estate, 419* (March 8, 1902).

[16]Quoted from Armstrong Committee Report, in William H. Price, "Life Insurance Reform in New York," *American Economic Association Quarterly* (December 1909), p. 18.

[17]Ray Ginger, *The Age of Excess: The United States from 1877 to 1914* (2nd ed.). New York: Macmillan, 1975, p. 185.

McKINLEY WRAPS HIMSELF IN FLAG

Mark Hanna, who managed McKinley's campaign for the nomination, made effective use of the American flag as a campaign symbol. At the GOP convention, Hanna distributed thousands of campaign buttons carrying only a replica of the flag as badges for McKinley. "From that moment this became one of the major themes of the Republican campaign—that McKinley's patriotism made him a national symbol coequal with the flag. The Republican campaign committee bought millions of flags and distributed them over the country. . . . The emphasis on a campaign of patriotism became particularly popular among upper-middle-class conservatives."[19] Later in the campaign, the GOP set October 31 as flag day and carried out major demonstrations in the nation's major cities. As Jones noted, "The Republican appropriation of the national flag as their campaign banner left Democratic campaign organizers in an infuriatingly frustrating position." Republicans today still exploit the flag as though they had a corner on patriotism.

Another important innovation in the Chicago headquarters was the organization of specially staffed bureaus to mobilize special interest groups on McKinley's behalf. Pamphlets were printed in German, French, Italian, Spanish, Swedish, Norwegian, Finnish, Dutch, and Hebrew. In his final financial statement, shown on page 218, Dawes listed expenses for a Colored Department, a Woman's Department, and a German Department. Bicycling had become a popular pastime in the 1890s, the days when a "Bicycle Built for Two" was a popular song, so Dawes set up a department, Wheelmen, to woo bicyclists. No specialized group was knowingly overlooked.

Alongside Heath's publicity bureau, another of McKinley's Ohio friends, William M. Hahn, directed a speakers' bureau that sent preachers of the Republican gospel to the far corners of the nation. In mid-September, Dawes wrote that Chicago headquarters had at that time 250 speakers working in the 27 states under its jurisdiction.[20] Here, too, special interest groups were singled out. Dawes, for example, wrote of sending Nils Haugen of Wisconsin to the state of Washington to appeal to Scandinavian groups.

As Dawes directed the highly organized publicity effort in Chicago, William McKinley converted his Canton, OH, home into a political Holy Land for visiting pilgrims. The GOP staged what one writer described as the "the greatest pilgrimage of American political history." He wrote:[21] "From mid-September until the last Saturday in October, special trains brought railroad men, millworkers, miners, potters, and workingmen of all kinds, school teachers, commercial travelers, bishops, preachers, evangelists, merchants,

---

[19]Jones, p. 291.
[20]Dawes to Bosworth, September 17, 1896, *Charles G. Dawes Papers*, Northwestern University Library.
[21]Timmons, p. 59.

TABLE 12.1
GOP Campaign Expenses for Chicago Headquarters, 1896
Chicago Headquarters

	Statement to November 21, 1896		
Received from Ellisworth		$ 70,158.00	
New York		$1,565,000.00	
Contributions (increased since			
last statement by furniture sold)	$ 187.67		
Stamps	940.00		
By Duffield	1,712.65		
	$2,840.32	327,167.59	$1,962,325.59
Chicago office expense		24,027.03	
" " salary		12,134.73	
Literary Dept. Printing		469,079.84	
" " Expense		15,919.34	
" " Salary		15,921.28	
Speakers' Dept. Salary		98,893.02	
" " Expense		43,824.84	
Colored Dept.		3,763.45	
Woman's Dept.		1,873.86	
Organization		274,189.64	
Wheelmen		5,234.18	
Rep. League		7,775.54	
States		902,752.54	
German Dept. Expense		3,344.36	
" " Salary		1,914.24	
Com'l Trav. Expense		9,578.56	
Com'l Trav. Salary		3,100.05	
Shipping Dept. Expense		46,693.84	
Shipping Dept. Salary		22,168.36	
Total Vouchers			$1,960,188.48
Cash on Hand			2,137.11
			$1,962,325.59
Estimated unpaid claims			
Speaker's Dept.		$1,200.00	
-Salaries		500.00	
Bills		975.00	
Bill at Canton		2,145.00	
Total		$4,820.00	
Campaign of 1896			
At NY Headquarters about		1,600,000.00	
Total Expenditures		3,562,325.59[18]	

[18]Charles G. Dawes, *A Journal of the McKinley Years* (Bascom Timmons, ed.). Chicago: Lakeside Press, 1950, p. 106.

bankers, Southern planters and Northern farmers, men of every trade and profession. Visitors would start arriving at dawn, and continue coming all day." All this was carefully planned, expertly staged. McKinley was determined that there would be no "Rum, Romanism, Rebellion" miscue in his tightly managed campaign. Jones explained:[22] "Information about each visiting delegation was sent to Canton several days in advance of the visit. If possible, copies of the speeches to be made by spokesmen for the delegations were obtained; and McKinley suggested changes, if he judged that discretion made them desirable."

The public opinion poll, today a basic element in political campaigns, had not been developed in 1896, but its need was seen, and apparently a poll of sorts was taken in a few states. A campaign worker, Theodore Stegner of Kansas City, MO, wrote Dawes on September 5, 1896, apparently suggesting a chain of letters be put out "from which could be ascertained the approximate vote cast in the United States." Dawes, replying on September 10, 1896, said:[23]

> We know from former elections what the approximate vote in the United States will be, and we know from the polls which are being taken in the several states what the vote is going to be this year. How to obtain more accurate and definite information than is to be obtained through a poll carefully taken, I cannot understand. In the close states such as Indiana, Michigan, Illinois, Iowa and Minnesota, a poll has already been taken and there will be at least one or two more taken between now and the day of the election. If you have any suggestions that would tend to obtain the vote more accurately and readily than that of the method of taking a complete poll of each election precinct, of course, we would be very happy to be informed of that fact.

Just what Dawes meant by his use of the word *poll* is not clear. In any event, the reliable poll based on a representative sample of voters would not be developed for 40 years, appearing first in the 1936 Presidential campaign.

BRYAN USED THE CAMPAIGN TRAIN

The Bryan campaign, by contrast, was not well organized and always pinched for money. Jones said: "It mattered little, Democratic strategists believed, that funds were lacking to satisfy the public hunger for pamphlets and platform speakers as long as Bryan was willing to travel over the nation and speak frequently to the immense crowds which met him everywhere."[24]

---

[22]Jones, p. 284.
[23]In Letterbook (outgoing) July 23–November 24, 1896, *Dawes Papers*.

Travel he did—according to Bryans' figures, he traveled 18,009 miles in his whistle-stop train campaign. But his efforts were in vain. Jones thought Bryan's failure came in the failure of labor to respond to the Democratic appeal and the Democrats' failure to effectively answer the Republican protective tariff propaganda directed to the city worker.

McKinley won easily though Bryan polled the largest Democratic vote up to that time. In historian Charles A. Beard's opinion: "Bryan was defeated by the new or hitherto lethargic voters who flocked to McKinley's banners— 2,000,000 more than had voted the Republican ticket four years previously." It is safe to say that the Republicans' unprecedented emphasis on publicity and pamphleteering played a part in winning these new adherents. In any event, the large-scale publicity bureau and the campaign train had become a part of national election campaigns in a nation whose electorate now stretched 3,000 miles across the continent.

The basic Presidential campaign pattern established in the 1896 Presidential campaign remained much the same until 1928 when it was modified by the use of radio broadcasting. The fundamental change in the United States' Presidential campaigns came in 1952 with the advent of the most powerful medium of all—television—that today dominates our political process—and not all to the public good.

THE GENESIS OF GOVERNMENT PUBLIC RELATIONS

Persuaded of the power of publicity to get themselves elected, officeholders gradually perceived the value of using this new weapon to stay in office. Similarly, bureaucrats in the expanding Executive branch of government saw publicity's value. Among the first of the latter breed to see the need for public relations was Major John Wesley Powell, explorer of the Colorado and architect of the U. S. Geological Survey. Named to head the new agency by President James A. Garfield shortly after he became President, Powell moved quickly to expand the concept and size of the new bureau. In the words of U. S. Senator Hilary Herbert: "Major Powell has the most ambitious scheme of geology ever conceived in the mind of man." Stegner observed:[25] "Among the things Major Powell had learned in a decade or more was the lesson [Ferdinand V.] Hayden had taught—that both collaborators and Congressmen were impressed by publications." To accomplish his expansive aims, Powell knew that he had to build strong scientific support as well as support in Congress. Consequently, publications began to appear with in-

---

[24]Jones, p. 302.
[25]Wallace Stegner, *Beyond the Hundredth Meridian*. Boston: Houghton Mifflin, 1954, p. 265.

creasing frequency, and in 1884, a division of publications was set up. John C. Pilling who had been doing the editorial work was designated as editor. As the publications multiplied, W. A. Croffut, an experienced editor and journalist, was hired in 1882.[26] Stegner labeled Croffut Powell's "press agent."

William Augustus Croffut was born in Redding, Connecticut, in 1835 and died in Washington, DC, August 31, 1915. A decision to learn phonography (shorthand) at the age of 15 led Croffut into a long career of newspaper and public relations work. Croffut entered journalism 1852, and early in his career, he went to "the far-off territory of Minnesota, accepting an offer which took me first to St. Paul, where I edited the *Times*, and later to the frontier village of Minneapolis, just struggling into life as St. Anthony's Falls, as editor of the Falls *Evening News*, and then of the state *Atlas*."[27] When Southern guns fired on Fort Sumter, the young cub enlisted in the First Minnesota Regiment at Fort Snelling, but after 3 months' reflection, he decided that he "greatly preferred writing to either shooting others or being shot." He was mustered out of the Army and took a job as a correspondent for the New York *Tribune* on the Potomac front.

Soon he was drafted to serve as secretary to President Lincoln's Secretary of the Treasury, Salmon P. Chase. Croffut found this work boring, and in 1863, he returned to the front as a war correspondent for the New York *Tribune*.

Croffut had a varied and interesting journalistic career that brought him into close contact with many of the great personalities of his time. For instance, in 1867, he worked as campaign secretary for P. T. Barnum when the fabulous showman unsuccessfully ran for the Congressional seat in Connecticut's Fourth District. After the Barnum campaign, he returned to the New York *Tribune* to work under Horace Greeley, whom Croffut described in his memoirs as "a queer compound of bone, brain and self-will."

In 1869, Croffut again headed West to spend a year in Madison, WI, where he worked as co-author of an encyclopedia with Lyman Draper, the man who was influential in building the Wisconsin State Historical Society, today one of the nation's leading archives. Unfortunately their encyclopedia was never published and resulted in a long and painful litigation. William B. Hesseltine, Draper's biographer, described Croffut as "an agreeable, genial, industrial young man with a knack for getting along with people." Croffut was a lively writer who always sought to make his copy interesting for his readers.

Croffut subsequently served on the staffs of other newspapers, including the New York *American*, the New Haven *Palladium*, and *The Washington Post*, where he served as editor for a time. Until the time he retired from active work at the beginning of the Woodrow Wilson Administration, Croffut

---

[26]William Culp Darrah, *Power of the Colorado*. Princeton, NJ: Princeton University Press, 1951, p. 278.

[27]W. A. Croffut, *An American Procession 1855–1914*. Boston: Little, Brown, 1931. [Croffut's reminiscences published posthumously.]

was closely identified with the Washington scene and knew every President from Fillmore to Wilson. He recalled of Lincoln's time:[28] "I often walked into the White House and went straight up to the private secretaries' room adjoining his own without seeing any person whatever." He was the author of several books.

That Croffut knew his way around Washington is evidenced in this recollection of Benjamin Perley Poore:[29]

> In the same era of enterprise [post-Civil War], the vice president of the Pullman Company, interested in building New York City's first elevated railroad, thought it advisable to make one of his early calls on Mr. William A. Croffut. Croffut had been a war correspondent for the New York *Tribune* and his editorial contacts were good. He was, therefore, the very man with whom to arrange a few articles "to create a favorable public opinion" against the day when shares in the undertaking should reach the market.

Croffut's newspaper experience and his wide range of contacts made him the right man for Powell's purposes.

The Survey's bureau of publications was divided into two divisions, one to provide illustrations and art work, the other to prepare publications and issue publicity releases. Understandably, Croffut's work brought him criticism in the agency. "Lester Ward, for instance, complained scathingly about the mutilation of one of his papers. Nevertheless, the Major had his eye on publicity—not for himself but for his bureaus."[30]

Whether Powell was the first one in the federal establishment to hire a full-time publicist is difficult to determine. Certainly his idea brought consternation to his scientific colleagues. Powell had learned publicity's value much earlier. Back in 1878, when he was lobbying for a consolidated geological survey, Major Powell made many trips "to newspaper offices to secure wide distribution of propaganda literature, and to the Capitol to importune members and Senators to support the measure, as well as to discussions of the measure in Congressional Committee rooms."[31]

USDA LEADS THE WAY

The Department of Agriculture, established in 1862 to "acquire and diffuse among the people of the United States information on subjects connected

---

[28]Starr, *The Bohemian Brigade.* New York: Knopf, 1954, p. 153.

[29]*Reminiscences of Sixty Years in the National Metropolis*, II. Philadelphia: Hubbard Brothers, 1886, p. 263.

[30]Darrah, p. 278.

[31]Joseph Stanley-Brown, mss., "An Eventful Career," 9, quoted in Darrah, pp. 248–249.

with agriculture in the most general and comprehensive sense of that word," led the way among the Executive agencies in developing public relations as a tool of administration and education. The department was established in February 1889, and in March, Jeremiah M. Rusk was named Secretary of Agriculture by incoming President Benjamin Harrison. Rusk, after observing that some 40,000 letters of inquiry reached his department during the first 10 months of 1889, decided that the public must get agricultural information more promptly and in more readable form. In his first annual report to the President in October 1889, he wrote: "Time and expense, ability and experience, lavished on the work of this Department can have no practical results unless we can lay their conclusions promptly before the people who need them."[32]

Rusk heeded W. O. Atwater's suggestion that a series of farmers bulletins be initiated to contain agricultural information expressed in very plain language, easily read by laymen. He directed that the increasing number of more plainly written bulletins be widely distributed and that advance sheets be prepared for the press. This new activity was carried on in the Secretary's office for some, time but in 1890, he established a Division of Records and Editing to improve the output of agricultural information. There was already a Division of Illustrations. In a few years, these two agencies were put together, but few other changes were made until "Tama" Jim Wilson of Iowa became McKinley's Secretary of Agriculture in 1897. He made many innovations in the department's expanding public information program but these came after the turn of the century.

During the latter part of the century, other government officials recognized the need for trained and experienced persons to prepare publicity releases. The Civil Service Commission, in the 1890s, conducted examinations for editorial clerks and editorial assistants to prepare official reports and to write pamphlets on governmental activities for public distribution. The publicity activities of the Executive Branch had not passed unnoticed by Congress, always jealous of threats to its power. In 1895, Congress passed the General Printing Act that forbade agencies to print any matter "except that which is authorized by law and necessary to the public business."[33] The conflict between Congress and the Executive Branch over the latter's expanding use of publicity, barely hinted at here, flared into the open near the end of the next decade. This conflict between the legislative branches and the Executive agencies over the propriety of government public relations has continued to this day, much to the detriment of the function in government.

---

[32]Quoted in T. Swann Harding, "Genesis of One Government Propaganda Mill," *Public Opinion Quarterly, 11*: (1947). p. 229.

[33]28 U.S. Statutes 601 (1895).

STATES SEE THE NEED

Understandably in the still predominantly agricultural nation, it was a state Department of Agriculture that took the lead among state governments. F. D. Coburn, Secretary of the Kansas Board of Agriculture, a man with a "peculiar gift for putting the best foot forward," is among the lost legion of pioneers. Starting in about 1893 he worked tirelessly for the next 20 years or so to publicize the glories of Kansas. Realizing that publicity was needed to attract capital and population to Kansas, Coburn "systematically conducted an unique campaign of publicity calculated to connect its [Kansas] accomplishments and possibilities with its name, and to counteract and correct some erroneous ideas excited by its somewhat spectacular history."[34] This was among the first efforts of states to promote their resources to industrialists, settlers, and tourists. Today the 50 states spend millions to attract industry and to promote tourism.

Coburn, assisted by his deputy, J. C. Mohler, and two clerks, spent something like $17,000 a year preparing reports and publicity releases to publicize Kansas' assets and promote improved farming. The department's biennial report grew to some 1,500 pages, "packed full of reports on various methods of advanced farming as well as of figures." Twenty thousand copies of this report were distributed to Kansas farmers, to prominent papers, and to various parts of the world.

Coburn also initiated a quarterly report and every 3 months issued 1,500 copies to disseminate information on improved farming practices. Weekly news releases were sent to the principal daily newspapers in the nation and to all the agricultural weeklies. Secretary Coburn didn't believe in release dates because he thought newspapers should "all have the same chance." Was all this publicity worth its cost? It was. As Harger pointed out, despite its trials of earlier years, in the first decade of the 20th century, Kansas gained 15% in population, Nebraska gained 11.8%, and Missouri 6% though "conditions were similar in all this group of states."[35]

BEGINNINGS IN THE ARMED FORCES

As indicated in chapter 8, "The First Public War," the Civil War brought public relations problems to both the Union and Confederate armies that both were ill-equipped to deal with. That war brought the first hazy beginnings of today's large corps of public affairs officers who dominate the news coverage of today's armed forces. The first reference I found of an official

---

[34]Charles M. Harger, "Publicity for a State," *Independent, LXXI,* August 31, 1911, p. 470.
[35]*Ibid.* p. 481.

recognition to inform the press and public is the establishment of the office of Chief Clerk in the Adjutant General's office in the War Department. According to *The Army and Navy Journal* of October 10, 1883, (Vol. 21, No. 12): "Among the Army orders placed on the little desk in the room of the Chief Clerk of the Adjutant General's office for the accommodation of the daily press on Tuesday last was one announcing the transfer of Major Fred W. Bentsen." A Major Azor Nickerson, who was forced to retire from the Adjutant General's office because of the sneaky way he had obtained a divorce, later claimed that the press had to use the output Adjutant General Drum furnished or not be given anything in the future. Be that as it may, it was the Spanish American War that brought the beginnings of today's massive public relations programs of the four armed services. Coming in the twilight of the 19th century, the Spanish American War marked the end of the United States' isolationism and limited military forces. The military entered that war with little strength and no public relations plans to cope with an aggressive, sensationalist press. Indeed, it was in many ways the newspapers' war. The metropolitan dailies, led by the Hearst and Pulitzer papers, were better prepared for the war than was the military. The sensationalist papers were already organized with press boat fleets in the Caribbean when the war broke, thought to have been brought about perhaps by the Hearst–Pulitzer circulation wars in New York.

By the time the war started, 100 correspondents had established themselves at Key West, FL. Correspondents shed the first blood, captured the first battle flag, and got their stories back despite many obstacles. Despite all the energy expended, the press' record in this unfortunate war was a spotty one. Along with vivid, accurate accounts there were stories loaded with rumors, distortions, and bias.

These adventuresome reporters led by Richard Harding Davis, both at the front and in Washington, forced the Army and Navy to give them some thought to dealing with the press. At the time of the war with Spain, the Army Adjutant General complained that newspersons ran wild in the War Department and read orders over the shoulders of staff officers, which they then published before their official release. As in the Civil War, censorship and military security again was a thorny problem for which no satisfactory solution was found; this time all the more important because of the greater pressure of the press and war correspondents for scoops and sensational material. The Army's view of this frenzied war reporting ran thus:[36] "During the Spanish War the success of the Cuban expedition of May, 1898, was seriously menaced by the news in the American press concerning the concentration at Tampa [Florida]. Every military movement was reported in the

---

[36]"Statement of a Proper Military Policy for the United States," War College Division, General Staff, U.S. Army, 1916, p. 5.

American newspapers, and the Spanish Government had, within two or three hours, complete accounts of the American preparation for war." The abrasive relations of press and military in this war is further reflected in this editorial in the *Army and Navy Journal*:[37]

> Our experience with the newspaper correspondents who reported operations in Cuba shows how given such writers are to misrepresentation and exaggeration. Great injustice was done to the service by ignorant comments on matters they did not understand by the society reporter, novelists, and other gentlemen without military training or knowledge who were sent to Cuba to represent the newspaper and fill their columns with stories designed for picturesque effect.

This comment is much like those voiced by military leaders during and after the Vietnam War.

The manner in which the press distorted the events in Cuba, violated military security, and made and broke generals by their reporting could not fail to drive home the need for some more orderly and systematic means of dealing with press and public opinion. These pressures forced the Army to accept the obligation of reporting directly to the people. Shortly after the start of the war, a correspondent whose name has been lost in time persuaded the War Department to issue information for the press each day by posting it on a bulletin board outside of the office of the Secretary of War. The Adjutant General began publishing casualty lists for the press, often causing reporters to be besieged by anxious kin.

The war with Spain gave the Navy a forceful demonstration in the effects of public opinion on strategy. Naval officers had a plan to take Havana before the arrival of Spanish reinforcements or to seize San Juan, Puerto Rico, and from there destroy the Spanish fleet upon its arrival in the West Indies. The Navy was given neither option; public clamor, fired by news reports, brought Congressional pressure to confine the Navy's role to blockade and cautious bombardments. Some ships were ordered held at Hampton Roads in reserve. The Navy extended a helping hand to war reporters in this war. There were reporters with Admiral Dewey, many embarked in ships off Cuba, and all were given aid in getting their dispatches to Key West. In the main, it was Navy Department policy to deal candidly with the newspaper persons who were covering the war in Washington and with the fleet.

In his diary, Secretary of the Navy Long wrote, after being beseeched for additional details on the sinking of the Maine: "The newspapermen cluster like bees about me. . . . They are gathering information for the public, and it is hardly worth while to be impatient with them when they are really the

---

[37]July 22, 1899, p. 1121.

avenues through which the public, very properly, gets its information."[38] Likewise, Naval commanders furnished whatever information they could:[39] "Admiral Sampson fully recognized the demand of the country for the fullest information which could be properly furnished, and placed no impediment int he way of this being supplied, beyond what military necessity demanded."

Such were the faint beginnings of military public relations in the United States. The Spanish American War had reinforced other trends developing in the society. As the United States moved onto the world stage as a new power, her citizens demanded more information from their government. The Spanish American War did much to instruct our military men in the need for sounder organizational structures and better information procedures and policies.

In contrast to the clumsy manner in which the Civil War generals dealt with the press, at least a few military men in the Spanish American War sensed the value of good press relations. The failure of General William R. Shafter as a consequence of his quarrels with the press and the success of General Leonard K. Wood, an able politician as well as solider, as a result of his attention to public relations was a lesson not likely to go unnoticed by rising young officers.

Shafter, the portly commander of the U. S. expedition, early showed his irritation with the press and refused to let war correspondent Richard Harding Davis land with the first troops on Cuban soil. Shafter's treatment of the correspondents caused one writer to remark that the general "never enjoyed a sense of what even the military of later years have come to speak of as public relations." One hostile account in 1898 pictured General Shafter "as a profane, cowardly, and incompetent soldier, a monstrosity of flabby flesh." Shafter's career suffered correspondingly.

On the other hand, the young Leonard Wood's star rose during the war and the ensuing occupation of Cuba and later the Philippines. Wood took special pains to establish good relations with the press. He was always ready to meet with reporters, to discuss events, and to have a quotable quip. General Wood, unlike Shafter, early recognized that the press performed a legitimate function on the battlefield. In contrast to the cold reception afforded the press at Shafter's headquarters, the Colonel Wood–Colonel Theodore Roosevelt Rough Riders welcomed the attention of the press. Later Wood's performance as governor of Santiago was exemplary, and he received wide recognition for this performance through favorable publicity from a friendly press. Wood even went to the extent of putting a reporter on his payroll, a move that later brought harsh criticism. Nonetheless from

---

[38]L. S. Mayo, *America of Yesterday.* Boston, 1923, p. 165.

[39]French Ensor Chadwick, *Relations of the United States and Spain,* I. New York: Scribner's Sons, 1909, p. 221.

the Cuban days until he unsuccessfully sought the Republican Presidential nomination in 1920, Leonard Wood showed great skill in public relations, and this in no small measure accounted for his varied and successful career.[40] The sharply contrasting lessons taught by Generals Shafter and Wood did not go unnoticed by the military in the years ahead.

---

[40]Foregoing based on Peter J. Foss, *Power and Prominence Through Publicity, a Study of the Publicity Campaigns of General Leonard Wood*, unpublished thesis, University of Wisconsin, 1968.

"Advertising"
Higher Education*

Author's Note: *History moves on many currents along the river of time. It is woven of many threads of a seamless fabric, thus it is difficult and arbitrary to shear it off at some arbitrary date. These last three chapters, which cover the antecedents of today's public relations in the noncorporate sector, inescapably lap over into the early years of the 20th century—years that I have labeled "The Seedbed Years: 1900–1917." Thus, these three chapters provide a bridge across the century line and presage the vast array of public relations practices that are now part and parcel of nonprofit, philanthropic, and educational institutions.

As early as the immediate post-Civil War years, a few farsighted educators saw the need to inform the public of the needs, benefits, and aims of higher education. The wise and innovative Charles W. Eliot testified to the importance of dealing with public opinion as early as 1869. In his inaugural address as president of Harvard College, Eliot said this of the duties of a college president: "He must . . . influence public opinion toward advancement of learning; and . . . anticipate the due effect on the university of the fluctuations of public opinion on educational problems . . . (and) of the gradual alteration of social and religious habits in the community. The university must accommodate itself promptly to significant changes in the character of the people for whom it exists."

---

*This chapter is condensed from two articles by the author that appeared in *The College and University Journal* under the title "Advertising Higher Education," Part I, Vol. 9, Fall 1970, and Part II, Vol. 10, January 1971. Reprinted with permission of Council for Advancement and Support of Education.

The University of Wisconsin, during the regime of the lively John Bascom, started a university press in 1870, which would be "devoted to the interests of the fast-growing university." Its first publication was a monthly periodical published in June of that year under the editorship of G. W. Raymor and James W. Bashford who asserted: "We have felt that the institution stood in need of no one thing more than a well-edited university journal, devoted to its interests—one that would make known its wants, advocate its rights, redress its wrongs; one that would be a firm supporter of the institution in all its interests."[1] The publication received some support from the regents of the university in the form of advertisements, but for 17 years it was operated as a private enterprise.

As the end of the century neared, a few educators were coming to see the need for publicity to recruit students, raise funds, and make known the results of pioneering research programs. For example, the University of Wisconsin, under President Charles Kendall Adams, in 1896 established a *Bulletin for Editors* within a rather feeble extension division. This small mimeographed sheet was sent out to weekly and daily newspapers in Wisconsin on a fortnightly basis. Within months, many editors in the state were using regularly the materials presented in the *Bulletin*, most of which reported findings on experiments conducted in the College of Agriculture.

But the extension program languished, and in 2 years the press bureau was discontinued. Though Wisconsin's initial attempt to establish a press bureau was short-lived, it did demonstrate that the news media welcomed such service. In 1896, *Science* magazine of New York wrote: "We are anxious to have news in a form that is authoritative. Would you forward items as early as it is desirable to make them public?"[2] From the *Midland Monthly*, Des Moines, IA, came a query in 1896: "We would be pleased to have well-written articles on the University of Wisconsin . . . sketchy in style and free of advertisements . . . not more than 4,000 words in length and accompanied by photographs."[3] President Adams, too, thought the infant publicity bureau of value. "It is believed that the *Bulletin* has done not a little to counteract the altogether false impression sometimes prevailing that athletic and social events form a chief or even a prominent part of university life." Nonetheless the regents discontinued the bureau, and Wisconsin did not have a publicity service again until 1904, when, under President Charles R. Van Hise, the bureau was reestablished and publication of the *Press Bulletin* resumed that September.

---

[1]C. W. Butterfield, *History of the University of Wisconsin*. Madison: University of Wisconsin Press, 1879, pp. 182–183.

[2]Letter from J. M. Cattell, *Science* magazine, Oct. 4, 1896, *Presidential Papers, Charles Kendall Adams*, University of Wisconsin Archives.

[3]Letter from Johnson Brigham, editor, March 23, 1896, *Presidential Papers, Charles Kendall Adams*, University of Wisconsin Archives.

The nation's private colleges, from Harvard on, had long been concerned with the problems of fund raising and student recruitment, attacking these problems with varying degrees of skill. The emergence of the strong public university dependent on taxpayer support in the latter part of the 19th century brought with it increased concern about ways to build popular support for higher education. The land grant college and its extension programs provided a healthy stimulus in this direction. This increased competition for support, plus expanding needs, forced private colleges to step up their efforts in the 1890s.

SEEDBED YEARS: 1900–1917

Prior to its establishment of a publicity office in 1897, the University of Michigan queried several other institutions in the Midwest. The results of this survey, recorded in the minutes of the University of Michigan Board of Regents for December 1897, give a partial picture of a few programs in higher education on the eve of public relations' Seedbed Years:

> In several of the western universities plans have recently been adopted, or are at present under consideration, for arousing public interest in these institutions by publishing at intervals authentic bulletins of university affairs. In answer to inquiries, President Thwing, of the Western Reserve University, writes that university news is collected and edited in the office of the President, and thence sent out to the newspapers of the State. Chancellor MacLean, of the University of Nebraska, reports that steps are being taken to furnish such items as may be of general interest to a newspaper union for use upon the "patent insides" of the country weeklies. President Swain, of Indiana University, expresses himself as holding it "a very important matter that the public should have adequate knowledge of the worth and workings of our colleges," and says, further, "We have encouraged our students to write to their home papers and have had a committee of the Faculty to keep the run of college news and place it at the disposal of these correspondents; and we occasionally have a little slip printed and sent out to the papers of our own state. While these are not always printed, enough of the papers publish them to make it worth while." President Jesse, of the University of Missouri, writes that any bit of important university news is embodied in a little bulletin of a page which is mailed to the editors of the state, he is anxious for the Trustees "to print a weekly newspaper in the University, to be edited by the Faculty, with some aid from the students. This paper would, by exchange, be laid on the desk of every editor in the state and would pay handsomely as a medium of advertisement." He adds that he expects to see it established within a year.

Public relations' Seedbed Years (1900–1917) brought innovative publicity programs to many colleges and universities, among them Harvard, Yale,

Columbia, and Pennsylvania in the Ivy League; Chicago, Michigan, and Wisconsin in the Big Ten. There were other pioneering programs developing in these years. As classical education gave way to curricula responsive to the needs of the 20th century, as the demand to extend knowledge beyond the confines of the campus grew, and as the need for money increased sharply to meet expanding demands, college administrators turned, sooner or later, to the use of publicity. As Veysey observed: "By 1900 the public-ity-conscious administrator found himself generally in charge of the new American university. Effortlessly blending the once distinct concepts of academic purpose, he sought to unite his constituents by providing them with the rhetoric of agreeable and uplifting ceremony."[4]

CHICAGO'S WILLIAM RAINEY HARPER SHOWS THE WAY

William Rainey Harper, dynamic builder of the new University of Chicago, did more than any other educator to harness the power of publicity to the cause of higher education. His methods and resulting success were observed and copied. The first University of Chicago, founded in 1858 on land donated by Senator Stephen A. Douglas, failed in June 1886. It had no President Harper to promote it, though it tried to hire him in its waning days. Subsequently two Baptist ministers—Thomas Wakefield Goodspeed and Frederick Gates—persuaded John D. Rockefeller to donate $600,000 of the million dollars needed to establish the University of Chicago anew. The rich Rockefeller, then approaching 50, was at this time moving from retail into "wholesale philanthropy," to use Gates' term. Incidentally, Gates came to be, in a few years, the oil magnate's chief adviser on his benefactions. Goodspeed and Gates successfully raised the other $400,000 in an intensive fund drive; then they and Rockefeller persuaded Harper, noted Old Testament scholar, to accept the presidency, a post he had declined 5 years earlier when the first Chicago was on its last legs. It was only after long deliberation that Dr. Harper accepted, and then only after being granted his demand that the university include a graduate school. In a letter of February 16, 1891, he agreed "to enter upon the work of the position . . . July 1, 1891."

Harper was determined to make the University of Chicago "from the very beginning an institution of the highest rank and character."[5] Faced with financial problems at the outset, the energetic young president determinedly set about a task he little cared for but one in which he came to be effec-

---

[4]Laurence R. Veysey, *The Emergence of the American University*, University of Chicago Press, 1965, p. 382.

[5]Letter from Harper to John D. Rockefeller, August 9, 1890. *William R. Harper Personal Papers*, University of Chicago Archives. Hereafter referred to as *Harper Papers*.

tive—that of raising money. Fortunately, Chicago's needs coincided with the beginnings of large-scale philanthropy in the United States. Among Harper's greatest attributes were his keen awareness of the importance of public opinion and his sure sense of publicity, qualities then rarely found in college presidents, most of whom came from the classics or from the ministry.

TWO EXTERNAL RELATIONS DIVISIONS

The roots of Harper's awareness of the need to promote support for a university were embedded in his concept of a true university: "Service for mankind wherever mankind is, whether within scholastic walls or without those walls and in the world at large." This philosophy was reflected in his plan for the University of Chicago, which called for three divisions—the university proper, the university extension, and the university press.[6] The latter two divisions were to disseminate university knowledge to people outside the university's walls. In addition to his religious conviction that it was the university's duty to discover and disseminate truth for the good of man, Harper was motivated by the practical necessity of winning public support. He was ever mindful of the first Chicago's failure.

Though, by Harper's own denial, the university did not have a bureau of publicity in its early years, it did regularly publish the *University Record* addressed to the public to improve public understanding of university affairs.[7] President Harper said of the *University Record*:[8]

> The *University Record* has been published weekly during the quarter. It has included important articles which were thought to be of interest to those directly or indirectly connected with educational work.
>
> The *Record* is intended to supply the trustees, the members of the faculties, the students, and particularly the friends of the University at a distance, with a correct statement concerning everything of importance which transpires at the University.
>
> It is expected that every alumnus will become a subscriber to the *Record* in order that he may thus keep himself in touch with the work of the University.

Reflected in these passages is Harper's awareness of the necessity of providing accurate information to the influential citizens who shape public opinion. Because of this awareness, Harper energetically courted influential Chicagoans with personal contacts, receptions, and parties. The Dean of Women from 1892 to 1925 wrote: "One of the first undertakings of the new

---

[6]*Official Bulletin* No. 1, University of Chicago, December 1890.
[7]William R. Harper, *President's Report: 1892–1902.* Chicago, 1901, p. xxviii.
[8]In "Quarterly Statement" *University Record, 1*(14). July 3, 1896, p. 228.

University was to establish friendly relations with the best and most helpful influences to be found in the city. It was fortunate in winning as friends many of the ablest and most cultured citizens."[9] Harper also used convocations, many of them held in downtown Chicago, to build goodwill because, in his words:

> Experience has shown that if [the convocation] is also a most desirable educational agency, inasmuch as in a community as large as that of Chicago, it is necessary for the University to contribute something to the general life of the city, in order that the city may continue to be conscious of the existence of the University. It is not sufficient to have the University's existence kept in evidence merely by athletic contests and student wranglings, the two subjects which the modern newspaper seems particularly interested in presenting to its readers.[10]

OPEN INFORMATION APPROACH

Harper constantly emphasized the importance of telling the university's story as widely and effectively as possible. "I have spoken to you frankly. It has been the policy of the university from the beginning to conceal nothing from its friends—the public."[11] In his *Decennial Report*, the president wrote: "Our feeling has been that the institution is a public institution and that everything relating to its inside history, including its financial conditions, should be made known." He correctly added that: "perhaps no other institution has shown a greater readiness to allow its internal affairs to be known and criticized."

This innovative president also made provisions for internal communications. On October 1, 1892, it was stated that on "Thursday at noon of each week the materials for announcement for the weekly bulletin should be handed to the Recorder." A sheet summarizing the coming week's activities was distributed to the faculty and students every Saturday. Eventually, this weekly bulletin was replaced by the much more detailed *Official Bulletin*, which provided a means of keeping the entire campus informed of university affairs and policies, a practice rare in universities of the 1890s.

Nor did Harper overlook the importance of courteous and careful treatment of guests visiting the campus. In her memoirs, Miss Talbot recalled: "I was once told by an academic official of wide experience that the official manners of the University of Chicago were the best in the country." To implement this policy, Harper established an information office to answer

---

[9]Marion Talbot, *More Than Lore: Reminiscences of Marion Talbot*. Chicago, 1936, p. 59.
[10]Harper, *President's Report*, pp. xviii–xix.
[11]William R. Harper, *Quarterly Calendar*, III:I. Chicago, May 1894, p. 18.

questions and direct visitors to their destinations. This office, later re-titled bureau of information, was cited in the *President's Report for 1911–12* as "a serviceable organization for the dissemination of information for students, members of the Faculty, and University visitors."

Harper was quite sensitive to the importance of maintaining good relations with the press to the end that his university was favorably and fully publicized, but this relationship gave him great difficulty. His presidency coincided with the emergence of the hotly competitive mass circulation newspapers; nowhere was this competition fiercer than in Chicago. From the university earliest years, the press took great interest in its activities. Even the classroom was invaded by reporters, for it was the practice of newspapers to buy stories from students.[12] Harper was delighted with the interest, but pained by the coverage. He once wrote a friend: "I wish very much that there could be enacted by a law in the state of Illinois inflicting the death penalty upon irresponsible reporters for the miserable way in which they misrepresented the truth."[13] Not all of his associations with newspersons were marked by such bitterness; he maintained a close, cordial relationship with James Keeley, editor of the *Chicago Tribune*, and often consulted him. Harper's correspondence plainly shows a strong concern for the way he appeared in the press.

As the university developed, President Harper was alternately pained by the lack of news attention or by what he deemed inaccurate reporting. In November 1904, he wrote his personal secretary:[14]

My dear Mr. Chandler:

We must take up the question of having press reports for the University functions. As a matter of fact, nothing was given in the Saturday papers about the action of the conference Friday afternoon, nor, so far as I can learn, were the names of the successful candidates Friday night announced Saturday morning, and only by accident was the matter taken up for Sunday morning. We must get some machinery into shape which will enable us to avoid this. I shall be glad to have you give your thought to it and talk to me about it.

Yours very truly,
W. R. Harper

He moved slowly getting "some machinery into shape." Nearly a year later, October 9, 1905, the following announcement was sent to the faculty:[15]

---

[12]Richard J. Storr, *Harper's University*. Chicago and London: University of Chicago Press, 1966, p. 223.

[13]Harper to D. J. Bailey, September 25, 1897, *Harper Papers*.

[14]Harper to H. P. Chandler, November 14, 1904, *Harper Papers*.

[15]William R. Harper to Members of the Faculties, October 9, 1905, *Harper Papers*.

TO MEMBERS OF THE FACULTIES:

It is not news to members of the faculties that the University has long suffered severely from misrepresentation in the press. For some time we have been wondering whether, by following the example of Columbia and Pennsylvania and appointing a special press representative whose business it should be to furnish the press with all the facts in regard to the University and detailing him to work up accounts of special features or developments in our life, we might not displace undesirable newspaper notices with accounts which should be interesting and at the same time accurate.

With a desire to test this plan Mr. Oscar D. Skelton has been appointed the press representative of the University for the coming academic year. It will be a great help in the work which we are undertaking if officers of the University will kindly communicate to Mr. Skelton, either in person or in writing through the Faculty Exchange, in which he will have a box, such items as seem to them proper for publication. He will be glad to take advantage of any clues that are given and work up accounts of such features of the life of the University as call for detailed treatment.

Finally, may I ask that officers of the University refer reporters to Mr. Skelton for information and treat him as the official channel of communication with the press. Only, of course, as newspaper men have confidence in him as a man conversant with all material facts and the best source of information will they consult him regularly, and only in this way can our relations with the press be centralized and responsibility fixed.

Counting on your cooperation in a policy which we hope will present the University to the public in a better light, I am,

                                        Very truly yours,
                                        William R. Harper

Thus, after years of battling with the press, President Harper initiated a program to "displace undesirable newspaper notices with accounts which should be interesting and at the same time accurate." Such a sophisticated approach to managing the news was rare among administrators in his era. Among other things, he saw the need to have all outbound communications channeled through a central office to solve a problem that plagues colleges to this day. He also saw the need to have a publicity director who had the confidence of the newspaper fraternity and faculty. The man he chose for this pioneering position was Oscar D. Skelton, a Canadian who held bachelor's and master's degrees from Queens University, Kingston. Skelton had worked for a few years in newspapers and from 1902 until 1905 was assistant editor of *Booklover's Magazine*.[16] Skelton's was only a part-time position because at the time he was working on his PhD degree in economics, which

---

[16]*Encyclopedia Canadiana*, IX. Ottawa, 1958, p. 323.

he received in 1908. He was ideally suited to gain the confidence of both the press and faculty.

PUBLICIST ACCEPTED BY NEWSPERSONS

The new publicity director took on his assignment with vigor and soon won credit for relieving administrative officers of interruption by reporters. The newspersons seemed to accept the arrangement and were quite content to consult Skelton exclusively.[17] Faculty members were less cooperative, either forgetting about the new publicity office or else choosing to deal with the press themselves, problems not uncommon on the campus today. Nonetheless, Skelton soon began sending out feature stories to the Chicago metropolitan newspapers and to New York newspapers, a service readily accepted by the press. He also paid much attention to the periodical press and with success, as the following table, compiled from *Reader's Guide to Periodical Literature, 1900–1909*, shows:

TABLE 13.1
A Comparison of the Increase in Quantity of Magazine Articles Written
About a Selected Sample of American Universities: 1900–1904 to 1905–1909

University	Quantity of Articles 1900–1904	Quantity of Articles 1905–1909	Variation
California	11	7	−4
Chicago	11	22	+11
Columbia	23	22	−1
Harvard	37	68	+31
Illinois	0	9	+9
Michigan	4	6	+2
Minnesota	1	4	+3
Wisconsin	2	13	+11
Yale	26	23	−3

The difference an organized publicity program made in getting attention in the nation's periodicals is clearly reflected in this table. The University of Wisconsin, for example, set up its news bureau in 1904 and soon stimulated much national attention for itself. In Chicago's case, Skelton doubled the number of periodical articles on Chicago in a 4-year period. Harvard's, Yale's, and Columbia's early publicity programs are likewise reflected. These results, in time, caused other university heads to set up competing publicity bureaus.

---

[17]H. P. Chandler to William R. Harper, October 16, 1905, *Harper Papers*.

STAGING EVENTS FOR ATTENTION

President Harper was equally aware of the value of the staged event in focusing attention on the university, and he used this technique with skill and style. He had originally planned to stage a formal opening in October 1892 but was dissuaded by Fredrick Gates, who argued that "already the institution has become extensively known."[18] The tranquil opening of the university with a simple assembly proved to be the exception, not the rule, in Harper's reign. Harper dated the university's beginning from the date he assumed the presidency, July 1, 1891, and duly celebrated the founding with a quinquennial celebration July 1–5, 1896, a decennial, June 14–18, 1901, and a sesquidecennial, June 12, 1906. He exploited the staged event fully 6 decades before a former Chicago professor, Daniel Boorstin, would damn such celebrations as "pseudo events."

To the best of Harper's knowledge, the Chicago Quinquennial was the first celebration of an academic institution's fifth birthday. Highlight of this quinquennial was the first visit of the university's founder, John D. Rockefeller, Sr., but this was by no means the only event. The celebration started with a graduate matutinal, a breakfast given by the president for the candidates for higher degrees and included a convocation, a luncheon for "associated alumni," a reception in honor of Mr. and Mrs. Rockefeller, seminars, and the laying of cornerstones for three laboratory buildings. This prolonged celebration of Chicago's fifth birthday, a rarity for its day, was, in the words of one guest, "the greatest festival in the educational history of the West."[19] Nor did its success escape the notice of other college presidents.

An even more extensive celebration marked Chicago's decennial, June 14–18, 1901. Once more the founder of the university and Mrs. Rockefeller were the honored guests for festivities that included the dedication of Nancy Foster Hall, the official opening of the school of education, and the laying of cornerstones for six new buildings. Again influential citizens and prospective donors were given special attention. Before the university opened, Harper had taken a firm stand against honorary degrees but, in time, he changed the policy, and for the decennial 11 such degrees were granted with the reluctant approval of the trustees. This special event was climaxed by the publication of the *Decennial Publications*, a project that grew from the initially planned 3 volumes to 28 volumes, published at a cost of $50,000. Though this put a severe financial strain on the university, Harper never

---

[18]Gates to Harper, May 13, 1892, *Harper Papers.*

[19]David Allan Robertson, *The Quarter-Centennial Celebration of the University of Chicago.* Chicago, 1918, p. 10.

waivered in his conviction that it was a wise investment. The celebration itself cost $5,268, a substantial public relations expenditure in those days.[20]

President Harper had prepared an elaborate program for a sesquidecennial to be held June 1906 to celebrate the university's fifteenth birthday, but on January 10 of that year he died. Because of President Harper's earnest desire that such an anniversary be observed, his successors went through with a dignified program that omitted the special festivities. The celebration commemorated President Harper and his work—a work that had laid the foundations for one of the nation's great universities. In this building, William Rainey Harper wisely used the arts and tools of public relations in a fashion few of his educational peers could match in that day or this.

In an era when most public relations programs were initiated in response to attacks from the muckraking journalists, and thus were of a negative nature, William Rainey Harper saw public relations as a positive means of gaining the requisite funds, faculty, and freshmen to build a university. At the Sesquidecennial, President Charles R. Van Hise of the University of Wisconsin, another able practitioner of public relations, who was greatly influenced by Harper's examples, said of President Harper:[21]

> It is doubtful if any other great university is so largely the work of one man as is the University of Chicago that of President Harper. In fifteen years there has been created at Chicago an educational institution of the first rank. This university will forever remain his great monument.

VAN HISE AND WISCONSIN

Among university presidents discernibly influenced by President Harper's public relations practices was Van Hise who, early in the 20th century, changed the University of Wisconsin from a small, provincial state university into an institution of national renown. Van Hise and Harper were close friends, and Van Hise often consulted the Chicago president until the latter's death. Like Harper, Van Hise showed the way in utilizing the power of publicity to build financial support, to extend education to the people, and to attract students to the campus. President Harper was one of the principal speakers at Van Hise's inaugural in 1904, and the Chicago president, speaking to Van Hise, said, among other things: "May I . . . beg you in your administration of the affairs of this University, to lay especial emphasis upon those features which sustain close relationship to the interests of the people. . . .

---

[20]"Decennial Expenses," an undated document in *Presidential Papers*, University of Chicago Archives.

[21]*Chicago Tribune*, January 11, 1906.

The University in the future must do for the people much that in the past has been done by the church. To accomplish this, it must touch the people directly and at first hand."[22]

The forces of progressive reform, a public relations-minded university president, and a discerning faculty member came together at Wisconsin shortly after the turn of the century to develop an effective publicity program, one later used as a model by other colleges.

In April 1903, geologist Van Hise became president of the University of Wisconsin; he brought to the new task a keen sense of public relations—a trait rare among scholars. As he wrote, sometime later: "The fundamental thing in securing results is the carrying of a campaign of education through the newspapers, through the national organizations, and through the schools, colleges, and universities."[23] Van Hise shared the goals of the Progressive movement being led in Wisconsin by his classmate and friend, Robert M. LaFollette. In the words of Theodore Roosevelt, Wisconsin, in the early years of the new century, was truly "a laboratory for wise experimental legislation aiming to secure the social and political betterment of the people." Van Hise, too, saw the importance of carrying university knowledge beyond the confines of the classroom to the people; he also saw the need to build a political base of support for the enlargement and extension of the university. This would require, he was quick to see, a public relations effort hitherto untried in most universities.

CREATION OF A "SPECTACULAR"

Observance of Harper's success and his earlier interest in conservation had convinced Van Hise of the importance of publicity as he embarked on his program to make Wisconsin a strong university of national reputation. One of his first moves as president was to make sure that the university was represented by exhibit in the St. Louis Exposition of 1904. Next he set in motion plans for celebrating Wisconsin's semicentennial in 1904. He delayed his inauguration until the semicentennial because he wanted to "make a deep impression upon the state and thus greatly strengthen the university."[24] To make this impression, Van Hise appointed a committee to combine Wisconsin's "fiftieth commencement, the presidential inauguration, and the semicentennial exercises into an unrivaled spectacular."[25] Van Hise arranged

---

[22]The Jubilee Committee ed. *The Jubilee of the University of Wisconsin.* Madison, 1904, pp. 64–65.

[23]Letter to Agnes C. Laut of *Outing Magazine*, March 4, 1909. *Presidential Papers*, University of Wisconsin Archives.

[24]Letter to Hon. August J. Myrland, October 9, 1903. *Van Hise Papers.*

[25]Donald C. Bauder, "University of Wisconsin Public Relations Policies under President Charles R. Van Hise," unpublished thesis, University of Wisconsin, 1960, p. 17.

for one professor to travel around the state promoting the *Jubilee*, a term for the celebration suggested by Van Hise. Professor Grant M. Hyde, who later served as a university publicist, termed Van Hise "a natural born public relations and publicity man."

The president asked a young English instructor, Willard Grosvenor Bleyer, to help out in publicizing the Jubilee by sending out occasional news releases. The two men observed several times that the press wasn't giving what they thought was adequate attention to the forthcoming Jubilee. Bleyer saw the need for an organized publicity program and urged Van Hise to reestablish the press bureau, which had been dropped just before the turn of the century. At Van Hise's recommendation, the University of Wisconsin Board of Regents voted April 19, 1904, "that some member of the instructional force be appointed editor of the university scientific bulletins and placed in charge of the University Press Bureau at an additional salary of $300, with the understanding that he do such editorial and press work as may be directed by the President, the cost to be charged to Printing and Advertising."[26] Bleyer took charge of the bureau 2 weeks later.

PUBLICITY IN SEARCH OF APPROPRIATIONS

Bleyer, who combined the qualities of scholarly thoroughness and journalistic sense, was fully aware of the explosion of knowledge then taking place and further that the news of knowledge was being either sensationally reported or not reported at all in the press. He saw an intensive publicity effort as extending knowledge to all citizens in the state and of building popular support for a university that had not been given adequate appropriations in the past. Bleyer ultimately gained fame as the influential pioneer in journalism education, which he started at Wisconsin on a credit basis in 1905. As a result, his pioneering work as a publicist has been little noted. Bleyer was born into a Milwaukee newspaper family; his father worked in the *Sentinel* circulation department until his death, and no less than five uncles held key positions on Milwaukee newspapers. As a student at Wisconsin, Bleyer had been editor of *The Daily Cardinal*, the university yearbook, and a literary magazine. He took his PhD in English, but his heart was in journalism. Bleyer threw himself into the task of organizing the press bureau. An intensive education program was started to teach other faculty members what was news, how to get it, how to report it, and the importance of full press coverage on the university's work.

In establishing the press bureau, the University of Wisconsin regents set down these objectives:

---

[26]*Records*, Board of Regents, April 19, 1904, University of Wisconsin Archives.

1. To give to the citizens of the state through the newspapers the results of the research that is being carried on at the University;

2. To keep the public informed in regard to the educational work of the University, and the constantly increasing opportunities for study in many fields offered by the University;

3. To furnish accurate reports to the newspapers of the official news of the University, including the meetings of the regents and faculty, and the work of officers of the University.

In a day in which scholars kept largely to their ivory towers, this was a precedent-setting document, presumably written by Bleyer.

Bleyer took charge of the reactivated press bureau May 2, 1904. Publication of the *Press Bulletin* began in September 1904. At first it was mimeographed, but Bleyer soon got permission to have it printed. The *Press Bulletin* was published regularly until 1948. Bleyer started on a half-time basis and had one assistant, Miss Alice Webb, who served as writer-secretary. By 1908, the press bureau was a lively news center and a steady stream of stories went to one or more of four mailing lists: (a) Wisconsin dailies, (b) Wisconsin weeklies, (c) agricultural and dairy papers that had readers in Wisconsin, and (d) metropolitan newspapers outside Wisconsin.

Reflecting an expanding definition of news, most editors, welcomed the service. Wrote one: "I think it is a capital idea of sending out notes of interest to the state press as you have been doing of late."[27] Desire for news of the university is reflected in the many letters Bleyer got complaining that other papers were breaking the release dates on his stories. Not all editors applauded; one scribbled across a press bureau envelope: "You might as well save time and postage and remove the *Berlin Journal* from your list as your documents invariably go into the wastebasket."

In a day of fierce competition among newspapers, Bleyer played editor against editor. In case of the canard or exaggerated story, Bleyer acted speedily and authoritatively. In July 1911, a sensational story that the university was requiring all its students to take a course in football so the coach could develop a better team broke in several Chicago newspapers. Bleyer immediately denied the allegation in a lengthy article in the *Press Bulletin* which he distributed throughout the Midwest. As the story worked its way eastward, Bleyer wrote each editor who printed the erroneous story. He wrote the editor of the *Boston Transcript*: "A course in punting and catching is taught at the university, and it is compulsory in part of the physical education program, but it is not meant to develop football heroes." The new publicist also moved in less obvious ways to counter unfavorable stories. In these years, the university was often attacked for teaching atheism; con-

---

[27]A. A. Washburn of *Horicon Reporter* to Bleyer, December 14, 1904, *Willard G. Bleyer Papers*, University of Wisconsin Archives.

sequently Bleyer sent out many feature stories emphasizing the religious side of campus life. He placed much emphasis on news of scientific development. He also promoted positive publicity in the nation's magazines.

RECOGNITION BY DESIGN

It was no accident that Wisconsin came to be widely publicized in these years; Bleyer was promoting the university in a time when he had few competitors. The first major recognition came in June 1907, when the *Saturday Evening Post* included Wisconsin in a series "Which College for the Boy?" authored by John Corbin. Only a month later William Hard, writing in *Outlook*, praised Wisconsin as a "kind of consulting engineer in the public life of the state." In 1909, Lincoln Steffens wrote an article of praise for Wisconsin in the *American Magazine*. The next month, Charles Johnston of *Harper's Weekly* wrote an article praising the university's close relationship with the state's lawmakers. An article by E. E. Slosson soon followed in the *Independent*, also one of profuse praise for Van Hise and his new extension system. Frank Parker Stockbridge wrote two articles on the university for *World's Work* in 1913. There were others.

Little wonder that other universities were soon writing to Wisconsin for advice on setting up a news bureau. By 1910, the press bureau had become a model. When the University of Illinois desired to change its public relations procedure, an official told Bleyer: "I have carefully examined a number of issues of both your press bulletin and mimeographed bulletins to the daily papers, and have been much interested. I beg leave to say that the combination of these two, it would seem to me, should constitute one of the most effective plans I have come across anywhere."[28] Bleyer asserted in 1913: "The University of Wisconsin is the only institution in the country that has maintained for nine years a continuous and consistent policy of newspaper and magazine publicity." In 1910, his secretary wrote him: "Those universities from which we have received exchange copies (which, so far as my knowledge extends, are all the institutions issuing such bulletins) are the University of Illinois; University of Michigan; Ohio State University; University of Kansas; Atlanta University, Atlanta, Georgia; Transylvania University, Lexington, Kentucky; Washington University, St. Louis; Colorado State Agricultural College, Fort Collins, Colorado; Cornell; Brown; and the University of Missouri."[29] Bleyer had given counsel to four of these on how to organize a publicity bureau, his correspondence shows.

---

[28]C. M. McConn to Bleyer, August 5, 1910. *Bleyer Papers.*
[29]Miss Webb to Bleyer, January 14, 1910. *Bleyer Papers.*

As the demand for journalism education mounted, Bleyer, from 1910 or so, sought to be relieved of his work as editor of the press bureau, and, on June 30, 1913, he was succeeded as publicist by Charles W. Holman, and the press bureau was once more placed in the university's extension division. Holman, then 27 years old and enrolled as a special student, received free tuition and $100 a month in salary. Holman's youthful brashness and friction with the College of Agriculture's new publicity man kept him in hot water much of the time. The College of Agriculture hired a full-time publicity man in 1908. Holman resigned in April 1915 and was replaced that July by a young journalism instructor, Mr. Grant Hyde, who held the post until 1928. Hyde later succeeded Bleyer as director of the University of Wisconsin School of Journalism in 1935 when the pioneer publicist and educator died unexpectedly on October 31, 1935, of a brain hemorrhage.

Though he was not the nation's first college publicist, Bleyer helped set the early patterns of publicizing higher education. He saw the need for educational institutions to take the initiative in getting a positive story told; he had a keen sense of news values and dealt profitably with editors and writers on their terms; and he had the academic standing to win faculty support for his new program. Bleyer "taught faculty members that it is not wise to withhold information from inquisitive reporters, for information voids often become filled with damaging rumor." Bleyer also worked to improve Wisconsin's alumni relations and made some innovations in the now highly specialized art of alumni relations. A biographer, appraising his public relations work, wrote:[30]

> Bleyer realized that the United States was losing a sense of community in the changeover from an agricultural to an industrial state. He realized that the increased tempo of living and the coming of a mechanized age were subordinating the individual in society. He also realized that effective communications must be reestablished before sound understanding could be achieved for any school or organization. Bleyer helped to do this at the University of Wisconsin.

And, in so doing, he helped establish sound public relations practices in the nation's colleges and universities.

UNIVERSITY OF MICHIGAN

The University of Michigan was among those institutions seeking Professor Bleyer's counsel, although that university had formally recognized its responsibility to release university news to the public as early as 1897. In

---

[30]Donald K. Ross, *W. G. Bleyer and the Development of Journalism Education*, unpublished thesis, University of Wisconsin, 1952, pp. 153–154.

October 1897, the Michigan regents voted to request the literary faculty "to report to the Board some general plan for getting University news before the people of the State."[31] At their December, 1897, meeting, the regents received a plan recommended by a committee headed by Acting President Harry B. Hutchins. This seven-man committee proposed:[32]

1. That a Bureau of News be organized with some member of the literary faculty in charge who would have the title University Editor.
2. That the University Editor be placed in charge of a part of the alumni publication and that this news section be regarded as an official publication of the University.
3. That the University issue every second week a small bulletin or newsletter to consist of material which would appear the following week in the Michigan *Alumnus*.

The committee urged that the editor be from the department of English composition so that "a small class of advanced students could eventually be organized to report systematically . . . the various interests of the University." This was recommended because, in the committee's view: "In this way the tedious labor of news gathering, which no member of the Faculty should be asked to undertake could be performed to some extent by members of the class as part of their regular work." The report was accepted by the regents, and Professor Fred Newton Scott, a member of the committee and a junior professor of rhetoric, was appointed university editor to implement the recommendations. The sum of $100 was appropriated to get the bureau started. On January 6, 1898, Scott began mailing the special news section of the *Alumnus* as a newsletter to Michigan editors. He continued in this post until the fall of 1900 when Shirley W. Smith became general secretary of the alumni association and took over editorial responsibility for the newsletter. Smith also used students to collect information.

This minimum, scantily financed program continued under President James Burrill Angell, and no major change occurred until Harry Burns Hutchins, a publicity-minded educator who had served as chairman of the committee in 1897, became Michigan's president. In the early years of this century Michigan's national publicity was generated mostly by its football power. With President Hutchins' regime came an increased awareness of the need for national publicity for Michigan's academic achievements and its need for funds. Hutchins was "favorable to enlarging the scope of the University. Thus, a course in journalism was provided in 1910 which was a

---

[31]*Minutes of University of Michigan Board of Regents*, October 20, 1897, University of Michigan Archives.

[32]*Minutes of University of Michigan Board of Regents*, December 22, 1897, University of Michigan Archives.

revival of Professor F. N. Scott's course in 'rapid writing' of 1890 . . . it led to a Department of Journalism in 1929."[33] Probably taking his cue from Presidents Harper and Van Hise, President Hutchins launched an extension service in 1912, aimed first at informing alumni and then educating adults generally.

That same year, 1912, Hutchins reestablished the position of university news editor and named Professor John L. Brumm, assistant professor rhetoric, editor. Like Bleyer at Wisconsin, Brumm pioneered journalism education at Michigan. Brumm, who continued in this post until 1928, broadened the scope of Michigan's publicity efforts and made a special effort to attract national attention. Hutchins, a Michigan product, gave much thought and time to the task of earning broad support for the university. He came to his presidency with a diverse background of experience that included teaching classics, history, and rhetoric. He was constantly guided by the conviction that people do their best "in an atmosphere of appreciation and friendliness."

President Hutchins took a special interest in the Michigan alumni and worked hard to persuade them to maintain a continuing interest in their alma mater. He saw the alumni as a lucrative source of funds that public colleges as well as private ones could tap, and from this belief came Michigan's highly effective alumni fund raising program. In 10 years of intensive effort, Hutchins helped organize 141 alumni clubs across the country and encouraged in them a sense of belonging to their alma mater. He went on long speaking tours to reach alumni and remind them of their obligation to Michigan. He constantly stressed the need for private gifts to supplement state monies. A biographer said of Hutchins: "His greatest monument . . . is the far-flung body of Michigan alumni whose organization he initiated, fostered, and animated year after year."[34] Like Harper and Van Hise, Hutchins saw public relations as one of his foremost tasks.

ILLINOIS' EDMUND JAMES

Another state university president who adopted a positive publicity approach in these Seedbed Years was Illinois University's Edmund J. James. James, in the words of E. E. Slosson, worked hard "to educate the public to the expressed approval of his ideal of a university instead of being content with a tacit permission to do what he likes."[35] For example, to gain approval of

---

[33]Howard H. Peckham, *The Making of the University of Michigan 1917–1967*. Ann Arbor: University of Michigan Press, 1967, p. 116.

[34]Shirley W. Smith, *Harry Burns Hutchins and the University of Michigan*. Ann Arbor: University of Michigan Press, 1951, p. xv.

[35]E. E. Slosson, *Great American Universities*. New York: Macmillan, 1910, p. 287.

a graduate school, James took his case to the legislature and public by means of a circular explaining the benefits of such a school. It was Slosson's view that Illinois gained in prestige through its aggressive publicity efforts.

Another means used by Illinois to build understanding of its program and needs was the advisory committee. Bridges to the then dominant agricultural leaders of Illinois were built in this way. James arranged for appointment of advisory committees to advise the Agricultural Experiment Station. He also worked closely with such organizations as the State Horticultural Society, the State Dairyman's Association, and the Live Stock Breeder's Association.

The Van Hises, Hutchinses, and Jameses were the exceptions more than the rule among academic administrators in these days. Typical of the more traditional academic view of publicity was Cyrus Northrop, president of the University of Minnesota. Slosson wrote of him: "President Northrop is opposed to university advertising, both the kind that is paid for and the kind that is otherwise obtained. He holds that true scholarship is modest and avoids publicity."[36]

The pioneering practices of Harper, Van Hise, and Hutchins gradually spread across the Midwest and then—after the formation of the American Association of College News Bureaus in 1917, now the Council for the Advancement and Support of Education—across the nation. Quite often these programs to promote publicity would provoke criticism from the conservative faculties of these years as they had from the start. One exception was the University of North Dakota where the faculty, as early as 1903, took the initiative in developing a public relations program for that institution. That same year, in addition to sending feature articles to newspapers, the faculty also asked the university to send a five-page circular to North Dakota high school graduates publicizing the values of the school. The next year, the student yearbook was sent to high schools in the state. A quarterly bulletin for editors and alumni was started in 1904, and in 1907, a semi-monthly newsletter for state newspapers was undertaken. North Dakota was at the same time welcoming the public to the campus at ever opportunity-staging high school days, public receptions, and open houses.[37] In 1914, to explain need for a larger state budget, the university sent out a bulletin, entitled "An Open Letter to the People of North Dakota." President Frank McVey defended his policies and the university's needs in two articles sent to the Grand Forks *Herald*. Here was a president of a state university who as early as 1914, saw the necessity of taking his case to the taxpayers.

---

[36]*Ibid.* pp. 162–163.

[37]Louis G. Geiger, *University of the Northern Plains, a History of North Dakota 1883–1958.* Grand Forks: University of North Dakota Press, 1958, pp. 180–182.

COMMUNICATION NEEDS

Such aggressive public relations tactics were clearly the exception, not the rule in those years. Probably more typical was the kind of situation that prevailed at the University of North Carolina. One historian observed that in relations with the general public, President Francis P. Venable lacked an understanding of the value of full communication between the university and its supporters, something of an understatement. In this period, 1900–1914, North Carolina did not have an organized news service. It relied upon the University *Record* for official reporting to the trustees, faculty, and General Assembly. The university's reporting barely reached beyond these narrow limits.[38] The alumni were not organized until 1911; an *Alumni Review* was started a year later. Official publications, generally, extended little beyond the campus walls.

At North Carolina, as at many institutions, the news that did go beyond the campus walls was dispatched by students earning money as newspaper correspondents in the manner of undergraduate Ivy Lee at Princeton. It was to deal with the problem of immature and often irresponsible student reporting that many colleges set up official news bureaus in the first instance. As Wilson noted, poor public relations resulted for North Carolina, for this method of reporting emphasized the sensational and controversial.

Astute faculty members, sensing the power of the emerging press, often took their differences to the newspapers, much to administrators' chagrin. For example, when, in November 1900, President Jordan of Stanford demanded the resignation of the prickly E. A. Ross from the faculty, Ross published his statement of the case in the San Francisco papers; an embittered controversy followed. Other faculty members issued vigorous public protests against the firing of Ross, who later became one of the nation's outstanding sociologists at Wisconsin.

Stanford, incidentally, appeared to rely solely on its president, David Starr Jordan, to spread its name. Jordan had the knack of writing books and articles in a popular style and was in great demand as a lecturer. Slosson found, in these years, that "Stanford University . . . has no extension department, gives no popular lecture courses, and is not remarkable for its literary productivity."[39]

Thus, the need for growing financial support to meet the expanding needs of higher education, the damages done by immature or irresponsible student reporting, and the increasing tendency of students and faculty to take their cases to the public served to stimulate the initiation of publicity programs in higher education in these Seedbed Years of public relations.

---

[38]Louis R. Wilson, *The University of North Carolina, 1900–1930, The Making of a Modern University.* Chapel Hill: University of North Carolina Press, 1957, p. 171.

[39]Slosson, p. 287.

COMPETITION FORCES STEP-UP

An editorial writer for *The Independent*, writing in the February 1, 1906, issue, took cognizance of the growing practice of colleges to "advertise," using mainly those methods that do not cost them anything—alumni banquets, commencement addresses, talks with high school seniors, magazine articles, and books. This writer thought competition was the prime stimulus for this "modern method of seeking the student," and supported the trend toward improved catalogs as well as "advertising in magazines and newspapers."

Adoption of the promotion methods developed in the worlds of entertainment and business brought, understandably, sour reactions from conservative scholars and writers. One such critic bitterly attached this trend "toward the commercialization of our institutions of learning," and said of the 20th century college president: "This notoriety the president offers to his millionaire patrons in lieu of dividends . . . a succession of press interviews becomes a more valuable asset than a magnum opus; a flash-in-the-pan reputation as a litterateur is more highly appreciated than years of faithful service as a teacher of international reputation as a scholar."[40] The cynical might think this anonymous writer was a frustrated aspirant for a presidency.

The writer of a letter to *The Nation* in 1910 roundly criticized "advertising" at the University of Pennsylvania, stating that the university was maintaining a "bureau of publicity," which has a weekly organ. He was provoked by an article in this weekly publication publicizing a professor's discovery, and wrote, in part, "one can hardly hope to find advertising agents of the requisite culture and judgment to represent matters of scholarship."[41] It should be noted that in these years advertising and publicity were often used as synonymous terms.

Another writer of a letter to *The Nation* that same year protested that "rumors are abroad that a Western institution is about to employ even the moving picture machine to flash its alluring university 'life' before the wondering gaze of prospective freshman [sic]."[42] Two years later, another observer saw university publicity efforts being patterned after those of corporations, adding: "Many colleges are private corporations anyway; and perhaps we ought not to protest if their advertising methods are not more scrupulously honest than those of other corporations."[43]

---

[40]"The American College President," *The Nation*, 77, 1903, p. 244.

[41]*The Nation*, 90 (May 19, 1910), p. 508.

[42]Louis J. Paetow, "University of Advertising," *The Nation*, 90, November 3, 1910, pp. 415–416.

[43]Neil E. Stevens, "Educational Advertising," *School Review*, 205, 1912, p. 582.

MIT HIRES PUBLICITY BUREAU

Another pioneer educator who early saw the value of publicity was Henry Smith Pritchett of the Massachusetts Institute of Technology, an early client of the nation's first publicity agency, the Publicity Bureau, founded in mid-1900 in Boston by three former newspapermen. MIT was then located on Boylston Street in Boston and thus was influenced by the Bureau's first client, President Charles W. Eliot of Harvard. Pritchett later, as head of the Carnegie Foundation, flayed "college advertising for the presences of the colleges of a great number of ill-prepared students."[44] Pritchett, as MIT president for 6 years, actively sought to publicize this then small institute. James Drummond Ellsworth recorded in his memoirs that MIT became a Publicity Bureau client in the early 1900s because "President Pritchett needed publicity at that time and was willing to pay for it."[45]

Ellsworth indicated the personal interest President Pritchett took in publicity: "It was customary for certain graduates of the Naval Academy at Annapolis to go abroad for a post graduate course in naval architecture and it was Pritchett's ambition to have them come to Tech instead. He thought that publicity would establish such a reputation for his institution, that he would attract the Annapolis graduates to Boston, and we were kept at the work until that result was obtained."

PUBLICITY SCORNED BY OLD PRO

Ironically, the most detailed and biting criticism of this trend to use publicity, paid and unpaid, to get funds and students came from Pritchett who, as president of the Carnegie Foundation, blamed college advertising "for the presence in the colleges of a great number of ill-prepared students who otherwise would be in local schools." He flatly asserted: "There are institutions of learning which live only by advertising."[46] He added, rightly, "that in the competition by advertising the weakest college can outshine the strongest university." Another objection to formal advertising, wrote Pritchett, "lies in the tendency to emphasize and advertise the weakest part of the institution." This was done, he contended, to fill the courses that were not full. Little wonder that the Carnegie president concluded: "Advertising so far as the student is concerned has been almost wholly bad."

Although Pritchett's criticism, which appeared originally in the *Fourth Annual Report of the President and Treasurer of the Carnegie Foundation,*

---

[44]"Advertising the College," *Harper's Weekly, 54,* 1910, pp. 9–24.

[45]James Drummond Ellsworth, *The Twisting Trail,* unpublished manuscript in Mass Communications History Center, Wisconsin State Historical Society, p. 120.

[46]"Advertising the Colleges," *Harper's Weekly, 54,* 1910, pp. 9–34.

1909, was directed primarily toward paid ads, particularly those in *Who's Who*, he included the growing publicity and alumni relations programs as well. He said the advertising methods of the state universities had, in the main, been indirect. Some did not use paid advertising. Of them, Pritchett wrote: "In the present crowded condition of the State universities of the Central West one reads with some degree of wonder in a single edition of a New York paper formal advertisements of the Universities of Wisconsin, Michigan, and Illinois." He also saw dangers in the trend of university publications and alumni relations. On these points, Pritchett said:[47]

> University publications under the advertising stimulus tend to assume more and more the nature of advertising remainders, not dignified or scholarly statements of the work and resources of a particular institution. . . .
> Still more far-reaching and influential is the advertising habit in affecting the organization of the university and its attitude to its own alumni and to the public. Most advertising is indirect. Representatives of the university travel over the country and meet the pupils in secondary schools. University professors are sent on long journeys to meet possible students. The alumni are organized into groups which in large measure drop the natural and desirable social relations of the alumni and become what are known in the West as "booster" clubs, their real reason for existence being to bring students and money to their university.

In those pioneering efforts to recruit students and get money through publicity and advertising, there were abuses and exaggerations. But in utilizing the emerging power of publicity, innovative college administrators were expanding the resources of higher education and extending its advantages to more persons, young and old. They also were shaping patterns of promotion that are in use today in most of our 2,000 collegiate institutions.

---

[47]*Ibid.* p. 34.

Nonprofit Groups See the Need
for Public Support

Understandably social reformers battling to win acceptance of new ideas and faced with the need of raising money through voluntary contributions were among the first to see the need for planned publicity to win public support. Among the first to realize the importance of an "enlightened public opinion and sympathy" was Charles Loring Brace, who founded the New York Children's Aid Society in 1853. Brace, a young clergyman and reformer, paved the way for the organization of the society with a series of articles in the *New York Daily Times* in late 1852 and early 1853 publicizing the sad plight of thousands of "vagrant" children in New York City.

Brace's family background well prepared him for his role as a social reformer with a sensitivity for the power of press and pulpit. On his mother's side, he was related to the Beecher family that produced preacher Lyman Beecher and propagandist Harriet Beecher Stowe. His father, John Pierce Brace, in his later years, edited the *Hartford Courant*. From his father, young Brace gained an appreciation of the power of the press.[1]

Brace was keenly aware of the importance of public opinion. In his first circular prepared for the trustees' consideration, he declared that "the Society has taken its origin in the deeply-settled feeling of our citizens that something must be done to meet the increasing crime and poverty among the destitute

---

[1]For an account of Brace's work see Miriam Z. Langsam, *Children West*. Madison: State Historical Society of Wisconsin, 1964. The only extensive biography of Brace is by his daughter, Emma Brace: *The Life of Charles Lording Brace, Chiefly Told in His Own Letters*. New York: 1894.

children of New York."[2] Brace soon came to realize that "one of the trials of a young Charity is raising money." He was among the first of social welfare pioneers to rebel against the then common cheap exploitation of human emotions, a problem that remains to this day. Tearful appeals, such as a pathetically crippled child pictured on a poster, were used then as they are used today in fund raising. Writing in 1880, Brace recalled:[3]

> I was determined to put this [raising money] on as sound and rational a basis as possible. It seemed to me, that, if the facts were well known in regard to the great suffering and poverty among the children of New York, and the principles of our operation were well understood, we could more safely depend on this enlightened public opinion and sympathy than on any sudden "sensation" or gush of feeling. Our Board fully concurred in these views, and we resolutely eschewed all raffles and pathetic exhibitions of abandoned children. . . . The solid ground for us was evidently the most rational one.

Brace was among the first of the reformers to realize that only an informed public support will prove to be a long-term support and that, conversely, emotional support is easy to arouse but quick to dissipate. "I was able to make use of the pulpits . . . throughout the Eastern United States," and "I made it a point, from the beginning, to keep our movements, and the evils we sought to cure, continually before the public in the columns of the daily journals." He wrote that he "was, in fact, often daily editor, in addition to my other avocations."[4]

CLARA BARTON BUILDS THE RED CROSS

Another reformer to the late 19th century, who utilized organized publicity to accomplish her goal, was the dedicated and determined Clara Barton, founder of the American National Red Cross, today a philanthropic giant but then a frail idea imported from abroad. This strong-willed, resourceful woman had become convinced of the urgent need for an American Red Cross (ARC) because of her experience in the Civil War and the Franco–Prussian War. She believed that no one could refuse to accept the Red Cross if they understood its principles. This called for a publicity effort of considerable magnitude, but her resources were quite limited.[5]

---

[2]Langsam, p. 8.

[3]Charles Loring Brace, *The Dangerous Classes of New York* (3rd ed.). New York: Wynisoop and Hallenbeck, 1880, pp. 280–283.

[4]*Ibid.* p. 282.

[5]For definitive history of ARC, see Foster Rhea Dulles, *The American Red Cross, a History*. New York: Harper, 1950. For a story of Clara Barton's life, see Ishbel Ross's *Angel of the Battlefield*. New York: Harper, 1956.

Consequently, Miss Barton did much of the work herself—writing letters, making speeches, and sending items to the newspapers. She also made frequent appeals to clergymen and engaged in Congressional lobbying. In 1878, she published an eight-page pamphlet, *The Red Cross of the Geneva Convention—What It Is*. It stressed two themes: (a) the Red Cross idea was good, and (b) America needed the Red Cross. The pamphlet got little notice at the time. In June 1879, Miss Barton spoke at Cape May, NJ, to the press associations of New Jersey, New York, and Pennsylvania and used the opportunity to thank the press for its "unwavering and generous kindness through the years." With such flattery, Miss Barton wooed editors for the role they were to play in the years ahead. She also spoke to many other groups. Miss Barton distributed handbills to Congressional offices and buttonholed legislators wherever she found them. Among her early converts were Congressman James A. Garfield who, after he became President, told Miss Barton to get on with organizing an American Red Cross.[6]

With this encouragement, Miss Barton brought 50 persons together at her house the night of May 21, 1881, to organize the Association of the American Red Cross. Included among the charter members were journalists Walter P. Phillips, Peter De Graw, George Kennan, and Colonel Richard J. Hinton. Three weeks later, Miss Barton was elected president, Kennan secretary, and Phillips and Hinton were elected to the Executive Board, the latter three "all giants in a day of thought-inducing journalism." Phillips was manager of the Washington office of the Associated Press at the time, and later became manager of the United Press. Kennan was Phillips' secretary in 1881. De Graw was on the AP staff in Washington and 2 years later, became Washington manager of the Associated Press. Hinton had come to the United States from Great Britain to cover the Civil War and had stayed on to continue his journalism career in the United States.

These newsmen were brought into the infant organization by the publicity-minded Clara Barton to, in the words of the new Red Cross Constitution, "collect and diffuse information touching the progress of mercy, the organization of national relief, the advancement of sanitary science, and their application."[7] Even before the Red Cross had received its charter from the District of Columbia in October 1881, Clara Barton had sent it on its first mission of mercy, which was widely publicized. In September of that year, fires ravaged the forests of Michigan, causing great destruction and leaving hundreds homeless. Miss Barton spread the word through the Associated Press that "everything is needed, everything is welcome." This publicity not only brought a national flood of gifts but also brought public awareness of the Red Cross. Two years later, Clara Barton wrote: "Not less than three

---

[6]Clara Barton, *The Red Cross*. Washington, DC: J. B. Lyon Co., Albany, NY, 1898, p. 104.
[7]*Ibid.* p. 47.

hundred periodicals and papers have, within the past two years, laid upon our desk graceful tributes of encouraging and fitly spoken words." She re-issued her pamphlet, *The Red Cross of the Geneva Convention*, and this time it brought over "five hundred editorial notices," which spoke of the little book in "approving and encouraging tones."[8]

Public relations problems, which have plagued the Red Cross from that day to this,were not long in appearing. During the yellow fever epidemic in Jacksonville, FL, in 1888 the arrival of the Red Cross was widely heralded. However, rumors soon circulated to the effect that many of the nurses were drunkards, thieves, and "women of the town." The *New York World* picked up the story and gave it top play.[9] Clara Barton had learned a fundamental publicity lesson—sin gets more coverage than virtue. In dealing with criticisms and unfavorable publicity she remained aloof, responding indirectly, if at all. She pursued with determination the more positive course of publicizing herself and the aims of her organization. In 1884, when she went to a Red Cross conference at Geneva she took a newspaper woman, Antoinette Margot, with her. Miss Margot sent glowing accounts of Miss Barton's honors and travels to both the *New York Tribune* and the *Daily Graphic*. Murray concluded that "except for the arch-suffragettes, no one woman remained so consistently in the limelight as did Clara Barton."[10]

Despite her advancing years, Miss Barton worked tirelessly to publicize the Red Cross. She reached the apogee of her effort in the intensively reported Spanish American War. This woman seemed to have knack of being in the place where news was being made. She lunched with Captain Charles D. Sigsbee aboard the *Maine* 2 days before it was blown up. As soon as she heard of the explosion, she cabled a message to the New York press, "I am with the wounded," in time to be included in the early press accounts. Although the Red Cross' assistance to soldiers and civilians in that brief war was meager and disorganized, widespread press coverage brought acclaim to the organization.

Indicative were the 116 stories on the Red Cross that appeared in newspapers during 1898. Not all these were favorable. There were occasional charges that field workers were holding back supplies from soldiers—a charge that was to repeat itself in every subsequent U.S. war.

As the 1890s drew to a close, the Red Cross idea had taken firm hold because Clara Barton had seen the need for publicizing it through every medium at her disposal. Charles Hurd, onetime Red Cross public relations man, wrote: "The years between 1882 and the Spanish American War were

---

[8]*Ibid.* p. 89.

[9]Robert K. Murray, "A Study of American Public Opinion on the American National Red Cross from Newspapers and Periodicals," *American Red Cross Magazine.* Washington, DC: 1950, p. 9.

[10]*Ibid.* p. 5.

marked by as strong a propaganda effort as could be mustered."[11] In the era of the press agent, Clara Barton practiced press agentry to obtain inexpensive and credible advertising for the struggling Red Cross.

SUCCESSFUL CONVENTION SAVES THE NEA

The power of imaginative, intensive promotion was clearly demonstrated to the educational world by the feat of Thomas W. Bicknell in staging a successful convention of the National Education Association (NEA) in Madison, WI, in 1884, which saved that faltering organization. This heavily promoted convention marked the turning point for what today is surely the world's most powerful educational and labor organization.

For most of its first 28 years, the NEA was on the brink of debt, its membership small and regional rather than national, and its meetings not well attended. The NEA's annual convention in 1883 had left the feeble organization with a $1,200 deficit and near dissolution. Thomas Bicknell's mandate as president of NEA was clear—to unify, nationalize, and strengthen the NEA. This he did with a masterful job of promotion and staging to make the 1884 convention NEA's turning point. The challenge brought forth the man to meet it.

By the time Bicknell emerged as leader of the NEA in 1883, he already had figured significantly in the establishment, development, and promotion of educational institutions. He possessed an intuitive ability to gain public support, a strong persuasive personality, and had a marked organizational ability; he was an innovator and leader. As a colleague observed: "People did what Thomas Bicknell told them to do because he had the sense to do what everyone wanted done."[12] While still a student at Brown University, Bicknell was elected to the Rhode Island General Assembly. A decade later, at age 34, he became Rhode Island Commissioner of Public Schools. His sense of weighing public opinion and evaluating the educational publics was evident in a letter written in that post:[13]

As leading educators of the town, you are to form and direct the public sentiment of the people on all questions which affect the welfare of the schools. By a thorough supervision of the schools, by public addresses and private conversations, by a constant encouragement of all the ennobling influences of a society, and by a constant check of all the demoralizing agents

---

[11]Charles W. Hurd, *The Compact Story of the American Red Cross.* New York: Hawthorn Books, 1959, p. 75.

[12]Edgar B. Wesley, *NEA: The First Hundred Years.* New York: Harper, 1957, p. 225.

[13]Bicknell, *Annual Report of the Commissioner of Public Schools of Rhode Island, 1869.* Providence: 1870, p. 19.

which would work our ruin, socially, politically and morally, we are called upon to hold up and carry forward the cause of education.

Bicknell had employed his political and public relations skills to preserve the American Institute of Instruction and promote the National Council of Education as an executive policy committee for NEA before confronting the task of staging a successful 1884 convention that would save and nationalize the NEA. Right after his election in July 1883, Thomas Bicknell set out to find a place for the meeting that would enable him to draw the crowds it would take to accomplish his educational and financial purposes. He wrote later:[14] "After a survey of the whole country, I chose Madison, WI, as the best place for the meeting. I established a press bureau and, assisted by the railroads, the whole country was supplied with literature as to the meeting and its privileges."

From the start, Bicknell knew that he was bucking a regionally oriented membership and an indifferent public, thus he saw the magnitude of his task. He conceived, planned, and promoted the convention with the virtuosity of a talented impresario. From September 1883 until the convention, Bicknell traveled some 12,000 miles by rail. He spent, altogether, 3 months arranging and promoting the event in advance. His successful efforts demonstrated his ability to see the need to activate the forces of internal communication, reach those influential in shaping public opinion, use publicity, and find others who would benefit from the convention to support the NEA's purpose. The key to his success came in a mutually supporting tie-up with railroads then engaged in intensive travel and settlement publicity campaigns.

Five major railroads saw the value of this tie-in and agreed to support NEA's promotional campaign—the Northern Pacific, the Chicago North Western, the Chicago–Milwaukee–St. Paul, the Grand Trunk, and Central Vermont.

The five lines cooperated in printing an estimated 250,000 pamphlets, circulars, and cards promoting the Madison convention. Seventy-five thousand maps containing information on the history and purposes of NEA, the convention program, special rates and post convention excursions were printed by these railroads and distributed in all 38 states. The railroads also bore the costs of publishing and distributing 100,000 copies of an illustrated 16-page convention booklet that was "scattered from one end of the country to the other."[15] "Railway Notes" columns in newspapers explained that the booklets were available to the public at local railroad stations. Copies of bulletins were also sent to other nations. Bicknell put the cost of these publications at $4,500. But the railroad's cooperation extended beyond convention publicity. Delegates were offered round-trip tickets at the usual one-way price, and for the first time in NEA history, the railroads offered

---

[14]In *History and Genealogy of the Bicknell Family.* Boston: 1913, p. 486.
[15]*NEA Proceedings*, 1884, p. 69.

to collect the $2 membership fee with the purchase of the ticket. The fees were turned over to NEA at a substantial saving in bookkeeping.

The upshot of Bicknell's imaginative program of planning and promotion was a convention that drew some 7,000 persons to Madison, then a small town of 12,000; a convention that enabled NEA to replace its perennial debt with its first endowment fund; a convention that dealt straight forwardly with the educational problems of the day and featured as speakers Alexander Graham Bell, Booker T. Washington, the U. S. Commissioner of Education, and the nation's prominent educators. Little wonder that "the 1884 meeting at Madison is cited as the turning point in the association's fortunes."[16] This was made possible by Bicknell's successful effort to enlist the railroads in a joint promotional effort, his establishment of a press bureau to publicize the event across the country, and his great public relations and organizational skills. The lesson taught by Bicknell of the NEA did not go wholly unheeded in the educational world.

As the end of the century neared, a few educators were coming to see the need for publicity to recruit students, raise funds, and make known the results of pioneering research programs.

ANTI-SALOON LEAGUE TEACHES NATION A LESSON

The pressure group organized to advance a cause or business interest or to oppose one developed impetus in this period. The Anti-Saloon League, which was to give a powerful if ill-fated demonstration of the power of organized publicity and political effort in the early 20th century, was founded in 1895. The League, which, eventually brought national prohibition, was erected on these pillars:

1. paid professional officers and workers giving their entire time to League activity;
2. a financial system based upon monthly subscriptions;
3. political agitation directed toward the defeat of wet and election of dry candidates;
4. concentration upon the liquor question—refusal to be sidetracked by other issues.[17]

This politico-ecclesiastical machine was soon embarked on a campaign of high-pressure propaganda against the evils of liquor.

---

[16]Bicknell, *Genealogy*, pp. 487–488.

[17]Peter Odegard, *Pressure Politics*. New York: Columbia University Press, 1928, pp. 6–9.

The League set out to turn the floodlight of publicity upon the saloon and the liquor traffic. Its object was not so much to form opinion as to mobilize for political action an already existing opinion. The very name Anti-Saloon League was chosen to focus interest on the institution that was the fountain of the poisonous product which the "Pledgers" shunned and the W. C. T. U. would outlaw. . . . The propaganda with which it proceeded to arouse the public conscience leaves little room for doubt that it regarded the institutions as hopelessly beyond reform or repair.[18]

The liquor interests had organized earlier. The New York State Brewers' and Malsters' Association, organized March 20, 1883, had frankly declared itself an antiprohibition association. The entry of the Anti-Saloon League into the battle forced the liquor interest to redouble their efforts. "The methods employed were essentially the same as those used by other pressure groups: publicity, organization of voters, and lobbying. Fancy-priced publicity agents prepared their literature; clever lobbyists secured favorable legislation, which high-salaried attorneys drafted and later defended before the courts."[19]

THE NAM IS CREATED TO FIGHT LABOR

The National Association of Manufacturers (NAM), for decades a sponsor of costly if somewhat ineffective public relations programs, was organized in 1895. Thomas H. Martin, editor of *The Dixie Manufacturer*, is given credit for conceiving this trade group. The NAM, a textbook example of a pressure group, came into existence to organize employers into a united front against the mounting power of organized labor, maintaining an "anti" posture from that day to this. The year before, there had been 750,000 working men out on strikes. But an equal emphasis in the founding of the NAM was the businessman's interest in getting into world trade. Over half of the original document was devoted to the problem of increasing U.S. markets abroad. The NAM's interest came to focus on domestic issues in a few years. In a very short time, the NAM was hard at work propagandizing against the 8-hour workday.[20] Another scholar, describing the NAM as "the most purposeful of all employer groups," wrote:[21]

From its inception in 1895 to the present time, the National Association of Manufacturers has vigorously (and often militantly) sought to further the in-

---

[18]*Ibid.* pp. 38–39.

[19]*Ibid.* p. 249.

[20]Richard W. Gable, *A Political Analysis of an Employers' Association—The National Association of Manufacturers.* Unpublished PhD thesis, University of Chicago, 1950, p. 3.

[21]Alfred S. Cleveland, *Some Political Aspects of Organized Industry.* Unpublished doctoral thesis, Harvard University, 1946, pp. 1–2.

terests of industrialists. These interests rationalized in terms of classical economic theory and the Spencerian doctrine of social evolution, include high profits, low taxes, and a maximum of industrial sovereignty. The Association has attempted to unite industrial and business opinion behind these objectives and in so doing has actively opposed organized labor, the bulk of social reform, and the participation of government in economic affairs. Much of this opposition has taken the form of extensive propaganda designed to influence the electorate.

Cleveland concluded that the NAM was primarily an opinion-molding rather than an opinion-representing pressure group. On the whole, particularly during the past 95 years, the NAM's elaborate and expensive public relations efforts have not been cost productive.

AMA TAKES ON THE ANTIVIVISECTIONISTS

The American Medical Association (AMA), which today also has an elaborate and expensive public relations program, launched its first public relations campaign in 1884 to defend the use of animals in medical experiments. The AMA, formed in 1847, had showed awareness of the importance of public opinion as early as 1855 when a resolution was introduced at its annual meeting in Philadelphia "urging the secretary of the Association to offer every facility possible to the reporters of the public press to enable them to furnish full and accurate reports of the transactions."[22]

At its 1884 convention, the AMA found it necessary to adopt a resolution defending animal experimentation and appointed a committee of seven to wage a campaign against antivivisectionists, a public relations task confronting the AMA from that day to this. The AMA *Journal*, however, did not take up this battle until 1893.

The AMA's conventions, its *Journal*, and its news releases served to stimulate news interest in medicine. The *Journal*, in an editorial July 4, 1891, observed: "It is apparent to even the careless reader of the daily papers that medical topics are receiving vastly more attention than ever before. It is even hinted that many large daily papers have a medical man on their staff; if such is the case they have generally succeeded in concealing the fact by displaying a phenomenal ignorance regarding medical subjects." Thus did the AMA serve to broaden the news spectrum and see the need for the issuance of reliable medical information.[23]

---

[22]Morris Fishbein, *History of the American Medical Association, 1847–1947.* Philadelphia: 1947, p. 61.

[23]For a history of the AMA, see Richard Harris, *A Sacred Trust* (rev. ed.). Baltimore, MD: Penguin Books, 1969.

JOHN MUIR ORGANIZES SIERRA CLUB

The now powerful and articulate conservation movement in the United States had its start with the founding of the Sierra Club in 1892 by the famed naturalist and conservationist John Muir, who served as its president from 1892 to 1914. Over time the name of the club has become synonymous with the bitter public battles over Yosemite National Park, the Upper Colorado, the Grand Canyon, and, in the 1960s, spearheading the Ecology Movement. Muir and his associates, using the Sierra Club as their weapon, carried the battle to save the nation's scenic and natural resources to the public with publicity and protest. Organized in San Francisco December 9, 1892, the Sierra Club set for itself these goals:[24] "To awaken public sentiment and frame laws regulating the grazing of sheep and cattle; to create forest reserves; to protect the watersheds; to establish national parks; to save the m;ore wonderful regions from destructive invasion of any sort, and finally to arouse the people themselves to a knowledge of the great, unexplored treasure house that lay neglected at their very doors."

Muir's organization of the Sierra Club came none too soon because the California lumbermen and stockmen were organizing a campaign to cut away nearly half the area of Yosemite National Park. These selfish interests got their bill through the House of Representatives in 1892 before Muir and his group got a counter-campaign under way. Before the bill came up in the Senate, Muir and the club swung into action. "The club memorialized Congress to defeat the bill, while Muir gave out interviews to newspapers that were taken up by the Eastern press. He also sent many personal telegrams to men influential in the Government."[25] The Sierra Club was able to get the House bill tabled, thus defeating the first, but far from the last, attempt to gut Yosemite. Next Muir mobilized the club's membership in a campaign to get Yosemite Valley added to the Yosemite National Park and this victory was achieved June 1906, with the support of President Theodore Roosevelt.

In this period, Muir worked tirelessly in "creating public sentiment and in making it effective" by writing articles for magazines on U.S. national parks, writing hundreds of letters, sending thousands of telegrams, and in stumping the country to generate interest in U.S. natural heritage. He built and guided well; when the Sierra Club celebrated its 75th anniversary, it had an annual budget of $2 million dollars, a membership of 60,000, and a long record of conservation victories to its credit. One biographer, Herbert F. Smith, well described Muir as a "one-man Madison Avenue of the transcendent beauty of the wilderness."

---

[24]Marion Randall Parsons, "The Sierra Club," *Annals of the American Academy of Political and Social Science, 35* (March 1910), p. 420.

[25]Linnie Marsh Wolfe, *Son of the Wilderness, The Life of John Muir.* New York: Knopf, 1945, p. 255.

Thus, John Muir spearheaded the conservation and ecology groups that in the latter half of the 20th century became a powerful movement to save and protect the environment. This is an unending battle because the Sierra Club was fighting for more protection and higher fees for the nation's grazing lands in the 1990s—a century after the Sierra Club was organized.

THE NEED TO REPRESENT
FOREIGN GOVERNMENTS EMERGES

Organized propaganda campaigns on behalf of foreign interests and governments, now a lucrative and controversial field of public relations, came in this watershed era. Just prior to the Spanish American War, a Cuban junta, represented in the United States by Cuban refugees and exiles, hired a young lawyer, Horatio S. Rubens, still in his twenties, to provide legal and public relations counsel for this junta. "The activities of Cuban sympathizers in America furnished the newspapers with much copy from the very beginning of the insurrection. While much of its was propaganda from the Cuban junta in New York, some of it was legitimate."[26] This junta used press releases and mass meetings to raise funds and promote support for the Cuban cause from 1895 on.[27] New York's exciting, controversial press of that day tended to set the news standards for the nation's press, and thus the preoccupation of the Hearst and Pulitzer papers with Cuba came to be reflected in other papers. Between March 1895 and April 1898 there were less than a score of days in which a story on Cuba did not appear in one of the New York newspapers. Rubens himself recounted: "The newspaper correspondents began to besiege the headquarters for written matter about Cuba. Secretaries of Congressmen needed background material."[28]

The *New York Journal* and the *New York Herald* used press releases and letters to the editor prepared by the New York junta office. "The New York reporters visited the junta offices at 4 o'clock each afternoon the days Rubens was in the city," he related. "I met them, answering their questions if possible and giving them whatever items the facts warranted."[29] The junta also had offices in Washington, DC, and Florida. The group set up press trips to Florida to publicize firsthand reports of refugees fleeing from Cuba. One historian ascribed much of the credit, perhaps too much, for the United States going to war against Spain to liberate Cuba to the junta. James D.

---

[26]Joseph E. Wisan, *The Cuban Crisis as Reflected in the New York Press 1895–1898*. New York: Columbia University Press, 1934, p. 69.

[27]Edwin Emery, *The Press and America*. Englewood Cliffs, NJ: Prentice-Hall, 1962, p. 432.

[28]*Liberty, the Story of Cuba*. New York: 1932, p. 108.

[29]*Ibid.* p. 204.

Squires wrote:[30] "The energetic Cuban junta in New York and the activities of prointervention American newspaper proprietors were largely responsible for convincing the American people that Spain was intolerably brutal in its conduct of the Cuban War and that intervention was not only the right, but the duty of the Nation." Typical of Rubens' methods was the publication in the *New York Journal* on February 9, 1898, of a photostatic reproduction of a letter to the Spanish minister in Washington that was derogatory to President McKinley. The Cuban agent had supplied the copy of the letter to the *Journal.*

The brief but dramatic Spanish American War which made the United States a world power, was but one of many profound convulsions that wrenched the United States of the Gay Nineties and cleared the way for not only a new century but a wholly new era, one in which representation of foreign governments became a major part of today's public relations practice.

---

[30]In *British Propaganda at Home and in the United States from 1914 to 1917.* Cambridge, MA: Harvard University Press, 1935, p. 11.

CHAPTER FIFTEEN

Promoting Social Change

PUBLICITY FOR SOCIAL WELFARE

As the late 19th century trends of industrialization, urbanization, and immigration gained momentum, the nation's social, health, and welfare problems grew in number, magnitude, and complexity. The crowding of more and more persons into cities brought the need for strong public health measures, the need for assistance for those trapped in poverty and illiteracy, and the need for recreation to ease the hard, grinding lives of many urban dwellers! The techniques of publicity developing in the business world were soon put to use by those who saw these problems and the need to generate public support for their solution. The rapid growth of industry, commerce, and finance that was causing U.S cities to grow rapidly was also creating sufficient surplus wealth to permit partial satisfaction of the increasingly urgent social needs. To move this money where it was needed would take organized fund-raising that would utilize the emerging expertise of public relations.

In the closing decades of the 19th century and in the Seedbed Years of the 20th, there came into the U. S. mainstream a new emphasis on social problems, which in turn, brought the creation of new social service and health organizations—some aimed at alleviating suffering of the poor, some aimed at bringing a better life to the underprivileged, and some aimed at combating the contagion of disease. As voluntary health and social welfare organizations multiplied in number, demands for consolidation and "business-like" efficiency in their operations were heard from increasing frequency from the wealthy.

Thus came in these years, councils of social agencies, welfare federations, alliances of charities, community funds, community chests, and new social concepts, all of which, in time, utilized publicity. As new problems arose, voluntary organizations were created to meet them. There were years of ferment, change, and increased social awareness. The tidal waves of revolt and reform set in motion by the Muckrakers and Theodore Roosevelt engulfed the fields of social welfare and public health as they had the business world.

The accelerating proliferation of national organizations seeking to improve society and to ameliorate the lot of the disadvantaged can be seen in the following list that shows that from the Civil War until the turn of the century, only 12 organizations dependent on public philanthropy were organized, compared to nearly twice that number—22—organized in the Seedbed Years of 1900–1917. This meant new demands on the philanthropist and increased competition among these organizations for public attention and support. A listing follows on page 266.

Growing realization of the need for public relations programs to undergird social welfare agencies can be traced in the proceedings of the National Conference of Social Work in these years. A more sophisticated understanding of the elastic term, *public opinion*, was dawning. A speaker at the 1904 conference said: "We are in the main governed by public opinion, but public opinion is a big term; it is the father of a big family of a lot of little public opinions." The next year, a speaker emphasized that the public had not only the right but the duty to know about operations of social agencies.

That same year, the relationship of public and charity organizations was referred to in terms of "education" of the public for sustained interest and support. It was suggested in 1906 that one of the duties of the chief executive of an organization was to keep in touch with popular opinion and to give all possible and proper publicity to his organization's work. Also, in this year, in a speech on fund-raising, a speaker said that personal solicitation of funds gave the collector the following advantage:[1] "He can meet the objections and keep the central administration in touch with the public sentiment, as such sentiment measures the work and value of the organization"—an early recognition of the two-way public relations concept.

From 1907 forward, the emphasis in this field began to shift from charity and relief to social work prevention and cure, bringing increased use of publicity to get these new concepts accepted. These years included an attempt to establish the role of publicity as an inherent part of social work because of this increased need for public support and understanding. This shift was reflected in the creation of a standing committee, Press and Publicity, in 1907. Prior to the 1908 conference, the committee sent out questionnaires to ascertain how social workers were "educating" the public through publicity. Questionnaires returned from 62 cities revealed that few charity organizations had planned publicity programs. Twenty organizations

---

[1]Walter S. Ufford, "Methods of Raising Funds for a Charitable Society," *Proceedings of the Conference of Charity and Correction*, 1906, p. 220.

TABLE 15.1
National Organizations Promoting Social Change

Prior to 1900	
Young Men's Christian Association	1866
National Women's Christian Temperance Union	1874
International Sunshine Society	1879
Salvation Army	1880
American Red Cross	1882
Needlework Guild	1885
Young Women's Christian Association	1886
American Humane Association	1889
Council of Jewish Women	1893
National Children's Home Society	1897
National Florence Crittenton Mission	1898
National Consumers' League	1899
1900–1917	
Society for the Friendless	1900
National Child Labor Committee	1904
National Tuberculosis Association	1904
Boys' Club Federation	1906
Playground and Recreation Association of America	1906
National Probation Association	1907
Federal Council of Churches of Christ in America	1908
National Association for the Advancement of Colored People	1909
National Committee for Mental Hygiene	1909
Boy Scouts of America	1910
American Association for Organizing Family Social Work	1911
National Federation of Settlements	1911
Camp Fire Girls	1912
National Organization for Public Health Nursing	1912
American Rescue Workers	1913
American Society for the Control of Cancer	1913
American Social Hygiene Association	1914
Girl Scouts	1915
National Committee for the Prevention of Blindness	1915
National Congress of Mothers and Parent-Teacher Associations	1915
National Association of Travelers' Aid Society	1917
National Committee on Prisons and Prison Labor	1917

paid no attention to publicity, 31 sent news to newspapers sporadically, and 11 were operating under some sort of publicity plan.[2]

This committee met and reported back to the conference in 1907, 1908, and 1909, discussing the need for social work publicity and formulating its justifications. The committee analyzed the shortcomings of social work

---

[2]H. Wirt Steele, "Publicity in Social Work," *Proceedings*, 1908, p. 263.

publicity and presented new methods and concepts to the conference. It also investigated the years the established practices of publicity in social work and found them to be few. Reflecting the dominance of the mass circulation daily among news media of that day, the committee adjudged the press to be the most effective method of reaching the public. It found that most social agencies proceeded on the assumption that they were trying to sell something the public did not want. Many of the appeals were directed exclusively to fundraising. The committee found that much of the publicity was defensive and emphasized individual, distressing, and sentimental cases, rather than putting forth meaningful programs of action for the whole community—a pitfall that Charles Loring Brace had warned against decades before. Furthermore, publicity was based on individual, other-worldly, evangelical traditions with the result that, in the committee's opinion, the case of the social agency was not stated in terms to catch and hold the attention of the public.

Midway in this Seedbed Era, publicity work was defined as:[3] "That by which a society interprets itself to the public. In a broader sense, it is interpreting a city to itself." The mature two-way concept voiced 2 years earlier by Ufford had not gotten through.

In this period, social workers were using these publicity media: news releases, paid advertisements, published reports, circulars, pamphlets, books, magazines, debates, lectures, stereopticon shows, exhibits, billboards, posters, and street car advertisements. The main reliance was put on newspaper publicity, but as a study of the conference proceedings shows, the newly emerged social worker had great difficulty in relating to the press and in getting responsible treatment of social welfare, a problem that plagued the field well into the 20th century.

In 1908, one speaker, urging more use of the newspaper, suggested as new methods of publicity: printing lists of contributors to fund campaigns, use of pictures, organizing public tours of inspection, and interviews with influential citizens. Another speaker criticized the press because it emphasized the material, not the spiritual struggles of people. In addition, he charged, newspapers focused on only one case or one neighborhood, instead of the whole city. He exhorted the press to eliminate the use of the words *charity, poor,* and *slums.*[4] Another speaker rightly pointed out that most "bad" stories were the result of incomplete information and uninformed reporters, suggesting the need for training social workers in journalism.

The next year, 1909, the committee on press and publicity appealed to newspaper reporters and magazine writers to do more to explain this new field to their readers. They asked more cognizance from the print media for

---

[3]A. W. McDougall, "Publicity in Charitable Work in Smaller Cities," *Proceedings,* 1908, p. 279.

[4]Charles F. Weller, "Publicity From the Point of View of a Social Worker," *Proceedings,* 1908, p. 277.

the great effort being made by social workers to better human living conditions. The committee, in its report, also charged social workers that it was
their duty to lend themselves to a campaign of publicity so that the public
might know the what, how, and why of charity and social work. A conference
speaker underlined this by saying that the social worker must have a sense
of news and know the channels of publicity. Few social workers of that day
felt the need nor were equipped to adequately communicate their programs
and needs to the lay public. Acceptance of the need for public relations
came slowly in this field. For instance, as late as 1925, a prominent Family
Welfare Association Worker told the National Conference of Social Work in
Denver: "I do not believe that our profession wants wholesale publicity
methods any more than the medical or legal professions."

By the end of the decade emphasis in conference sessions had shifted
from exhortation on the need for publicity to the details of ways and means,
indicating growing acceptance of the function. At the 1910 conference, the
press and publicity committee suggested a general outline for a campaign
of publicity, the first of its kind, based on the assumption that for any single
piece of publicity work, whether it is "educational propaganda or raising
funds," the psychological principles involved in education of the public are
the same as those used by classroom teachers. One speaker amplified this
by suggesting that the attention of the public must be seized by some
legitimate device of the publicist—through pictures, typography, a headline
"with a neatly turned phrase"—and this interest must be sustained and turned
to action.[5] He added: "The fundamental duties and functions of a given
society should condition the nature of the advertising and of the appeals."

Lewis was one of the first in social work to link performance with publicity
as the effective means of gaining public support. He further suggested that
successful publicity meant continuous publicity with frequent new plans
and advocated that the secretary or publicist of an organization should study
type faces and advertising methods. Social work publicity got no attention
again until the 1913 conference when a speaker discussed exhibits as a
means of publicizing a program on child welfare.

EVART ROUTZAHN PIONEERS PUBLICITY
IN SOCIAL WORK

The first publicist to emerge in response to this developing need for expertise
in interpreting social and health needs to the pubic was Evart G. Routzahn,
who was born in Dayton, OH, in 1869 and educated in the public schools
of that city. In his twenties, Routzahn drifted into YMCA work, one of the

---

[5]O. F. Lewis, "Publicity and Charitable Finance," *Proceedings*, 1909, p. 346.

first social work fields to develop in the United States. Routzahn, who devoted 28 years of his life to promoting support for health and welfare services, took his first fulltime publicity job in 1906 when he joined the newly organized National Tuberculosis Association. The Tuberculosis Association had been organized in Atlantic City, NJ, in 1904. Formation of this national association was stimulated by the work of a Pennsylvania society to fight this then common disease in 1892 and the first comprehensive analysis of the extent of the disease in the United States undertaken by the Charity Organization Society of New York in 1903. With the advent of bacteriology, physicians saw TB as a medical problem, but the burgeoning field of social work felt it could not ignore a disease that seemed to be both cause and effect of poverty and distress.

The National Tuberculosis Association, one of the first of the voluntary organizations, brought leaders in medicine and welfare into a common cause. The only funds in sight were membership dues and donations. This made the association's founders painfully aware of the need to gain publicity to attract a wide membership. Yet, these organizers declined the offer of a New York firm to handle publicity for the association, deciding instead to publish the *Transactions* of annual meetings as a way of keeping members informed. The directors also made arrangements to send members the *Journal of Outdoor Life*, published at Saranac Lake.

The association quickly learned the value of publicity. The only capital the new group had was the ability and prestige of its members; it needed funds to educate the public and to combat the disease. The answer came in the development of the now traditional TB Christmas Seal, a lucrative though expensive way of raising money. This novel idea for raising funds to fight tuberculosis was developed in Denmark and first publicized in this country by Jacob A. Riis, a Danish immigrant whose crusading journalism did much to spur reform in this era. (Riis was the father of Roger William Riis, pioneer practitioner in the 1920s and co-author of an early book on publicity.) In 1907 in Wilmington, DE, Miss Emily Bissell read with avid interest Riis' article, "The Christmas Stamp," in the July 6 issue of *Outlook*. She saw the possibility that a similar stamp might help raise a few dollars desperately needed for penniless consumptives in an open-air shack being run by her cousin, Dr. Joseph P. Wales, to prove that fresh air was the proper treatment for tuberculosis.

Miss Bissell, at the time secretary of the Delaware Red Cross, sketched a rough design—a half-wreath of holly centered with a red cross and crowning the words, *Merry Christmas*. Her fellow officers in the Red Cross were not enthusiastic about the idea but agreed to go along if the national Red Cross organized approved. It did, and thus made fund-raising history. Initially Miss Bissell saw this as only a local fund-raising effort. However, her intensive promotional efforts caused such brisk sales in Wilmington that she decided to spread the campaign to Philadelphia. In this move, she learned the value of publicity, a lesson that her colleagues in the Red Cross learned with her.

December 13 Miss Bissell went to nearby Philadelphia to solicit the support of the editor of the *North American*, a crusading newspaper interested in the new social movements. A call on the paper's Sunday editor was unavailing. He told her he just couldn't see linking Christmas with "the curse." Rebuffed, she next turned to the conductor of a column, "The Optimist," she read regularly, Leigh Mitchell Hodges. He quickly caught Miss Bissell's enthusiasm for the idea, seeing "a flaming banner to head the fight against a dread foe." He grabbed a sheet of the stamps from Miss Bissell and rushed downstairs to see E. A. Van Valkenburg, editor in chief. The editor, too, was quickly sold. "Drop what you're doing and give this your whole time. Take all the space you need. Ask her to send us fifty thousand stamps by tomorrow." Columnist Hodges boomed the sale of the seals with publicity in the *North American*. "All the make-it-known methods of a modern newspaper were set going—'scarehead' stories on Page One; endorsements from civic, religious, and political leaders; the Postmaster General's approval of Christmas Stamp sales in post office lobbies. Pictures of the stamp peppered its papers."

The immediate result of this frenzied effort on the part of Emily Bissell, columnist Hodges, and a few other dedicated volunteers was to sell 400,000 of the new Christmas stamps in 18 days and clear about $3,000. One third of this amount was raised in Philadelphia by the Hodges *North American* publicity campaign. This sum equalled one fifth of the national association's total 1906 budget of $15,000—far too little for the task the association had undertaken.

Miss Bissell's success begat repetition and, ultimately, imitation. She persuaded Miss Mabel T. Boardman and others in the American National Red Cross to undertake a nationwide Christmas seal campaign the next year. The 1908 nationwide Christmas stamp sale was carefully planned and heavily promoted. Howard Pyle designed the 1908 seal, and the American Bank Note Company and the Bureau of Engraving and Printing collaborated on its production. Sales were handled through Red Cross state branches in 33 states, through women's clubs, and certain of the local tuberculosis societies. These agents were given 80% of the proceeds, the other 20% sent back to the Red Cross for preparing and promoting the seals. The national return reached $125,000 in 1908, and $200,000 in 1909. Such a painless way of raising money and the use of publicity in raising it were not likely to go unnoticed for long.

The leaders of the TB crusade soon saw the publicity was needed for more than money. At the first annual meeting in 1905, it became clear to the founders that the association would be primarily a promotional and educational society to build support for the fight against TB with a public health program as its ultimate goal. "The public must first be aroused; this would inspire the formation of voluntary societies which would then campaign for necessary laws and institutions."[6]

Given its objective of arousing interest in TB, the association moved to develop a publicity program; it first utilized the medium of exhibits, then highly popular in a nation without motion pictures, radio, or television. As Shryock noted, "From the day of the Philadelphia Centennial of 1876, Americans had been accustomed to going to these affairs in droves." After 1 year's experience with exhibits, the directors decided to organize a display that could be shown in one city after another. Evart Routzahn was hired to direct the first traveling exhibit, which was shown in 16 U. S. cities, in Mexico City, and Toronto, between December 1905 and May 1907 and was visited by 370,000 persons. This national exhibit program spawned others at the state level. For example, in Maryland, a Baltimore & Ohio coach was rented, and it was parked at every village along the B & O route in Maryland. The coach's arrival was heralded by the explosion of an aerial bomb that could be heard for 5 miles. Loud gramophone music was played to lure crowds. In 1908, the association started a second exhibit under the direction of W. L. Cosper to tour the states west of the Mississippi. Routzahn worked out the schedules for these exhibits with local committees who had the responsibility of publicizing them. Lecturers were used in conjunction with the exhibits to advocate support of the local TB society. These exhibits, in Shryock's judgment, "attracted good crowds and centered attention on the tuberculosis problem." Typical was the International Tuberculosis Congress exhibit of 1908—designed by Routzahn—which presented in graphic form what was at that time the latest information on TB, its nature, treatment, prevention and control—an exhibit viewed by more than a million persons in Washington, New York, Philadelphia, and elsewhere.[7]

Though the exhibit was effective, the association came to see that other channels of publicity were needed and, in 1908, established a Publicity Bureau which Shryock incorrectly termed "probably the first of its kind in the country." The association was one of the first to utilize a special day or week as a publicity gimmick. In 1910, it set aside a Tuberculosis Sunday and urged clergymen to discuss the menace of TB from their pulpits; in response to criticism this was later changed to Tuberculosis Day to avoid objections on denominational grounds. In 1915, the idea was converted to Tuberculosis Week, one of the first of the hundreds of weeks that now crowd U.S. calendars. The annual meeting also served to get publicity for the association. In 1917, the association launched the Modern Health Crusade to stimulate interest of children in the sale of Christmas seals, developed to

---

[6]Foregoing information on origins of TB association from Richard Shryock, *National Tuberculosis Association, 1904–1954*. New York: National Tuberculosis Association, 1957, pp. 59–96.

[7]Philip Jacobs, *The Tuberculosis Worker*. Baltimore, MD: Williams and Wilkins, 1923, p. 19.

finance the association's program, but this crusade was primarily an effort in health education.[8]

The Tuberculosis Association was one of the nation's first users of the motion picture as a means of communication. Its first picture was made in 1910 by the Edison Company and entitled, "The Red Cross Seal." For the next several years, until the Edison Company went out of film production, the company annually made a film promoting sale of the TB Christmas seals with such titles as "The Awakening of John Bond," "The Price of Human Lives," and others. In 1916, the association produced its first motion picture, a two-reel film entitled "The Great Truth."[9]

In response to the growing demand from the proliferating social agencies for help and to the increased recognition of the value of publicity, the Russell Sage Foundation, in 1912, established a Department of Surveys and Exhibits to serve "as a clearing house for advice and information on social surveys and exhibits, and for field assistance in organizing surveys and exhibits." Like publicity, the social survey was in its infancy. Shelby M. Harrison, formerly of Pittsburgh, PA, skilled in the then rudimentary techniques of the survey, was named director and started work July 1, 1912. Routzahn was appointed associate director September 1, a position he held until his retirement.

Harrison stated the purpose of the department thus:[10] "The purpose was something more than centralizing of inquiries regarding surveys and exhibits. Behind that was a conviction that the survey, including the exhibit and other popular methods of educating the pubic, was proving a sound and effective measure for preventing and correcting conditions that are wrong, and for quickening community forces that are showing promise."

The work of Harrison and Routzahn initially was collecting information about surveys and exhibits and making this available to social agencies, studying improved methods of popular education, and disseminating practical guides to workers in these fields. It also lent advice and assistance to local groups. Exhibits prepared at Russell Sage under Routzahn's direction were of four main types: large temporary exhibitions serving as the central feature of the community campaigns, traveling exhibits designed for durability and convenience in setting up and transporting, posters that could be mounted on panels, and special features for the publicity "weeks" that were coming into vogue.

One of the first persons to be hired in the new department was Miss Mary B. Swain, a former English teacher. She and Routzahn fell in love, courted, and then married in 1914 as they worked day and night to build

---

[8]*Ibid.* p. 65.

[9]*Ibid.* p. 81.

[10]Quoted in John M. Glenn, Lilian Brandt, and F. Emerson Andrews. New York: *Russell Sage Foundation 1907–1946*, I, 1947, p. 177.

understanding of publicity's value in the social welfare field. They worked tirelessly as a team until his retirement in 1934; then Mrs. Routzahn carried on the work until she retired in 1945. Routzahn died in 1939. This couple blazed new publicity paths in promoting social change, he in the field of public health, she in the field of social work. The woman who succeeded Mrs. Routzahn at the Sage Foundation, Mrs. Sallie Bright, said of the Routzahns:[11] "Mr. Routzahn was the spark that powered them to their accomplishments. Mrs. Routzahn didn't have his keen imagination but she effectively complemented him in many ways. He was primarily interested in the health field, she in social welfare. He was a great gadgeteer and exhibits were always his first love. As a former English teacher, she was more interested in the written word. He was utterly uninhibited as a person; she was more sedate. They worked well together and accomplished much for our field."

CLAIRE M. TOUSLEY ANOTHER PIONEER

Another pioneer in social work public relations was Miss Claire M. Tousley, who served on the staff of the Charity Organization Society (COS) of New York from 1913 until she retired from its public relations post in 1955. The COS later became the Community Service Society as the term *charity* lost acceptability. Miss Tousley, a 1911 graduate of Oberlin College, joined th COS staff after a year's work as a teacher in a Minnesota school for dependent children. At the COS she started out as a case worker, but in a year or so, her aptitude for pubic relations was recognized so she was "asked to come down to headquarters to help the Board raise money and work with the volunteers" by the COS president, Robert W. DeForest. "As I got into this work, I felt that we needed to tell our story to the public, that there was a lot of interpreting to do that wasn't being done."[12] DeForest, head of the Russell Sage Foundation, was of the old school who believed that deeds spoke for themselves and thus a publicity program was unnecessary. He resisted for a time Miss Tousley's plea to develop a publicity program—a common attitude in those days.

She won her point in 1916 when the *Morning World* printed a sob-sister story about a man, his wife, and his children which made the family the object of public curiosity and ridicule, a story that "almost ruined this family." "So I walked down to the *Morning World* and said that I thought this was very bad and that they ought to use an agency like ours to check out such stories beforehand. I asked them that after this they call me and check and

---

[11]Interview, New York City, March 10, 1960.
[12]Interview, New York City, June 9, 1964.

that if we didn't handle it right away they could go ahead and print the story. For about two years they called me on every such case."[13] This incident coupled with the fact that COS was not raising enough money to meet its needs persuaded DeForest to change his mind.

"The first thing I did when Mr. DeForest said we'd try having publicity was that I went around to all newspaper editors and city editors and I asked them that if I wrote up what I thought was a story, would they go over it, and if it wasn't right would they tell me? They were good enough to do this and I was amazed." The publicity program paid off as the organization raised $80,000 beyond its quota of that year—1916. Miss Tousley was aided and influenced by the Routzahns. "I knew Evart and Mary Swain Routzahn very well and I used to talk over ideas with them a good deal. They taught me a lot." Miss Tousley held that it was important for the social work publicist to know his or her subject as well as publicity techniques. She described herself in the twilight of her career as "a social worker who believes very earnestly in public relations as an honest way to tell your story to the public."[14] Full-scale development of a public relations program for the COS would come in the 1920s.

NEED FOR MONEY PROVIDES IMPETUS FOR PUBLICITY

With the boom in national voluntary organizations came the concomitant need to finance such organizations through subscriptions, dues, and donations. Demands on the public to give escalated and the techniques to get people to give money multiplied in the years from 1900 through World War I when the fund drive reached a new level of intensity and results. In response to the nonprofit agency's need for money, modern techniques were developed: the public fund drive, the beginnings of the Community Chest, now commonly known as the United Fund, and the employment of fund-raising and public relations specialists.

The short-term, intensive campaign to raise money by bombarding the public with strong emotional appeals and by recruiting scores of volunteers to solicit many times their number had its origins in the Young Men's Christian Association (YMCA). First developed to raise money for YMCA buildings, the successful techniques were soon put to use in the annual appeals of other charitable and social agencies to build hospitals, churches, colleges, civic centers, Boys' Clubs, and to finance national health and welfare associations. The systematic solicitation of the public for gifts quickly proved its worth after the first whirlwind drive was put together for a Washington, DC,

---

[13]*Ibid.*
[14]*Ibid.*

YMCA in 1905. In the preceding 55 years, the YMCAs of the United States had accumulated a total capital investment of $35 million in buildings and endowment. In the next decade, 1905–1915, this amount was increased by another $60 million for capital funds through the publicity-supported campaign method of raising money.[15]

The architects of today's fund drive were two YMCA secretaries, Charles Sumner Ward and Lyman L. Pierce. These two energetic, resourceful and imaginative fund-raising pioneers knew well the value of publicity and promotion in paving the way for a drive to raise money. In their long careers as fund-raisers, they trained the early leaders in this vocation and set the patterns for this work. Understandably, the early 1905 model campaign constructed by these two men, working together in Washington, has been expanded and strengthened over the years. Although examples of the "whirlwind" campaign can be found in the YMCA as early as 1884, it was a 30-day campaign to raise $85,000 in 1 month to reach the required sum of $350,000 for a new YMCA in the nation's capital that became the prototype for today's fund drive.

ROCKEFELLER PUTS CHARITY ON A "BUSINESS BASIS"

The United Way campaign, which today raises billions of dollars each year in some 2,500 communities in the United States and Canada, had its birth in Cleveland, OH, in 1913 when charitable fund-raising could be described in this way:[16]

> At present our philanthropic activities rely chiefly upon "personal equation" methods of raising funds. Mrs. Earnest lunches with Mrs. Gushing and describes a visit to the day nursery that is suffering dreadfully for want of money; Miss Prominent invites a selected list to a parlor meeting where the needs of some worthy hospital or church or club are touchingly presented. After appeals in person begin to affect one's invitations to dinner and other social functions the paid collector is tried.

Such personal begging among the well-to-do proved to be increasingly inadequate for the United States' mounting social needs. This led to more and more publicity-fueled fund drives. This, in turn, brought increasing concern on the part of both givers and seekers ever the multiplying number

---

[15]The history of fundraising in the United States is told in Scott M. Cutlip, *Fund Raising in the United States: Its Role in America's Philanthropy.* New Brunswick, NJ: Rutgers University Press, 1965, or Transaction Press, 1990.

[16]William H. Allen, *Modern Philanthropy. A Study of Efficient Appealing and Giving.* New York: Dodd Mead, 1912, pp. 311–312.

of fund solicitations—a problem still with us. The much-solicited business-man saw the need to bring "efficiency" to fund-raising and fund disburse-ment. Among those most insistent on more efficiency in philanthropy was John D. Rockefeller, then a Cleveland resident. He saw charity as "the busi-ness of benevolence." The first definitive response to these pressures came in Cleveland when, on the afternoon of March 1, 1913, a group of business-men, civic leaders, and welfare workers organized the prototype of today's United Way: The new financial federation was called the Cleveland Federa-tion for Charity and Philanthropy; the latter word was added because for the first time such agencies as the YMCA and YWCA were included. After a clever bit of arithmetic, the federation was announced as embracing 57 agencies, because its first executive secretary, Charles Whiting Williams, "decided that we would use the number 57 that is well known now through Mr. Heinz and his pickles."[17] Cleveland's move was not the first community effort to federate local money-seeking groups, but it became the successful model of the Community Chest and latter-day United Fund, due mainly to the public relations skills of the federation's first paid executive, Whiting Williams, and his utilization of publicity.

In forging a productive pattern for community fund-raising, Williams and his associates demonstrated the value of public relations in this burgeoning field. Another pioneer in social welfare public relations, William J. Norton, noted:[18] "Cleveland founded its federation on a wealth of evidence, planted it in extremely fertile soil, and promptly announced it to the world. Its federation succeeded from the start; it was advertised from the start; it prompted a dozen other cities to do the same thing; and it deserves to be known as the originator of the modern movement."

Whiting Williams was serving the president of his alma mater, Oberlin College, as a fund-raiser and publicity agent when he was offered the Cleve-land post. He was, in the words of an associate, "a pretty good propagandist." Shortly after taking over, Williams hired a full-time publicity man for the federation, Elwood Street, who had covered the federation's founding as a reporter for the Cleveland *Leader*. This is the first known instance of a charitable fund-raising federation employing a full-time person for publicity. This started Street on a fruitful lifetime career in the community chest–social welfare field. Street had worked his way through Western Reserve University by freelance newspaper writing and photography, getting his A.B. degree in 1912. In 1917, Street left the Cleveland federation to organize Louisville, Kentucky's, Federation of Social Agencies. The new department, called "The Social News Bureau," was set up to serve all federation agencies.

---

[17]From the manuscript of a talk by Elwood Street, given in 1949, supplied to the author by Mr. Street.

[18]In *The Cooperative Movement in Social Work*. New York: Macmillan, 1927, pp. 68–69.

WILLIAMS AND STREET SET THE PATTERN

Williams and Street, both skilled writers with a flair for public relations, energetically set about the task of selling the new federation concept to Cleveland—and to the nation. *The New York Times* of April 6, 1913, in a story that has the mark of a press release waxes: "Nothing quite like this 'Cleveland Federation for Charity and Philanthropy' has ever been seen in any city anywhere." In this story, the federation's chief architect, Martin A. Marks, stressed the importance of informing the public to create "a large and united body with a public opinion that could be appealed to for the taking of progressive steps." He saw as one of the federation's values spending the money "which now goes simply to making one form of charity seem more attractive than another" on the more constructive "broad social and philanthropic education."

Today's competitive, expensive fund-raising public relations campaigns make Marks a poor prophet. Williams, too, saw the value in eliminating competing appeals and instead of offering an integrated view of a city's social needs. Of his new publicity bureau, he said: "This bureau is able to interpret to the public the whole of a given social problem in a way that is impossible for any one organization touching only part of that problem."

Articles explaining and praising the new federation plan, written by Williams, were published in the February 1, 1913, issue of *Survey*, in the October 1913 issue of *Review of Reviews*, and in the December 20, 1913, issue of *Saturday Evening Post*. In the *Review of Reviews*, Williams reported: "The almost daily inquiries—received by wire as well as by post—from the leading municipalities of the entire country would indicate that the problem which Cleveland is thus attacking is one of nationwide proportions." Typical of the national publicity spreading word of the new plan, was "Putting the 'Cleave' in 'Cleveland,' " in the July 5, 1913, issue of *Survey*, an article that presumably came from either Williams or Street. The story praised the Cleveland federation as a plan for "benevolence by cooperation in place of benevolence by competition."

This intensive emphasis on publicity in the rather staid charity field brought questions and criticism. Williams and Street, one or both, replied to their critics in the February 1916 issue of the *Social Bulletin*, which they had started in 1913:

IS PUBLICITY NECESSARY?

"Why should you put so much stress on publicity?" officers of the Federation are often asked.

"Because we believe that work done for the community's welfare is the community's business," we answer.

The policy often adopted by charitable agencies in the past, with the order, implied or stated, that "you give us the money and we'll do the work," has no room in the Federation.

Not only do we believe that the public is entitled to exact facts as to income and expenditure, number of workers, number of people aided, but, also, that the public is entitled to as much of the human details of this service as possible though "human interest" stories and pictures, so that support of these activities may seem not merely a blind duty, but also as a pleasure backed by intelligence.

More than that, we believe that it is the business of charitable organizations in touch with harmful social conditions to present these conditions to the public, so that public opinion, warned, may see the removal of these conditions and the ultimate elimination of necessity for charities and philanthropies.

Such is the basis for the Federation's continued endeavors at publicity through the newspapers, window posters, Social Bulletin, motion pictures, stereoptican talks and speakers on a great variety of welfare topics.

This was revolutionary thinking in the strait-laced charity field of that day, and it took decades for it to be fully accepted by givers and social workers alike. In fact, faint echoes of such criticism can be heard in this day. Routzahn, Swain, Williams, and Street not only shaped new welfare institutions they shaped and advanced social work public relations, today a major field of public relations practice.

Epilogue

It is a truism that "practice should be informed by history." In the words of Patricia Lewis, president of the National Society of Fund Raising Executives: "Our future will be surer if we understand our past." Today's astute public relations practitioners should take the time to read these stories of the forerunners of modern public relations and not shrug them off as ancient, or worse, irrelevant history. A careful reading will reveal instructive elements of modern public relations.

Experience, especially in public relations, often provides the greatest, and often most painful, leaning lessons. These are stories of our past, valuable not just for their own inherent interest as an historical record, but for the pain they might save, or more happily, the inspiration they might engender.

In the exaggerated publicity hype of the new American colonial settlements on the Atlantic Coast, there is a basic lesson far too many of today's practitioners have yet to learn: Building false hopes in hyping a product, service, or a candidate's message inevitably leads to disappointment and disillusionment, with the ultimate losses paid by the sponsor (often followed by loss of the account by the practitioner). No glowing accounts sent back to England could alter the reality that would lead to bitter disappointments on the part of our intrepid forebears.

Who among today's workers in the public relations vineyards could not profit from the fundamentals of propaganda developed by Samuel Adams and his brave band of revolutionaries and insurrectionists? They seized their day by casting a clear unwavering eye on necessity of an organization to implement actions made possible by a public relations campaign. The political consultants' arguments will come to naught if there is not an organization to raise either money or hell and get people either into the voting booths or onto the streets.

We have also seen in this history the skillful use of symbols that are easily identifiable and that arouse emotions (e.g., the Star of David or the Cross of Christ, in some cases aflame) and the use of slogans that compress complex questions in a memorable phrase (e.g., "Vote No on the Monkey Wrench Tax Bill").

We have seen the use of staged events that attract the media and get an issue on the public news agenda; the importance of putting your side of the story before the public in such a way that your interpretation of events comes to be the most widely accepted version of what actually happened (e.g., "The Horrid Boston Massacre" or in a more recent version, "The Saturday Night Massacre" of Watergate). Some today call it slant and spin.

Above all, we have seen antecedent practitioners grapple with the perennial necessity of a sustained, organized, tactically efficient campaign, operating under a well-planned strategy that will ultimately break through the citizens' meager budget of time or interest to pay attention to affairs outside their own lives. History can be instructive, and those who study it are saved many trips down blind alleys that have been mapped before.

The monumental struggle Alexander Hamilton, James Madison, and John Jay waged to win ratification of the United States Constitution, which governs our lives to this day, demonstrates far better than any other public relations campaign the far-reaching effect of public relations' unseen power. Allan Nevins was not exaggerating when he termed this campaign "the greatest work ever done in the field of public relations."

It is this Constitution that makes possible the advocacy role of public relations, combined with freedom of thought, freedom of speech, freedom of assembly, and the right to petition our governors guaranteed in law.

It is this Constitution that protects a democratic public information system in which the practitioners play such a vital role as they seek to make heard the voices of institutions, industries, and individuals above the roar and tumult of the crowded public opinion marketplace.

It is this Constitution that permits advocacy of all points, no matter how repugnant or reprehensive, that characterize today's public relations battles, whether over reproductive rights, sexual orientation, taxation, national defense, the economy, or how to help the less fortunate.

As mentioned in the preface, John Milton in his historic *Areopagitica* written 300 years ago, argued that free people should let truth and falsehood grapple freely in the public opinion marketplace, because he held "who ever knew Truth put to the worse in an open and free encounter." In waging campaigns for individuals, causes, institutions, or candidates for public office, practitioners are serving the Miltonian principle of free and robust debate that makes U.S. democracy the viable, although often shaky and seldom calm, instrument of governance that it is.

Yet, there are current doubts that the Miltonian ideal prevails in the face of increasingly powerful interests that assault the public interest, especially in legislative halls. Many thoughtful observers of today's society fear that Milton's marketplace of ideas is breaking down, that this self-righting process is seriously imbalanced by the large, money-stuffed war chests and armies of skilled communicators that the powerful special interests can put into the field of debate. One of these observers, Professor Conrad Fink, a veteran Associated Press reporter and executive, maintained: "Our public opinion marketplace is under assault by the manipulators of ideas—not *communicators* but *manipulators*."

Those who serve ethically and effectively the Miltonian self-righting process fulfill a principle embedded in historic decisions of United States Supreme Court Justices Oliver Wendell Holmes, John M. Harlan, Louis D. Brandeis, Robert H. Jackson, Hugo Black, William O. Douglas, and William Brennen. Justice Holmes first enunciated this principle in 1919 with his "clear and present danger" test of free speech. As a result of this and subsequent decisions of the Supreme Court, the rights to the First Amendment to the Constitution have now been absorbed into the due process clause of the Fourteenth Amendment. Justice Harlan termed this "the nationalization of the First Amendment."

In those decisions, and reaching back beyond them to the ratification of that very Constitution, the public relations practitioner's advocate role was embedded as an essential ingredient in the process of democracy.

The emergence of John Beckley as President Thomas Jefferson's "eyes and ears" in the dawn of our political party system presaged the role of today's political consultant—campaign manager, a role that has reshaped our national political process. Today his successors have grown to a mighty army.

I will be so bold as to suggest that the young achievers in President Clinton's White House could profit from a study of Amos Kendall's strategies and tactics in winning support for the Jacksonian Revolution. Just for example, Jackson's "Thinking Machine," as Kendall was called, carefully researched the financial terrain from Baltimore to Boston before launching Jackson's battle against Nicholas Biddle's Bank of the United States. This first major corporation versus government public relations contest had a profound effect on the nation's financial system—then and now. There just might be lessons here in today's epic struggle that arrayed the insurance companies and the American Medical Association against President Clinton's efforts to bring rationality and reform to the nation's health-care system.

Perhaps among the significant contributions of the history written here is the content that rescues Amos Kendall from the attic of U. S. history and tells anew the impact of this able, intelligent man on the United States in the first half of the 19th century. Amos Kendall shaped and built support for the Jacksonian Revolution, which changed the role of the political parties in the American electoral system and changed the nation's banking system. Later on, as Postmaster General, he overhauled and modernized—for its time—our postal system and then capped his career by making the nation's telegraphic system—in partnership with the telegraph's inventor Samuel F. B. Morse. For the lack of an adequate biography these and other accomplishments of Kendall have been lost in the oubliette of history.

There are other lessons to be learned by the careful reading in the pages. For example, the United States' large corporations, or at least a few of them, have yet to learn the folly of the Buccaneers and their blunders in the post-Civil War era of expansion, exploitation, and abuse of the public interest, abuses that brought the reforms of Theodore Roosevelt and his Square Deal. Among them, but by no means alone, are the Exxons, the Dow-Cornings, the Sears, and worst of all, the tobacco industry—and its merchants of ill public health and death.

This volume closes with the end of the 19th century and the beginnings of the 30th century that brought profound change to the United States and the world. Democracy's flames consumed tyranny's madness, miracle drugs saved millions, and workers, men and women, went back to work. The pace picked up and has led, at breakneck speed, to a world of instant communication, globe-girdling jets, a white-hot competitive world economy, space exploration, cyberspace, and the information highway. Along with these changes came others.

The cost of progress arrived at the same time as millions of lives were consumed and altered in two globe-encircling wars, a great economic depression, and repeated quakes and after shocks to the global job base, tremors that shook the assumed value of work down to its very foundations. Decay and disenfranchisement ate their fill in the guts of cities; a decline in moral values showed itself in the increasing tawdry cheapness of much of our media contents; illegal drugs and concomitant violent crimes seized and killed many. Terrorists arrived to kill on two fronts: direct and random. Thermonuclear weapons that had once killed directly stalked us and threatened randomly everyone everywhere for most of 50 years.

These situations, and their multiple aftermaths and fallouts, are but a few listed on history's unresolved balance sheet. They pose a difficult challenge to today's public relations practitioner. The practitioner's role, ideally, should be one of communication, conciliation, and consensus building. It requires fortitude and manifold skills to pick up an agenda such as this, much less find a way to see it through. To see our way through the myriad of problems that will confront us in the 21st century, there is, in my view, a compelling need to reassess the components of our public information system.

This is my last work in a career that has spanned 62 years in newswork, public relations, and education of two generations of public relations practitioners. As I pass the baton on to the present generation of journalists, practitioners, and educators, I do so with a sense of deep concern for the vitality and integrity of the nation's public information system, the public information system on which we must depend to govern ourselves and do the nation's business. America's public relations practitioners, some 150,000 strong, wield a major influence in that system by providing nearly half of the mainstream media's daily content. Their effort is to put a favorable spin on the news in the interest of the client, not the public's interest. Of course there are times when the two coincide. The U. S. military's control of the news of the Gulf War with Iraq in 1991 was a perfect example how news sources, guided by public relations officials, can control and shape the news with the truth a casualty.

Propagandist, press agent, public information officer, public relations or public affairs officer, political campaign specialists, trade association lobby-ists—all are protected in our democratic system by the same First Amendment rights that journalists enjoy, enabling them to play a far more important opinion-making role that the public perceives, or that journalists (who them-selves are only some 130,000 strong) are willing to admit. It is safe to say that more than 40% of today's media content originates in the word proc-essors and fax machines of public relations specialists. The thrust of their work is always the same—to mobilize public opinion in the interest of a paying client. Their hope is to set the public agenda in their favor. These professional case-pleaders play to win. And usually do. The some 100 million dollars the insurance, medical, and health industries spent to kill President Clinton's proposal for health reform in 1993–1994 is a case in point. Robin Toner wrote in *The New York Times* of September 4, 1994:

> That the (Constitutional) system was simply overwhelmed by millions of dol-lars worth of lobbying, polling and advertising. That it was whip-sawed by two years of strategizing and manipulation by the top consultants and theo-reticians in both parties. That Americans were taken on an emotional 18 month journey that produced not a new consensus but paralysis.[1]

A common complaint of our time is that Washington has lost touch with the people of this nation and it is time to throw the rascals out and set term limits on their service in Congress. Another case that can be made is that our lawmakers have been paralyzed by the growing number of public relations specialists, lobbyists, and by our new radio "talk show democracy." Today's Washington is wired for quadrophonic sound and wide screen video, swamped by fax, computer messages, 800 numbers, and CNN to every citizen in every village in the nation. Its every act or failure to act to blared to the

---

[1]For a carefully documented account of this lobbying effort, see: The Center for Public Integrity: *Well-Healed Inside Lobbying for Health Care Reform*. Washington, DC, 1994.

public thanks to C-SPAN, open-meeting laws, financial disclosure reports, and campaign spending rules, and its every misstep is logged in a database for use of future opponents. When a Rush Limbaugh can swamp Congressional switchboards with 500,000 calls in one day to defeat legislation to control professional lobbyists, Milton's self-righting theory seems out of whack.

The campaign specialist has become a major segment of today's public relations vocation—and a disturbing one. Since Richard Nixon's campaigns of 1946 against Representative Jerry Voorhis and 1950 against Representative Helen Gahagen Douglas each of our political campaigns appears to reach a new low in mean spiritedness. Negative television advertising, fashioned by these campaign specialists, is debasing the coin of respect and credibility in our political system. This course, if continued on its downward spiral, can destroy the people's confidence in their governors and in their government. The mean spiritedness and lack of mutual respect between candidates reached its nadir in 1994. These practitioners ought to reassess their role in democratic government.

I have equal concerns with the other major element in our public information system—the mainstream news media and their increasing tabloidization. At the turn of this fading century, we developed a wholly new concept of journalism—third person objectivity with editorial opinions relegated to the editorial page. This was brought about by the birth of the national press associations which sought to serve newspapers of all political faiths. In the view of Everette E. Dennis, Director of the Freedom Forum Media Studies Center: "That delineation is no longer clear as U. S. newspapers and television . . . have begun to leave behind their search for impartiality, however flawed that quest might have been. Now, many leading papers have replaced impersonal descriptive reports on their front pages with heavily interpretative news analysis, which used to be featured in sidebars." Dennis says the result is a "more manipulative, more partisan press, one given to setting agendas. . . ."

Beyond this the press has become cynical and thereby contributing to the sense of cynicism and distrust of our major institutions including the press itself. Thomas E. Mann of the Brookings Institution has sensed this: "We're now at a point of believing it's all a scam, everyone is looking out for his own interest and the job of the reporter is to reveal the scam." By casting doubt on everyone, a cynical brand of journalism may be undermining its own credibility, as well as that of other institutions.

In short, it is time for the journalist and the practitioner to take stock of their work and to determine if what they are doing is truly in the public interest as both journalists and practitioners profess to serve.

Courage to those who give it a try.

Index